COMPUTER NETWORKS

Nastaran Nazar Zadeh

TAP

Toronto Academic Press

COMPUTER NETWORKS

Nastaran Nazar Zadeh

Toronto Academic Press
4164 Lakeshore Road
Burlington ON L7L 1A4
Canada
www.tap-books.com

Email: orders@arclereducation.com

ISBN: 978-1-77956-291-3

ABOUT THE AUTHOR

Nastaran Nazar Zadeh is a highly experienced computer engineer, researcher, and advisor in the fields of robotics, artificial intelligence and computer science. She holds a Master of Science in Computer Engineering from Mapua University of the Philippines and pursed her Ph.D. in Electronic Engineering at the same institution. With over seven years of teaching experience, Nastaran has taught electronic and computer engineering programs at several reputable academic institutions, where she has also led numerous thesis studies. Her research focuses on developing robotics systems with A.I. and machine learning, which enables her to stay up-to-date with the latest advancements in the field and implement cutting-edge technologies.

Table of Contents

List of Figures

List of Tables

PREFACE

In the 21st century, we have witnessed some remarkable new technologies that have significantly altered our way of life. This significant transformation began in the late 20th century with the emergence of the internet in 1995. The internet has introduced new methods of operation, tools, and devices that are highly beneficial in educational institutions, businesses, and virtually every other sector. Despite originating in 1989, the internet now hosts an immense amount of data, approximately 1.2 million terabytes, contributed by major corporations such as Google, Amazon, Microsoft, and Facebook. The internet is home to a vast array of content – with over 4.5 billion accessible websites, and even more content residing in the deep web, which surpasses the size of the commonly used internet.

Shortly after the inception of the internet, email emerged, followed by a variety of other online platforms including e-commerce websites, social media, online enterprises, digital learning, e-government services, cloud storage, and more. These platforms began to surface between 1995 and the early 2000s. Presently, there is a multitude of internet-based technologies utilized across various domains such as business, science, engineering, healthcare, and beyond. These technologies have become integral to our daily lives, with most individuals utilizing them whether by choice or necessity. Due to advancements in computing power and the decreasing cost of data storage, both governmental bodies and private enterprises are amassing vast quantities of information. Computer networking is about connecting computers together so they can talk to each other and share data. Basically, a computer network is just two or more computers hooked up together. This makes it easier for people to communicate with each other.

The aim of this book, "Computer Networks," is to provide a comprehensive foundation in the principles and practices of computer networking. It is designed to cater to undergraduate students in computer science, information technology, and related fields who are seeking to gain a thorough understanding of network concepts, architectures, protocols, and technologies. The textbook aims to equip readers with the knowledge and skills necessary to understand the complexities of modern networks, including the Internet, LANs, WANs, and wireless networks.

Through a blend of theoretical concepts and practical applications, the textbook introduces fundamental networking concepts such as the OSI and TCP/IP models, network topologies, routing algorithms, network security, and network management. It emphasizes not only the technical aspects of networking but also explores critical issues like network security, data communication protocols, and the latest networking trends and technologies. Intended to serve both as a learning resource and a reference, this textbook includes numerous examples, case studies, and exercises to reinforce learning and encourage practical application of concepts.

–Author

CHAPTER 1

Computer Networks and Services

LEARNING OBJECTIVES

After studying this chapter, you will be able to:

- Define the fundamentals of computer networking
- Evaluate the various types of network services
- Discuss on numerous types of network

INTRODUCTORY EXAMPLE

FANTSUAM FOUNDATION'S COMMUNITY WIRELESS NETWORK

Kafanchan is a community of 83,000 people located 200 km northeast of Abuja, in central Nigeria. Kafanchan used to be known as a busy and thriving town as it was the host of one of the main junctions of the national railway. When the railway industry was booming, almost 80% of Kafanchan's population relied on it in one way or another. Following the complete breakdown of the Nigerian railway system, the population of Kafanchan has been forced to go back to its original source of income, which is agriculture.

Kafanchan is a poorly connected area in terms of fixed telephony and Internet connectivity. Today, no fixed telephony (PSTN) is available in the area and GSM only just arrived in 2005. However, the GSM coverage is just as poor as the quality of the service. At the moment, SMS services are the most reliable communication service because voice conversations tend to cut off in the middle and suffer heavy noise.

Poor access to electricity brings further challenges to the people of Kafanchan. The national electric power company of Nigeria, generally known as NEPA (National Electric Power Authority), is more commonly known to Nigerians as "Never Expect Power Always". In 2005, NEPA changed its name to Power Holding Company of Nigeria (PHCN).

Kafanchan is receiving power from NEPA on an average of 3 hours per day. For the remaining 21 hours, the population relies on expensive diesel generators or kerosene for illumination and cooking. When NEPA is available on the grid, it provides an unregulated voltage in the range of 100–120 V in a system designed for 240 V. This voltage must be regulated to 240 V before most loads can be connected. Only light bulbs can be fed straight to the grid power since they can handle the low voltage without damage.

Project Participants

Given the challenging background of Kafanchan, how could anyone come up with the idea of establishing the first rural Wireless ISP in Nigeria there? Fantsuam Foundation did, and they made it happen. Fantsuam Foundation is a local, non-governmental organization that has been working together with the community of Kafanchan since 1996 to fight poverty and disadvantage through integrated development programs. Fantsuam's focus lies on microfinance, ICT services, and social development in rural communities of Nigeria. Becoming the first rural wireless ISP in Nigeria was part of their mission to be a recognized leader in the provision of rural development initiatives, as well as the foremost rural knowledge economy driver in Nigeria.

The Wireless ISP of Fantsuam Foundation, also known as Zittnet, is funded by IDRC, the International Development Research Centre of Canada. IT +46, a Swedish-based consultancy company focusing on ICTs for development, has worked together with the Zittnet team to provide technical support for wireless communications, bandwidth management, solar energy, power backup systems, and VoIP deployments.

Network Operating Center (NOC)

A new Network Operating Center was established to host the power backup system and server room facilities. The NOC was designed to provide a place safe from dust, with good cooling capabilities for the batteries and the inverters. The NOC uses natural methods and is made from locally available materials. The building comprises four rooms: a battery storage room, a server room, a working space, and a room for equipment storage. The battery storage room hosts seventy 200 Ah deep cycle batteries, as well as five inverters (one of them pure sine wave), two solar regulators, power stabilizers, and DC and AC disconnects. The batteries are stacked vertically on a metal shelf structure for better cooling.

The server space accommodates a rack unit for servers and a fan. The room has no regular windows, to avoid dust and overheating. The server room and battery room face south to improve natural cooling and to help keep the room at an appropriate temperature. The server room and the battery space require effective low-cost/low-energy cooling as they need to operate 24x7. To achieve this goal, natural cooling techniques have been introduced in the NOC design: small fans and extractors and thick walls of bricks (double width) in the direction of the sunset. The south side of the building hosts 24 solar panels in a shadow-free area on its metal roof. The roof was designed with an inclination of 20 degrees to host the panels and limit corrosion and dust. Extra efforts have been made to keep the panels easily reachable for cleaning and maintenance. The roof has also been strengthened in order to carry the extra load of 150–200 kg. The NOC building is constructed of locally produced laterite mud bricks. The material is cheap since it is frequently used and comes from the top layer of soil. The bricks are produced locally by hand using a low-tech pressing technique. The NOC is unique for its kind in Kaduna State.

Physical Infrastructure: A Communication Mast

Most potential clients of Zittnet are located between 1 km and 10 km from the premises of Fantsuam. To reach these clients, Fantsuam established a communication mast on their premises. In October 2006, a 45m (150-foot) tall self-standing mast was installed at Fantsuam Foundation. The mast was equipped with grounding and lightning protection, as well as a mandatory signal light. A metal ring was buried at the base of the tower at a depth of 4 feet. All three legs of the mast were then connected to the grounding circuit. A lightning rod was mounted at the highest point of the mast to protect the equipment against lightning strikes. The rod is made of pure copper and is connected to the earth ring at the base of the mast using copper tape. The signal light mounted at the top of the mast is a requirement from the Civil Aviation Authorities. The light is equipped with a photocell that enables automated switching based on the level of ambient light. This way, the light comes on at night and goes off during the day.

Clients

The clients are free to use the Internet access for any purpose. For example, Isaiah Balat is reselling vouchers (that he bought from Fantsuam) to his clients. His Internet café hosts 10 computers that are all connected to Zittnet. The clients purchase vouchers from the owner with a margin of 25% over the price offered by Fantsuam. In return, clients that do not have access to a computer connected to Zittnet can access the network through the PCs at Isaiah Balat's café. The New World Hotel is another client that aims to create a similar business model but on a larger scale. They will provide wireless Internet access to all of their rooms and offer access to Zittnet's uplink by reselling vouchers. Other clients, like the General Hospital and the Jagindi Street Clinic, are using the Internet access for professional and private use without reselling access to their clients.

INTRODUCTION

A group of linked computers is known as a computer network. Nodes refer to computers connected to a network. Computers can be linked wirelessly using radio waves or through cabling, typically an Ethernet cable.. Computers that are connected can share resources such as file servers, printers, Internet access, and others. A network is a multifunctional link that enhances the capabilities of a single computer.

A computer network is made up of two or more computers connected to one another in order to exchange data electronically. In addition to physically joining computers and other communication devices, a network system performs the crucial job of creating a unified architecture that enables a range of equipment types to transfer data almost seamlessly. IBM's Systems Network Architecture (SNA) and ISO Open Systems Interconnection (OSI) are two well-known architectures.

Wide-area networks (WANs) and local-area networks (LANs) are the two fundamental types of networks. LANs use links (wires, Ethernet cables, fiber optics, Wi-Fi) that send data quickly to link computers and peripheral devices in a constrained physical area, like a lab, business office, or college campus. A local area network (LAN) usually comprises multiple desktop computers, printers, and large-capacity disk storage units known as file servers. These devices allow all computers connected to the network to access a shared collection of files. LAN operating system software enables users to share printers and storage devices, communicate with one another, and access centrally located processors, data, or programs (instruction sets) all at once. It does this by interpreting input and providing instructions to networked devices. LAN users can connect to WANs and other LANs. Bridges, or similar devices, serve as transfer points connecting LANs with comparable architectures. "Gates," which change data as it travels between systems, connect LANs with disparate architectural styles.

Wide Area Networks (WANs) link computers and local networks to larger networks across extensive geographical regions, such as continents. Although their users typically access the networks via a modem (a device that allows computers to communicate over telephone lines), they may link the computers via cables, optical fibers, or satellites. The Internet, a vast network of gateways and networks connecting billions of computer users worldwide, is the biggest WAN.

1.1. FUNDAMENTALS OF COMPUTER NETWORKING

→Learning Objectives

- Discuss on open systems interconnection (OSI)
- Access the useful protocol for networking
- Elaborate the various network topology
- Learn about the unique identifiers of network

A computer network is an assembly of computing hardware, including computer systems, that is connected via communication channels to enable resource sharing and communication among various users.

It is this network that evolved to become what we now call the internet.

Networks are used to:

- Facilitate communication via email, video conferencing, instant messaging, etc.
- Enable multiple users to share a single hardware device like a printer or scanner.
- Enable file sharing across the network.
- Allow for the sharing of software or operating programs on remote systems.
- Make information easier to access and maintain among network users.

There are many types of networks, including:

- Local Area Networks (LAN).
- Global Area Networks (GAN).
- Personal Area Networks (PAN).
- Home Area Networks (HAN).
- Wide Area Networks (WAN).
- Campus Networks.
- Metropolitan Area Networks (MAN).
- Enterprise Private Networks.
- Internetworks.
- Backbone Networks (BBN).
- Global Area Networks (GAN).
- The internet.

It is the connection of several devices together, usually referred to as hosts connected via multiple paths in order to send and receive media or data. Additionally, there are various devices or mediums that facilitate communication between two distinct devices, collectively referred to as network devices. Examples include Hub, Bridge, Switch, Router.

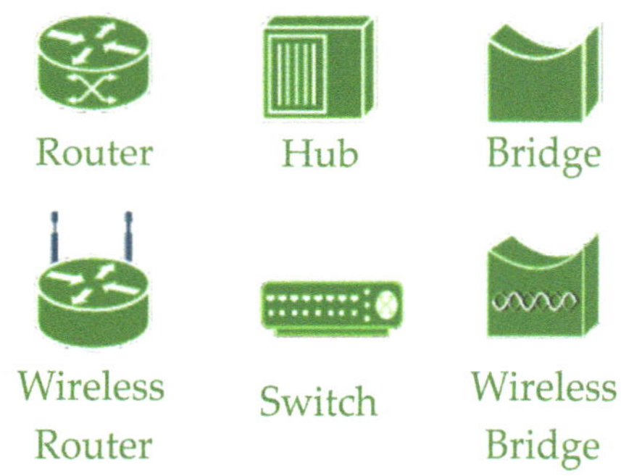

Figure 1.1. Example of computer network parts (Source: Medium.com, https://miro.medium.com/v2/resize:fit:640/format:webp/0*rkjdV8aVrpovzJv.png).

Network topology refers to the design pattern that links devices together. like the Daisy chain, Ring, Mesh, Star, and Bus.

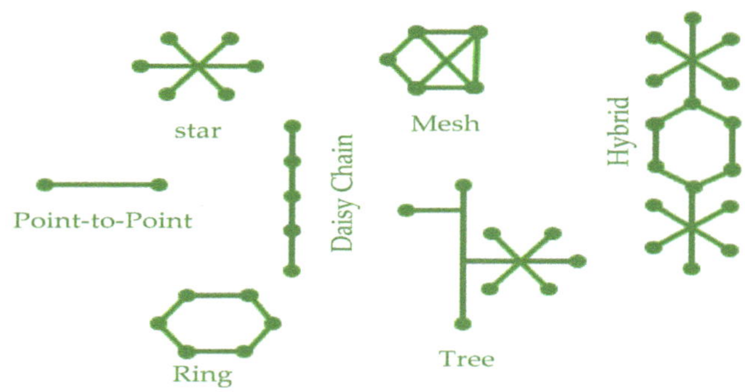

Figure 1.2. Format of computer network topology (Source: Medium.com, https://miro.medium.com/v2/resize:fit:640/format:webp/0*DZGU9Yd2VSSBfeSW.png).

1.1.1. Open Systems Interconnection (OSI)

It is a reference model that details the functions of every layer as well as standards for communication protocols. A conceptual framework for comprehending relationships is called a reference model. The OSI reference model serves as a guide for software developers and vendors to ensure interoperability of their digital communication products and programs. It also provides a clear framework for describing the various functions of a networking or telecommunication system.

Keyword

Network device is hardware or software that establishes and maintains a secure and effective internet connection.

When describing their goods and services, the majority of telecom vendors try to align them with the OSI model. Furthermore, although OSI is helpful in directing discussion and assessment, it is rarely used in practice. This is due to the fact that, unlike the OSI model, few network products or common tools maintain related functions in clearly defined layers. The internet is defined by the TCP/IP protocol suite, which does not map exactly to the OSI model.

To simulate or track the transmission or reception of data over a network, IT specialists employ OSI. According to this model, sending and receiving data is divided into seven layers, each of which is in charge of carrying out particular functions.

The fundamental idea behind OSI is that communication between two endpoints in a network can be separated into seven different groups, or layers, of related functions. Every user or program that communicates uses a device capable of providing those seven levels of functionality. Each layer in this architecture provides support to the layer above it, which in turn provides support to the layer below it. Data will therefore flow down through the layers of the source computer, across the network, and then up through the layers of the receiving computer in any given message between users. The only layer in the stack that isn't able to provide services to a higher level is the application layer.

Applications, operating systems, network card device drivers, and networking hardware work together to provide the seven layers of function, which let a system send a signal over a network Ethernet or fiber optic cable, or via Wi-Fi or other wireless protocols.

1.1.2. Protocol

A protocol is a collection of guidelines or formulas that specify how two entities can communicate over a network; there are distinct protocols defined at every OSI model tier. DHCP, FTP, UDP, ARP, TCP, and IP are a few examples of these protocols. In the field of computer science, protocol refers to a collection of guidelines or practices used to transfer data between electronic devices like computers. A preexisting agreement defining the information's format and the sending and receiving protocols is required for computers to exchange data. Without a protocol, a computer transmitting data might send it in 8-bit packets, whereas a computer receiving the data might anticipate receiving it in 16-bit packets. International or industry-wide organizations create protocols. A set of guidelines for implementing networking communications between computers, OSI (Open Systems Interconnection) is arguably the most significant computer protocol.

The norms and guidelines for communication between network devices are specified by a network protocol. Network protocols include formatting rules that define the way data is formatted into sent and received messages, as well as mechanisms for devices to recognize and establish connections with one another. In addition, certain protocols facilitate data compression and message acknowledgment for dependable and/or high-performance network communication.

All contemporary computer networking protocols send and receive messages in the form of packets, which are messages divided into parts that are gathered and put back together at their destination. These packets are sent and received using packet switching techniques. Thousands of distinct computer network protocols have been created, each with a specific function and setting in mind.

1.1.2.1. Internet Protocols

A group of related network protocols that are also some of the most popular are part of the Internet Protocol (IP) family. Higher-level protocols like TCP, UDP, HTTP, and FTP all interface with IP to offer extra features in addition to Internet Protocol itself. Likewise, IP coexists with lower-level Internet Protocols such as ARP and ICMP. Lower-level protocols in the IP family typically communicate with network adapters and other computer hardware, whereas higher-level protocols in the IP family typically interact more directly with applications like web browsers.

Remember

Computer networking is the branch of computer science that deals with the ideation, architecture, creation, maintenance, and security of computer networks. It is a combination of computer science, computer engineering, and telecommunication.

1.1.2.2. Wireless Network Protocols

Thanks to Wi-Fi, Bluetooth, and LTE, wireless networks have become commonplace. Network protocols designed for use on wireless networks must support roaming mobile devices and deal with issues such as variable data rates and network security.

1.1.2.3. Network Routing Protocols

Routing protocols are specialized protocols created especially to be used by internet network routers. A routing protocol has the ability to recognize other routers, control the routes—the paths that connect network message sources and destinations—and perform dynamic routing. Routing protocols commonly used are BGP, OSPF, and EIGRP.

1.1.2.4. How Network Protocols Are Implemented

Some network protocols are supported by software services that are integrated into modern operating systems. Programs that support the high-level protocols required for an application to operate, such as web browsers, are contained in software libraries. In direct hardware (silicon chipsets), support is implemented for a few lower-level TCP/IP and routing protocols for better performance.

Binary data, which is made up of ones and zeros that encode messages, is contained in every packet that is sent over and received over a network. The majority of protocols include a brief header at the start of every packet to hold the sender and destination of the message. Some protocols conclude with a footer as well. Every network protocol has the ability to recognize messages of a particular type and handle headers and footers when transferring data between devices. A protocol family is a collective term for a set of interoperable network protocols at both higher and lower levels. Traditionally, network students study the OSI model, which divides network protocol families into discrete layers conceptually for educational purposes.

1.1.3. Network Topology

The arrangement of a network which comprises of nodes and connecting lines via sender and receiver is referred as network topology. The various network topologies are:

1.1.3.1. BUS Topology

The bus topology is multipoint. A single, lengthy cable acts as the network's backbone, linking all devices. Taps and drop lines are utilized to connect nodes to the bus cable. A drop line is the part of the main cable that links to the device. A tap is a connector that establishes contact with the metallic core of a cable by either splicing into the main cable or piercing the sheathing of a cable. As a signal travels along the backbone, it loses some energy and transforms into heat. Consequently, as it travels further, it weakens. Due to this, a bus can only accommodate a specific number of taps and a certain distance between taps.

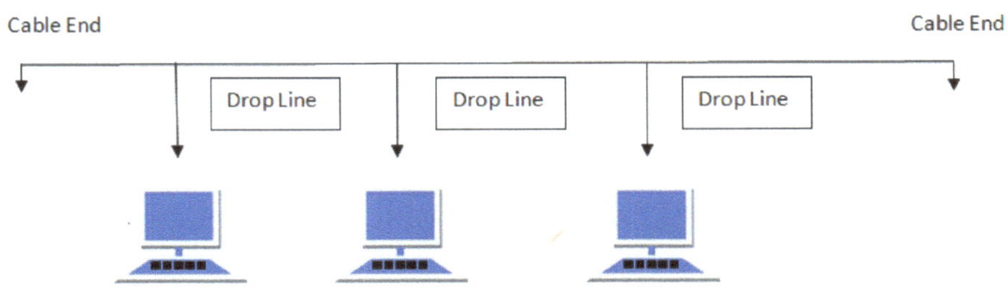

Figure 1.3. Functionality of bus topology (Source: Computernetworks969, https://i0.wp.com/www.studytonight.com/computer-networks/images/Figure5.png).

a. Features of Bus Topology

1. It transmits data only in one direction.
2. Every device is connected to a single cable

b. Advantages of Bus Topology

1. It is cost effective.
2. Cable required is least compared to other network topology.
3. Used in small networks.
4. It is easy to understand.
5. Easy to expand joining two cables together.

c. Disadvantages of Bus Topology

1. Cables fails then whole network fails.
2. If network traffic is heavy or nodes are more the performance of the network decreases.
3. Cable has a limited length.
4. It is slower than the ring topology.

1.1.3.2. RING Topology

Each device in a ring topology has a unique point-to-point connection with just the other two devices on either side. From device to device, a signal is transmitted in a single direction around the ring until it reaches its target. Every gadget in the ring has a repeater built in. A device's repeater regenerates the bits and transmits them when it receives a signal meant for another device.

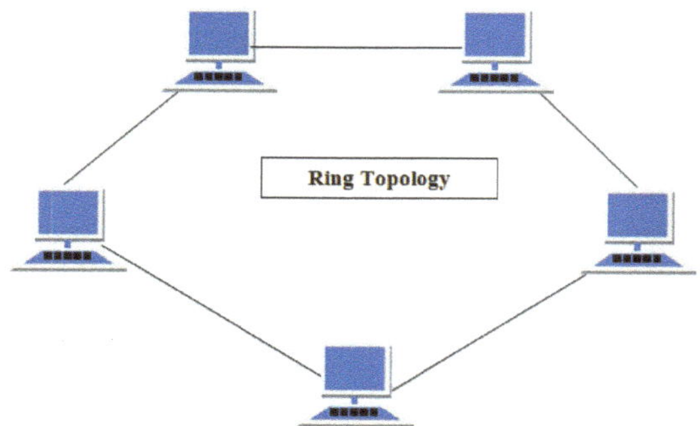

Figure 1.4. Structure of ring topology (Source: Geeksforgeeks, https://media.geeksforgeeks.org/wp-content/uploads/20200526102238/Untitled-Diagram-153-1.png).

a. Features of Ring Topology

1. For a ring topology with 100 nodes, many repeaters are needed because, in order to get to the 100th node, data must travel through 99 nodes. This is why in large ring topologies with lots of nodes, repeaters are used. Therefore, the network uses repeaters to prevent data loss.
2. The transmission is unidirectional, but it can be made bidirectional by having 2 connections between each Network Node; it is called Dual Ring Topology.
3. In Dual Ring Topology, two ring networks are formed, and data flow is in the opposite direction in them. Also, if one ring fails, the second ring can act as a backup to keep the network up.
4. Data is transferred in a sequential manner, bit by bit. Data transmitted has to pass through each node of the network until the destination node.

Remember

Computer networking is the branch of computer science that deals with the ideation, architecture, creation, maintenance, and security of computer networks. It is a combination of computer science, computer engineering, and telecommunication.

b. Advantages of Ring Topology

1. Transmitting network is not affected by high traffic or by adding more nodes, as only the nodes having tokens can transmit data.

2. Cheap to install and expand

c. Disadvantages of Ring Topology

1. Troubleshooting is difficult in ring topology.
2. Adding or deleting the computers disturbs the network activity.
3. Failure of one computer disturbs the whole network.

1.1.3.3. STAR Topology

Every device in a star topology has a dedicated point-to-point link connecting it to the hub or central controller. There's no direct connection between the devices. Unlike mesh topologies, star topologies don't allow direct communication between devices. When a device needs to send data to another, it goes through the controller, which then forwards it to the other connected device. That's how the controller acts as an intermediary.

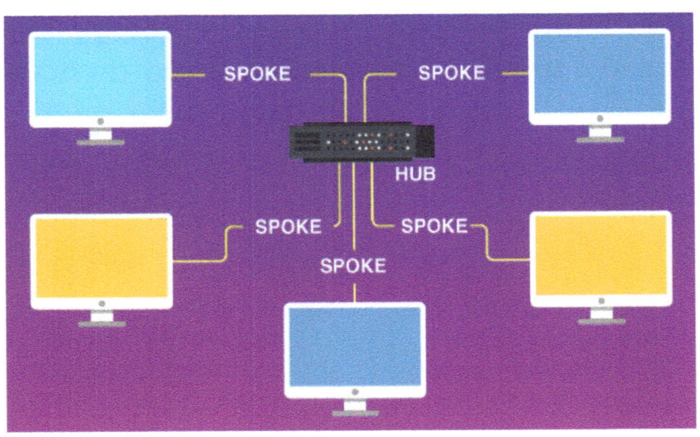

Figure 1.5. Arrangement of star topology (Source: BYJU'S, https://cdn1.byjus.com/wp-content/uploads/2022/07/star-topology.png).

a. Features of Star Topology

1. Every node has its own dedicated connection to the hub.
2. Hub acts as a repeater for data flow.
3. Can be used with twisted pair, Optical Fiber or coaxial cable.

b. Advantages of Star Topology

1. Fast performance with few nodes and low network traffic.
2. Hub can be upgraded easily.
3. Easy to troubleshoot.
4. Easy to setup and modify.
5. Only that node is affected which has failed, rest of the nodes can work smoothly.

c. Disadvantages of Star Topology

1. Cost of installation is high.
2. Expensive to use.
3. If the hub fails, then the whole network is stopped because all the nodes depend on the hub.
4. Performance is based on the hub; that is, it depends on its capacity.

1.1.3.4. MESH Topology

The link to other nodes or devices is point-to-point. There is a connection between every network node. Mesh can link n devices with its n(n-1)/2 physical channels. There are two techniques to transmit data over the Mesh topology: they are:

1. Routing; and
2. Flooding.

a. MESH Topology: Routing

According to network specifications, each node in routing has a routing logic similar to how routing logic guides data to take the shortest path to its destination. Alternatively, routing logic that avoids those nodes, etc., based on information about broken links. For the purpose of reconfiguring the failed nodes, routing logic is even an option.

b. MESH Topology: Flooding

Since flooding transfers the same data to every network node, routing logic is not needed. Since the network is strong, data loss is extremely unlikely. However, it causes unnecessary strain on the network.

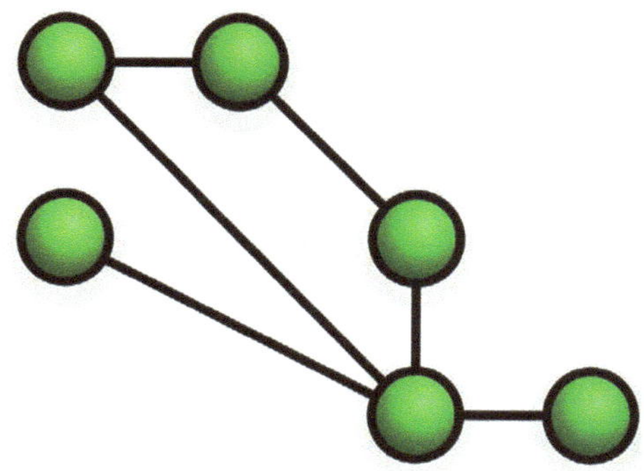

Figure 1.6. Networking of mesh topology (Source: Wikipedia, https://upload.wikimedia.org/wikipedia/commons/thumb/9/97/NetworkTopology-Mesh.svg/800px-NetworkTopology-Mesh.svg.png).

a. Types of Mesh Topology

1. **Partial Mesh Topology**: In this topology, some of the systems are connected in the same fashion as mesh topology, but some devices are only connected to two or three devices.
2. **Full Mesh Topology**: Each and every node or device is connected to each other.

b. Features of Mesh Topology

1. Fully connected.
2. Robust.
3. Not flexible.

c. Advantages of Mesh Topology

1. Each connection can carry its own data load.
2. It is robust.
3. Fault is diagnosed easily.
4. Provides security and privacy.

d. Disadvantages of Mesh Topology

1. Installation and configuration is difficult.
2. Cabling cost is more.
3. Bulk wiring is required.

Remember

Mesh networks offer high redundancy because there are multiple paths for data to travel between any pair of nodes. If one link or node fails, data can still be routed through alternative paths.

1.1.3.5. TREE Topology

It has a root node and all other nodes are connected to it forming a hierarchy. It is also called hierarchical topology. It should at least have three levels to the hierarchy.

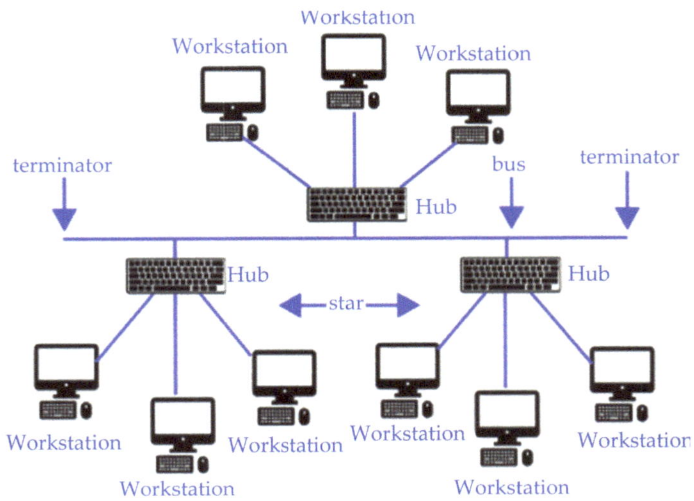

Figure 1.7. Features of mesh topology (Source: Pinterest, https://static.javatpoint.com/tutorial/computer-network/images/tree-topology-advantages-and-disadvantages.png).

a. Features of Tree Topology

1. Ideal if workstations are located in groups.
2. Used in Wide Area Network.

b. Advantages of Tree Topology

1. Extension of bus and star topologies.
2. Expansion of nodes is possible and easy.
3. Easily managed and maintained.
4. Error detection is easily done.

c. Disadvantages of Tree Topology

1. Heavily cabled.
2. Costly.
3. If more nodes are added maintenance is difficult.
4. Central hub fails, network fails.

1.1.3.6. HYBRID Topology

It's a mix of two or more topologies and comes in two different varieties. A hybrid topology (ring topology and star topology) is formed when two topologies are connected in an office setting. For example, one department uses ring topology while another department uses star topology..

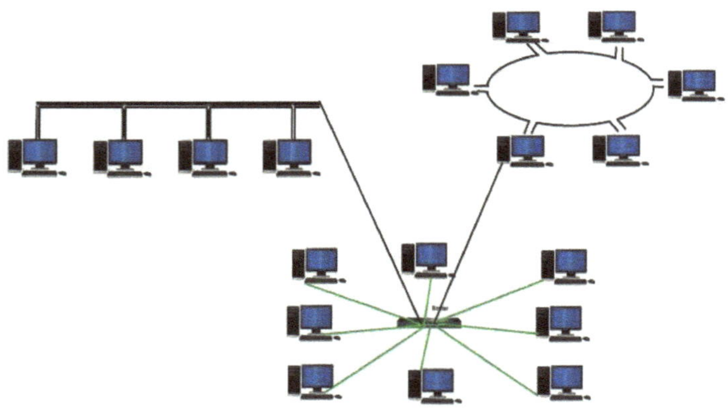

Figure 1.8. Structures of hybrid topology (Source: JavaTpoint, https://static.javatpoint.com/tutorial/computer-network/images/tree-topology-advantages-and-disadvantages.png).

Did you know?

In the 1970s and 1980s, Ethernet emerged as a popular networking technology developed by Xerox PARC, which later became a standard known as IEEE 802.3. Ethernet initially used a bus topology, but it later evolved to support various topologies, including the star topology.

a. Features of Hybrid Topology

1. It is a combination of two or topologies
2. Inherits the advantages and disadvantages of the topologies included

b. Advantages of Hybrid Topology

1. Reliable as Error detecting and troubleshooting is easy.
2. Effective.
3. Scalable as size can be increased easily.
4. Flexible.

c. Disadvantages of Hybrid Topology

1. Complex in design.
2. Costly.

1.1.4. Unique Identifiers of Network

A string of numbers or alphanumeric characters linked to a single entity inside a system is called a unique identifier, or UID. That entity can be addressed using a UID in order to be accessed and interacted with. Anything that has to be identified differently from other entities, including machines, websites, businesses, and individual users, can be given a unique identifier. These unique values can be allocated incrementally, arbitrarily generated by an algorithm, or selected by the user. The assignment of these distinctive values is typically contingent upon the requirements of the particular application.

The process through which users register for a website or service is the most well-known application of unique identifiers. In order to distinguish themselves in user logs, customers are frequently given a username or user ID by the business they are registering with. Afterwards, security and log-on uses are made of these identifiers.

In a physical supply chain, UIDs are also commonly used. Manufacturers often attach a serial number to the entire product or specific parts of a larger component, such as computer parts. This practice allows consumers to trace the product back to its original manufacturer in case of issues like malfunctions, defects, or recalls. The healthcare sector also makes frequent use of unique identifiers. Instead of the patient's name, a personal code is generated for reporting medical information. This approach not only addresses patient privacy concerns but also eliminates the possibility of duplicate reports. Regarding host names, a hostname is a unique device name assigned to each device in a network. To view your machine's hostname, simply type "hostname" in the Administrator Mode command prompt and press "Enter."

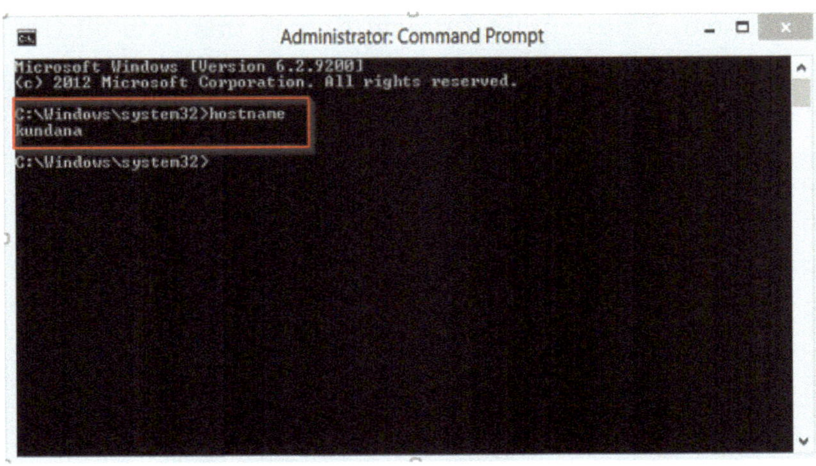

Figure 1.9. Unique identifiers of network (Source: Geeksforgeeks, https://media.geeksforgeeks.org/wp-content/uploads/hostname.png).

- **IP Address (Internet Protocol address):** The system's network address over the network is also referred to as the Logical Address. The Internet Assigned Numbers Authority (IANA) assigns an IPv4 (Version 4) address to each device on the Internet so that it can be uniquely identified in the global web. The IP address has a length of 32 bits. Consequently, 2^32 IP addresses are available

Keyword

Network interface card (NIC) is a hardware component, typically a circuit board or chip, installed on a computer so it can connect to a network.

to us. In the command prompt, type "ipconfig" and hit "Enter" to obtain the device's IP address.

- **MAC Address (Media Access Control address):** The NIC (Network Interface Card) is linked to the unique identifier of every host, which is also referred to as the physical address. At the time of manufacture, the NIC is given a MAC address. The MAC address has the following length: 12 nibbles/6 bytes/48 bits. Type "ipconfig/all" into the command prompt and hit "Enter" to obtain the MAC address.
- **Port**: A port is a logical channel that an application can use to send and receive data. Numerous applications can be running on a single host, and the port number of each application allows for its identification. Since port numbers are 16-bit integers, there are 216 ports available, which are divided into the following categories:

PORT TYPES	RANGE
Well known Ports	0 – 1023
Registered Ports	1024 – 49151
Ephemeral Ports	49152 – 65535

Number of ports: 65,536 Range: 0 – 65535

Type "netstat -a" in the command prompt and press 'Enter', this lists all the ports being used.

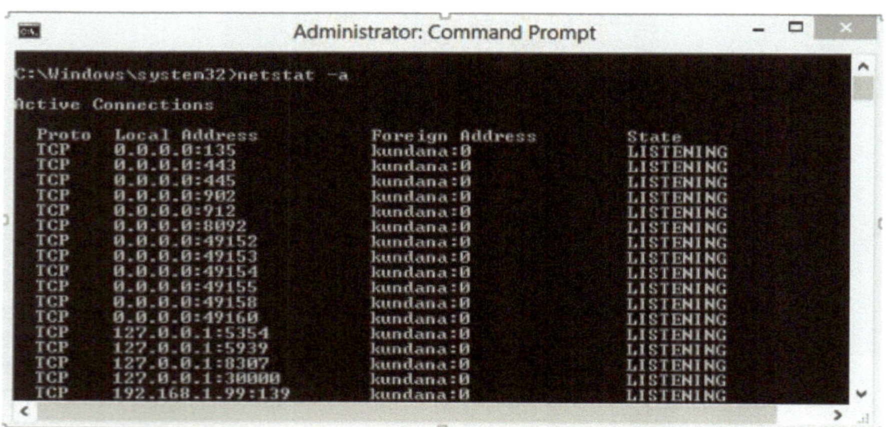

Figure 1.10. Identification of active network connection (Source: Geeksforgeeks, https://media.geeksforgeeks.org/wp-content/uploads/ports.png).

- **Socket**: The unique combination of IP address and Port number together are termed as Socket.
- **DNS Server**: The domain name system is known as DNS. In essence, DNS is a server that translates URLs, or web addresses (e.g., www.google.com), into

the IP addresses that match them. It is not necessary for us to retain the IP addresses of every single website. You can find the IP address of the domain you're looking for by using the 'nslookup' command. This also provides details about our DNS server.

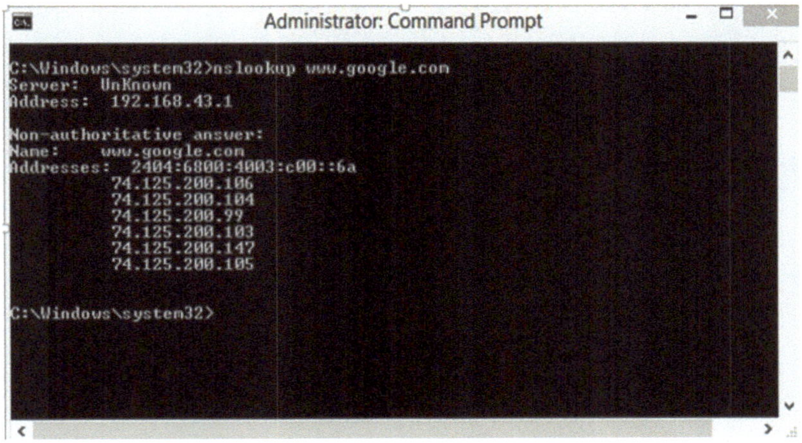

Figure 1.11. Translation of web addresses or URLs (ex: www.google.com) into corresponding IP addresses (Source: Geeksforgeeks, https://media.geeksforgeeks.org/wp-content/uploads/nslookup.png).

- **ARP:** Address Resolution Protocol is what ARP stands for. It is employed to translate an IP address into the matching physical address (i.e., MAC Address). The Data Link Layer uses ARP to determine the Receiver's machine's MAC address.
- **RARP:** Reverse Address Resolution Protocol is what RARP stands for. As the name implies, it accepts a physical address as input and outputs the device's IP address. However, since DHCP entered the scene, RARP has become outdated.

Did you get it?

1. Differentiate the functionality of bus topology and hybrid topology.
2. What are the unique identifiers of network?

1.2. TYPES OF NETWORK SERVICES

→Learning Objectives

- Examine the strategy of user management
- Know about the email management
- Find the process of printer sharing
- Give an overview on system administration

A vast array of connectivity and software tools that are distributed to computers connected to a network and overseen by a central team are collectively referred to as network services. When several computers are connected to a central server or to each other, the result is a networked computer environment. Shared files and utilities are accessible from a central location to all computers. This kind of environment has many benefits, from improved quality control to performance and issue management. System administration, email, printing, and user management are the four categories of network services. Desktop computers are referred to as client computers or workstations in a networked environment.

The servers are normally kept in a separate, temperature-controlled room that is frequently housed in a different structure than the areas where the workstation users are situated. Network cables, which are used to transfer data packages within the network, are used to provide access. Additionally, these cables offer access to the Internet, usually following a path via a network switch or central server. A variety of functions are included in user management, such as assigning rights, privileges, and access in addition to creating user names and passwords.

Email is a widely used tool for productivity that typically requires an Internet connection. Policies in many organizations govern the email software, maximum storage limits, and file sizes for transmission. Most companies provide their employees with company-specific email addresses, which necessitates the setup and maintenance of an email server. Shared printing is one of the key network services required in any organization. All users can send printing tasks to a central unit, eliminating the need for individual printers at each desk. This device often serves as a multifunction printer, scanner, and copier. Many businesses utilize specialized printer management software to handle document flow and protect sensitive information.

An essential network service for system administration is the ability to manage all workstations from a single location. The administrator is responsible for installing new software, updating operating systems, and ensuring all workstations run the same software versions. In many businesses, workstations are locked, granting only the system administrator permission to install updates or launch new applications. This practice reduces staff time spent on computer maintenance and enhances the overall quality of the network.

Keyword

System administration is the field of work in which someone manages one or more systems, be they software, hardware, servers or workstations.

1.2.1. User Management

Effectively managing users and their accounts to grant them access to a range of IT resources, including storage systems, networks, devices, apps, systems, and SaaS services, is known as user management, or UM. Administrators can grant access and take control of user accounts through user management, also known as user access management. A user management system is a fundamental security tool that is a crucial component of identity and access management (IAM).

In an organization's IT infrastructure, user management enables administrators to add, edit, and remove user accounts. An administrator can establish a user account for a newly hired employee, outlining the user's role, permissions, and access rights, for instance. The administrator grants the necessary permissions when a user needs access to particular resources, like files or applications. These rights specify what an individual is allowed to do on the network of the company and what they are not. A sales representative, for example, might only have access to customer information pertinent to their position, whereas a marketing manager might have access to marketing tools and data.

User management simplifies the process of granting and controlling access to IT resources overall. It guarantees that users have the rights to carry out their jobs efficiently while upholding security and compliance standards inside the company. An individual's access to devices, software, and services can be managed through a system called user management. Its main objectives are to monitor usage and manage permissions for actions and access.

Remember

User management is a system to handle activities related to individuals' access to devices, software, and services. It focuses on managing permissions for access and actions as well as monitoring usage.

Functions of user management include:

- Providing users with authenticated access
- Supporting set up, reissuing, and decommissioning of users' access credentials
- Establishing access privileges based on permissions

Accounts connected to software licenses can also be monitored by user management at every stage of their existence. This makes sure that everyone using the software has licenses for it, and that these can be reclaimed and reissued when they're not in use.

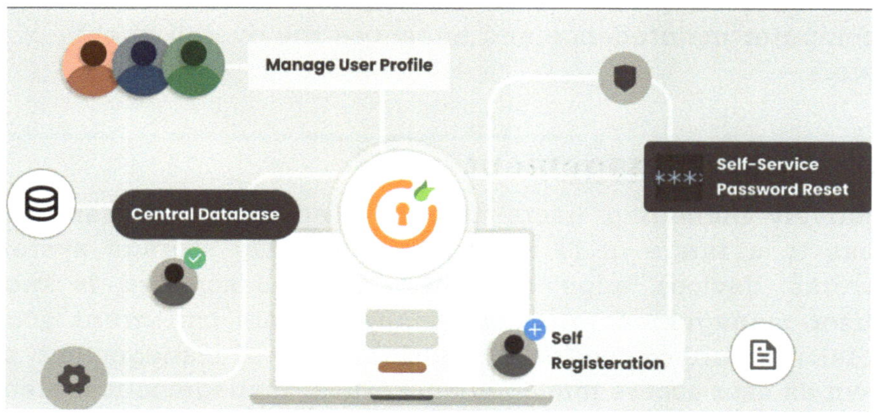

Figure 1.12. Administrators to manage users and the actions they are permitted to take on objects.

Source: https://www.miniorange.com/images/user-management/user-management.webp

User Management and the Cloud

User management in cloud applications and resources calls for increased caution. To handle the spread of users and the proliferation of accounts, IT departments must develop and oversee more intricate policies. IT teams also have to keep track of the different user management systems that the cloud service providers use, which complicates this already difficult task. This is due to the fact that user management in the cloud varies based on the service provider and the kind of deployment. Here are two popular approaches to cloud user management:

1. **Identity and Access Management (IAM):** The technology, regulations, and procedures gathered here are employed to oversee user accounts and associated access (i.e. e. humans) and functions (i.e. e. scripts or services). IAM is connected to roles or users. Permissions based on a user's job are

defined using a system called Role-Based Access Control, or RBAC.

2. **Resource Access Management (RAM):** Policies specify who can access a resource and what actions can be performed. RAM is tied to the resource rather than to a user or role.

Benefits of User Management

User management software can help organizations gain productivity, security, and cost savings.

- Productivity benefits with user management software

  Software-enabled user management automatism boosts productivity and reduces waiting times by mirroring modifications (e.g., adding, changing, and deleting users) between various platforms. Moreover, it streamlines the process of creating users, roles, and groups, which lessens the administrative teams' workloads.

- Cost-savings benefits with user management software

  Software usage can be tracked with the help of user management software to guarantee the best possible licensing. It is possible to reassign licenses that are no longer required. Software agreements that are no longer required may be terminated. For organizations looking to optimize license distributions, knowing how many devices a user has activated under their license is helpful. It also aids in budgeting for software in the future.

- Software license compliance benefits with user management software

  By monitoring users and their usage, user management software helps organizations make sure license agreements are followed. Additionally, this makes reporting easier in the event of an audit.

- Security benefits with user management software

  Security benefits from user management software are substantial. Unauthorized access can be avoided through the support of stringent access controls. Further reducing insider threat is the speed with which systems can be swiftly locked down or removed. Root cause analysis, remediation in the event of a data breach, and forensic audits are further features supported by user management software.

User Management—Benefits from Security and Beyond

Software tracking and management has always been a little tricky. This complexity has only grown as a result of the widespread use of cloud applications, which may have also made user management more crucial. Organizations are more vulnerable to possible data breaches as user anonymity increases and perimeters become more permeable. In order to prevent internal and external users from gaining unauthorized access to files, applications, systems, and devices on-premises and in the cloud, IT can maintain control over users' activities and reinforce other security measures with the aid of user management. One advantage of user management is that its advantages go beyond IT defense, which is not the case with other security solutions. Through optimized license usage, it lowers costs, which has an impact on finance.

Lastly, it helps with the onboarding and decommissioning of corporate identities for contractors and employees, which benefits IT operations and human resources (HR).

1.2.2. Email Management

Email is just the abbreviated version of "electronic mail," which is a system for sending, receiving, and storing electronic messages. It is also sometimes written as e-mail. With the growth of the Internet, its popularity has increased almost universally worldwide. Email is now frequently used as the go-to form of communication for both personal and professional matters.

Email messages typically arrive in the recipient's account in a matter of seconds. Images and various types of formatted documents are now easily included as attached files, so they usually contain more than just text. Furthermore, sending or receiving emails no longer requires a computer in front of you. Various mobile devices, including tablets and smartphones, enable correspondence management while on the go. Emails can move easily across different kinds of servers on different networks and between computers running different software thanks to standardized protocols that users use to send and receive messages. SMTP, or simple message transfer protocol, makes it possible for messages to be sent and received. Users can retrieve and store messages over time using additional protocols like Internet Message Access Protocol (IMAP) and Post Office Protocol (POP).

In the beginning, processing mail required a program known as "client software." Email clients come in a variety of forms; some are free to use, some require payment, and some Internet service providers even bundle them into their packages. Although client software is still in use today, a more adaptable approach has gained popularity recently. Webmail is another well-liked method of accessing email in addition to client software. As an extra bonus, the majority of service providers allow users to access their mailboxes via the Internet from any computer or other web-connected device. There are email services that are made especially to use the Internet as their main interface. These websites, known as "portals," have gained a lot of popularity because they typically allow users to register for a free email account and provide access to a calendar, news, search engine, and many other resources from one location.

Although the exact date of the invention of email is somewhat unknown, Ray Tomlinson, an American, is widely recognized as the father of the modern version. Prior to Tomlinson, users could communicate with one another via messages, but only if they had the same computer connected. Not even after computers were networked could messages be directed to a specific user. Tomlinson was credited with one of the most significant inventions in communication of the 20th century because he came up with a method to address mail to specific users. Tomlinson came up with the idea of identifying the user's name and the computer that they were using. Because of this, the standard email address format was username@usercomputer. With the exception of the user computer being frequently substituted with the name of a service provider, this standard has not altered significantly over time.

Legally speaking, email is typically regarded as a private communication medium, similar to phone conversations or even handwritten letters. While specifics may differ depending on the country, it is usually prohibited to access, read, or publish someone else's messages without authorization. Nonetheless, it is crucial to realize that hackers can easily intercept electronic mail. Furthermore, a lot of businesses demand that workers sign a consent form authorizing the business to read and keep track of all emails sent and received from company email addresses. The fact that every electronic message becomes a virtually permanent record of the conversation raises additional privacy concerns.

When a message is marked for deletion, it is taken out of the user's account's visible queue; however, deleted emails are infamously recoverable, so one should never assume that the message is permanently lost. Emails are likely to remain in existence on both the recipient's end and many of the servers they traversed, even if the sender uses specialist software to completely remove all traces of the message from their computer. As such, it is foolish.

Email's impact is too great to be understated. For instance, the USPS reports that it processes 485 million pieces of mail every day. Comparatively, in the US, 39.6 billion emails are sent each day. Stated differently, the volume of electronic mail handled by providers surpasses 81 times that of the world's largest postal system. Examining how much the use of traditional "snail mail," as it is now commonly called, has been impacted by electronic mail may be equally instructive.

Beginning in the latter half of the 1990s and continuing steadily ever since, the postal service, like many other postal services around the world, has seen dramatic declines in volume and revenue; this is partially due to the increasing amount of personal and business correspondence that is now delivered by email.

Did you know?

In 1994, Information Cybernetics, a company in Cambridge, Massachusetts, developed tools for pattern analysis and categorization of emails and other electronic communication channels. The platform of tools was called EchoMail. The first company to adopt EchoMail was AT&T. JC Penney adopted EchoMail in 1997.

1.2.2.1. Management Procedure

Currently, email is the de facto standard for business communication within organizations. The organizational standards pertaining to information and records must include email as well as adherence to it, just like any other form of business information and record. Email is now extremely important to business and is used in every part of all organizations. Information workers spend many hours a day reading, replying to, and working together via emails, with the email client serving as their main business application. Many people's definition of email management is as simple as taking emails off a server and putting them in a repository. However, in order to properly handle it, all of the other types of documents and records must also be categorized, stored, and possibly destroyed in accordance with established business policies and standards. The methodical regulation of the volume and caliber of electronic messages sent and received by an organization is known as email management.

Email servers within the organization are negatively impacted by the large amounts of emails stored in sent, deleted, and inboxes, which also pose a risk to the organization. The purpose of email servers was never to store so many emails and transfer control of that data outside of the company. A company's effort and expenses when responding to eDiscovery and disclosure will increase if it is unable to manage its email system and meet its legal preservation obligations in the event of litigation or government investigations.

Emails sent and received by staff members are centrally recorded by email management systems. Retention periods and access controls can be used to manage emails in addition to using a classification scheme to manage this content. To manage and retrieve this information, metadata related to the emails can be collected. One of the most popular uses for email management is email archiving. These solutions, in their most basic form, copy or delete messages from the messaging app and store them elsewhere. Some of these solutions archive the attachments but leave the messages unarchived, replacing them with a stub or a link from within the message. Systems for managing emails are a component of a larger solution. Records management programs, which include personnel, activities, and policies and procedures applicable to the entire organization, are essential.

Email is an information type that is often treated differently than others even though it shouldn't be. The reasons for different treatment are many and reflect:

- The sheer volume of messages involved, which dwarfs the number of other document types in play on a daily basis
- The informality with which they can be created and forwarded: everybody does it, all the time, with the simple click of a mouse
- The ease with which documents can be attached, even if they're not supposed to be.

These factors make it difficult to fully understand email management as a discipline and wrestle it to the ground. Organizations will often default to one or more of a number of unacceptable options that they think constitute management but really don't. Organizations may decide the best way to manage email is by doing one or more of the following:

- Saving all email messages forever
- Saving all email messages in the messaging application
- Setting arbitrary mailbox sizes for all users
- Declaring "email' as a record series
- And, of course, the ever-popular "Doing nothing"

The best answer is to ensure your organization has strong policies in place to govern such things. And yet, we know full well that not every organization does. According to a 2009 AIIM study on the subject:

- Only 10% of organizations have completed an enterprise-wide email management initiative,
- Only 20% currently are rolling out a project, and
- Even in larger organizations, 17% have no plans to do so.

There is much that organizations need to determine:

- When to declare an email, copy of a message or an entire thread/ conversation a record
- Determine what to base the record decision upon – sender, receiver, type of content, attachments, text within the email, etc.

1.2.3. Printer Sharing

The process of granting access to one or more printers to numerous computers and devices linked to the same network is known as printer sharing. Depending on the permissions the administrator has set for each user, every node or device on the network can print to any shared printer and, to a limited extent, modify the printer settings. A computer can share a printer with other computers on the same network if it is connected to a printer that supports printer sharing. As long as the shared printer is set up correctly on one computer, that computer can share it regardless of how old or new it is. The *operating system* (OS), which manages communication between computers and devices on the network as well as the printer itself, makes sharing possible. The computer connected to the shared printer receives print requests from other networked computers and uses them to initialize the printer before forwarding print jobs to it. Regretfully, the person initiating the print job still needs to manually retrieve the actual printouts.

Keyword

Operating System (OS) is a collection of software that manages computer hardware resources and provides common services for computer programs.

To enable printer sharing in Windows 7 and 8, navigate to the Network and Sharing Center icon, click "Change advanced sharing settings," and then select the "Turn on file and printer sharing" radio button under "File and printer sharing." Each computer (Client PC) in a network shared environment sends data via a server PC, which is managed centrally, as shown below. This kind of computer is frequently referred to as a "Print Server" or "Server."

In a Network Shared environment:

- It is possible to use both print and scan functions from a server PC, but only print from client PCs. (Note: Only if your Brother machine has a scan function.)
- Client PCs cannot use the shared printer when a server PC is turned off.

1.2.3.1. Peer-to-Peer

Every computer sends and receives data to every device directly in a peer-to-peer setting. File access and machine sharing are not controlled by a single central server. We recommend using the peer-to-peer printing method, as shown below, if your Brother device is compatible with wired or wireless Ethernet networks.

- In a Peer-to-Peer environment,
- It is easier to configure than the Network Shared printing method.
- Client PCs can print to the printer at any time.
- No need to be concerned if the Server PC is turned on or not.
- You can use the print and scanning functions of the Brother

machine. The functions available on the Peer-to-Peer connection vary depending on the machine. For details, we recommend you check the machine specification.

1.2.4. System Administration

Managing a hardware and/or software system is known as system administration. A system administrator is responsible for handling various tasks such as backups, granting user access, managing user accounts, ensuring system security, monitoring system health, and allocating system resources like disk space. IT professionals typically work on system administration for an organization, ensuring that computer systems and associated services operate smoothly. The responsibilities of system administrators are diverse and can vary based on the types of computer systems they maintain, but they often involve common tasks that can be approached in different ways.

Tasks like installing new hardware or software, setting up and maintaining user accounts, managing computer systems such as servers and databases, and preparing for and addressing system outages are common. Additional duties may include providing guidance to computer users, assisting with light programming or scripting to streamline system workflows. While having some programming knowledge can be beneficial, system administration is not primarily a programming role. Modern Microsoft Windows systems often use PowerShell for detailed system information, while Linux and UNIX systems offer a variety of programming languages like Bash, Perl, and Python. While proficiency in these languages is not mandatory, reaching an intermediate level can enhance your understanding of system operations and improve efficiency in daily tasks.

Access control, user management, backup and recovery, and system monitoring are among the duties of system administration. Usually, backup, recovery, and system monitoring features are combined into a single application for the entire company. Role assignment and user creation are examples of user management functions. Using the same login ID and password to access various systems within an organization is known as single sign-on, or SSO. Software libraries frequently integrate authorization and authentication into a single component. A computer network's overall functionality, including network security, the individual PCs and hardware connected to the network, as well as any software the computers may be running, are all under the control of computer system administrators. Computer system administrators must regularly upgrade hardware and software, troubleshoot any issues that arise during upgrades, and consult with staff regarding upcoming system upgrades in order to achieve the goal of satisfactory system functioning. Nowadays, the majority of system administrator jobs demand at least a bachelor's degree in computer science, with US and larger corporations setting the standard.

When it comes to system administrator tools, computer users are more likely to think of physical, tangible items like cables, power cords, and various analyzers that are intended to measure and analyze signal problems and system efficiency than people in the industry. Punchdown tools, sometimes referred to as punch-down tools or Krone tools, are the only tools that a system administrator can truly use that resemble tools. Wires are inserted into tiny spaces inside computers using punchdown tools. Software created for various purposes is also included in the system administrator tools. System administrator software, sometimes referred to as admin source tools, is not visible to end users, in contrast to the software utilized on network user PCs. Rather, it provides the system administrator with a variety of data, including software usage trends, computing speeds across different programs and databases, and software updates that are installed automatically but need the system administrator's approval. System security-related software is another category of software that is deemed necessary for system administrators. These kinds of software support safe business transactions, preserve data privacy, and provide. Many of the tasks that once required continuous attention from network system administrators are now automated and are regarded as essential administrator tools of the trade. Numerous native tools, also referred to as system administrator tools, come pre-installed with the software that they are meant to manage. Third-party vendors sell other kinds of automated software made to make system administrator tasks easier.

Did you get it?

1. What are the useful factors for user management?
2. Determine the management procedure of email networking.

1.3. TYPES OF NETWORK

→Learning Objectives

- Understand the local area networks (LAN)
- Describe the personal area networks (PAN)
- Know about the home area networks (HAN)
- Learn about the wide area networks (WAN)
- Discuss on campus networks
- Give an overview on metropolitan area networks (MAN)
- Examine the enterprise private networks
- Define the purpose of internetworks
- Define the backbone networks (BBN)
- Explain the purpose of global area networks (GAN)

A computer network is an assembly of interconnected computers that facilitates computer-to-computer communication and resource, data, and application sharing. A collection of two or more linked computer systems is called a computer network. A network connection can be made with wireless or cabled media. Hardware and software are used in every network to link computers and other devices.

A computer network is a type of digital communications network that permits resource sharing between nodes. Computer networks use connections (data links) between nodes to facilitate data exchange between computing devices. These data links are set up using wireless technologies like Wi-Fi and cable technologies like twisted pair or fiber-optic cables.

Network nodes are computer systems on a network that start, route, and end data. Network addresses are typically used to identify nodes, which can include networking hardware like switches and routers as well as hosts like PCs, phones, and servers. When two of these gadgets can communicate with each other, regardless of whether they are directly connected, it is considered that they are networked together. Application-specific communications protocols are typically layered (i.e., transported as payload) via additional, broader communication protocols. To maintain the dependability of this formidable collection of information technology, expert network management is needed.

A vast array of services and applications are supported by computer networks, including access to the World Wide Web, digital video and audio, shared use of printers, fax machines, application and storage servers, email and instant messaging, among many other things. Different computer networks have different bandwidths, transmission media for carrying their signals, communications protocols for managing network traffic, sizes, topologies, traffic control mechanisms, and organizational goals. The Internet is the most well-known computer network.

Remember

Computer networks may be classified by many criteria, including the transmission medium used to carry signals, bandwidth, communication protocols to organize network traffic, the network size, the topology, traffic control mechanisms, and organizational intent.

There are many different types of networks, which can be used for different purposes and by different types of people and organizations. Here are some of the network types that you might come across:

1.3.1. Local Area Networks (LAN)

A local area network, or LAN, is a collection of peripherals and computers that are connected to a server within a specific geographic area via a wireless link or shared communications line. As few as two or three users in a home office or several hundred users in a corporation's central office can be connected to a local area network. In order for network nodes to share resources like printers or network storage, LANs are set up by homeowners and information technology (IT) administrators. Cables, switches, routers, and other hardware are needed for LAN networking in order to connect users to internal servers, websites, and other LANs that are a part of the same wide area network (WAN). The two main methods for making LAN connections available are Ethernet and Wi-Fi. A specification called Ethernet makes it possible for computers to talk to one another. Wi-Fi connects computers to LANs via radio waves. While Ethernet and Wi-Fi speeds increased and connectivity costs decreased, other LAN technologies, such as Token Ring, fiber distributed data interface (FDDI), and ARCNET, fell out of favor. A wireless LAN's cost and flexibility make it potentially better than a wired LAN connection in many circumstances. People who work exclusively with smartphones, tablets, and other mobile devices are common among companies that view WLANs as their main source of connectivity. Virtual LANs, which enable network managers to logically divide and group network nodes without requiring significant infrastructure changes, were made possible by the trend toward virtualization.

Networking is integrated into many operating systems, such as Apple OS X and Microsoft Windows. This means that connecting computers in a network is not too challenging, as long as the network administrator has a fairly modern laptop or desktop PC. To set up a wireless network, the administrator will need an Ethernet cable to connect the wireless router to the main PC or server, as well as a wireless router connected to a broadband connection. This setup will allow other computers with built-in or connected wireless networking hardware to detect wireless signals and join the local area network.

1.3.1.1. Characteristics of a LAN

LAN sizes can vary quite a bit. A local area network (LAN) consists of devices connected through a home internet connection. In small businesses, LANs connect around a dozen to a hundred PCs with printers and file storage. The largest LANs are managed by a server that handles file storage, routes files to printers and scanners, and shares data among devices. The devices on a LAN are typically located in the same building as the network, distinguishing it from other networks like the internet. These devices—computers, printers, scanners, and more—connect wirelessly to a router through a Wi-Fi access point or via an Ethernet cable. It's possible to connect multiple LANs together using radio waves or phone lines.

1.3.2. Personal Area Networks (PAN)

A network built around a person's workspace is called a personal area network. The device owned by the individual serves as the hub of the network, to which other devices are connected. Wireless personal area networks are another option. A group of networked devices without a centralized network system is called a personal area network. These networks are frequently built with the aid of a mobile computing device, like a laptop or smartphone. It doesn't really matter how the devices are connected, so Bluetooth™ is just as likely to be used in a personal area network as Wi-Fi™ or network cables. A personal area network connecting to the Internet was not common in the past, but with the increasing popularity of Wi-Fi™ and mobile Internet, that has changed.

A local area network (LAN) is a type of network that is commonly constructed using a centralized routing system. These central systems, which are typically routers, establish wired or wireless connections with each device on the network. The router is used by the system's devices to communicate with one another. The priority and sequence of transferred traffic are also set by the router. Finally, the router is the means by which the LAN communicates with the Internet. Building a personal area network involves some slight variations. All connected devices typically connect to one main hub, though daisy-chaining devices together is an option if the hardware permits it. The linked devices connect to one another through this central device. After that, they simply function as regular extensions of the central device, managing movement and operation priorities in the same manner as any of its regularly installed systems.

The building of the network takes precedence over the techniques utilized to establish a personal area network. As a result, there are numerous standard techniques utilized in their construction. The practice of wiring computers together was widespread in the past, but with the advent of wireless connections, it has become less common. Certain devices in the network may use Bluetooth in addition to wireless technology. The effective broadcast distance of a personal area network's individual components is the only real restriction, aside from those resulting from construction. The effective broadcast range of Wi-Fi™ and Bluetooth™ is approximately 30 feet (10 meters). This indicates that two of the pieces could be as much as 60 feet (20 meters) apart under normal circumstances. It is possible to expand that even further if the device supports multiple connections.

> **Keyword**
>
> **Network cabling** is the physical infrastructure that connects computers and other devices to a network.

1.3.3. Home Area Networks (HAN)

Home environment devices are connected by a home area network. Personal computers, iPads, iPhones, printers, TVs, and other gadgets may be included. The Home Area Network, or HAN, is a network that makes it easier for devices in close proximity to a home to communicate with one another. An internal network used for energy monitoring and control is called a home area network, or HAN. It monitors energy consumption and connects to the electric meter of the utility company so that the homeowner can see what energy is being used and where. Additionally, it serves as a means for the utility to manage the air conditioning and heating in order to conserve energy. Moreover, the HAN offers a practical method for turning appliances on and off. A home area network, or HAN for short, is a kind of network that enables multiple computers and other network devices in a room to share resources, including internet connectivity. Any device with a TCP/IP connection can access the internet these days thanks to a router installed in practically every home. This covers the standard desktop or laptop, as well as the newest home appliances (IoT), smartphones, smart TVs, gaming consoles, and security cameras.

A typical architecture of a Home Area Network:

Internet service providers provide fiber-optic networks that are directly connected to homes, offering lightning-fast VoIP, gaming, and TV streaming services. A TCP/IP connection between the Internet Service Provider and the home router is used for all communications. In order to guarantee complete Wi-Fi signal coverage inside the house, we typically have one or more wireless access points.

- Computers such as desktops, laptops, netbooks, and tablets
- Network-attached storage (NAS) device
- Network Printers
- Smartphones connected via Wi-Fi
- Smart speakers

- Smart TV's and DVRs (access to services such as Netflix and YouTube)
- Stereo systems with network connectivity that allow a user to easily access their music library stored on a PC or NAS
- Video game consoles for multiplayer games and social network integration
- Security alarms
- Garage door and gate openers
- HVAC (keeping your house warm or cold)
- Smoke/CO detectors
- Media Players or Streaming Devices like Apple TV

1.3.4. Wide Area Networks (WAN)

A wide area network extends over a greater area of space, typically within a radius of several kilometers. Wide area networks, or WANs for short, are communications networks that connect local computer networks to a wider, functional network that can span both domestic and foreign locations by utilizing current technology. The local area network and the metropolitan area network, on the other hand, offer communication inside a constrained geographic area. It is frequently desirable to link computer networks, particularly for companies that run multiple locations. Utilizing the current telephony technology makes this the easiest to do, starting with the local area network and progressing to the wide area network. Fiber optics are essentially used to establish a connection between networks that are housed in various facilities. This usually entails using PSTN (public switched telephone network) technology or POTS (standard phone lines). A third option for creating a network, ISDN (integrated services digital network) solutions, became very popular in the 1990s, primarily due to the drawback.

Did you know?

WANs are often built using leased lines. At each end of the leased line, a router connects the LAN on one side with a second router within the LAN on the other. Because leased lines can be very expensive, instead of using leased lines, WANs can also be built using less costly circuit switching or packet switching methods.

A wide area network, or WAN, enables businesses to utilize shared resources to run their operations. For instance, many retail pharmacies use one to assist consumers who fill prescriptions at one of their locations. Once a customer is in the pharmacy's common customer database, they can fill a prescription at any of the company's locations—even when they're on vacation in a different state.

Wide area networks are useful for businesses as well. With this kind of wide area network application, internal operations like sales, marketing, production, development, and accounting can also be shared with approved locations. Employees can work from almost anywhere by using this to combine disparate location-based computer networks into a single computer network for the entire company. In the event that a natural disaster damages or renders one facility unusable, staff members simply relocate and continue working using the shared network at their new location.

1.3.5. Campus Networks

A campus network is like a local area network (LAN) used by government agencies, universities, businesses, and similar organizations. It usually covers a group of nearby buildings. In a campus network, you'll find a set of connected LANs exclusive to a business, government body, academic institution, or similar establishment. Typically, a campus includes a cluster of adjacent buildings. While users in a campus network are not as spread out as in a wide area network (WAN), they may be more geographically dispersed than in a single LAN. Campus networks in colleges and universities connect various buildings like administration offices, housing complexes, lecture halls, libraries, student centers, sports facilities, and more within a specific town or neighborhood. Important departments and staff members work in buildings linked by corporate campus networks. The corporate campus network, within a limited geographic area, acts as the user-facing part of the larger corporate network. In an ideal campus network, every node is connected to every other node via optical fiber media, utilizing Gigabit Ethernet or 10-Gigabit Ethernet technology. In certain places, such as university student centers or libraries, where multiple users concurrently use portable and mobile devices like notebook and tablet computers for research and communication, Wi-Fi hot spots or even a hot zone comprise the user end of the network. Occasionally, the phrase "campus network" refers to a group of geographically dispersed Internet users who share a common interest. Examples of such groups include the International Sustainable Campus Network (ISCN), a forum that assists colleges, universities, and businesses in their pursuit of sustainability in research and teaching, and the Roosevelt Institute Campus Network, a nationwide student initiative.

Keyword

Switched Multimegabit Data Service (SMDS) is a public, packet-switched service aimed at enterprises that need to exchange large amounts of data with other enterprises over a wide area network on a nonconstant or bursty basis.

1.3.6. Metropolitan Area Networks (MAN)

Networks that cover an area the size of a metropolitan area are known as metropolitan area networks. A Metropolitan Area Network, or MAN, is made up of several interconnected Local Area Networks (LANs) that may also be connected to a Wide Area Network (WAN). A Metropolitan Area Network, or MAN, is a sizable computer network that reaches across a city or a sizable university campus. Long-term internet connectivity is the main goal of the Metropolitan Area Network (MAN). Several LANs are typically combined into a MAN (Metropolitan Area Network) to create a network. An optical fiber setup makes up the backbone of this extensive network, known as the Metropolitan Area Network (MAN).

The three technologies that are most frequently used to create MAN (Metropolitan Area Network) networks are Switched Multi-megabit Data Service (SMDS), ATM (Asynchronous Transfer Mode), and Fiber Distributed Data Interface (FDDI). The most commonly used is ATM (Asynchronous Transfer Mode). Digital data transfer technology is known as ATM (Asynchronous Transfer Mode). It was created in 1980 with the goal of enhancing real-time data transfer across a single network. Similar to a cell relay system, ATMs (Asynchronous Transfer Mode) divide data into fixed, equal-sized packets that are transferred gradually. During a video conference, the ATM (Asynchronous Transfer Mode) was used to access clear audio and video results. ATMs' qualities have made it possible for them to serve as the foundation for wide area data networks.

Asynchronous Transfer Mode, or ATM, combines packet switching and circuit switching features to transfer data even in real time. The data transfer over LAN standard FDDI has a range extension of about 200 kilometers. Several thousand users' data transmission can be supported with the aid of FDDI. It is known as the MAN (Metropolitan Area Network) technology for this reason. Fiber distribution data interface, or FDDI, gets its name from the fact that its fundamental infrastructure is built on optical fiber. SMDS technology is used when transferring data via a connectionless service. Data is transferred by storing information in the header and traveling independently over any network to reach its destination, according to connectionless services. Data transfers via SMDS technology result in the formation of tiny data packets, much like those seen in ATMs. Nevertheless, datagrams—unreliable data service provider's data packets—can be transmitted over great distances thanks to SMDS. These days, microwave and infrared signals are used to establish MAN (Metropolitan Area Network) links.

Between LAN and WAN is typically where MAN (Metropolitan Area Network) is located. Connecting geographically separated LANs is the usual use for it. In order to create a communication link between two independent LAN nodes, MAN's objective. Optical fiber is typically used to create a metropolitan area network, or MAN. Routers and switches are used to set up the network. An active port that manages the filtering of data, typically in the form of frames, is called a switch. Every switch functions as two ports: on the one end, it handles data filtering, and on the other, connection management. Another tool to help with network connectivity is a router. The data packets are assisted by the router in determining the best course of action. To put it another way, it monitors the transfer of data. An area of up to 50 km is typically covered by MAN (Metropolitan Area Network).

The Metropolitan Area Network, or MAN, is situated between the LAN and the WAN. As a result, it lowers the cost associated with setting up a wide area network while also improving data handling efficiency. The Metropolitan Area Network, or MAN, provides centralized data management. You can link numerous fast LANs together with it. Data transfer has been made easier by telephone companies all over the world thanks to an underground optical fiber network. The effectiveness and speed of data transfer are improved by these optical fibers. A speed of nearly 1000 Mbps is available to you thanks to the optical fibers. A WAN with a speed of 1.45 Mbps will cost you more money than it will benefit you. On the other hand, a metropolitan area network provides you with a total speed of 1000 Mbps at the lowest possible cost.

1.3.7. Enterprise Private Networks

An organization connects its sites via an enterprise private network, allowing the locations to share resources. An enterprise private network is a type of computer network that enables large corporations with several dispersed offices to securely connect those offices to one another via a network. Sharing of computer resources is the primary purpose of an enterprise private network.

Enterprise Private Networks fulfill the original function of private networks, which was to share resources while protecting data. Businesses create enterprise private networks to link their various locations, which include offices, manufacturing facilities, retail stores, warehouses, and other company sites. In order to exchange resources. Enterprise Private Networks, or EPNs, are a cutting-edge illustration of how information technology benefits the business sector. Businesses can easily expand their operations by connecting various departments that are spread out across remote locations and frequently do not have connectivity with one another through a private network.

Keyword

Public network is a wireless or wired network that computers and devices you don't trust are connected to.

This has a wide range of effects because it significantly affects a company's ability to be sustainable. Different business divisions can benefit from the increased connectivity and resource mobility that comes with integrating an enterprise private network. Enterprise private networks place a high value on privacy, which is typically protected by a combination of security controls and tunneling protocols like the Layer 2 Tunneling Protocol. Internet service providers, or ISPs, use a type of computer networking protocol called L2TP, or Layer 2 Tunneling Protocol. Such a protocol exists only to facilitate private network functions, like VPN and EPN. Although Layer 2 Tunneling Protocol is a session layer protocol, it resembles the Data Link Layer Protocol found in the OSI reference model quite a bit.

A User Datagram Protocol, or UDP, is included in the Layer 2 Tunneling Protocol to facilitate communication. IPSec, or Internet Protocol Security, is used as an encryption protocol since the original version of this protocol lacked any features that could have maximized data security, confidentiality, and encryption.

1.3.7.1. How Does It Work?

To create a secure environment, an EPN model enforces a private network with numerous restrictions. One of the core features of an enterprise private network that businesses hope to utilize is security. A network of this kind is set up so that no device operating outside of the EPN can attempt to connect to the network. This kind of model can only be accessed by registered devices according to the network model. Access points and routers have settings encoded in them that determine which devices are allowed access. It is named EPN because of its integration into the business organization's dimensions and the value it adds in such a core area. A public network and an enterprise private network are completely different from one another. An internet connection and an access point are necessary for a public network to function.

It is interesting to note that there are not many differences between public and private networks. Both regions use hardware technology and the infrastructure pretty much in the same ways. The only modern differences between them are the addition of security measures and access privileges. To put it another way, the terms "private" and "public" just indicate that both types of networks are understood. Setting up a private network like EPN in an organization would involve several steps. The reason for this is that it is intended to be highly encrypted and secure with restricted access. Thus, in order to achieve the goal of integrating such a network, organizations must concentrate on these specific areas. Enterprise private networks are becoming increasingly important to how businesses run and make use of their resources, particularly when it comes to sharing critical business data. Because web servers are exposed to the internet and can become targets of cyber security breaches, it is necessary to monitor and ensure their protection. Installing firewalls is also necessary to increase security.

1.3.7.2. Benefits of Using EPN

Considering the intended purpose of enterprise private networks, it can well be said that they have a number of plausible benefits to a business. These are discussed below:

- **Maximum security** – It is necessary for an organization to implement stringent security measures. Cyberattacks can occur on networks, and sensitive information stored in some company data runs the risk of being lost or obtained by unauthorized individuals. Even so, enterprise private networks are an excellent way to ensure that security risks are minimized and that the company can more easily manage its critical operations since data circulation is essential to long-term business operations. This is a key factor in the majority of businesses' decision to use enterprise private networks, despite the setup hassles and initial expenses that may arise.
- **Cost-cutting measure** – At the end of the day, a strong return on investment requires minimal overhead. The majority of businesses implement stringent policies to ensure their continued profitability. One important method of achieving this is by reducing major costs, of which the use of enterprise private networks is a prime example. Reducing the expense of physically moving resources and company data from one place to another is possible by sharing crucial data over the network to which key stakeholders can gain access. Meanwhile, a significant amount of precious time is saved because any type of resource or data can be uploaded over the network in a matter of minutes.
- **Centralization** – An organization's ability to continue operating is yet another essential component. Departments within a company can freely share resources with one another by connecting through an enterprise private network. Time savings are made possible by it,

allowing businesses to continue working toward meeting their daily requirements gradually.

In the end, enterprise private networks, or EPNs, continue to be cutting-edge technology that offers genuine advantages to an organization. With the newest Cisco technologies, the platform provides competitive training. From QoS implementation and firewalls to unified computing and unified communications, it covers a broad spectrum of topics and experiences. For CCNA, CCSP, CCIP, and CCNP certifications, QuickStart unquestionably provides the best training. To ensure that everyone understands the fundamental concepts and skills of computer networking, a variety of courses and training programs are offered.

1.3.8. Internetworks

Internetworks join disparate networks to form a more expansive network. Creating a vast, international network is commonly referred to as "internetworking." Internetworking is the process of utilizing intermediary devices, such as routers or gateways, to connect various networks. Internetworking uses the Internet Routing Protocol and a common data communication protocol to ensure data communication between networks that are owned and operated by various entities. The Internet is the world's largest collection of geographically dispersed networks, yet they are all connected by the same protocol stack—TCP/IP. Working on the internet requires that all networks that are connected employ the same protocol stack or communication techniques.

A computer network consists of several computers connected to one another via networking hubs and switches. Every single network node or segment is configured with a similar protocol or communication logic, which is typically TCP/IP, to enable communication. Internetworking is the process by which two networks that use compatible or identical communication protocols exchange information.

Routers and other internetworking devices are used to implement internetworking as well. These are actual hardware components with the capacity to link various networks and guarantee error-free data transfer. They are the fundamental components that make it possible to work online and form the foundation of the Internet. The process of connecting several computer networks to create larger networks is known as internetworking. With the use of intermediary devices called gateways, various network types can be connected to function as a single, sizable network. The foundation of the current Internet was created through internetworking, which was developed in response to a number of problems that arose during the early development of personal computers. Many people use various networks on a daily basis without even recognizing it. While a home user might stream music to a laptop over a wireless network, a businessperson using a smartphone to check email uses a cellular network. While large wired networks are the norm in the corporate world, rural users may use dial-up to access their ISP's network. Despite their disparate technological backgrounds, all of these networks can connect to one another thanks to internetworking.

The idea of packets—tiny, discrete data units—is essential to connecting various network types. Modern computer networking is built on packets, which are not limited to any particular network technology. Alternatively, packets can be inserted into frames—which are made for particular network technologies—instead of standalone units. This configuration makes it possible to use packets from one kind of network on another. Packets can be transferred between these various networks by special devices known as gateways or routers, which support multiple networking technologies.

Internetworking gradually evolved in response to various challenges. The first computer-to-computer connections were established by "dumb" terminals, which had limited processing power and were linked to powerful mainframes. Local Area Networks (LANs) came into existence as personal computers (PCs) began replacing terminals. Despite the numerous advantages, productivity suffered as LANs were self-contained and unable to connect with other LANs. Organizations with multiple locations encountered difficulties in sharing resources like file servers, printers, and other equipment, as well as exchanging information.

In the early 1970s, American researchers involved in the Advanced Research Project Agency Network (ARPANET), a network supported by the defense department, began exploring the idea of linking their network with other early networks. This exploration led to the development of the Transmission Control Protocol and Internet Protocol (TCP/IP) as it became evident that existing network protocols were not ideal for internetworking. By the late 1970s, two additional networks had been integrated into ARPANET through TCP/IP, marking a significant milestone in the Internet's development.

Throughout the 1980s, ARPANET was used to connect an increasing number of LANs to one another as well as new networks. ARPANET was superseded by a network constructed by the National Science Foundation (NSF) in 1989. From there, a sizable "network of networks" known as the Internet emerged when local networks were linked to the NSF's network via TCP/IP and associated protocols.

Keyword

National Science Foundation is an independent agency of the United States federal government that supports fundamental research and education in all the non-medical fields of science and engineering.

1.3.9. Backbone Networks (BBN)

A backbone is a key part of a network that helps nodes communicate and provides a channel for sharing information. Backbone networks are crucial for a network's stability. The backbone's role is to bring together different parts of the network to create a unified entity while maintaining their individuality. This allows multiple networks to work together for specific tasks and data sharing. Nowadays, there are many examples of backbone networks in action. One common scenario is setting up an infrastructure that allows networks at a company's main office and satellite locations to operate independently yet collaboratively. This type of network backbone can enhance coordination efforts by enabling data sharing between dispersed sales offices and the corporate sales office.

College campuses also frequently use a similar approach to connect local networks in different buildings to a central system for data exchange. Backbone networks typically use various communication techniques to establish connections and transfer data. This may involve a mix of wired and wireless components, such as Ethernet connections or dial-up telephone connections for remote locations with limited connectivity options. Additionally, backbone networks often have secondary connection options available for flexibility. For example, even when traveling for business with only a hotel phone line, employees may still connect to the backbone through alternative processes.

Differentiating between backbone networks and Internet backbones is crucial. Even though an internal backbone may allow remote access to networks through the Internet, interconnected networks within businesses remain closed unless the right credentials are provided for access. Even if an employee can access a few networks connected to the backbone, they may not have access to other networks in the community if the backbone network's architects design the communication process to restrict entry. This ensures data sharing among authorized users while helping maintain the integrity of each network within the system.

1.3.10. Global Area Networks (GAN)

An international network that links networks worldwide, like the Internet, is called a global area network. A network made up of several interconnected networks that span an extensive geographic area is referred to as a global area network (GAN). The term and the Internet, which is considered a global area network, are somewhat interchangeable. Geographically speaking, GANs are much more extensive than local area networks (LAN) and wide area networks (WAN). The primary challenge for any GAN is moving user communications from one local coverage area to the next since a GAN is utilized to support mobile communication across multiple wireless LANs. A broadband GAN is the most sought-after type of GAN. The broadband GAN is a global satellite Internet network that enables phone calls using portable terminals. These terminals offer broadband Internet access to laptop computers located in remote areas.

Did you get it?

1. What are Home Area Networks (HAN)?
2. What distinguishes Enterprise Private Networks from other network types?

FOCUS ON CAREERS

NETWORK ENGINEER

A network engineer is a professional responsible for designing, implementing, and maintaining the intricate systems that allow computers and devices to communicate and share resources within an organization. These professionals play a crucial role in ensuring the reliability, security, and performance of network infrastructure. Network engineers design network layouts and architectures, considering factors such as scalability, redundancy, and security requirements. They are adept at configuring and managing networking equipment such as routers, switches, firewalls, and load balancers to establish robust connectivity and enforce security policies. Monitoring network performance and identifying and resolving issues promptly are essential aspects of their job.

Overall, network engineers are instrumental in maintaining the backbone of an organization's IT infrastructure, enabling seamless communication, collaboration, and access to resources across the network while safeguarding against potential security risks.

A Network Engineer usually plans and manages networks to ensure they function as intended. Network Engineers are the integral cog of an IT system. People usually confuse Network Technicians with Network Engineers. Network Technicians usually assist with daily IT and troubleshooting tasks while Network Engineers deal with high-level tasks that involve designing and improvising the network.

Network Engineer Requirements

To excel in a network engineer role, candidates must meet specific job requirements, such as:

- A bachelor's degree in computer science (or a related field).
- Relevant certifications, such as Microsoft, Cisco, Citrix, VMware.
- Knowledge of network protocols, including TCP/IP, DNS, and DHCP.
- Experience with network hardware (routers, switches, and firewalls)
- Familiarity with network monitoring and management tools.
- Excellent problem-solving and analytical skills.
- Strong communication and teamwork abilities.

Responsibilities of a Network Engineer

Network engineers often work closely with other IT teams to integrate network services with other systems and applications. They are also responsible for ensuring compliance with relevant industry regulations and standards, particularly regarding data security and privacy. Continuous learning is essential in this field, as network engineers must stay updated with the latest technologies, protocols, and best practices to adapt to evolving network demands and emerging cyber threats. Strong analytical and problem-solving skills, along with attention to detail, are essential for success in this role.

- Maintain and control computer networks and associated computing environments like software for systems, software applications, equipment, and configurations.
- Running operations for disaster recovery and backups of data where possible.
- Data, applications, and hardware are protected by organizing, preparing, and enforcing network security measures.
- Troubleshooting, diagnosing, and solving hardware, software, and other issues affecting the network and device.
- Replacing defective hardware components of the network where possible.
- Maintain, customize, and track the device and email applications for virus protection.
- Network performance monitoring to decide whether any changes are required.

Conferring with network users on solving issues with current networks.

- Use master consoles to control network and computer system output.
- Coordinating access to the use of computer networks.
- Plan, install, and test networking devices, hardware for computers, and devices for operating systems.

Expect

- The work is office-based, although you may need to work across different sites, depending on the size of the organization and its network. More frequent travel may be involved if you work as a consultant.
- Jobs are available throughout the UK in organizations with large, sophisticated IT systems or with consultancies providing support to clients.
- The job can be challenging, particularly when things go wrong, as companies are dependent on their computer networks.
- Women are underrepresented in the job and the gender imbalance across the IT industry is a recognized issue. Steps are being taken to redress the balance. See Women in Technology and BCSWomen for more information and job vacancies.
- Systems support roles such as network engineering involve less programming, so you should consider this before committing to a career in this area if that is something you really enjoy.

Qualifications

You'll usually need a degree in a subject such as:

- computer science
- computer software/computer systems engineering
- computer systems and networks
- electrical/electronic engineering
- mathematics
- network security management
- physics.

It may be possible to enter this career without a degree, provided you have significant experience. There are many Level 4 network engineering apprenticeship opportunities and you can search for them using Find an apprenticeship. To find out more, see Apprenticeships.

Employers will usually expect you to do further study to get professional qualifications if you don't already have them. For example, many colleges and private training organizations participate in the Cisco Networking Academy program, which provides certification at several levels for students and network professionals.

Skills

You will need:

- An up-to-date knowledge and understanding of your employer's business and industry needs, as well as the technical demands
- To recognize the importance of customer focus and/or of serving the needs of the end user
- Excellent communication skills for communicating with staff who aren't technically trained
- The skill to take on a variety of tasks and pay attention to detail
- Analytical and problem-solving ability
- Teamwork skills and the ability to feel comfortable working with different teams, clients, and groups of staff across an organization
- Organizational skills and the ability to prioritize your workload.

Work Experience

Relevant work experience, for example through vacation work and summer placements, is useful as recruiters often look for evidence of skills developed through project work and placements.

Experience in related areas such as IT support, service, and repair can be useful if you want to move into network engineering.

Being on the user end of IT systems is also helpful as this will give you an idea of the types of problems that may arise.

Find out more about the different kinds of work experience and internships that are available.

Employers

You can work for any organization with large, sophisticated IT systems. Typical employers include:

- banks and building societies
- retail groups
- large government departments
- schools, hospitals and local authorities
- utility companies
- transport providers
- management consultancies.

Some organizations, including many local authorities and other public sector bodies, outsource all their IT systems to specialists, so these specialist companies often have vacancies for people with networking skills.

Network engineers can be employed by a large IT company to manage the firm's own systems or work in their contract services.

Large companies, such as Microsoft, provide an extensive range of installation and customer support services and they recruit graduates and experienced staff into all areas of IT support.

There are also many small consultancies that work by setting up and managing systems for organizations that are too small to warrant full-time IT support.

Look for job vacancies at:

- CWJobs
- efinancialcareers
- Technojobs

Recruitment agencies specializing in IT, such as Hays, also have vacancies, although these are more useful once you've built up some solid work experience. While large companies usually have a structured graduate recruitment procedure, you can approach small businesses and IT consultancies on a speculative basis, ensuring your CV stresses your personal, as well as technical, abilities. Contracting may be an option once you've gained substantial experience – visit Contractor UK for more information. Most job sites include contractor roles as well.

Other job titles used for this area of work include:

- network architect/computer network architect
- network/helpdesk support
- support/security/systems engineer
- IT/systems support engineer
- network administrator
- first/second-line support
- VoIP/Cisco engineer.

Career Prospects

Your career path will depend, to a certain extent, on the size of the organization you work for and the scope of its IT systems. With experience, you can progress to senior network manager and network management positions. Some network engineers choose to broaden their careers into other IT, customer-related, or management functions. Technical or infrastructure project management and network architecture are possibilities. Those who start as help-desk technicians can sometimes progress to network engineer posts, then on to senior network support, and finally network controller (mainly involved in decision-making, staff management, and advice on future strategy). This may be the typical route in an organization such as a large bank or a major government department.

A CLOSER LOOK

Computer networking is the backbone of modern communication and information exchange, enabling devices to connect and interact with each other across various geographic locations. At its core, networking involves the establishment of connections between computers, servers, routers, switches, and other devices to facilitate data transmission, resource sharing, and collaboration. The architecture of a computer network typically follows a hierarchical model, with multiple layers of protocols and technologies working together to ensure seamless communication. Protocols such as TCP/IP govern how data is transmitted and received, while devices like routers and switches manage traffic flow within the network.

One of the fundamental concepts in networking is the distinction between local area networks (LANs) and wide area networks (WANs). LANs connect devices within a limited geographical area, such as a home, office, or campus, using technologies like Ethernet or Wi-Fi. WANs, on the other hand, span larger distances and connect multiple LANs together, often utilizing leased lines, fiber-optic cables, or satellite links. The internet itself is the most extensive WAN, providing global connectivity to billions of devices worldwide.

Security is a critical aspect of computer networking, as networks are susceptible to various threats, including unauthorized access, data breaches, and malicious attacks. Network security measures such as firewalls, intrusion detection systems, and encryption protocols help safeguard sensitive information and prevent unauthorized access to network resources.

Advancements in networking technology are constantly pushing innovation and shaping the digital landscape. Emerging trends like 5G connectivity, edge computing, software-defined networking (SDN), and the Internet of Things (IoT) are changing how networks are designed, deployed, and managed. These developments bring faster data speeds, lower latency, increased flexibility, and scalability, creating new opportunities for applications like autonomous vehicles, augmented reality, and smart cities.

SUMMARY

- A computer network is a group of linked computers. Nodes are computers connected to a network, either wirelessly using radio waves or through cabling like an Ethernet cable.
- Wide Area Networks (WANs) connect computers and local networks to larger networks across extensive geographical regions, like continents.
- A computer network is a group of computers connected by communication channels to share resources and communicate with users.
- The fundamental idea behind OSI is that communication between two endpoints in a network can be separated into seven different groups, or layers, of related functions. Every user or program that communicates uses a device capable of providing those seven levels of functionality.
- Specialized routing protocols are designed for internet network routers. Each device in a ring topology has a unique point-to-point connection with only the other two devices on either side.
- Every device in a star topology has a dedicated point-to-point link that connects it to the hub, or central controller.
- Hostname is a special device name that is assigned to each device in the network. In the Administrator Mode command prompt, type "hostname" and hit "Enter" to see your machine's hostname.

MULTIPLE CHOICE QUESTIONS

1. **Combination of two or more networks are called**
   a. Internetwork
   b. WAN
   c. MAN
   d. LAN
2. **Which topology covers security, robust and eliminating traffic factor?**
   a. Mesh
   b. Ring
   c. Star
   d. Bus
3. **National Internet Service Provider (ISP) networks are connected to one another by private switching stations called**
   a. Network Access Points
   b. Peering Points
   c. National ISP
   c. Regional ISP

4. Multipoint topology is

a. Bus
b. Star
c. Mesh
d. Ring

5. A communication path way that transfers data from one point to another is called

a. Link
b. Node
c. Medium
d. Topology

6. Which of the following devices operates at the Data Link layer of the OSI model?

a. Router
b. Hub
c. Switch
d. Bridge

7. What protocol is used for transferring files over the Internet?

a. FTP
b. HTTP
c. SMTP
d. TCP

8. Which networking device works at the Application layer of the OSI model?

a. Router
b. Switch
c. Hub
d. Proxy server

9. In TCP/IP, what is the maximum number of addresses in the IPv4 address space?

a. 256
b. 2^{32}
c. 2^{64}
d. 2^{128}

10. What protocol is used to translate domain names to IP addresses?

a. DNS
b. DHCP
c. ARP
d. ICMP

REVIEW QUESTIONS

1. What is the Open Systems Interconnection (OSI) model, and what are its different layers?
2. What is network topology, and what are the common types of network topologies?
3. How does email management contribute to efficient communication within organizations?
4. What are the key responsibilities of system administrators in managing computer systems and networks?
5. What are Personal Area Networks (PANs), and what are some examples of devices commonly used in PANs?

Answer to Multiple Choice Questions

1. (a)	2. (a)	3. (b)	4. (a)	5. (a)
6. (d)	7. (a)	8. (d)	9. (b)	10. (a)

REFERENCES

1. Daniel, B., (2008). The Salsa20 family of stream ciphers; Chapter. In: Matthew, R., & Olivier, B., (eds.), New Stream Cipher Designs. Springer-Verlag.
2. Guido, A., Isaac, K., & McKeown, N., (2004). Sizing router buffers. ACM SIGCOMM Computer Communication Review.
3. Joan, D., & Vincent, R., (2002). The Design of Rijndael: AES – The Advanced Encryption Standard. Springer-Verlag.
4. Mills, D. L., & Kamp, P. H., (2000). The nanokernel. Proc. Precision Time and Time Interval (PTTI) Applications and Planning Meeting (423–430). Reston VA.
5. Mogul, J., Mills, D., Brittenson, J., Stone, J., & Windl, U., (2000). Pulse-Per-Second API for Unix-Like Operating Systems, Version 1 (p. 31). Request for Comments RFC-2783, Internet Engineering Task Force.
6. Neal, C., Yuchung, C., Stephen, G. C., Soheil, H. Y., & Van, J., (2016). BBR congestion-based congestion control. ACM Queue, 14(5).
7. Stefania, C., Bruce, D., Arjen, K. L., Walter, L., Peter, M., Brian, M., Herman Te, R., et al., (2000). Factorization of a 512-bit RSA modulus. Advances in Cryptology — EUROCRYPT 2000, Lecture Notes in Computer Science (Vol. 1807). Springer-Verlag.
8. Vladimir, B., Suman, B., Marco, G., & Sangho, O., (2008). Wireless device identification with radiometric signatures. Proceedings of the 14th ACM International Conference on Mobile Computing and Networking (MobiCom '08).

CHAPTER 2

Network Model and Standardization

LEARNING OBJECTIVES

After studying this chapter, you will be able to:

- Prepare for the OSI model
- Know about the multiplexing and switching
- Discuss on transmission control protocol (TCP)
- Learn about the user datagram protocol (UDP)

INTRODUCTORY EXAMPLE

THE OSI MODEL FOR CLOUD COMPUTING AND VIRTUALIZATION

Cloud computing is now crucial for online businesses as it helps them store, access, and process data efficiently at lower costs. The OSI model enables seamless operation and interoperability between different systems. All layers of the OSI model closely align with cloud computing, which is essentially the delivery of on-demand computing resources over the Internet. OSI provides a framework for encompassing the various components involved in cloud computing. At the lower layers of OSI, we find virtualization technology. Virtualization creates virtual instances of operating systems and storage within a physical infrastructure, allowing for efficient resource utilization, scalability, and flexibility in the cloud environment. There are two main layers of the OSI model that enable cloud computing: the Application Layer and the Network Layer. The Network Layer routes and transmits data across networks to deliver them to client devices, while the Application Layer defines the standards for clients to access cloud-based applications.

INTRODUCTION

A network's core is its networking software. It helps admins deploy, maintain, and monitor networks. Traditional networks use specialized hardware like switches and routers with integrated networking software. Software-defined networking (SDN) separates software from hardware, making it easier to innovate and adapt quickly. Network software allows admins to access network operations, unlike software applications for end users. Its main role is to facilitate users' access to network resources seamlessly.

- The basic functionality of network software includes:
- User management: Enables administrators to add or remove users from the network.

File management: Allows administrators to define the location of data storage and user access to that data.

Network standards establish the guidelines for communication between devices connected to a network, ensuring the interoperability of networking technologies. In order to reduce the possibility of incompatibility, networking standards are in place to help guarantee that products from various vendors can operate together in a network. Our dictionary of networking standards provides a glossary of key terms you should know. If the various network standards in use today were published in print, they would fill volumes upon volumes of text. They range from wireless networking standards like 802.11a and Gigabit Wi-Fi to wired networking standards like Ethernet and Gigabit Ethernet. The standards themselves specify the functions for which these network standards are intended. For instance, you need to use one standard to talk over the phone network and another to communicate over the Internet. Nearly everything that we encounter in a day is determined by standards. Both your TV's television signal and the cover on your "to-go" coffee cup adhere to standards. While some standards, like the television signal, are unregulated, others are, such as the new High-Definition Television (HDTV) standard developed in part by the Advanced Television System Committee (ATSC) or the National Television System Committee (NTSC).

2.1. THE OSI MODEL

→Learning Objectives

- Understand the purpose of application layer.
- Learn the responsibilities of the presentation layer.
- Explore the management of session layer.
- Comprehend the mechanisms used in the transport layer.
- Study the useful concepts in the network layer.
- Understand the framing detection in the Data Link Layer.
- Familiarize signaling in the Physical Layer.

The ISO/OSI model, which stands for International Standards Organization/Open System Interconnection, is a commonly used reference model for network communication between two end users. Understanding the network's operation can be helpful for addressing future issues. The significance of the OSI model cannot be overstated. Most networking suppliers and users recognize the importance of network computing products adhering to and fully supporting the networking standards established by this model.

Connecting a vendor's products to those of other vendors becomes relatively easy when they comply with the standards set by the ISO model. Conversely, the more a vendor strays from these guidelines, the more challenging it becomes to integrate their offerings with those of other vendors. Deviating from the communication standards fostered by the model would make software development efforts significantly more difficult for a vendor. They would need to develop all the necessary software from scratch instead of building on existing work done by other vendors.

The challenge arises when a vendor's products cannot easily integrate with those of other vendors, impacting their marketability. This, in turn, presents a significant issue for vendors. The ISO model provides a networking architecture for implementing protocols layer by layer. While each layer functions independently, it also supports the layer above it and is supported by the layer below it. The layers are divided into two groups. When a message is sent to or from a user, the upper layers come into play. On the other hand, when a message passes through the host computer, the lower layers are involved. Messages destined for the device target the higher layers, while those meant for another host do not get forwarded to the upper layers.

Layers of OSI model are as follows:

- Application layer
- Presentation layer
- Session layer
- Transport layer
- Network layer
- Data link layer
- Physical layer

2.1.1. Application Layer

The application layer provides users, whether software or human, with network access. It supports services like email, remote file access, transfer, shared database management, and other distributed information services, offering user interfaces for them.

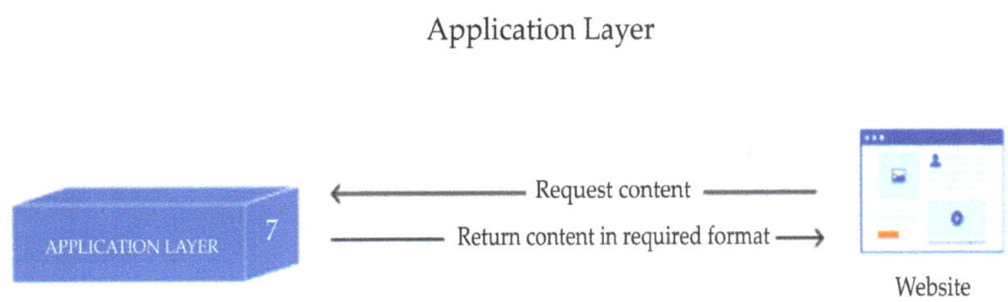

Figure 2.1. The request context of application layer (Source: Cloudflare, (https://cf-assets.www.cloudflare.com/slt3lc6tev37/2rcDKpr4WLqoyAZ7GDKkyJ/7cab96402de7ac5465b86e617da3da4e/osi_model_application_layer_7.png).

Specific services provided by the application layer include:

- *Network Virtual Terminal*: A network virtual terminal is a software version of a physical terminal that allows a user to log on to a remote host. To do so, the application creates a software emulation of a terminal at the remote host. The user's computer communicates with the software terminal, which then communicates with the host, and vice versa. The remote host believes it is communicating with one of its own terminals and allows the user to log on.
- *File Transfer, Access, and Management (FTAM)*: This application allows a user to access files on a remote computer (to make changes or read data), retrieve files from a remote computer, and manage or control files on a remote computer.
- *Mail Services:* This application provides the basis for email forwarding and storage.
- *Directory Services*: This application provides distributed database sources and access to global information about various objects and services.

2.1.2. Presentation Layer

Data received is converted into a format that the intended application can understand at the presentation layer. Think of the work at this layer as a translation task. For example, data is often encrypted at the presentation layer before being sent to other layers for transmission. Once received, the data is decrypted and sent in the expected format to the application.

The presentation layer's specific responsibilities include translation and encryption.

- *Translation*: Translation involves ensuring interoperability between different encoding techniques used by various computers.
- *Encryption:* Encryption is essential for maintaining privacy when transmitting sensitive information. It involves transforming the original information into another form for

sending over the network, with decryption reversing this process to restore the message to its original form.

- *Compression*: Data compression reduces the number of bits to be transmitted. Data compression becomes particularly important in the transmission of multimedia such as text, audio, and video.

Keyword

A **remote computer** is a computer that you can connect to from another location and control as if you were physically present. It's also known as a remote desktop.

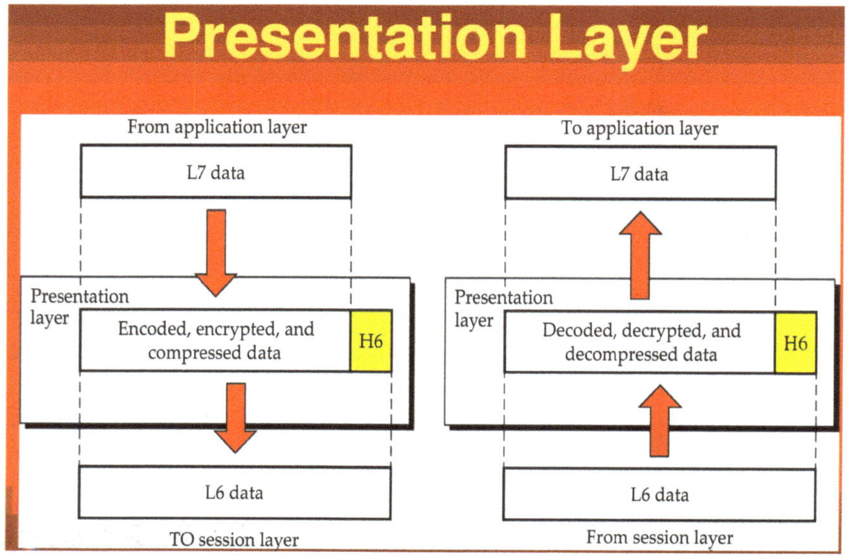

Figure 2.2. Presentation layer (Source: Thenationaltv, https://f002.backblazeb2.com/b2api/v1/b2_download_file_by_id?fileId=4_za8a2358db1d7f91b68b30916_f102f662b1ec69f3a_d20190909_m073653_c002_v0001114_t0001).

2.1.3. Session Layer

Establishing, maintaining, and terminating connections take place at the session layer. This usually refers to network-based application requests for data. As the actual data flow is managed by the transport layer, the session layer serves as an announcer, informing the programs and applications sending and receiving data when their requests are fulfilled. The session layer synchronizes data transmission, to put it technically.

Specific responsibilities of the session layer include:

- Dialog Control: The session layer allows two systems to enter into a dialog. It allows the communication between two processes to take place either in half-duplex (one way at a time) or full-duplex (two ways at a time). For example, the dialog between a terminal connected to a mainframe can be half-duplex.

- Synchronization: The session layer allows a process to add checkpoints into a stream of data.

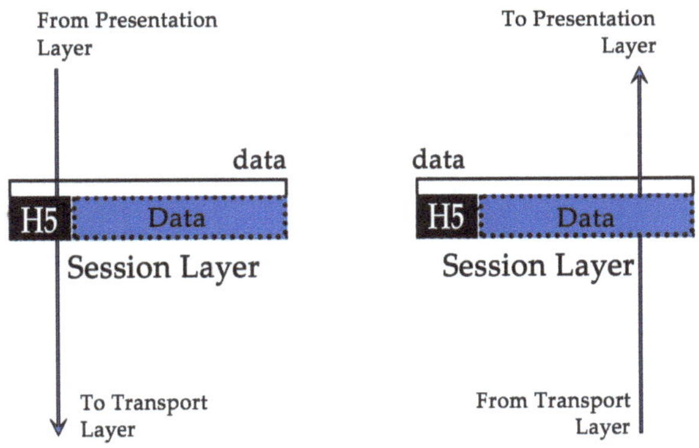

Figure 2.3. Session layer (Source: Open4tech, https://open4tech.com/wp-content/uploads/2019/09/session-layer.png).

2.1.4. Transport Layer

Transmission of data over the network is handled by the transport layer. The data is conceptualized at this level more as a conversation than as individual packets. This is achieved by using protocols, which are referred to as "rules of communication." The protocols monitor the entire transmission of numerous packets, looking for errors in the conversation, acknowledging successful transmissions, and requesting retransmission in the event that errors are found.

Remember

Transport layer services are conveyed to an application via a programming interface to the transport layer protocols.

Specific responsibilities of the transport layer include:

- *Service-Point Addressing*: Multitasking is a common feature of computers. Because of this, delivery from one computer to another or from one computer's running program to another computer's running program is referred to as source-to-destination delivery. Hence, a sort of address known as a service-point address (or port address) needs to be included in the transport layer header. While the transport layer delivers the complete message to the appropriate process on that computer, the network layer delivers each packet to the right machine.
- *Segmentation and Reassembly*: A message gets split into transmittable chunks, each with a sequence number attached. These numbers help the transport layer identify and replace lost packets during transmission, as well as correctly piece together the message upon reaching the destination.
- *Connection Control*: There are two types of transport

layers: connection-oriented and connectionless. With a connectionless transport layer, each segment is sent to the destination machine's transport layer as an independent packet. In contrast, a connection-oriented transport layer establishes a connection with the destination machine's transport layer before sending the packets. The connection is closed once all data is transmitted.

- *Flow Control*: Flow control, similar to the data link layer, is managed by the transport layer. However, at this level, flow control is implemented end-to-end rather than over a single link.
- *Error Control*: The transport layer shares the responsibility for error control with the data link layer. Error control at this layer occurs end-to-end, ensuring that the entire message reaches the receiving transport layer without any errors (loss, duplication, or damage). Retransmission is commonly used to rectify errors.

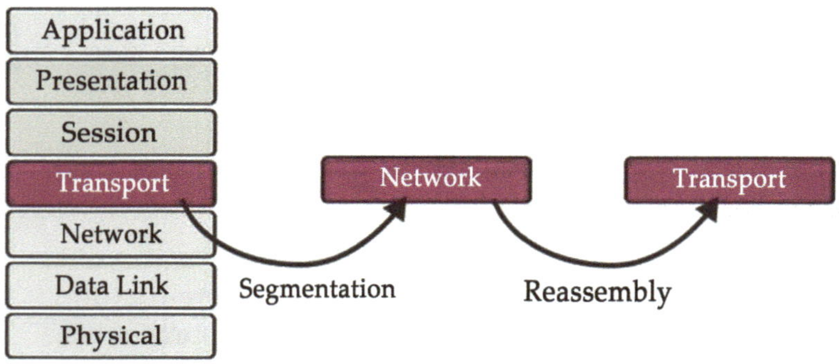

Figure 2.4. Transport Layer in OSI Networking System (Source: Fiberbit Technology Co.Ltd., http://fiberbit.com.tw/wp-content/uploads/2013/06/transport-layer-in-osi-networking-model-system.jpg).

2.1.5. Network Layer

The network layer is responsible for sending a packet from its source to its destination, possibly over several networks. The network layer ensures that every packet reaches its destination from its point of origin, while the data link layer handles packet delivery between two systems connected by the same network (links). Network layers are typically unnecessary when two systems are linked to the same link. However, source-to-destination delivery is often achieved by the network layer if the two systems are connected to separate networks (links) with connecting devices between the networks (links).

Specific responsibilities of the network layer include:

- **Logical Addressing:** The data link layer's physical addressing scheme resolves the local addressing issue. To differentiate the source and destination systems, a packet requires a different addressing system when it crosses the network boundary. In addition to the logical addresses of the sender and recipient, the network layer adds a header to the packet originating from the upper layer.
- **Routing:** Devices that link separate networks or links to create an internetwork, also known as a network of networks, or a large network, route packets to their

intended destination. These devices are known as routers or gateways. This is one of the functions performed by the network layer.

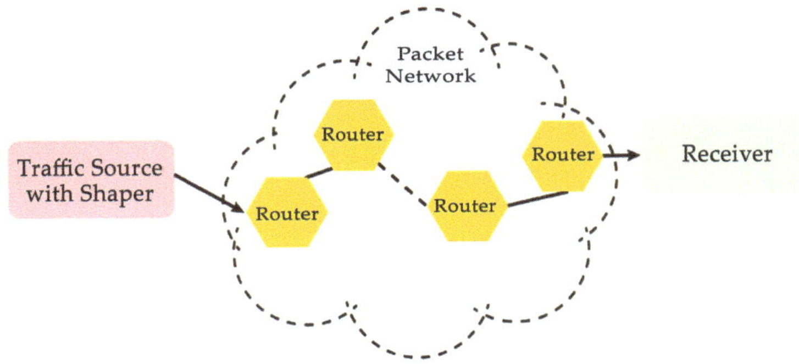

Figure 2.5. Network layer process (Source: Geeksforgeeks, (https://media.geeksforgeeks.org/wp-content/uploads/20230419121402/Forwarding-2-(2).png).

2.1.6. Data Link Layer

Information gets transformed at the data link layer into coherent "packets" and frames that are sent to higher layers. Essentially, the data link layer changes information from the upper layers into raw data that can be sent over the physical layer and unpacks raw data that comes from the physical layer. Another task of the data link layer is to correct and compensate for errors that occur in the physical layer.

Did you know?

In some networks, such as IEEE 802 local area networks, the data link layer is described in more detail with media access control (MAC) and logical link control (LLC) sublayers. This means that the IEEE 802.2 LLC protocol can be used with all of the IEEE 802 MAC layers, such as Ethernet, Token Ring, IEEE 802.11, etc., as well as with some non-802 MAC layers such as FDDI..

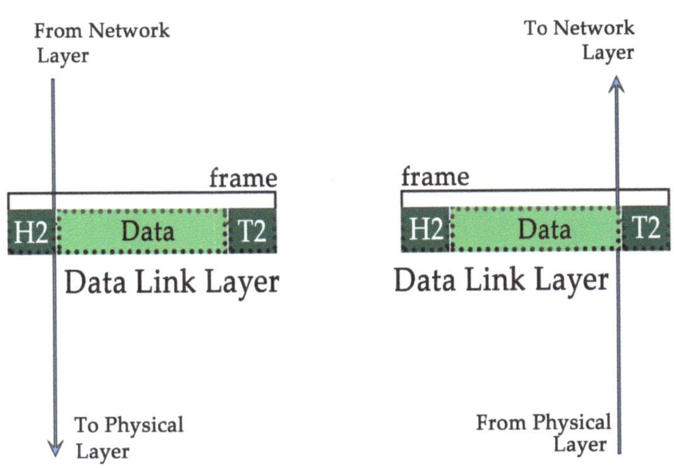

Figure 2.6. Framing of data link layer (Source: Open4Tech, (https://open4tech.com/wp-content/uploads/2019/09/data-link-layer.png).

Specific responsibilities of the data link layer include:

- **Framing**: The data link layer divides the stream of bits received from the network layer into manageable data units called frames.
- **Physical Addressing**: If frames are to be distributed to different systems on the network, the data link layer adds a header to the frame to define the physical address of the sender (source address) and/or receiver (destination address) of the frame. If the frame is intended for a system outside the sender's network, the receiver address is the address of the device that connects one network to the next.
- **Flow Control:** If the rate at which the data is absorbed by the receiver is less than the rate produced by the sender, the data link layer imposes a flow control mechanism to prevent overwhelming the receiver.
- **Error Control**: The data link layer adds reliability to the physical layer by adding mechanisms to detect and retransmit damaged or lost frames. It also uses a mechanism to prevent duplication of frames. Error control is normally achieved through a trailer added to the end of the frame.
- **Access control**: When two or more devices are connected to the same link, data link layer protocols are necessary to determine which device has control over the link at any given time.

Keyword

Fiber optics is the technology used by internet services such as Verizon Fios home internet to transmit information as pulses of light through strands of fiber made of glass or plastic over long distances.

2.1.7. Physical Layer

The physical layer of a network includes cables, fibers, cards, switches, and other components. This layer changes digital data into signals for transmission over wires. These signals can be electrical or non-electrical like optics or other encoded pulses. The physical layer's role in networking is to enable data transmission. Troubleshooting the physical layer is likely easier due to the need for hardware connections, but building or repairing it can be challenging.

Figure 2.7. Physical layer (Source: simplilearn, https://www.simplilearn.com/ice9/free_resources_article_thumb/Working_And_Implementation_Of_Physical_Layer_In_The_OSI_Model_2.png).

The physical layer is concerned with:

- *Physical Characteristics of Interfaces and Media*: The physical layer defines the characteristics of the interface between the devices and the transmission medium. It also defines the type of transmission medium.
- *Representation of Bits:* The physical layer data consists of a stream of bits (a sequence of 0's and 1's) without any interpretation. The physical layer defines the type of encoding (how 0's and 1's are changed to signals).
- *Data Rate:* The transmission rate, the number of bits sent each second, is also defined by the physical layer. In other words, the physical layer defines the duration of a bit, which is how long it lasts.
- *Synchronization of Bits:* The sender and receiver must be synchronized at the bit level. In other words, the sender and the receiver clocks must be synchronized.
- *Line Configuration:* The physical layer is concerned with the connection of devices to the medium. In a point-to-point configuration, two devices are connected together through a dedicated link. In a multipoint configuration, a link is shared between several devices.
- *Physical Topology:* The way that devices are connected to form a network is specified by the physical topology. Devices can be linked together using one of four topologies: bus (every device on a common link), ring (every device connected to the next, forming a ring), mesh (every device connected to every other device), or star (devices connected through a central device).
- *Transmission Mode:* The physical layer also specifies whether two devices will transmit in a simplex, half-duplex, or full-duplex fashion. One device can only send while the other can only receive in simplex mode. One-way communication is used in the simplex mode. Two devices can send and receive simultaneously when using the half-duplex mode. Two devices can send and receive simultaneously when they are in full-duplex (or just duplex) mode.

Did you get it?

1. When to use transport layer in OSI model?
2. Where do you use data link layer in OSI model?

2.2. MULTIPLEXING AND SWITCHING

→Learning Objectives

- Examine the various types of multiplexing
- Discuss on the techniques of switching
- Know about the digital multiplexers
- Learn about the digital demultiplexers
- Execute the multiplexers as PLDS

Multiplexing is the process of combining several signals (analog or digital) for transmission over a single line or medium. Multiple low-speed signals are combined for transmission over a single high-speed connection in a common form of multiplexing. A multiplexer (MUX), which combines N input lines to produce one output line, is used to multiplex data (many to one).

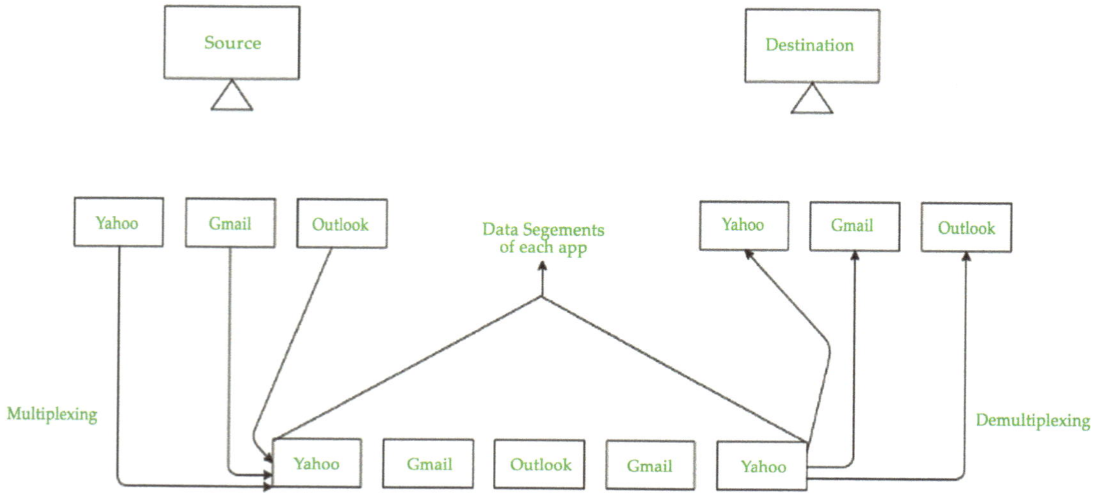

Figure 2.8. Multiplexing (Source: Geeksforgeeks, https://media.geeksforgeeks.org/wp-content/cdn-uploads/CN_Multiplexing-1.jpg).

As a result, a multiplexer (MUX) has one output and multiple inputs. A device known as a demultiplexer (DEMUX) is used at the receiving end to split the signal into its component signals. DEMUX therefore has multiple outputs and one input. Four input lines are fed into the multiplexer, which outputs one output line. This single line combines and transmits the signal from four distinct devices. A demultiplexer at the receiving end splits this signal from a single line into its original signals, which are then sent to the four separate receivers.

2.2.1. Types of Multiplexing

Types of multiplexing are as follows:

- **Frequency-division multiplexing (FDM):** An analog multiplexing technique called frequency-division multiplexing (FDM) combines analog signals. When the combined bandwidths of the signals to be transmitted are less than the bandwidth of a link (measured in hertz), FDM is used. Different carrier frequencies are modulated by the signals produced by each sending device in FDM. After that, the modulated signals are combined into a single composite signal that the link is able to carry. Enough bandwidth separates the carrier frequencies to allow for the modulated signal. The different signals travel through these channels, which are these bandwidth ranges. Strips of unused **bandwidth** can be used to divide channels, i.e., guard bands, to prevent signals from crossing over. Furthermore, carrier frequencies shouldn't obstruct the original data frequencies.
- *Wavelength-Division Multiplexing (WDM):* It is an analog method of combining optical signals through multiplexing. WDM is designed to leverage the high data rate capacity of fiber-optic cables. The data rate of metallic transmission cables is lower than that of optical fiber. When a fiber-optic cable is used for a single line, its available bandwidth is wasted. Multiplexing allows us to combine multiple lines into a single one. Although optical signals sent through fiber-optic channels are used for the multiplexing and demultiplexing processes, WDM and FDM are conceptually identical. The concept remains the same: combining various signals with different frequencies. These frequencies are extremely high, which makes a difference.
- *Time Division Multiplexing (TDM):* This method of digital multiplexing converts multiple low-rate channels into a single high-rate channel. Unlike FDM, which shares a portion of the bandwidth, TDM is a digital process that enables multiple

Keyword

Bandwidth is how much information you receive every second, while speed is how fast that information is received or downloaded.

connections to share the high bandwidth of a link. Instead of sharing bandwidth, time is shared. Each connection occupies a specific time slot in the link. By combining digital data from various sources, a time-shared link is created. It is worth noting that analog data can still be generated by the sources; it just needs to be sampled, converted to digital data, and then multiplexed using TDM.

2.2.1.1. Types of TDM

Types of TDM are as follows:

- **Synchronous TDM**: A frame is created by gathering a round of data units from every input connection. A frame is split up into N time slots if there are N connections, one for each unit and each input line. Each slot has a Tin duration, each frame has a T duration, and the input unit has a T duration. To ensure data flow, the output link's data rate needs to be N times higher than the connection's data rate. Frames are used to organize time slots. A frame is made up of one full cycle of time slots, one for every sending device. Each frame in a system with N input lines has N slots, and each slot is designated to carry data from a particular input line.
- **TDM interleaving**: Two fast-rotating switches, one on the multiplexing side and one on the de-multiplexing side, can be seen. The switches spin simultaneously and in opposite directions at the same speed. As the switch opens in front of a connection on the multiplexing side, that connection has the chance to send a unit onto the path. Interleaving is the term for this procedure. By opening the switch in front of a connection, the de-multiplexing side allows that connection to receive a unit from the path.
- **Statistical Time-Division Multiplexing:** A reserved slot is assigned to each input in the output frame during synchronous TDM. If there are input lines with blank data, this could be inefficient. To increase bandwidth efficiency, statistical time-division multiplexing dynamically assigns slots. An input line receives a slot in the output frame only if it has a slot's worth of data to transmit. The number of slots in each frame during statistical multiplexing is less than the total number of input lines. Round robin, the multiplexer checks each input line; if a line contains data to send, it is assigned a slot; if not, it skips the line and checks the one after it.

Remember

Time-division multiplexing is used primarily for digital signals, but may be applied in analog multiplexing in which two or more signals or bit streams are transferred appearing simultaneously as sub-channels in one communication channel, but are physically taking turns on the channel.

2.2.2. Switching

A collection of connected nodes, referred to as switches, make up a switched network. Switches are devices that can establish temporary connections between two or more connected devices. Some of these nodes are linked to the end systems (computers or phones, for instance) in a switched network. Others are only used in routing. Types of switching of network are as follows:

- *Circuit Switching:* Physical links connect a group of switches in a circuit-switched network. A dedicated path consisting of one or more links connects two stations. On each link, though, each connection only uses one dedicated channel. FDM or TDM is typically used to divide each link into N channels. Electrical switching occurs at the physical layer.
- *Packet Switching:* A message is split up into multiple segments or packets when using packet switching. Every packet is handled as an independent communication. Then, a continuous sequence of these packets is sent to each station. It is possible for packets from different messages to be transmitted together or for the same message to be sent over multiple lines. A packet's source and destination addresses, as well as its packet address, are listed in its header. When the packets arrive at their destination, they put themselves back together to form the original message.

The packet switching common network is made up of stations, nodes, and transmitted parts. The benefits of packet switching are as follows:

- The first, and most significant, advantage is that, because each packet is brief, the communication links between the nodes are only used to send one message at a time during packet transmission. Longer messages need to be sent in a series of packets, but they don't need a dedicated link to be sent in between each packet. This allows for a much more equitable distribution of the resources across all of the links. It is implied that packets from other messages may be sent between the packets of the message being sent from A to Ddot.
- "Pipelining" is a further benefit of packet switching. When packet 1 is sent from C to D, packet 2 is sent from B to C, packet 3 is sent from A to B, and so on. At the same time, packet 1 is sent from C to D. This concurrent use of the communication links results in increased efficiency. Despite the fact that a header is included in each packet rather than in each message, the overall latency for transmission across a packet network may be significantly lower than for message switching.
  - *Message Switching:* All communications sent to any computer system connected to the network are received by the central switching station in a message switching network. A message is then stored in its buffer memory. Every message includes its intended recipient's address. Messages are forwarded to their addresses as soon as lines become available. The store and forward method is another name for message switching.

2.2.3. Digital Multiplexers

Multiplexer is short for multiplexing. A circuit known as a multiplexer is used to choose and direct any one of the many input signals toward an output signal. A single pole multiposition switch is a basic illustration of a non-electronic multiplexer circuit. Numerous electronic circuits make extensive use of multiposition switches. On the other hand, circuits with high operating speeds need an automatic multiplexer selection. This is not a task that a mechanical switch can complete effectively. As a result, electronic components are used in the construction of the multiplexers that perform high-speed switching. Analog and digital data are handled by multiplexers. Relays and transistor switches are the building blocks of multiplexers used in analog applications. Standard logic gates are used in their construction for digital applications. A circuit with multiple inputs but only one output is known as a digital multiplexer, and it is utilized in digital applications. Control signals allow any input to be directed toward any output. The 2-to-1, 4-to-1, 8-to-1, and 16-to-1 multiplexers are among the few types of multiplexers.

2.2.3.1. Understanding 4-to-1 Multiplexer:

There are 4 input bits, 2 control bits, and 1 output bit in a 4-to-1 multiplexer. The bits D0, D1, D2, and D3 are the four inputs. Output Y receives only one of these transmissions. The value of AB, the control input, determines the output. Which input data bit is sent to the output depends on the control input. For example, as Figure 2.9 illustrates. The upper AND gate is active and the other AND gates are inactive when AB = 00. Consequently, data bit D0 is sent to the output, resulting in Y = D0.

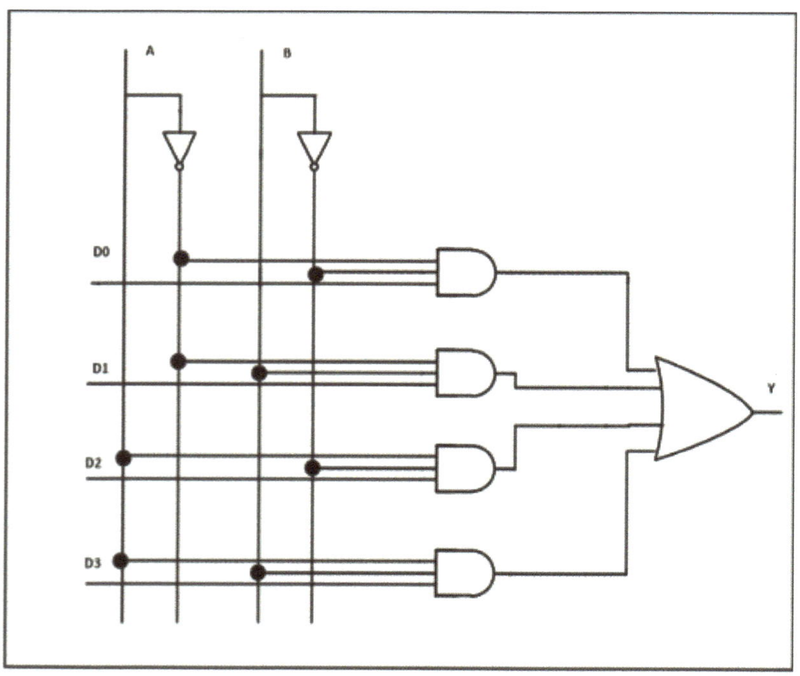

Figure 2.9. 4-to-1 multiplexer (Source: EEWeb, https://www.eeweb.com/wp-content/uploads/articles-articles-4-to-1-multiplexer-circuit-diagram-1387783580.jpg).

If the control input is changed to AB = 11, all gates are disabled except the bottom AND gate. In this case, D3 is transmitted to the output and Y = D3.

- An example of a 4-to-1 multiplexer is IC 74153 in which the output is the same as the input.
- Another example of a 4-to-1 multiplexer is 45352 in which the output is the complement of the input.
- An example of a 16-to-1 line multiplexer is IC74150.

2.2.3.2. Applications of Multiplexers

Multiplexers are used in various fields where multiple data need to be transmitted using a single line. There are some applications of multiplexers:

- *Communication System:* Transmission systems, relay and tributary stations, and communication networks are examples of systems that facilitate communication. With a multiplexer, a communication system's efficiency can be significantly increased. Multiplexers enable the simultaneous transmission of several types of data, including audio and video, over a single transmission line.
- **Telephone Network**: Using multiplexers, several audio signals are combined onto a single line for transmission in a telephone network. This allows for the isolation of several audio signals until the desired audio signals are eventually received by the intended parties.
- **Computer Memory**: A large amount of memory can be added to a computer by using multiplexers, which also reduce the number of copper lines needed to connect the memory to other components of the computer circuit.
- **Transmission from the Computer System of a Satellite**: A multiplexer can be used for the transmission of data signals from the computer system of a satellite or spacecraft to the ground system using the GPS (Global Positioning System) satellites.

Keyword

Tributary station means an aeronautical fixed station that may route, receive, or transmit messages or digital data but does not relay except for the purpose of serving similar stations connected through it to a communication center.

2.2.3.2. Chaining Multiplexers

Up to four MPEG encoders can be multiplexed and controlled by the MIDI MUX. Multiple multiplexers must be chained together if more than four services are to be encoded on a single transport stream.

2.2.3.3. How to Connect the Multiplexers:

The TS input of the subsequent multiplexer must be connected to the TS output port of the multiplexer before it can be chained. It makes no difference which TS input port is used for chaining because all of the input ports on the Mini MUX and MIDI MUX are equal. The output device should be connected to the TS output of the final multiplexer in the chain. The transport stream clock should go with the data so TS input port and TS output port should be configured as follows for chaining:

- TS Output: Clock Direction: generate
- TS Output: Frame size: 188 Byte
- TS Output: Clock rate
- TS Input Mode: External click

The total clock rate of all TS sources linked to the multiplexer plus an extra 10% as a safety precaution should equal the transport stream clock rate. Assume a Midi Mux has four linked encoders, each with a 4,000 Kbit/s data rate set. This results in a total data rate for this Midi Mux's TS output of 16,000 Kbit/s. The TS Output Clock rate should be set to 18,000 Kbit/s with the safety margin. After receiving this stream at one of its TS inputs, the subsequent Midi Mux in the chain adds three more services from encoders linked to the remaining three TS inputs, each with 4,000 Kbit/s. This means that the output of this Midi Mux is seven times 4,000 Kbit/s. One sets the TS output to 32,000 Kbit/s with the safety margin.

2.2.4. Digital Demultiplexers

When you have one too many, it's demultiplexed. A circuit with one input and multiple outputs is known as a demultiplexer. Any input can be directed to any output by using a control signal. There are various types of demultiplexers, such as 1-to-2, 1-to-4, 1-to-8, and 1-to-16. The general idea of a demultiplexer with one input signal, m control signals, and N output signals is illustrated in Figure 2.10.

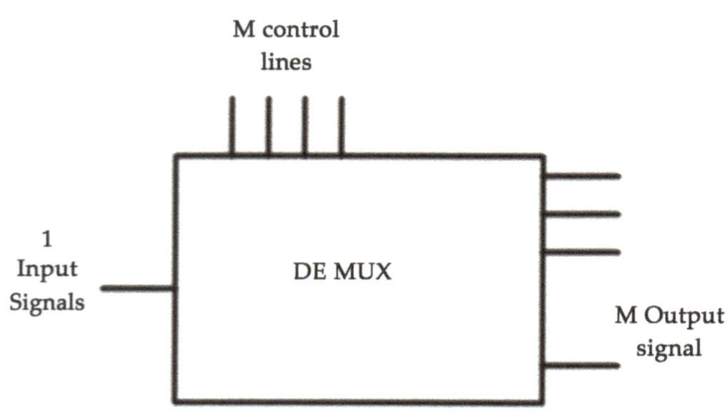

Figure 2.10. Digital demultiplexers (Source: IPUNOTES, https://i0.wp.com/www.electronicshub.org/wp-content/uploads/2013/12/Demultiplexer-Pin-Diagram.png).

2.2.5. Multiplexers as PLDs

Typically, one or more interconnect arrays used by programmable logic devices (PLDs) are programmed using an array of memory cells (e.g., EEPROM, flash EPROM, flash EEPROM, or EPROM cells) to create the different PLD interconnections that are necessary for a particular design. Because PLD complexity can be increased on a regular basis due to technological advancements, increasing the size of the programmable interconnect array is also necessary to reach the desired PLD complexity. Regretfully, the programmable elements of the programmable interconnect array consume a large portion of the die size and power. Furthermore, the programmable elements used in the programmable interconnect array cause capacitive loading, which significantly reduces speed. As a result, a larger programmable interconnect array uses more power and operates at a slower pace. Therefore, the programmable elements themselves become a more important and limiting factor as larger PLDs are designed.

Multiplexer 101's requirement for a discrete control signal for each multiplexer connection is one issue with this PLD. For PLD designs that require a small number of multiplexers, this arrangement is fine; however, PLD designs that require a large number of multiplexers also require a larger number of control signals. Multiplexers are commonly arranged in arrays with 450 multiplexer connections, which consist of 126 input lines × 3 connections per input line (including input pad and feedback connections) + 36 ground connections + 36 UIM connections. Up to six of these multiplexers can be found in a typical PLD, necessitating 2700 multiplexer connections and 2700 control signals. These control signals are unnecessarily complicated to route through a PLD.

Any multiplexer input line to any multiplexer output line can only have two entry points with conventional multiplexers. Put differently, a previous art multiplexer had two output lines that could be connected to each input line. Routing signals through the multiplexer becomes very challenging if a particular user design calls for multiple input signals to be routed into a function block (which includes AND array 102, multiplexer 101, and macro cells 103). One must switch different multiplexer input signals to different lines if routing through the multiplexer is not possible. Usually, this is done with the help of the programming software used to configure the PLD.

In such a case, the input lines are accessed via different multiplexer ports. Unfortunately, this approach is undesirable because:

- If an input signal is an external signal that is received via a specific PLD pin, it may not be possible to place the signal on the desired pin;
- If an input signal is received from a macro cell within the PLD, the signal must be placed in a different macro cell, thereby exacerbating the placement problem; and
- Moving an input signal to a different input line of the multiplexer implies that the signal is moved globally, i.e., for all multiplexers associated with all other function blocks. For large PLDs, there are many function blocks, thereby increasing the probability that a particular routing for one multiplexer adversely affects the routing of the other multiplexers to which the signal is propagated.

Consequently, in order to enable the reliable implementation of complex user designs without significantly increasing the PLD's size or power requirements or adding needless complexity, a multiplexer that offers effective and flexible control and routing options is needed.

Did you get it?

1. What is the function of digital multiplexers?
2. How can multiplexers be implemented as PLDs?

2.3. TRANSMISSION CONTROL PROTOCOL (TCP)

→Learning Objectives

- Find the TCP header format
- Clarify the connection establishment and termination
- Examine the sliding window and flow control
- Discuss on congestion control

The Internet connection suite consists of two protocols, one of which is the Transmission Control Protocol. The basis of almost all Internet traffic is formed by the combination of this protocol and the Internet Protocol. Because these protocols are practically indispensable in their usage and depend entirely on one another to function properly, the Internet connection suite is commonly referred to as TCP/IP (Transmission Control Protocol/Internet Protocol).

The Internet Protocol is in charge of routing and transmission, while the Transmission Control Protocol disassembles and reassembles data. Small data bursts known as packets make up the majority of *Internet traffic*. Along with some optional extra information, these packets include details about the data's origin and destination. The Internet Protocol sends the packets over the Internet, while the Transmission Control Protocol creates and reassembles them.

Consider moving a document from a distant computer to a local one to demonstrate this procedure. The Internet protocol decides how the document needs to be moved between the computers after the computer receives the move command. Next, the transmission control protocol is requested by the Internet protocol to divide the document in a particular manner. The document is then divided into packets by TCP, which are then sent out via the Internet protocol. TCP starts reassembling the document packets as soon as they reach the local computer. It first makes sure that it has all of them and that they are in good condition. If not, it requests the necessary parts and waits for them to be delivered. Once it has all the parts, it assembles the document by rearranging them according to the correct order. The computer is then notified that the file has arrived by the Internet protocol. The great majority of Internet usage consists of these procedures. Every interaction in programs like file transfer systems, email clients, and web browsers uses this fundamental back-and-forth process. Information can be sent between unrelated programs and systems without conversion thanks to this unified system. Given that this is the fundamental building block of the Internet, there isn't much variation in the protocol.

This allows for backward compatibility between systems across the Internet. Older machines might disconnect permanently due to protocol changes. Since the system is quite straightforward, it usually doesn't require extra care or monitoring, even without regular updates. TCP is often referred to as a byte stream, connection-oriented, transport layer protocol with reliable delivery.

Keyword

Internet traffic is the flow of data within the entire Internet, or in certain network links of its constituent networks.

- **Byte Stream Delivery:** The network layer below and the application layer above are interfaced by TCP. Applications use 8-bit byte streams to transfer data to TCP. The sending TCP is then responsible for segmenting or demarcating the byte stream so that the receiver can receive the data in digestible chunks. The term "byte stream delivery service" comes from the fact that there are no "record boundaries."
- **Connection-Oriented:** Before two communicating TCPs can exchange data, they must first agree upon the willingness to communicate. Analogous to a telephone call, a connection must first be made before two parties exchange information.
- **Reliability:** A number of mechanisms help provide the reliability TCP guarantees.
    - *Checksums:* Every TCP segment has a checksum that the recipient uses to identify errors in the data or TCP header.
    - *Duplicate data detection:* Because packets in packet-switched networks may be duplicated, TCP records the bytes it receives in order to remove duplicate copies of data that have already been received.
    - *Retransmissions:* To ensure data delivery in the event of data loss or damage, TCP must implement retransmission schemes. Data reception success is verified by the sender receiving positive acknowledgements from the recipient. Retransmission is required due to a timeout period (see timers below) and a lack of positive acknowledgements.
- *Sequencing:* Packets may be delivered out of order in packet-

switched networks. TCP's responsibility is to correctly sequence the segments it receives so that the byte stream data can be sent to an application in the correct order.

- *Timers:* When sending data, TCP keeps track of a number of static and dynamic timers. Within a set amount of time, the sending TCP waits for the recipient to respond with an acknowledgement. The sender may retransmit the segment if the timer runs out before getting an acknowledgement.

2.3.1. TCP Header Format

A TCP segment is the entirety of the TCP header and TCP contained in a single packet. All valid TCP segments have the format shown in Figure 2.11. The header is 20 bytes in size when no options are selected. We will quickly go over each field in the provided TCP header.

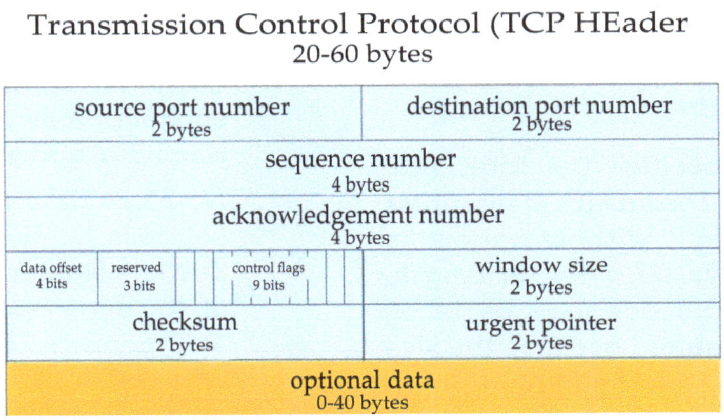

Figure 2.11. TCP Header Format (Source: Github, (https://i0.wp.com/www.electronicshub.org/wp-content/uploads/2013/12/Demultiplexer-Pin-Diagram.png).

2.3.1.1. Source Port

A 16-bit number that indicates which sending host application the TCP segment came from. There are three ranges for the port numbers: registered ports (1024 through 49151), private ports (49152 through 65535), and well-known ports (0 through 1023). TCP uses port assignments as an application layer interface. For instance, on TCP hosts, the TELNET server is always by default assigned to the well-known port 23. A single, globally unique TCP connection is defined by a complete pair of IP addresses (source and destination) and a complete pair of TCP ports (source and destination).

2.3.1.2. Destination Port

A 16-bit number identifying the application the TCP segment is destined for on a receiving host. Destination ports use the same port number assignments as those set aside for source ports.

2.3.1.3. Sequence Number

A 32-bit number identifying the current position of the first data byte in the segment within the entire byte stream for the TCP connection. After reaching $2^{32} - 1$, this number will wrap around to 0.

2.3.1.4. Acknowledgment Number

A 32-bit number identifying the next data byte the sender expects from the receiver. Therefore, the number will be one greater than the most recently received data byte. This field is only used when the ACK control bit is turned on.

2.3.1.5. Header Length

A 4-bit field that specifies the total TCP header length in 32-bit words (or in multiples of 4 bytes if you prefer). Without options, a TCP header is always 20 bytes in length. The largest a TCP header may be is 60 bytes. This field is required because the size of the options field(s) cannot be determined in advance. Note that this field is called "data offset" in the official TCP standard, but header length is more commonly used.

2.3.1.6. Reserved

A 6-bit field currently unused and reserved for future use.

2.3.1.7. Control Bits

- *Urgent Pointer (URG):* If this bit field is set, the receiving TCP should interpret the urgent pointer field.
- *Acknowledgment (ACK):* If this bit field is set, the acknowledgment field described earlier is valid.
- *Push Function (PSH):* If this bit field is set, the receiver should deliver this segment to the receiving application as soon as possible. An example of its use may be to send a Control-BREAK request to an application, which can jump ahead of queued data.
- *Reset the Connection (RST):* If this bit is present, it signals the receiver that the sender is aborting the connection and all queued data and allocated buffers for the connection can be freely relinquished.
- *Synchronize (SYN):* When present, this bit field signifies that the sender is attempting to "synchronize" sequence numbers. This bit is used during the initial stages of connection establishment between a sender and receiver.
- *No More Data from Sender (FIN):* If set, this bit field tells the receiver that the sender has reached the end of its byte stream for the current TCP connection.

Did you know?

In May 1974, Vint Cerf and Bob Kahn described an internetworking protocol for sharing resources using packet switching among network nodes.

- **Window:** Data transmission window size, a 16-bit integer used by TCP for flow control. The data acceptance limit of the recipient is indicated by this number to the sender. Although there is a "window scale" option that allows for even larger windows to be used, the maximum value for this field would limit the window size to 65,535 bytes.
- **Checksum:** A TCP sender uses the data fields and TCP header contents

to calculate a value. The same computation will be used to compare this 16-bit value with the value the receiver produces. The receiver can be extremely certain that the segment arrived undamaged if the values match.

- **Urgent Pointer:** Under some conditions, a TCP sender might need to alert the recipient to urgent data that needs to be handled by the receiving application right away. When the last byte of urgent data in the segment ends is indicated to the receiver by this 16-bit field.
- **Options:** A TCP sender and receiver can use a number of optional parameters to provide additional functionality. The length of this field will vary depending on the option(s) selected, but because of the size of the header length field (4 bits), it cannot be longer than 40 bytes. The maximum segment size (MSS) option is the most often used option. Using this option, a TCP receiver informs a TCP sender of the largest segment size it will accept. For different flow control and congestion control strategies, other options are frequently used.
- **Padding:** Because options may vary in size, it may be necessary to "pad" the TCP header with zeros so that the segment ends on a 32-bit word boundary as defined by the standard.
- **Data:** Although not used in some circumstances (e.g., acknowledgment segments with no data in the reverse direction), this variable-length field carries the application data from TCP sender to receiver. This field, coupled with the TCP header fields, constitutes a TCP segment.

2.3.2. Connection Establishment and Termination

Over packet-switched networks, TCP offers a connection-oriented service. Connection-oriented designates that two endpoints are connected virtually. Any virtual connection goes through three stages. These phases include data transfer, connection termination, and connection establishment.

2.3.2.1. Three-Way Handshake

In order for two hosts to communicate using TCP, they must first establish a connection by exchanging messages in what is known as the three-way handshake. The diagram below depicts the process of the three-way handshake.

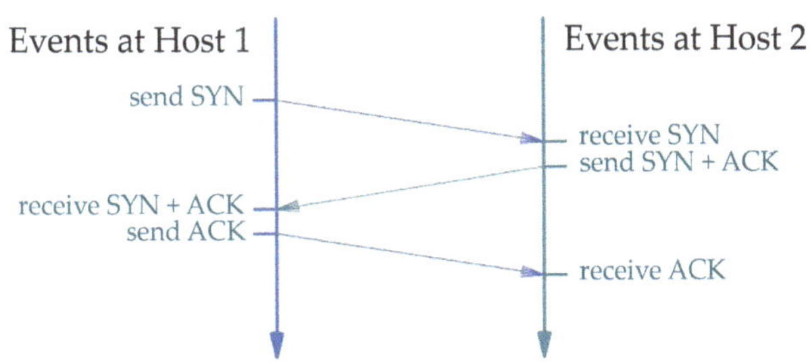

Figure 2.12. TCP Connection Establishment (Source: Birkbeck, University of London, https://www.dcs.bbk.ac.uk/~ptw/teaching/IWT/transport-layer/retransmission.gif).

Three TCP segments are exchanged between two hosts, Host 1 and Host 2, as shown in Figure 2.12. Events in time are depicted as you read down the diagram. First, Host 1 sends a TCP segment with the SYN control bit set and an initial sequence number (ISN), which we represent as the variable x in the sequence number field, to establish the connection. Host 2 receives this SYN segment at a later time, processes it, and replies with a TCP segment of its own. The SYN control bit is set and its own ISN, represented as variable y, is contained in Host 2's response. Additionally, Host 2 sets the ACK control bit to signal that data beginning with sequence number x+1 should be contained in the next anticipated byte from Host 1. After receiving Host 2's ISN and ACK, Host 1 sends Host 2 a final acknowledgment segment to complete the connection establishment process. In this instance, Host 1 sets the ACK control bit and uses the acknowledgment number y+1 in the acknowledgment field to indicate the next expected byte from Host 2. Each sender's segment includes an exchange of source and destination ports to use for this connection in addition to the information displayed in the above diagram.

> **Keyword**
>
> **Initial sequence numbers (ISN)** refers to the unique 32-bit sequence number assigned to each new connection on a Transmission Control Protocol (TCP)-based data communication.

2.3.2.2. Data Transfer

As long as there is data to send and the sender stays within the window that the recipient has advertised, a basic TCP implementation will add segments to the network for a recipient. The receiver transmits positive acknowledgments back, indicating its location in the byte stream, as it accepts and processes TCP segments. The "window," which indicates how many bytes the recipient is currently willing to accept, is also included in these acknowledgments. The byte stream may have a "hole" if data is lost or duplicated.

A receiver that has accepted a byte stream will keep acknowledging the most recent contiguous place in the stream. The sending TCP will do nothing but wait for the application to insert data into the byte stream or for data to arrive from the other end of the connection if there is nothing to send. The sender must stop transmission and wait for additional acknowledgments and an advertised window size greater than zero before continuing if the amount of data queued by the sender reaches a point where the amount of data sent will exceed the receiver's advertised window size. Timers are employed to prevent unresponsive connections and deadlocks. Transmissions are delayed in order to increase efficiency.

2.3.2.3. Connection Termination

A connection must be fully closed in four segments in order for it to be released. TCP requires four segments because it is a full-duplex protocol, which means that each end needs to shut down on its own. Figure 2.13 depicts the phase of connection termination.

In this scenario, the application executing on Host A instructs TCP to close the connection. As a result, Host A and Host B generate the first FIN segment. Upon receiving the initial FIN segment, Host B promptly notifies its destination application of the termination request and acknowledges the segment. In the event that Host B's application also chooses to terminate the connection, it sends its own FIN segment, which Host A processes and acknowledges.

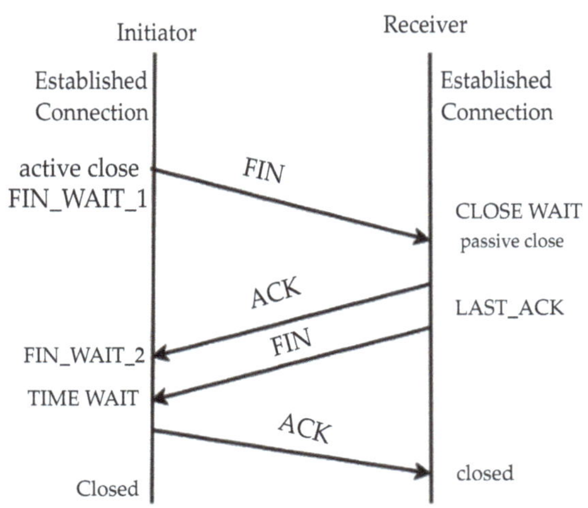

Figure 2.13. TCP Connection Termination (Source: Geeksforgeeks, https://open4tech.com/wp-content/uploads/2019/09/session-layer.png).

2.3.3. Sliding Window and Flow Control

The primary objective of the technique known as flow control is to properly align the sender's transmission rate with that of the receiver and the network. A sufficiently high transmission rate is essential to ensure optimal performance and prevent network or host overload. It is important to note that congestion control and flow control are distinct concepts. Congestion control primarily deals with managing network intermediate devices, such as IP routers, to avoid overload. TCP's primary approach to controlling flow is through the window field, as mentioned earlier. The window field adjusts the flow rate of the byte stream between communicating TCPs during data transfer.

In this basic example, a 4-byte sliding window is utilized. The window "slides" from left to right as bytes in the stream are sent and acknowledged. Determining the window size and the rate at which to adjust it is a critical aspect.

2.3.4. Congestion Control

In packet-switched networks, congestion is a significant problem that can occur. In communication networks, congestion is the state in which performance suffers due to an excessive number of packets in one area of the subnet. A network may experience congestion if the load on it (i.e., packets transmitted to the network) exceeds the network's capacity (i.e., the maximum quantity of packets a network can manage). Flow control is not the same as congestion control. One sender outrunning a single receiver (e.g., flow control) is a data link problem (i.e., a link between points). Being a network layer problem, congestion control addresses what occurs when there is more data in the network than can be sent with acceptable packet delays, no dropped packets, etc. Whereas congestion control is global, flow control is local. Confusion can be avoided by reducing the amount of traffic that a specific host sends over the network via a flow control mechanism. Congestion is influenced by numerous design parameters at the data link, network, and transport layers. Eliminating the issue is aided by setting each of these with the goal of avoiding congestion. For instance, a flooding routing algorithm produces a large number of redundant packets despite being quick. Overly strict data link layer timers can result in unnecessary packet retransmissions.

Remember

A version of the leaky bucket, the generic cell rate algorithm, is recommended for Asynchronous Transfer Mode (ATM) networks in UPC and NPC at user–network interfaces or inter-network interfaces or network-to-network interfaces to protect a network from excessive traffic levels on connections routed through it.

2.3.4.1. Traffic Shaping

The inherent burstiness of computer network traffic is one of the reasons for congestion. To smooth out or modify the offered traffic as a function of time is known as traffic shaping. Bursty traffic is more difficult to handle than smooth traffic. While a subnet might be able to process 10 million packets in an hour on average, it most likely won't be able to process 10 million packets in a minute and nothing for the next fifty-nine minutes. The concept of agreeing to a flow specification with a network service provider is related to traffic shaping. A flow specification outlines the kind of traffic you plan to send over the internet and the level of service quality you anticipate receiving back.

Some of the quality of service parameters are:

- loss sensitivity (number of lost bytes per unit of time)
- loss interval (the unit of time for calculating loss)
- burst loss sensitivity (how long of a loss burst can be tolerated)
- minimum delay (how large of a delay before the app notices)
- maximum delay variation (the variance or jitter in the inter-packet delay)
- quality of guarantee (how serious the spec is to the application)

2.3.4.2. Leaky Bucket Algorithm

A buffer that changes an uncontrolled, erratic traffic flow into a controlled, steady, and predictable flow. A traffic source and the subnet are placed between the buffer and the source. The buffer functions as if it were a single server queue with a set maximum length. Once the buffer is full, packets added to it are dropped. Either a certain number of packets per unit of time or a total number of bytes per unit of time (useful if packet sizes vary significantly) may be drained from the buffer onto the subnet. Token buckets are a variation of leaky buckets. At a predetermined rate, tokens are added to the bucket. To exit the bucket, a packet needs to take hold of and destroy a token. Senders only need to wait for a token to become available; packets are never lost. Certain applications benefit from bursts, which are permitted (up to the number of tokens in the bucket) and compromise with source requirements and congestion.

2.3.4.3. Choke Packets

Using output lines whose utilization has surpassed a certain warning level, routers send unique choke packets back to hosts while keeping an eye on how their output lines are being used. By sampling it on a regular basis and combining the new value (either in use, f = 1, or not in use, f = 0) with the current value for U, the utilization can be estimated. The weight a determines how quickly the router reacts to changes:

$$Unew = a * Uold + (1-a) * f$$

When the sending host receives the choke packet, it reduces the flow of traffic it is sending to the subnet (often done by factors of 1/2, 1/4, 1/8, etc., as needed). Then, it stops watching for choke packets, since other packets that are in transit will probably also cause the congested router to send more choke packets. When a packet is forwarded on a congested line, it is marked so that downstream routers don't also generate choke packets for the sending host corresponding to the same packet.

2.3.4.4. Load Shedding

When routers run out of buffers, they behave as follows. They can try to select the best packets to discard if needed. This depends on the data link layer error strategy and the application. Older packets may create gaps in the received packets and could lead the data link layer to use a go-back-n strategy, which is worse for file transfers than discarding newer packets. It's probably better to discard old data (already obsolete?) and keep new packets for real-time voice or video. Lowering transmission rates for lower priority packets is necessary to encourage the application to mark packets with priority. Instead of waiting for congestion to take over, it seems better for routers to start dropping packets as soon as congestion seems likely.

Did you get it?

1. Which types of control bits used in TCP networking?
2. How to use three-way handshake procedure for connection establishment and termination?

2.4. USER DATAGRAM PROTOCOL (UDP)

→Learning Objectives

- Understand the structure and purpose of Protocol Headers.
- Explore the challenges and considerations of implementing TCP over Wireless Links.
- Identify the key characteristics of Wireless Media.
- Learn about various TCP Performance Enhancements.
- Examine the evolution of Wireless Systems and their impact on TCP.
- Gain knowledge about IP Networks and their functionalities.
- Study techniques for Network Security and Performance Analysis.

One of the main network protocols used to send data over the Internet is the User Datagram Protocol. It is a component of the Internet Protocol Suite, which sets the rules for how computers connect to servers and to one another via IP networks. An application can send datagrams, or messages, to other hosts via the User Datagram Protocol without the need to first set up specific transmission channels or data paths. Compared to other methods, this one is less dependable but allows for faster communication. Data transmission is the main objective of the User Datagram Protocol. It offers no protections against data corruption during transmission or to guarantee that the information actually arrives. If error checking is necessary, the protocol assumes that the computers involved in the communication will take care of it.

A stateless protocol is the User Datagram Protocol. In other words, it handles every information request as a separate transaction. The benefit of running this way is that the server can handle more traffic because ongoing conversations don't require storage space to be assigned. The User Datagram Protocol is actually superior to more dependable communication techniques in some circumstances. For example, it enables the delivery of messages without the lag time brought on by error checking. This is why time-sensitive applications frequently use it. Voice over IP, a popular streaming media application, is an example of this kind of application. For servers that process a large number of tiny requests, the User Datagram Protocol is also helpful. The server can reply to each request more quickly because it doesn't have to allocate storage or establish connections before speaking. All users will experience faster service as a result. For this reason, servers that host online games frequently use the User Datagram Protocol.

Applications and upper-layer protocols can use UDP as a minimal, erratic, best-effort message-passing transport. UDP and its variant UDP-Lite are distinct from other transport protocols in that they do not create end-to-end connections between communicating end systems. As a result, UDP communication has little associated end system state and incurs no overhead during connection establishment or teardown. These features make UDP a very effective communication transport for some applications, but they also make it unreliable and lack inherent congestion control. Applications must be thoughtfully designed because UDP has a second unique feature: it offers no inherent congestion control. On many platforms, applications have the ability to send UDP datagrams at the line rate of the link interface, which is frequently much higher than the available path capacity [RFC 4505].

UDP is being used more and more frequently as a tunneling protocol. In this scenario, one tunnel endpoint encapsulates the packets of another protocol inside UDP datagrams and sends them to another tunnel endpoint, which forwards the original packets that were part of the payload after decapsulating the UDP datagrams. Tunnels can be used to create virtual (private) networks by creating virtual links that, in the physical Internet topology, appear to connect distant locations directly. Since many middleboxes along the path support UDP transmissions, using UDP as a tunneling protocol is appealing when the payload protocol is not supported by them. There is no communication security offered by UDP. Applications must thus independently provide security services using extra protocol mechanisms to safeguard their communications against message forgery, tampering, or eavesdropping.

Keyword

Service access point (SAP) is the point at which a service begins (ingress) or ends (egress) and represents the access point associated with a service.

2.4.1. Protocol Header

Sending UDP packets doesn't require a connection to be established between the computer and the recipient. Due to the fact that a UDP datagram can only contain a maximum payload of 65,507 bytes for IPv4 and 65,527 bytes for IPv6, it can only be carried in a single IP packet. Large IP packet transmission typically necessitates IP fragmentation. Fragmentation should be avoided since it reduces the effectiveness and dependability of communication. A computer must fill in the relevant fields in the UDP header (PCI) before forwarding the data and header for IP network layer transmission in order to send a UDP datagram.

The UDP header consists of four fields each of 2 bytes in length:

- Source Port (UDP packets from a client use this as a service access point (SAP) to indicate the session on the local client that originated the packet. UDP packets from a server carry the server SAP in this field)
- Destination Port (UDP packets from a client use this as

a service access point (SAP) to indicate the service required from the remote server. UDP packets from a server carry the client SAP in this field)

- UDP Length (The number of bytes comprising the combined UDP header information and payload data)
- UDP Checksum (A checksum to verify that the end-to-end data has not been corrupted by routers or bridges in the network or by the processing in an end system. The algorithm to compute the checksum is the BN . This allows the receiver to verify that it was the intended destination of the packet because it covers the IP addresses, port numbers, and protocol number, and it verifies that the packet is not truncated or padded because it covers the size field. Therefore, this protects an application against receiving corrupted payload data in place of, or in addition to, the data that was sent. In cases where this check is not required, the value of 0x0000 is placed in this field, in which case the data is not checked by the receiver.

2.4.2. TCP over Wireless Links

TCP makes the assumption that congestion is the main cause of packet losses. TCP reduces network utilization in response to congestion by shrinking its congestion window. However, in wireless networks, fading and mobility, as well as the high bit-error rate of the transmission medium, can cause losses. TCP continues to respond to losses in accordance with its congestion control scheme, which reduces network utilization needlessly.

Wireless wide area networks (WWANs) like CDPD and GPRS networks, as well as wireless local area networks (WLANs) like 802.11 networks, can both be represented by this model. On the other hand, nodes in ad hoc networks can arrange themselves to create communication routes, and no infrastructure—such as base stations (BSs)—is necessary. Multiple wireless hop configurations are possible with satellite networks. Though we also categorize approaches where this isn't always the case, we primarily look at configurations where the wireless link is the last hop.

2.4.3. Characteristics of Wireless Media

A number of inherent characteristics of wireless media affect TCP performance including:

- Channel Losses: While frames are being transmitted, signals carried by wireless media are susceptible to substantial interference from other signals, which results in losses owing to bit modification. Even with error correction techniques, these losses are challenging to recover from at the link layer and usually necessitate retransmission. Either the transport layer (TCP) or the link layer can handle retransmission. Frequent losses at the link layer have an impact on TCP performance because TCP by design assumes that all losses are caused by congestion and calls the congestion control algorithms when it detects a loss.
- Low Bandwidth: Wireless links may have low bandwidth, which occasionally causes the base station to experience excessive buffering. Due to the possibility

of packets being dropped at the base station or being transmitted back-to-back over the wireless link, long observed round trip times may arise.

- Signal Fading: When a wireless host is mobile, fading usually takes place. Physical interference from things like weather, obstructions, unavailable channels, and areas where multiple cells overlap can cause signal fading and blackouts. Blackouts of this kind may last for extended periods of time.
- Mobility across Cells: Handling connection handoff is a necessary part of a wireless host's mobility. The base station may retain connection state regarding the transport layer, which may also require handoff, in addition to the link layer state that needs to be transferred. Other issues, such as the previously mentioned signal fading, are highly likely to arise when a host travels between cells.
- Channel Asymmetry: Channel contention resolution is typically asymmetric. More transmission time is granted to the sending entity than to the receiving entity. As a result, when channel access is allowed, TCP acknowledgments may be queued for transmission at the receiving entity's link layer and sent back-to-back. This may result in bursty traffic and longer round trip times as recorded by the TCP sender, which lower the TCP connection's throughput.
- Link Latency: High latencies can occur on wireless links. When these delays account for a sizable portion of the round trip times that TCP observes, TCP sets its retransmission timeouts to high values, which negatively impacts TCP performance. Such situations arise in satellite networks and wireless wide area networks. High variance in the measurements is another factor.

2.4.4. TCP Performance Enhancements

2.4.4.1. Transport Layer Solutions

The primary cause of TCP's decreased performance over wireless links is the misinterpretation of wireless losses for congestion. As a result, there are many suggestions for suitable TCP modifications. In cellular communications (CC) systems, packets can be lost or delayed during handoffs. After the handoff is complete, recovery from these losses should begin immediately without waiting for a timeout. TCP is able to accomplish this by getting the right signals from lower layers. Alternatively, TCP can use lower layer mobility hints to heuristically identify handoff-related losses. TCP can avoid skipping the congestion avoidance phase by not halving the slow start threshold during recovery in order to account for these losses. Another method involves the transparent closure of the receiver's advertised window by wireless link endpoints, which chokes TCP senders during handoffs. Subsequently, the sender stops all running timers and begins periodically checking the recipient's window.

Congestion avoidance aids in assessing the new link's capacity following handoffs. But for other wireless losses, recovery can be achieved with only retransmissions. TCP connections can be divided by using routers connected to both wireless and wired links as pivot points because end-to-end retransmissions are slow. This results in the splitting of end-to-end connections into distinct TCP sessions for the wired and wireless portions of the path. Over the wireless links, a different protocol designed for error recovery could be used in its place. Since acknowledgments may arrive at the sender before data packets reach their destination, split schemes defy end-to-end TCP semantics. Throughput must be decreased because acknowledgments must be delayed in order to maintain TCP semantics. Due to the fact that packets are processed twice by TCP and a sizable amount of per-connection state is retained, pivot points incur significant overhead.

2.4.4.2. Link Layer Solutions

This is accomplished in CC systems by non-transparent mode RLPs. Another approach is to carry out IP-level local error recovery, which is a link layer task, similar to Snoop TCP. By preserving the state of each TCP connection as it passes through a pivot point, Snoop keeps track of TCP data and acknowledgments. Snoop employs local timers in conjunction with the loss indications provided by duplicate acknowledgments to transparently retransmit lost data. It does this by caching unacknowledged TCP packets. It avoids redundant TCP recovery by hiding duplicate acknowledgments from the TCP sender that indicate wireless losses. Snoop avoids link layer control overhead by taking advantage of the data contained in TCP packets. Without going against TCP semantics, it performs better than split TCP schemes. Additionally, by suppressing duplicate TCP acknowledgments, it prevents incompatible local and TCP retransmissions. It is necessary for Snoop to locate the TCP receiver immediately following the pivot point.

TCP acknowledgments are returned too late for effective recovery when a wireless host is transmitting data to a remote receiver; they might even indicate congestion losses. In this case, TCP requires Explicit Loss Notification (ELN) in order to differentiate between wireless losses and congestion. The Snoop agent sets an ELN bit in TCP headers and propagates it to the recipient, who then echoes it back to the sender, if it detects a loss unrelated to congestion. Queue length data can be used by Snoop to heuristically differentiate wireless errors from congestion. The TCP sender retransmits the lost packet without using congestion control after receiving an ELN notification. ELN works with most topologies, but it necessitates modifications to router algorithms. Furthermore, only after a round trip time has passed and an acknowledgment with the ELN bit set has been returned can a lost packet be retransmitted.

While CC system RLPs can retransmit data in parallel with TCP, they are not subject to the layering violations of Snoop, which analyzes TCP headers at the IP level. However, this is uncommon with completely dependable RLPs, and it is avoided by RLPs that give up on error recovery after a few fruitless tries. Unlike TCP modifications, link layer schemes operate at the local level with low round trip delays that enable quick recovery. Their primary drawback is that they only provide one recovery level, which might not be suitable for all higher layer protocols and applications.

2.4.5. Wireless System Evolution and TCP

Higher speeds and better support for packet data services are the trends for CC systems. The microcells, or small areas with higher user densities, will have the fastest data rates available. By allocating multiple TDMA slots for every data circuit, the High Speed

Circuit Switched Data (HSCSD) system is a GSM extension that offers bit rates of up to 56 Kbps. An extension of packet switched GSM is the General Packet Radio Service (GPRS). Bit rates of up to 171 Kbps can be achieved with GPRS through dynamic TDMA slot reservation. Presently available implementations offer user throughput of 20–40 Kbps. There will be about 2% of Internet packet loss, according to experiments. Wideband CDMA is the foundation of UMTS, the third generation European CC system that supports both packet switched and circuit switched modes at different bit rates.

Keyword

Explicit Loss Notification (ELN) is a mechanism by which the reason for the loss of a packet can be communicated to the TCP sender.

Phase one offers GPRS-like services with bit rates as high as 384 Kbps; later phases will offer up to 2 Mbps in certain locations. The GSM EDGE/IS-136 HS system in the USA will offer bit rates between 270 and 722 Kbps, or even more than 2 Mbps in certain places. Many FH spread spectrum systems, like Bluetooth, which offers bit rates of 400–700 Kbps, are examples of short-range (in-room) systems, or Personal Area Networks (PANs), that are intended for low bit rates. Bluetooth's radio link-level interoperability with IEEE 802.11 is seriously flawed, even though it should offer TCP performance comparable to low-end WLANs.

This problem is being worked on by the IEEE 802.15 project, which defines a PAN standard based on Bluetooth. The Local Multipoint Distribution System (LMDS) will use the 28 or 40 GHz frequency bands to provide broadband fixed wireless Internet access at very high speeds. A Wireless Local Loop (WLL) system called LMDS gives fixed hosts access to bandwidth between one and two GHz. We have observed that LMDS can reliably carry TCP traffic and that it makes use of strong link layer FEC schemes.

2.4.6. IP Networks

Developed in the 1970s, the Internet Protocol (IP) is the main network protocol used on the Internet. IP and Transmission Control Protocol (TCP) are frequently used together on the Internet and numerous other networks; this combination is known as TCP/IP. IP enables computers connected to a network to have unique addresses. The Internet Protocol version 4 (IPv4) standard, which has IP addresses that are four bytes (32 bits) long, is used by the majority of networks. A 16-byte (128-bit) address is one of the standard features of the more recent Internet Protocol version 6 (IPv6). Packets are the units of data organization on an Internet Protocol network. Every IP packet consists of the message data itself as well as a header that contains information about the source, destination, and other details about the data. On layer 3 of the

OSI model, IP operates. As a result, it can operate over a variety of data link interfaces, such as Ethernet and WiFi.

Communication between computing devices is facilitated by networks. Every computer (host) connected to a network must employ the same communication protocols in order to communicate with one another.

A computer network that uses Internet Protocol as its communication protocol is known as an Internet Protocol network. Every computer connected to an IP network needs to have a unique IP address that identifies it as a host. A collection of hosts that utilize Internet Protocol for network layer communication and share a physical connection is referred to as an Internet Protocol-based network, or IP network. In an IP network, the IP addresses are contiguous, meaning there are never any gaps between them.

2.4.6.1. Address Types in an IP Network

Within a given range of IP addresses used in every IP network are special addresses reserved for:

- Host Addresses
- Network Addresses
- Broadcast Addresses

An IP network also has a subnet mask. Each computer has a value stored on it called the subnet mask, which enables it to distinguish between IP addresses on an external network and IP addresses that are part of the network to which it is connected.

2.4.6.2. Host Address

The address of a specific host on an IP network is referred to as its IP address. Each host on a network must have a unique IP address. Typically, this IP address falls neither at the beginning nor at the end of the range of network IP addresses, as the first and last IP addresses are reserved for specific purposes. Apart from the first and last IP addresses, all addresses within the IP network range are considered host addresses. Hosts on a network can communicate directly with each other on a one-to-one basis thanks to their IP addresses. This type of communication is known as unicast communication. A host IP address consists of two parts: a network part and a host part. The network portion of the address identifies the IP network to which the host belongs, while the host part uniquely identifies an individual host.

Did you know?

The dominant internetworking protocol in the Internet Layer in use is IPv4; the number 4 identifies the protocol version, carried in every IP datagram. IPv4 is described in RFC 791 (1981).

2.4.6.3. Network Address

The IP address that appears first in the range is the network address. More specifically, the host portion of the IP address with all binary bits set to zero is the address that is the network address. The network address serves as a means of communication between hosts that offer specific network services. In actuality, communication almost never uses the network address.

2.4.6.4. Broadcast Address

The final IP address in the range is the broadcast IP address. More specifically, the IP address in which every binary bit in the host section of the address is set to one is the broadcast address. A reserved broadcast address enables one host to broadcast a message to every other host on the network. This is known as broadcast communication, and since the last address in a network is where the host portion is all ones, it is used for broadcasting to all hosts. This unique address is occasionally referred to as the all hosts address. It is possible to designate a different address as the broadcast address than the last address with certain vendors. Keep in mind that every network has unique broadcast and network addresses. The host component of a network address does not always have a zero in its decimal representation.

2.4.7. Network Security and Performance Analysis

The goal of network security is to prevent unwanted access to the underlying computer network infrastructure. The network administrator is in charge of it, and it involves ongoing effectiveness assessment and monitoring.

Every business that uses computers should be very concerned about network security, which is the set of precautions a company takes to safeguard its computer system. A hacker or rival with access to sensitive or important data could cause data loss or even the system's total destruction if network security is compromised. A network has reached appropriate security when a user must pass through multiple security levels in order to gain access to the desired network. A system is more secure the more layers it contains. Because he has administrator rights on the system, the systems administrator is frequently in charge of network security. Actually, the mainframe server and any associated computer terminals should only be accessible administratively by the systems administrator and his helpers. This will assist in preventing any unauthorized employees from altering any data on the servers within the company.

In addition, a systems administrator will construct a secure firewall for the network that might have sentinel software that automatically blocks unauthorized programs from accessing it and an encryption layer. Restrictions on websites that might contain malicious coding or malware that installs itself on a user's computer can also be applied by the administrator to employees' computers. Programs to remove malware and adware are available for both networks and individual computers. Flexibility is one issue that typically comes up with this kind of security. Management must strike a compromise between security concerns and workers' need to access websites for work.

It takes communication between management, the systems administrator, and staff for network security to function and for staff members to be able to use it. Security lapses are expensive and harmful to output and efficiency, as demonstrated by the experience with prior network and email viruses. U.S. Businesses invest millions of dollars annually in network security solutions. A multi-pronged attack is the best defense a company can have against breaches. A network can be kept secure with the help of firewalls that prevent single points of access, astute systems administrators, regular security updates, and early anti-adware software installation.

The different wireless network security methods are:

2.4.7.1. Wired Equivalent Privacy (WEP)

This technique encrypts data as it travels between computers on the network using a key that is set. This key is needed during wireless network setup in order to encrypt and decrypt sent data. This is a comparatively outdated method of network security, and it is not too difficult to crack the WEP key.

2.4.7.2. 802.1X Authentication

Particularly, 802.1X is utilized for both wired and wireless 802.11 networks. Most often, networks in offices use this kind of authentication. When a user requests access to the network, their identity is verified by an authentication server.

2.4.7.3. Wi-Fi Protected Access (WPA)

The most popular approach to secure wireless networks is this one. Information is encrypted and only those with permission can access the network when using Wi-Fi Protected Access. This encryption method has been updated and is known as WPA2. Because it is more secure than WPA, it is advised to use it. Nevertheless, older wireless devices (such as MP3 players) and access points might not support WPA2.

Did you get it?

1. What are the various TCP Performance Enhancements?
2. How does the evolution of Wireless Systems impact TCP?

A CLOSER LOOK

The network model serves as a foundational framework for communication and data exchange within computer systems. It delineates how devices within a network interact, communicate, and share resources. At its core, the network model comprises various layers, each responsible for specific tasks such as data transmission, addressing, and error detection. This modular approach ensures efficiency, scalability, and interoperability across heterogeneous network environments.

Standardization plays a pivotal role in the development and implementation of network models. By establishing uniform protocols, interfaces, and technologies, standardization facilitates seamless communication between diverse devices and systems. Key organizations such as the Institute of Electrical and Electronics Engineers (IEEE) and the Internet Engineering Task Force (IETF) play instrumental roles in defining and refining networking standards. These standards encompass a wide array of aspects, including data formats, communication protocols, security measures, and network topologies.

The network model and standardization are intricately intertwined, with standards providing the guidelines and specifications for implementing various layers and protocols within the network model. For instance, the OSI (Open Systems Interconnection) model, a prominent network model, delineates seven layers, each governed by standardized protocols and interfaces. These standards ensure that devices from different manufacturers can communicate effectively, fostering compatibility and interoperability.

Moreover, standardization fosters innovation and market growth by providing a common framework upon which developers can build new technologies and services. It enables seamless integration of diverse networking technologies, fostering the development of sophisticated applications and services.

ROLE MODEL

Christopher S. Strachey: One of the founders of denotational semantics, and a pioneer in programming language design and computer time-sharing.

Biography

Born on November 16, 1916 into one of England's more prominent families, Christopher Strachey was educated at Gresham's School, Norfolk, and at King's College, Cambridge. He spent the war years in radar research, after which he spent several years as a schoolmaster. His career in computing did not effectively begin until 1951 when he started to program the machines at the National Physical Laboratory and Manchester University, while still a master at Harrow School.

In 1962, he also began work in the University Mathematical Laboratory, Cambridge, where, in the nominal position of "part-time research assistant," he worked on the CPL programming language. In 1965, he wound up his consultancy and resigned from Cambridge in order to form the Programming Research Group at Oxford University. Under his leadership, the group quickly established an international reputation in the theory of programming. At Oxford, in collaboration with Dana Scott, he produced the work of which he was most proud, the foundation of denotational semantics; this work was just beginning to bear fruit when he died in 1975.

Returning to King's in October 1938 for a fourth and final year, he graduated in the summer with a "lower second" in the natural sciences tripos. This mediocre result was a considerable disappointment, and it dashed any hopes he had entertained of a research studentship. Obliged to find an occupation of some kind, he accepted a post as a physicist with Standard Telephones and Cables Limited (STC) at a salary of £4 per week.

Strachey began work in the Valve Development Laboratories of STC, London, in August 1939, just a month before the declaration of war with Germany.

Most of his time at STC was spent as one member of a small team led by J.H. Fremlin (later a professor at the University of Birmingham), investigating the theoretical design of centimetric radar valves. Strachey's particular contribution was the derivation of analytical formulas for valve parameters and their experimental verification. His mathematical work involved the integration of differential equations, some of which proved particularly intractable; so, with colleague P.J. Wallis, he began to obtain numerical solutions using a differential analyzer. He later came to regard this experience with a computing machine as being something of a turning point, and his interests in computing were aroused generally at this time; he began to read the literature on the subject, and from time to time he also assisted STC colleagues in computational tasks.

In July 1944 Strachey left Fremlin's group and was transferred to London to work in the STC Radio Division. This work was concerned with electrical and mechanical design, which he found much less to his taste than the theoretical work. Strachey had never liked the atmosphere of the STC laboratories (either at Ilminster or at London), which he found "rather narrow-minded and sordid."

Strachey began as a "physics-cum-mathematics" master at St. Edmund's in October 1945, at a salary of £335 per annum.

He seems to have been a thorough schoolmaster: his lessons were meticulously prepared, and he spent much effort coaching his pupils for public examinations. After many applications to other schools, he was finally offered a position at Harrow School and left St. Edmund's in the spring of 1949.

Strachey began teaching at Harrow School in September 1949, at a salary of £600 a year. Securing a post at Harrow, one of Britain's leading public schools, was a real advancement to his career.

Strachey spent many of his evenings organizing societies and clubs. He was particularly keen on the science society and gave talks on topics such as interplanetary travel and the surface tension of soap films. He also played bassoon in the school orchestra, an instrument he had taught himself at St. Edmund's.

Against this background of busy "schoolmastering," Strachey's interest in computing had been largely dormant since leaving STC. Of course, computers were very much in the air in the late 1940s, and he no doubt read the semipopular articles.

His first exposure to a stored-program computer occurred in January 1951 when, through a mutual friend, he obtained an introduction to Mike Woodger of the National Physical Laboratory (NPL).

Back at Harrow, he began to write a program to make the Pilot ACE play draughts. This was typical of his early attempts at programming: anyone with more experience or less confidence would have settled for a table of squares. He got the idea of using the machine to play draughts largely from an article by Donald Davies of NPL, "A Theory of Chess and Noughts and Crosses," that had appeared in the June 1950 issue of Penguin Science News.

The following spring, Strachey learned from Woodger of the Ferranti Mark I computer that had just been installed at Manchester University. This machine had a much larger store than the Pilot ACE, with correspondingly greater scope for Strachey's kind of programming. Alan Turing, who was then assistant director of the Manchester University Computing Machine Laboratory, had written the programmer's handbook for the machine, and Strachey had known him just well enough at King's College that he could ask for and receive a copy.

He visited the Manchester Mark I for the first time in July 1951. When Strachey explained his ideas for a draughts-playing program, Turing was much impressed and suggested that another interesting problem would be to make the machine simulate itself, in the fashion of the interpretive trace routines developed for the Cambridge University EDSAC. Strachey was attracted by this idea and temporarily put the draughts program to one side. The final trace program was some 1,000 instructions long-by far the longest program that had yet been written for the machine, although Strachey was unaware of this.

Shortly after, Strachey received a letter from M.H.A. Newman, professor of pure mathematics at Manchester, complimenting him on the quality of his programs (which had been reported by Turing), and saying that he hoped to be able to offer him a post in the laboratory when one became available. Before he could do so, however, Strachey came to the notice of Lord Halsbury, managing director of the National Research and Development Corporation (NRDC). In November 1951 he was formally offered a post as technical officer with NRDC at a salary of £1200. Strachey formally began as an employee of NRDC on June 3, 1952.

During the first week of September 1952, Strachey attended the second ACM National Conference, held at the University of Toronto. The conference was timed to coincide with the inauguration of the FERUT, the second Ferranti Mark I, which had been installed in the Computation Centre of the university.

NRDC had agreed to loan Strachey to the University of Toronto to help with programming the calculations for the St. Lawrence Seaway project. Strachey spent all of October and November, and part of the following spring, on the program. The program was very long-about 2,000 instructions-and the input data tape was estimated to be one and a half miles in length.

During his time in North America, Strachey visited various research labs and computer manufacturers in the US, conducting a detailed study of different computers' order codes. He was one of the first in Britain to recognize the importance of this subject. In early 1954, he began discussions with Ferranti about designing a new machine, the Ferranti Packaged-Circuit Computer (FPC, later known as Pegasus). He convinced Ferranti to establish a small department to create a programming system for the machine, actively participating in its development. The Pegasus programming system was a significant achievement in British programming during the 1950s and had a profound impact.

Strachey, though relatively new to computing, was 38 years old when he started working on Pegasus, displaying great energy and maturity. The project thrived under his leadership, which was never as strong in subsequent endeavors.

In the late 1950s, multiprogramming (also referred to as time-sharing) gained popularity. Strachey's concept of time-sharing aimed to maintain direct interaction between programmers and machines while benefiting from the efficiency of multiprogramming. He applied for a time-sharing patent in February 1959, causing some tension with Kilburn's group at Manchester due to similarities with the Atlas project. In March 1959, after eight years at NRDC, Strachey announced his decision to resign and pursue freelance director and consultant roles. Strachey formally started activities as a private consultant on June 1, 1959, operating from his private address of 9 Bedford Gardens, Kensington. As part of his consultancy agreement with Ferranti, Strachey undertook to deliver a scientific autocode for the new ORION computer. To do this work, he took on a full-time employee, Peter Landin, in January 1960. Landin spent only part of his time on the autocode; with Strachey's encouragement, he spent the remainder of his time on a theoretical study of programming languages. It gave Strachey a certain ironic satisfaction that he was financing "the only work of its sort being carried out anywhere (certainly anywhere in England)" (Strachey 1971). Landin's work, which concerned the application of Church's lambda calculus to programming language semantics, was described in a classic paper, "The Mechanical Evaluation of Expressions."

As well as financing Landin's theoretical studies, Strachey was also prominent in the public debate on programming languages, particularly Algol. For example, at the 1959 UNESCO conference in Paris, he was in fine form, holding forth on the deficiencies of Algol while perched on the edge of a table on the platform, his legs swinging.

Strachey became well known for his outspoken view that Britain had fallen seriously behind the US in the field of programming. The main reason for the poor progress in Britain, Strachey perceived, was the small size of British machines. It was simply not possible to implement a LISP compiler on a machine the size of Pegasus, which was then the workhorse of most university computer centers.

In June 1962, Wilkes invited Strachey to work full-time in the University Mathematical Laboratory, Cambridge, to participate in the development of a new programming language and compiler for the Titan computer. Strachey accepted enthusiastically and began work the following month. A considerable financial sacrifice was involved, for the salary that Wilkes was able to offer was very modest compared to the consultancy fees he was then able to command.

The CPL (Cambridge Programming Language) project got off to a most promising start. By mid-August, the project group, which consisted of Strachey, Baron, and David F. Hartley, had produced an outline proposal. In the autumn, the group began to collaborate with Eric Nixon and John N. Buxton of the London University Computer Unit, so that CPL could also be used on the London University Atlas.

Concurrent with the CPL activity at Cambridge, it must be recalled that Strachey was also in business as a private consultant, with an office, a secretary, and his principal assistant Peter Landin to support. From mid-1963, he was actively seeking an opportunity to lead a university research group in the theory of programming. At first, it was hoped to set up a research unit in the Mathematical Laboratory at Cambridge, but this proved unsuccessful. In January 1964, Strachey also unsuccessfully competed for the chair of Computing Science at Imperial College, University of London. Finally, he secured the support of Leslie Fox, who succeeded in obtaining a DSIR grant to set up a programming research group at Oxford University in July 1965.

Although DSIR support for the Programming Research Group (PRG) started in July 1965, Strachey didn't move to Oxford until April 1966. The work on CPL continued. In June, Strachey gathered the full CPL group for a meeting, and it was decided, probably due to his enthusiasm for revising earlier drafts, that Strachey should edit and distribute the final version of the CPL reference manual. Throughout the rest of 1966, Strachey and David Park kept working on CPL and preparing the reference manual, titled the CPL Working Papers.

In the latter half of 1967, Strachey penned "Fundamental Concepts in Programming Languages," one of his most significant and lengthy papers, which, as usual, remains unpublished in its original form. Like much of Strachey's work at Oxford, though, the paper had a significant impact through private circulation.

Since starting at Oxford, Strachey had limited his external activities to focus on his academic work. For instance, he stepped down from his directorship of CAP in 1967, although he remained a shareholder and a consulting fellow. He became less involved in British Computer Society matters. He did participate in the computer science subcommittee of the SRC and gave occasional external lectures and did some consulting, but these activities were much less frequent compared to the early 1960s. On one memorable occasion, he collaborated with Stanley Gill and Alex d'Agapeyeff to address a Labour Party Science and Technology Committee, and in July 1973, he took part in a television debate on the Lighthill report on AI research in Britain.

Strachey's research into mathematical semantics took a significant step forward in 1969 through his collaboration with Dana Scott. Scott, a mathematical logician at Princeton University at the time, was on a sabbatical leave in Europe when he first met Strachey at a lively meeting of IFIP Working Group 2.2 in Vienna during Easter.

Scott's contribution was to provide a sound mathematical basis for the lambda-calculus models that Strachey used in his formal semantics. Strachey had first used this device in 1964 in his paper "Towards a Formal Semantics," but now conceded it was "gravely lacking in mathematical rigour."

Strachey decided, early in 1973, to submit an essay for the Adams Prize of Cambridge University, an award that has secured the reputation of many distinguished British mathematicians over the years. The subject for the Adams Prize for 1973-1974 was "Computer Science excluding Hardware," and the competition was open to persons admitted to a degree of the university. Apart from its obvious practical value as the kind of tangible evidence that would impress a Royal Society election committee, winning the Adams Prize perhaps meant something deeper to Strachey in terms of recognition from the alma mater. The essay for the Adams Prize dominated the remainder of his life.

The Adams essay included an important historical account of the development of the Oxford semantics and a final reworking of his "Fundamental Concepts in Programming Languages." The essay, with a few sections still unwritten, was finally dispatched to the Cambridge University Registry at the very end of 1974. The effort of writing the Adams essay took its toll on Strachey, and early in 1975 he spent several weeks away from Oxford resting. He returned to Oxford in the spring, where he continued to work with Milne at completing the essay and revising it into book form. In a matter of weeks, however, he contracted an illness diagnosed as jaundice; he obeyed the usual dietary restrictions and made an apparent recovery, but the illness quickly returned. He died of infectious hepatitis on May 18, 1975. The winner of the Adams Prize was announced shortly after Strachey's death. The submission of Strachey and Milne did not win.

Strachey made three important technical contributions to computing in Britain: the logical design of computers, the design of programming languages, and the development of denotational semantics. Strachey was responsible for a strong current of influence in the design of programming languages. Perhaps more important than any details of a particular language was the example that Strachey set: his whole approach to the subject and his way of going about things. Donald Michie made this point well when he wrote in 1971: Today an "invisible college" of programming theory exists throughout the Universities of Britain. Almost every member of this "college" was guided along the path at some stage by Strachey's direct influence. Developments of theory may in the long run prove decisive in helping to clear the hurdles of software engineering which still lie ahead (Michie 1971).

SUMMARY

- A network's foundational component is its networking software. Administrators can use it to deploy, maintain, and keep an eye on networks. Conventional networks consist of specialized hardware, like switches and routers, which combine networking software into the whole setup.
- The ISO/OSI model, which stands for International Standards Organization/ Open System Interconnection, is a commonly used reference model for network communication between two end users. To solve future issues, it can be useful to have a fundamental understanding of the network's operation.
- Transmission of data over the network is handled by the transport layer. The data is conceptualized at this level more as a conversation than as individual packets. This is achieved by using protocols, which are referred to as "rules of communication."
- The network layer makes sure that every packet makes it from its point of origin to its destination, while the data link layer manages the packet delivery between two systems connected by the same network (links).
- The physical layer of a network consists of the actual cables, fibers, cards, switches, and other electrical and mechanical components. This layer converts digital data into signals so that they can be transmitted over a wire.
- Multiplexing is the process of combining several signals (analog or digital) for transmission over a single line or medium. Multiple low-speed signals are combined for transmission over a single high-speed connection in a common form of multiplexing.

MULTIPLE CHOICE QUESTIONS

1. Which organization developed the OSI (Open Systems Interconnection) model for network architecture?
   a. IEEE
   b. ISO (International Organization for Standardization)
   c. IETF (Internet Engineering Task Force)
   d. ITU (International Telecommunication Union)
2. Which layer of the OSI model is responsible for providing end-to-end communication between applications?
   a. Application Layer
   b. Transport Layer
   c. Network Layer
   d. Data Link Layer

3. Which TCP/IP model layer corresponds to the OSI model's Physical and Data Link layers?
   a. Network Access Layer
   b. Internet Layer
   c. Transport Layer
   d. Application Layer
4. Which organization is responsible for the development of TCP/IP standards and protocols?
   a. IEEE
   b. IETF (Internet Engineering Task Force)
   c. ISO (International Organization for Standardization)
   d. ITU (International Telecommunication Union)
5. Which of the following is not a characteristic of the TCP/IP model?
   a. It is a hierarchical model.
   b. It is based on a set of protocols developed for the ARPANET.
   c. It consists of four layers: Application, Transport, Internet, and Network Access.
   d. It was developed before the OSI model.

REVIEW QUESTIONS

1. What mechanisms are used in the transport layer?
2. How is framing detection understood in the Data Link Layer?
3. What are the various types of multiplexing?
4. What is the purpose and functionality of digital multiplexers?
5. How is connection establishment and termination clarified?

Answer to Multiple Choice Questions

1. (b) 2. (a) 3. (a) 4. (b) 5. (c)

REFERENCES

1. Alderson, D., Li, L., Willinger, W., & Doyle, J. C., (2005). Understanding internet topology: Principles, models, and validation. IEEE/ACM Transactions on Networking, 13(6), 1205–1218.
2. Bhandarkar, S., Jain, S., & Reddy, A., (2005). Improving TCP performance in high bandwidth high RTT links using layered congestion control. Proceedings of the 3rd International Workshop on Protocols for Fast Long-Distance Networks.

3. Bresnahan, J., Link, M., Khanna, G., Imani, Z., Kettimuthu, R., & Foster, I., (2007). Globus GridFTP: What's new in 2007. Proceedings of the 1st International Conference on Networks for Grid Applications. Article 19.
4. Kelly, T., (2003). Scalable TCP: Improving performance in highspeed wide area networks. ACM SIGCOMM Computer Communication Review, 33, 83–91.
5. Leith, D., & Shorten, R., (2008). Next generation TCP: Open questions. Proceedings of the 6th International Workshop on Protocols for Fast Long-Distance Networks.
6. Magoni, D., & Pansiot, J. J., (2002). Internet topology modeler based on map sampling. Proceedings of the 7th International Symposium on Computers and Communications (ISCC 2002) (pp. 1021–1027).
7. Mahadevan, P., Hubble, C., Krioukov, D., Huffaker, B., & Vahdat, A., (2007). Orbis: Rescaling degree correlations to generate annotated internet topologies. ACM SIGCOMM Computer Communications Review, 37(4), 325–336.

CHAPTER

3

Local Area Network/Wide Area Network

LEARNING OBJECTIVES

After studying this chapter, you will be able to:

- Prepare for the OSI model
- Know about the multiplexing and switching
- Discuss on transmission control protocol (TCP)
- Learn about the user datagram protocol (UDP)

INTRODUCTORY EXAMPLE

LOCAL AREA NETWORK DESIGN AND CONFIGURATION IN AN ORGANIZATION

When it comes to setting up a Local Area Network (LAN) for an organization, it's all about taking a systematic approach to meet the needs of users while ensuring security, reliability, and scalability. LANs are crucial for internal connectivity, data exchange, resource access, and seamless communication within the organization. A well-thought-out LAN design involves considering elements like network topology, hardware selection, addressing schemes, security measures, and management protocols. Choosing the right topology is key in LAN design as it dictates how devices are connected within the network. Common topologies include star, bus, ring, and mesh. In organizational setups, the star topology is often favored for its centralized management and ease of troubleshooting. Each device connects to a central switch, enabling efficient data transmission and network management.

Hardware selection is vital in LAN configuration, with switches, routers, access points, and cabling infrastructure forming the network's backbone. High-performance switches with adequate port density and throughput are essential to meet the organization's bandwidth needs. Routers facilitate interconnectivity between LANs and provide access to external networks, while access points enable wireless connectivity for mobile devices and remote access.

Addressing and subnetting schemes are essential for efficient resource allocation and network management. Implementing a structured IP addressing scheme using IPv4 or IPv6 addresses helps organize devices logically and simplifies troubleshooting. Subnetting enables the segmentation of the network into smaller, manageable subnets, improving performance and security by controlling traffic flow and minimizing broadcast domains.

Security measures are paramount in LAN configuration to safeguard sensitive data and protect against unauthorized access or malicious activities. Implementing firewalls, intrusion detection/prevention systems, and access control lists (ACLs) helps enforce security policies and restrict access to authorized users only. Encryption protocols such as WPA2/3 for wireless networks and VPNs for remote access ensure data confidentiality and integrity.

Scalability is a crucial consideration in LAN design, as organizations need networks that can accommodate growth and expansion over time. Designing a scalable LAN involves deploying modular hardware, implementing redundant links for high availability, and adopting protocols such as Spanning Tree Protocol (STP) to prevent network loops and ensure stability.

INTRODUCTION

A computer network that is located within a constrained physical space, such as a house, school, office building, computer lab, or collection of buildings, is known as a local area network, or LAN. Workstations and personal computers that are networked together to form a local area network (LAN) can access and share data and devices, including printers, scanners, and data storage devices, from any location on the LAN. Higher data transfer and communication rates, as well as the absence of the need for leased communication lines, are characteristics of local area networks (LANs). Digital data is sent over serial transmission lines by local area networks. Because it allows for relatively high transmission speeds by sending character blocks at a time, synchronous transmission is typically used.

A wide area network, or WAN, is a communications system that connects many different locations, like cities, states, or nations. They can be more public to link smaller networks together, or they can be more private to connect sections of a business. The simplest way to comprehend what a wide area network (WAN) is to consider the internet as the largest WAN in the world. Because it connects numerous smaller local area networks (LANs) or metro area networks (MANs) via the use of ISPs, the internet is a wide area network (WAN). A company may, on a smaller scale, have a WAN that connects its headquarters, smaller branch offices, and cloud services. In this scenario, the WAN would be utilized to link all of those corporate divisions.

The ultimate goal is always to enable communication between various smaller networks located in different places, regardless of what the WAN connects or how far apart the networks are from one another. A wide-area network, or WAN, is one that spans a sizable geographic area. A wide area network (WAN) links several smaller networks, such as metropolitan area networks (MANs) and local area networks (LANs). This guarantees that users and computers in one place can communicate with users and computers in other places. Either a private network or the public transmission system can be used to implement a WAN.

3.1. LOCAL AREA NETWORK

→Learning Objectives

- Trace the historical development and milestones of local area networks (LANs).
- Identify different types of LAN architectures and topologies.
- Analyze the role of LAN applications in enhancing productivity and efficiency in business environments.
- Define the characteristics and attributes that distinguish LANs from other types of networks.
- Identify the different types of devices commonly found in LAN environments.
- Explore the hardware components and infrastructure required to establish and maintain a LAN.
- Analyze the advantages and benefits of deploying a LAN in a computing environment.
- Explain the importance of protocol standards in ensuring interoperability and compatibility in LAN environments.
- Explore the standards and specifications that govern LAN technology and operations.

The network is privately owned and is known as the local area network. A network is an assembly of computers and other devices that are linked together to exchange data. A local area network, or LAN, is a type of network that can function over a small physical area, such as a few kilometers in size, which could be an office, factory, or collection of buildings. Widely used in a range of computers, LANs allow resources (e.g., printers) and communication of data. To share resources, LANs connect the workstations and personal computers in the offices. The resources that need to be shared can be data, software, or hardware such as a printer. For computer communications, a local area network, or LAN, is a type of shared packet network with limited distance. Every machine in a LAN is linked by a single cable. A LAN can have data rates as high as 100 Mbps, with a range of 4 to 16 Mbps. A local area network (LAN) can also simply refer to the hardware and software that enable device networking. In this regard, Ethernet and Local Talk are two different types of LANs. The Local Talk protocol is called AppleTalk.

Hardware, protocols, and cabling standards comprise the parts that LANs use. Ethernet, Token Ring, TCP/IP, 5MB,

NetBIOS, NetBeui, IPX/SPX, Fiber Distributed Data Interchange (FDDI), and Asynchronous Transfer Mode (ATM) are some examples of LAN protocols.

LANs can be identified from other kinds of networks based on their topology, size, and transmission technology. A limited local area network (LAN) is one that can cover a comparatively small area. LANs employ cable-based transmission technology. Conventional LAN technology has very low error rates and can transmit data at 10 Mbps to 100 Mbps. But LAN technology today can transfer data at up to 10 Gbps. For broadcast LANs, a variety of network topologies are possible. One client machine is the master machine in a linear cable network (Bus) at any given time, and it is only permitted to transmit. Every other machine doesn't send any data. The ring is the second kind of broadcast LAN. There, LAN speeds of 4 and 16 Mbps are used. Another illustration of a ring network is FDDI.

3.1.1. The Evolution of LAN

The office setting makes extensive use of PCs and desktop computers, so it became clear that the cost of connecting a printer or FAX machine to every single computer would be prohibitive. It also takes time to copy files to a disk and transfer them between computers in order to print them. Significant savings resulted from connecting computers so they could share a printer and files. When 10 Mbps Ethernet cards first appeared in 1982, they were highly priced. Even in 1988, 10 Mbps Ethernet was still functional in small installations and offered respectable performance for large LANs. Congestion started to appear on large installations by 1990. As a result, alternatives to 10 Mbps cards were gaining traction. Installing a switched architecture was one of these options instead of building a hub-based architecture.

For smaller installations, 10Mbps switched LANs were offering serviceable performance in 1996. At this point, shared Ethernet at 100 Mbps was an incredible technology. By 1998, large LANs and small LANs alike were using switched 100 Mbps and switched 10 Mbps Ethernet, respectively. As more people start using video conferencing on large LANs, 100 Mbps starts to become limited. Gigabit Ethernet cards can now be purchased. The 10 Mbps cards have been superseded. Currently, the market offers 10/100, 10/100/1000 auto-sensing cards. The future of autosensing is dual-mode technology. Despite its increasing popularity, Gigabit Ethernet LANs are ten times faster than 100Mbps LANs. ALOHA was the original protocol from which Ethernet evolved. ALOHA was primarily utilized in satellite-based packet radio networks for communication. To put it briefly, an earth station sends some data and then waits for an acknowledgment (ACK) when the data is ready. It will time out and send the same message again if it does not receive an ACK. Up until the transmission is successful, the sender never gives up. Determine the maximum number of users to guarantee an area with the aid of traffic analysis.

3.1.2. LAN Technology

In the information age, local area networks, or LANs, are now widely used. The advent of low-cost computers and the requirement for hardware resources and information sharing in an office setting paved the way for the development of low-cost local area networks (LANs). LAN technologies are intended to link computers together over short distances (e.g., inside one structure or space). Modern LANs are cheap, incredibly dependable, and simple to set up and maintain. An interface card is required for a computer in order to connect to a LAN. This interface card is seen by the computer as any other I/O device. When data is transmitted to the interface card, it is received by another computer connected to the same communication medium (copper wire, coax cable, optical fiber, or through the air) at a specific radio frequency. The application can see through the communication channel that is being used.

Keyword

Communication medium is a channel or route in the communication process through which a sender communicates their message to the receiver.

Because LANs have altered the economics of computing, they have become incredibly popular. Cheap computers can now be used to share access to shared resources like printers, large storage banks (disks), and application software. LANs facilitate group and collaborative work by allowing users to share information. Ethernet is arguably the most widely used LAN technology. Ethernet communicates between various LAN stations via a broadcast mechanism. When a station wants to talk to another station, it just listens to the channel and, if no one is talking, sends its data onto the communication medium along with the station's numerical address. Each station scans the communication medium for information transmitted with its address. If it detects such information, it receives it and forwards it to the relevant application program.

3.1.3. LAN Applications

Local Area Networks can be utilized to provide any or all of the following facilities (see Figure 3.1):

1. The interconnection of all computers, terminals, PCs, and other workstations within a department or building.
2. The effective communication between all devices attached to the network, regardless of their vendor.
3. The sharing of expensive peripheral resources attached to the network such as disks, printers, plotters, central processors, and databases.
4. The standardization of wiring, hardware, and software required for communication and applications.
5. The establishment of a foundation for continued growth and the expansion of a distributed computing environment.

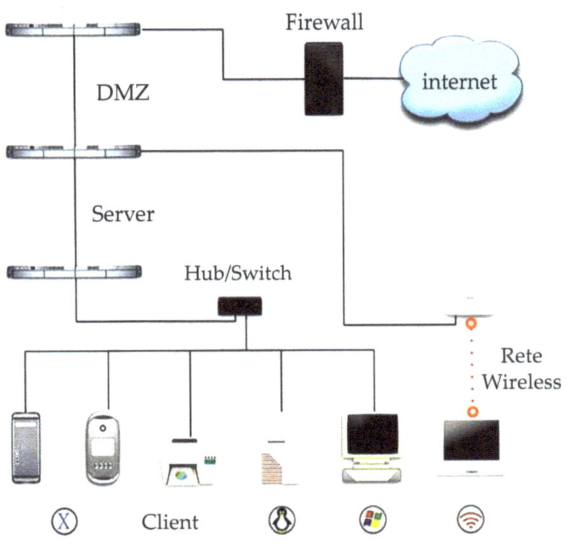

Figure 3.1. Example of a typical LAN application (Source: Quora, https://qph.cf2.quoracdn.net/main-qimg-9682d6e2cd0628b9e7ddb061c8237166-pjlq).

3.1.4. Characteristics of a LAN

A LAN can be characterized by means of hardware and software components and a set of protocols.

Hardware components of a LAN are:

- *The Server:* A server is a computer on a network that offers services to other workstations and clients. Data management is a LAN server's main objective. It safeguards, keeps, and retrieves the data. A server also transmits data to authorized remote users and requesters on the network. The type of server and its configurations are primarily determined by the reason behind the LAN's construction. Depending on the kind of service they offer, servers can be categorized. Numerous services could also be offered by a single server. The servers are listed below in different categories according to the kind of service they provide.
- *File server and disk server:* A file server provides different client pieces with disk storage space (of several gigabytes) in response to data requests from application programs running on client workstations. When multiple clients request data at the same time, it also maintains data consistency. Any application running on a workstation within a LAN that uses a file server can request a file involving the local operating system. The server receives the file request from the workstation and processes it before sending the necessary file straight to the workstation. File servers and disk servers are comparable. The distinction lies in the fact that when an application operating on a workstation makes a request for a particular file on a file server, the workstation's local operating system communicates with the file server to obtain the necessary data. The application can access the necessary file directly from a disk server without the help of the local operating system.
- *Database server:* A subset of file servers make up these servers. They give their clients access to enormous databases. Data from databases is kept on optical, CD-ROM, and hard disk drives. The DBMS, which is more advanced than the straightforward file I/O access technique, is contained in it. Data redundancy is removed by DBMS, enabling transparent data distribution for the user. Unlike a file server, which sends the entire

file to the requesting client, a database server only extracts the pertinent data and sends it.

- *Print server:* Each workstation or node on a LAN shares one or more printers. The job of a print server is to collect data from multiple workstations, store it on disk, and send it to the printer. Print spooling is the term for this process. Nowadays, print services are integrated into file servers. Any PC connected to the network can act as a print server in many LAN architectures.
- *Gateway server:* A gateway server is used to provide connectivity to other networks. The GIAS (Gateway server of VSNL, India) is a gateway server that provides connectivity to all other networks on the Internet for the Indian segment of the Internet. A gateway server also provides connectivity to dissimilar networks.
- *Communication server:* Communication servers are more diverse than other servers. The main functions of a communication server are linking client workstations on the LAN with mainframe computers, sharing a pool of modems among the client stations, and communicating with other LANs as well. Examples of the most popular LAN servers include Novell Netware LAN Server, Microsoft Windows NT Server or Windows 2000, IBM OS2 Server, etc.
- *Workstations:* The clients that utilize the network server's services are workstations, also known as nodes. Special software is installed on workstations so they can communicate with the server and use the services. Examples of workstations include Microsoft Windows NT Workstation, Windows 2000 Workstation, IBM Workstation, Sun Workstation, and so on.
- *The Transmission Media for LAN:* To build a LAN, a variety of transmission media is used. Optical fibers, coaxial cables, and twisted pairs are the most widely used types. Wired LANs are those that use any type of such transmission media. It is also possible to build LANs without using cables or transmission media. These LANs are referred to as wireless LANs.

Communication Equipment

- Repeater: A repeater operates at layer 1. It has just enough intelligence to determine the incoming signals at layer 1 and then sends out a clean stream of signals built from scratch, eliminating noise. A repeater has one incoming and one outgoing line, extending the distance a signal may be sent over a transmission media.
- **Hub:** A hub is a multi-port repeater. Any incoming signal is repeated on all other outgoing lines. A hub functions at layer 1.
- **Bridge**: A bridge has more intelligence than a hub or repeater. This device separates two segments of a single LAN. A bridge operates at layer 2 by examining the destination address in the frame header. By consulting a table, the bridge determines if the frame needs to pass on to the other segment. Only certain frames may pass, those with the correct MAC address.
- **Switch:** A switch is a multi-port

bridge that operates at layer 2. It looks at MAC layer addresses like a bridge, consults a table, and determines if a frame needs to be sent on one of the attached lines. Multiple connections can occur through a switch simultaneously as long as they do not compete for the same line. A switch, like a bridge, does not divide a LAN into two LANs but reduces unnecessary traffic on LAN segments.

- **Router** A router is more intelligent than bridges and switches. It functions at layer-3. At layer-2 all incoming frames are checked for errors and then they are delivered to layer-3. A layer-3 datagram has an address that permits it to be sent across internetworks (interconnected networks). This requires a single global addressing scheme. The router finds the layer-3 address and consults a table that it keeps. There the router will learn which attached line to send the datagram on. A router provides facilities to the stations on the LAN to access other networks.

3.1.5. Devices

A LAN device is essentially any device directly connected to a local area network. Through a shared access point like a router, devices on the same local area network can usually share files, access resources, and connect to the Internet. To ensure they stay cool and secure from tampering, many LAN devices we use daily are stored in protected server rooms. The definition of a LAN has remained unchanged for over 20 years, even as the devices within a LAN continue to evolve. A local area network, or LAN, is a small data network that can be set up in a home or office, enabling devices like PCs to share services and resources. Ethernet and Wi-Fi (802.11x) are the most popular LAN technologies nowadays, with older technologies like Token Ring rarely used. Essentially, any device in your home, workplace, or classroom directly linked to a local area network via Ethernet cable or Wi-Fi adapter is considered a LAN device. When two devices are connected through the same access point, such as a router, they can typically share files, access resources, and use the Internet. Many LAN devices we use daily are kept secure and cool in server rooms.

Remember

A LAN comprises cables, access points, switches, routers, and other components that enable devices to connect to internal servers, web servers, and other LANs via wide area networks.

3.1.5.1. LAN Devices You See Daily

LAN devices include the router and modem found in the majority of homes and small offices, as well as computers, tablets, and smartphones that are linked to a network. If your smart appliances are networked, they can also function as local area networks (LANs). These can range from IP-based webcams and network printers to Blu-ray players, smart TVs, and game consoles. These days, some manufacturers are producing smart ovens, dryers, and washers that, once set up for your home network, can also function as LAN devices. Any device that is directly connected to a local area network can be considered a LAN device in the most basic sense. When two devices are connected by the same access point—such as a router—they can typically share files, access the same resources, and use the Internet. Numerous LAN devices that you might use on a daily basis are kept cool and safe from tampering by being kept in secure server rooms.

3.1.5.2. LAN Devices in a Large Network

Large corporations' and educational institutions' networks often contain extra network equipment that isn't typically found in a home. Among them are servers, which are powerful PCs that store data and applications and control network access using stored passwords. Advanced networking equipment like switches, firewalls, and routers are also utilized in large networks. These networking devices manage traffic and direct data to the appropriate devices, similar to a home router. The key distinction is their sophisticated management software and ability to handle numerous connections simultaneously.

3.1.6. Hardware Devices for LAN

When two or more PCs are connected, a local area network, or LAN, is established. The hardware added to a local area network (LAN) as it expands can include routers, wireless access points, servers, switches for connecting hardware (such as computers and printers), and wireless access points.

3.1.6.1. Switches

The main piece of hardware in LANs that allows network communication is a switch. Cabling is run to every hardware device on the network in order to create a LAN. Switches are used to allow data flow and connect hardware cabling throughout a local area network. Every switch has ports built in for network connections; the quantity of ports depends on the switch's size. Switches have features like quality of service to prioritize different kinds of LAN traffic and redundant power supplies that allow them to operate around the clock, seven days a week.

3.1.6.2. Wireless Access Points

Wireless access points can be added to the LAN to increase flexibility and lessen the need for cabling. This hardware device allows for workplace mobility by transmitting radio waves to computers through antennas. Common locations for installations include conference rooms and open spaces like cafeterias. To expand network services, the access point is connected to a LAN switch. It's crucial that this device has security features, such as data encryption, when connecting it to a LAN.

3.1.6.3. Servers

Servers are business-class PCs that provide collaboration tools, antivirus protection, messaging, and other services to the office. Similar to switches, servers run around the clock, seven days a week, to satisfy the demands of the office. Multiple processors, larger memory, and power supplies are features found in servers. To ensure uptime, server components can be changed while the machine is operating. Servers are housed in secure data centers and computer rooms and are built for high availability.

3.1.6.4. Thin Client

Installing desktop computers is an option provided by thin client hardware. Thin clients are hardware devices with a smaller profile and fewer components. These devices consume less power, leading to reduced operating costs. They establish a LAN connection and provide ports for a keyboard, mouse, and monitor. Workers rely on servers to access application services through thin clients. Unlike desktop computers with local file storage capabilities, thin clients depend on storage connected to the LAN. This centralized approach to providing application services and file storage simplifies management and enhances security.

3.1.7. LAN Advantages and Services

A local area network (LAN) consists of personal computers (PCs) that connect and share resources like printers and storage via phone lines or cables. LANs are typically confined to a single building or a small area, but this is not a strict rule. The area could be a home or workplace with only a few devices, or it could span a larger space like an entire office building with numerous devices. The common feature of all LANs, regardless of size, is connecting devices within a limited area. The benefits of networking devices within a LAN include file sharing, printing to shared printers, using a single internet connection, and more. Larger LANs may include dedicated servers for email, global user directories, and other shared corporate resources.

A LAN has the following advantages:

- They work on higher operating speed than WAN and MAN.
- They suit the requirements of a specific organization.
- They are easy to install and maintain.
- hey exist as connected (wired) and wireless configurations.

LAN can provide the following services. They are:

- **File-based services.** File transfer between nodes inside a local area network (LAN). When a new transaction is made on behalf of a customer, for instance, the file containing the specific customer's detailed transactions is transferred from the server to the client in a typical local area network (LAN) used for local banking. Additionally, it offers effective means of data retrieval and storage. The presence of multiple copies of an identical file facilitates the essential synchronization required for file updates. In order to enable safe recovery in the event of a failure, LANs additionally offer backup for vital data. Additionally, it offers the ability to encrypt data so that only specific individuals may access it.
- **Print services.** Applications may use one or more printers, modems, and fax machines that are connected to a local area network (LAN). These devices can be shared by several clients. Many clients can safely share printers and other similar devices thanks to print services. These services are available on all modem LANs.
- **Application-based services**. Higher processing power may be needed for client-side applications. The power of servers exceeds that of clients. A server's processing power can be shared by multiple clients over a local area network (LAN). A good illustration of this is with application servers.

- **Mail and message-based services.** One useful tool for information sharing on a network is electronic mail (e-mail). Emails can be sent to another user or stored. On the Internet, there are a lot of free mail servers that offer their users free mail services.
- **Database services**. Storing and retrieving data in databases is another requirement of a client to control and manipulate the data. Database servers are the most popular ones that service the need of clients.

Keyword

Database server is a server that uses a database application to provide database services to other computer programs or computers, as defined by the client–server model.

- **Distributed data services**. When data is distributed, it is possible for more than one client system to share the data. Though the databases appear physically distributed, there is a single logical view given by the database server. There are many issues involved in sharing a single file by more than one client. Consistency issues are very seriously tackled when updating shared files.
- **Remote services**. Linking a LAN with a remote computer or a mainframe is another required service.

This feature is used to access remote databases available on large mainframes.

3.1.8. Protocol

A local area network is one that operates within a structure, such as a home office, business, or office. LANs are utilized in confined geographic areas. Within a constrained network distance, LANs can transfer data at speeds of up to 10Mbps. Peer-to-peer networking and client-server networking are the two forms of network architecture that can be used in local area networks. Ethernet and Token Ring connections are the most often used types in local area networks (LANs).

The ability of LAN protocols to effectively transfer data over shorter distances—a few hundred feet, for example—through a variety of media—including copper cabling—sets them apart. There are various "layers" of the "Open Systems Interconnect," or OSI, model, and distinct protocols for various uses. Generally speaking, lower level, or physical, layers are meant to be described when a protocol is referred to as "LAN." The most widely used LAN protocols are "Fiber Distributed Data Interface," or "FDDI," "Ethernet," and "Token Ring." By far the most popular kind of LAN protocol is "Ethernet." It is identifiable by its typical "CAT5" copper cable medium and is found in homes and offices all over the world. To exchange data, all systems connect to a switch or hub.

The outdated LAN technology known as "Token Ring" is becoming less common. The fundamental idea behind "Token Ring" is that only the intended recipient can read a single "token" that is transferred between systems or via a hub. The term "FDDI" describes the fiber cabling method used to transfer LAN traffic. When greater security is needed or longer distances—typically between floors or buildings—are needed, fiber cabling is utilized. Multiple network protocols can be used by LANs (Local Area Networks) to define their networks. The OSI Data Link Layer defines these protocols.

- **ARP (Address Resolution Protocol):** Converts IP address to MAC Address. An ARP cache is maintained in the system that has a table mapping of IP address to MAC address in the Network.
- **RARP (Revers Address Resolution Protocol):** Convers MAC address to IP Address

Classifications of LAN transmissions:

- **Unicast:** Data is transmitted from source to a destination system
- **Multicast:** Data is transmitted from source to multiple destinations using a special multicast IP address

Did you know?

The development and proliferation of personal computers using the CP/M operating system in the late 1970s, and later DOS-based systems starting in 1981, meant that many sites grew to dozens or even hundreds of computers.

3.1.9. LAN Standards

A local area network, or LAN, is a type of data communication network that links computers or terminals within a building or a constrained geographic area. Both wired and wireless connections between the devices are possible. Standard LAN technologies include IEEE 802.11 Wireless LAN, Ethernet, and Token Ring.

- **Ethernet:** The most popular LAN technology, as defined by IEEE standards 802.3, is Ethernet. Ethernet's widespread use is due to its simplicity in understanding, implementation, and maintenance, as well as its ability to enable low-cost network implementation. Additionally, Ethernet allows for flexibility in terms of permitted topologies. The Physical Layer and Data Link Layer are the two OSI model layers in which Ethernet functions. Since we primarily work with DLL, the protocol data unit for Ethernet is the frame. Ethernet uses CSMA/CD as its access control mechanism to handle collisions. Ethernet employs the Manchester Encoding Technique.

Since we are talking about IEEE 802.3 standard Ethernet, therefore, 0 is expressed by a high-to-low transition, a 1 by the low-to-high transition. In both Manchester Encoding and Differential Manchester, Encoding Baud rate is double of bit rate.

Baud rate = 2* Bit rate

Ethernet LANs consist of network nodes and interconnecting media or link. The network nodes can be of two types:

- **Data Terminal Equipment (DTE):** DTEs are typically the final devices that change signals received into user information or vice versa. Personal computers, workstations, file servers, print servers, and other devices commonly referred to as end stations are examples of DTEs. These devices are either data frames' source or destination. The data terminal equipment can consist of one unit or several units that are networked together and fulfill all the necessary tasks to enable user communication. DTE and users can communicate with each other.

- **Data Communication Equipment (DCE):** The intermediary network devices, or DCEs, are responsible for receiving and forwarding frames over the network. They could be stand-alone gadgets like routers, network switches, and repeaters, or they could be communications interface units like modems and interface cards. The DCE may be a component of the DTE or intermediate equipment and carries out tasks like coding and signal conversion.

Currently, these data rates are defined for operation over optical fibers and twisted-pair cables:

i) **Fast Ethernet**. Fast Ethernet refers to an Ethernet network that can transfer data at a rate of 100 Mbit/s.

ii) **Gigabit Ethernet**. Gigabit Ethernet delivers a data rate of 1,000 Mbit/s (1 Gbit/s).

iii) **10 Gigabit Ethernet**. 10 Gigabit Ethernet is the recent generation and delivers a data rate of 10 Gbit/s (10,000 Mbit/s). It is generally used for backbones in high-end applications requiring high data rates.

- **ALOHA**. The University of Hawaii project included the design of the Aloha protocol. It allowed packet radio networks to be used to transfer data between computers on various Hawaiian Islands. At the data link layer, Aloha is a multiple access protocol that suggests a way for multiple terminals to access the medium without causing a collision or interference.

There are two different versions of ALOHA:

1. **Pure Aloha**: Pure Aloha is a decentralized, easy-to-implement protocol that is not slotted. The stations in Pure Aloha simply send frames whenever they have data to transmit. Prior to transmission, they do not verify if the channel is busy. In case two or more stations transmit simultaneously, collisions occur, leading to the destruction of frames. Upon sending a frame, each station expects to receive an acknowledgment from the recipient. If the acknowledgment or frame is not received within a specified time frame, the station assumes it has been lost and retransmits the frame after a certain waiting period.

   This unpredictability helps in reducing collisions. While this approach works well in small networks with light traffic, it performs poorly in heavily loaded networks. This limitation led to the development of Slotted Aloha. To ensure the effectiveness of Pure Aloha, certain conditions must be met:

1) All frames should be of the same length.

2) Stations cannot generate frames while sending or attempting to send frames.

3) The population of stations uses a Poisson distribution to determine how to transmit, including new

frames and previously collided frames.

Vulnerable Time = 2 * Tt

Efficiency of Pure ALOHA:

Spure= G * e^-2G

where G is number of stations wants to transmit in Tt slot.

Maximum Efficiency: Maximum Efficiency will be obtained when G=1/2

(Spure)max = 1/2 * e^-1 = 0.184

which means, in Pure ALOHA, only about 18.4% of the time is used for successful transmissions.

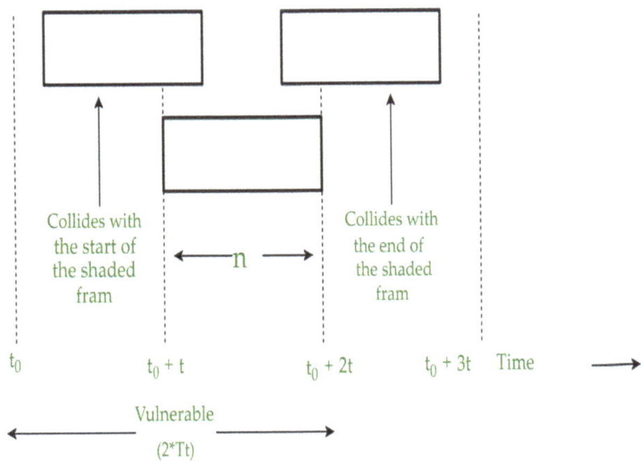

Figure 3.2. Throughput and rate of transmission of the frame (Source: Geeksforgeeks, https://media.geeksforgeeks.org/wp-content/uploads/20230710122406/ETHERNET_2.webp).

2. **Slotted Aloha:** The only real difference between this and Pure Aloha is how transmissions happen. Rather than sending the message at the exact moment of demand, the sender holds off. The shared channel's time is split into distinct intervals known as Slots in slotted ALOHA. Only at the start of the slot are the stations allowed to send a frame, and each slot can only have one frame sent. A station must wait until the start of the following time slot if it is unable to get the frame onto the channel at the start of the slot. If two stations attempt to send at the start of the same time slot, there is still a chance of a collision. However, compared to Pure Aloha, the number of collisions that could occur is still significantly decreased, and performance is significantly improved.

   Collision is possible for only the current slot. Therefore, Vulnerable Time is Tt.

Efficiency of Slotted ALOHA:

*Sslotted = G * e^-G*

Maximum Efficiency:

(Sslotted)max = 1 * e^-1 = 1/e = 0.368

Maximum Efficiency, in Slotted ALOHA, is 36.8%.

Did you get it?

1. What are the different types of devices commonly found in LAN environments?
2. What hardware components and infrastructure are required to establish and maintain a LAN?

3.2. WIDE AREA NETWORK

→**Learning Objectives**

- Identify common WAN protocols and their characteristics.
- Describe the functions and features of WAN devices.
- Learn how to connect WAN devices to establish a wide area network.
- Explore strategies for managing and optimizing wide area networks.
- Describe various types of WAN connections available in networking.
- Identify key WAN standards and their significance in networking infrastructure.
- Explore the configuration and usage of WAN ports in wide area network setups.
- Acquire the skills necessary to design and implement a wide area network.

Wide area networks, or WANs for short, are communication networks that connect local computer networks to a wider, functional network that can span both domestic and foreign locations by utilizing current technology. On the other hand, the local area network and the metropolitan area network offer communication inside a constrained geographic area. It's often desirable to link two computer networks together, especially for companies with multiple locations. Using current telephony technology makes this process easier, starting with the local area network and moving on to the wide area network. Fiber optics are commonly used to establish connections between networks in different facilities. This typically involves using PSTN (public switched telephone network) technology or POTS (standard phone lines). Another option for network creation emerged in the 1990s: ISDN (integrated services digital network) solutions. This was mainly because it became more cost-effective to expand the network across international borders.

A wide area network, or WAN, allows businesses to use shared resources to operate. For example, many retail pharmacies use it to help customers who fill prescriptions at their stores. Once a customer is in the pharmacy's common customer database, they can fill a prescription at any of the company's locations—even when they're on vacation in a different state. Businesses also benefit from using wide area networks. With this kind of wide area network application, internal operations like sales, marketing, production and development, and accounting can also be shared with approved locations. Employees can work from almost anywhere by using this to combine disparate location-based computer networks into a single computer network for the entire company. In the event that a natural disaster damages or renders one facility unusable, staff members simply relocate and continue working using the shared network at their new location.

The current GPRS, EDGE, or 3G mobile network is expected to be used for the Wide Area Network because it is widely accessible and has coverage in the majority of the UK. The crucial aspect in this situation is that data from the Personal Connector must be routinely sent to the distant servers for examination. Installing a software program on a mobile device allows it to interact with both the server application and the Personal Connector. This software, known as service integration software, is essential for facilitating the communications needed for the analysis of data on smart clothing.

There may be times when the mobile network doesn't receive any signal, preventing data from being sent to distant servers. In such situations, data is retrieved from the Personal Connector and stored on the mobile device. The Personal Connector holds onto this data until the end servers can be reached and the data transfer is completed successfully. Each piece of data is time-stamped and assigned a message sequence number. This two-stage process enhances the overall service reliability, ensuring that information can be transmitted to the far-end servers once the wide area mobile network is accessible. This eliminates the need to wait for data transfer from the Personal Connector to be successful.

In a normal scenario,

- This application polls the Personal Connector,
- Retrieves the information,
- Checks the timestamps and message sequence numbers of this information,
- Sets up a connection to the far-end servers,
- Sends the information to the far-end servers,
- Receives an acknowledgment from the far-end servers with the message sequence number of the last information received,
- Completes Cyclic Redundancy Checks (CRC) successfully, and
- Sends a 'Success' message back to the Personal Connector with the message sequence number and receives an acknowledgment, sent by the Personal Connector.
- All pointers and information are now updated. A timeout occurs, and the data is resent in failure scenarios, such as when acknowledgments are not received or CRC malfunctions. Whether it is GPRS or 3G, this software program will provide the interface to the selected mobile network. The software program can be updated in the future in response to changes in the wide area network, which could involve Wi-Max or any other technology selected for 4G mobile. Establishing a reliable protocol is essential for the complete data transfer process from the home network to the distant servers through a wireless wide area network.

3.2.1. WAN Protocol

Packet-switching exchange nodes (PSEs) are the hardware that drops traffic onto the wires connecting sites in standard-sized packets, delivered in order, with error correction. X.25 is one of the oldest protocols used to deliver WAN traffic. Leased lines, dial-up phone services, and Integrated

Services Digital Network (ISDN) connections are examples of the physical links. It's not as common these days.

The replacement for X.25 is frame relay. Frame Relay divides data into frames of varying sizes and leaves it up to the endpoints to handle packet loss and error correction. The overall data rate is accelerated by these discrepancies. Furthermore, Frame Relay uses fewer dedicated connections to build mesh networks, resulting in fewer physical circuits and a financial savings for businesses. Once more, frame relay was once very popular but is now less so. The main distinction between frame relay and asynchronous transfer mode (ATM) is that data is divided into uniformly sized packets known as cells. Cells facilitate the blending of various traffic classes onto a single physical circuit and increase the ease with which service quality can be guaranteed. ATM's drawback is that, due to its use of relatively small cells, a disproportionately large portion of each cell's contents is taken up by the headers. As a result, frame relay uses bandwidth more efficiently overall than ATM. Additionally, ATMs are becoming less popular with business clients.

Keyword

Integrated Services Digital Network is a set of communication standards for simultaneous digital transmission of voice, video, data, and other network services over the digitalized circuits of the public switched telephone network.

Today, a lot of corporate data is transported across WAN links using multi-protocol label switching. MPLS routers in an MPLS network can swiftly determine where to forward packets and assign them to the appropriate class of service based on short header segments known as labels. As traffic moves between sites, this enables the operation of various protocols inside MPLS packets while allocating the proper priority to various applications. One protocol that is frequently carried within MPLS is Internet Protocol (IP), which became more widespread in the 1990s. The Wide Area Network, or Internet, rose to prominence recently because it is so widely used and makes business management and information sharing possible everywhere in the world. The operation of this complex WAN structure is governed by a set of rules and standards, just like any other type of activity. The technologies or protocols known as WAN protocols control how effectively WANs operate. These significantly affect business continuity, which is important for enterprises.

Depending on the features they support and the protocols governing those features, technological appliances can operate effectively. Wide Area Networks, or WANs, employ a variety of networking tools and technologies. They are not the same as what Local Area Networks (LANs) use. The majority of WAN technologies and protocols are Layer 2 (data link layer) protocols. Asynchronous Transfer Mode (ATM), Frame Relay, Point-to-Point Protocol (PPP), Synchronous Optical Network (SONET), Synchronous Digital Hierarchy (SDH), and X are the main WAN protocols that are currently in use, as well as a few additional WAN protocols. Gaining a deeper comprehension of these ideas is crucial because they provide the foundation for improving Internet applications, which in turn helps businesses compete in the market. A quick summary of some of the most significant protocols is provided below.

- **Asynchronous Transfer Mode:** The packet switching protocol known as ATM allows data traffic to be encoded into discrete, pre-sized cells. The foundation of this protocol is connection-oriented technology. It functions by creating a virtual circuit between two endpoints even before any data is exchanged. A mechanism for routing traffic on a data stream with fixed 53-byte packets is established by the ATM protocol suite. Fixed-sized cells reduce the need for switching and multiplexing. Two systems on the network must notify each intermediate switch about service requirements and traffic parameters for communication to be established. ATM operates over layer 1 links to provide data link layer services as a cell relay protocol. ATM's inherent circuit-switched and packet-switched network properties make it ideal for real-time media transport and wide area network data networking. ATM Adaptation Layers (AALs) enable a variety of services. Between the ATM layer and an upper layer, the AAL transfers the ATM cells. It carries out a crucial task known as Segmentation and Reassembly (SAR). While information is being received from the higher level, data is divided into ATM cells.
- **Broadband Access**: High-speed Internet access is referred to as broadband, or broadband Internet access, and because of its high data transmission rate, it is one of the most widely used WAN protocols. Through broadband, speeds of up to 256 kbit/s are possible. In most places, cable modems and digital subscriber line (DSL) are the standard broadband technologies. Fiber-optic cables and Very High Bitrate DSL (VDSL or VHDSL) are two examples of more recent technologies that have developed. Modem technology is the foundation of DSL, which allows Internet access over copper phone lines. A Digital Subscriber Line Access Multiplexer is used to connect multiple DSL users to the high-speed network (DSLAM). The telephone company connects available DSL lines to the ATM network by using the DSLAM to aggregate data transmission from those lines. After demultiplexing the signals at the transmission endpoint, a DSLAM forwards the data to a DSL connection.

The various DSL connection types—ADSL, HDSL, SDSL, IDSL, and VDSL—collectively called xDSL are what create the connection between the phone company and the office. Discrete Multitone Technology (DMT), Simple Line Code (SLC), Carrierless Amplitude Modulation (CAP), Multiple Virtual Line (MVL), and Discrete Wavelet Multitone (DWMT) are some of the modulation technologies used in Digital Subscriber Lines. The foundational network system of the early WAN protocols, the Integrated Services Digital Network (ISDN), offers digital phone connectivity and permits high-speed simultaneous transmission of data, voice, video, and graphics over standard communication lines using bearer channels. In addition to telephone networks, packet-switched networks can also be used to transmit ISDN. Primary Rate Interface (PRI) and Basic Rate Interface (BRI) are the two fundamental types of ISDN service. Large enterprises and other users who need more capacity can use PRI, which offers a total of 1536 kb/s. BRI is limited to 160 kb/s for individual users.

- **Frame Relay.** Frame Relay is a WAN protocol that is only for internetworking Local Area Networks (LANs), or the transfer of data between LANs and WAN endpoints. It is based on packet-switching technology. Network providers frequently use frame relay, a low-cost technique, to encapsulate data and voice between LANs connected by a wide area network. A private or leased line will connect the user to a frame relay node. Frame relay enables data transfer between user devices across numerous switches and routers at both the physical and data link layers. The amount of frame relay technology being used has been steadily declining as a result of advancements in other technologies. However, this affordable WAN protocol with continuous connectivity at 64 kb/s is still in use in rural areas that have not yet had access to DSL or cable modem.
- **Point-to-Point Protocol**. A direct connection between two nodes can be established via serial cables, fiber optic links, exclusive radio links, cellular phones, telephone lines, and trunk lines using the PPP data link protocol. Customers frequently use point-to-point protocol, a WAN protocol, to access the Internet via dial-up. Connection establishment over synchronous and asynchronous circuits is facilitated by this protocol. Encapsulation is a crucial component of PPP, whereby PPP frames are encapsulated in a lower layer protocol to provide framing and other functions like transmission error detection. The two common encapsulated PPP forms are Point-to-Point Protocol over ATM (PPPoA) and Point-to-Point Protocol over Ethernet (PPPoE). They are used to carry out tasks similar to those that DSL services complete.
- **SONET/SDH**. Light Emitting Diodes (LEDs) or lasers are used in the multiplexing WAN protocols Synchronous Optical Networking (SONET) and Synchronous Digital Hierarchy (SDH) to facilitate the transport of multiple digital bit streams over the same optical fiber. SDH and SONET are two closely related protocols that use circuit mode communication as their foundation. Instead of using copper cables, SDH tests the compatibility of optical-fiber-based digital telephone links. When widely implemented, SONET/SDH allows multiple ISPs to concurrently share an optical fiber without interfering with each other's traffic load. Time division multiplexing (TDM) protocols are physical layer protocols that provide uninterrupted connections without requiring packet mode communication.
- **X.25**: X.25 is a packet-switched network-based WAN protocol for WAN communications. It delineates data exchange and control of information within a user appliance,

Data Terminal Equipment (DTE), and a network node, Data Circuit Terminating Equipment (DCE). X.25 comprises physical links such as packet-switching exchange (PSE) nodes for networking hardware, leased lines, and telephone or ISDN connections. Its unique functionality is its capacity to work effectively on any type of system that is connected to the network. X.25, although replaced by superior technology, continues to be in use. It utilizes a connection-oriented service that enables data packets to be transmitted in an orderly manner.

- **WAN solutions to address specific needs.** To maintain its wide area network (WAN) infrastructure, which is the foundation of communication, any business needs improved technology solutions. Technological innovators provide a full range of WAN solutions that are specifically designed to fortify an organization's WAN infrastructure. Advanced features offered by these technology products include data compression, VPN security, encryption capabilities, WAN acceleration, optimization, dependability, security, and dynamic load balancing of incoming and outgoing data traffic. These solutions are essential to the competitive business world as they determine whether wide area networks remain stable and help organizations meet their business continuity objectives.

3.2.2. WAN Devices

In situations where a company or organization has locations that are geographically far apart, it will be necessary to connect these locations in order to share, exchange, and manage data or communication. In order to accomplish this, the company requires a Telecommunication Service Provider (TSP) to establish connections between the local area networks at each location. Long-distance, expansive area networks are overseen by telecommunications service providers. Voice and data communications are carried over different networks by TSPs. Wide Area Networks (WANs) are the networks that link Local Area Networks (LANs) in distinct geographic locations.

WANs' Main Function:

1. WANs generally connect devices that are separated by a broader geographical area than can be served by a LAN.
2. WANs use the services of carriers, such as telephone companies, cable companies, satellite systems, and network providers.
3. WANs use serial connections of various types to provide access to bandwidth over large geographic areas.

3.2.2.1. Modems

When transmitting and receiving information, modems allow digital data to be sent over analog media. A voice band modem translates digital signals generated by a computer, which are 1s and 0s, into voice frequencies that can be sent over the telephone network's analog lines. To be input into a computer or network connection, the sounds are converted back into a digital signal on the other end of the connection by another modem.

3.2.2.2. CSU/DSU

A combined piece of equipment called a Channel Service Unit (CSU) and Data Service Unit (DSU) is used to monitor line clocking and frame synchronization. It is also capable of error detection at the physical layer; in a way, it functions like a modem.

Remember

Wide-area network (WAN) optimization is a collection of techniques that improve WAN performance metrics such as throughput, congestion, and latency. WAN design, technology choices, and traffic flow arrangements all affect WAN performance.

3.2.2.3. Access Server

Concentrates dial-in and dial-out user communications. An access server may have a mixture of analog and digital interfaces and support hundreds of simultaneous users.

3.2.2.4. WAN Switch

A multi-port internetworking device used in carrier networks. These devices typically switch traffic such as ATM and operate at the Data Link layer of the OSI reference model. Public switched telephone network switches may also be used within the cloud for circuit-switched connections like Integrated Services Digital Network (ISDN) or analog dial-up.

3.2.2.5. Router

A router provides internetworking between the LANs and WAN access interface ports that are used to connect to the service provider network. These interfaces may be serial connections or other WAN interfaces. With some types of WAN interfaces, an external device such as a DSU/CSU or modem (Analogue, Cable, or DSL) is required to connect the router to the local point of presence (POP) of the service provider.

Core Router

A router that resides within the middle or backbone of the WAN rather than at its periphery. To fulfill this role, a router must be able to support multiple telecommunications interfaces of the highest speed in use in the WAN core, and it must have the ability to forward IP packets at full speed on all of those interfaces. The router must also support the routing protocols being used in the core.

3.2.3. Connecting Your Wide Area Network (WAN) Devices

The connection between your router and the service provider must be established before you can utilize any type of WAN connection.

The type of connection will dictate your next steps. Commonly used interfaces include ISDN ports, serial ports, or Channel Service Units/Data Service Units (CSU/DSU).

- **Serial ports.** A serial port is a primary method to connect the router to your service provider's network. Depending on your service provider, you may be provided with a CSU/DSU. The CSU/DSU readies your digital data for transmission over a telephone company network that may not support digital signals, similar to a modem (modulator/demodulator). These devices connect to the T1 link or service provider connection, which in turn links to your router.

  Data Terminal Equipment (DTE) refers to end-user devices, while Data Communications Equipment (DCE) refers to telephone company devices, categorizing the connection into two device types. In your interactions with the service provider, your router acts as the DTE, and the service provider's communication devices act as the DCE. In the realm of computing, a computer serves as the DTE, and a modem as the DCE. To test your network equipment before deployment, you can utilize a specialized serial cable known as a back-to-back serial cable, designed with distinct ends for DTE and DCE. Essentially, one end of the cable that connects to your router links to the DTE, while the end connecting to the service provider's equipment links to the DCE.

- **Integrated CSU/DSU**. Integration of the CSU/DSU components into routers has grown in popularity as a way to cut costs or simplify systems. You can have the CSU/DSU functionality built into your router's circuitry, saving you from having to place another large device in your communications room. The disadvantage is that you might have to replace your router if you choose to switch the kind of connection you have. As a result, Cisco developed the WAN Interface Card (WIC) port, which enables you to reuse your current router and switch at a minimal cost the type of service provider connection you use.

- **ISDN ports.** Instead of using WIC ports that are already set up for ISDN environments, Cisco has produced and marketed routers with a fixed configuration due to the increasing popularity of ISDN connections. Although you have few options for connectivity, if you don't plan on switching up the connection types you use with your service provider, the cost of these routers may be appealing.

Q: What is the key architectural components of WAN?

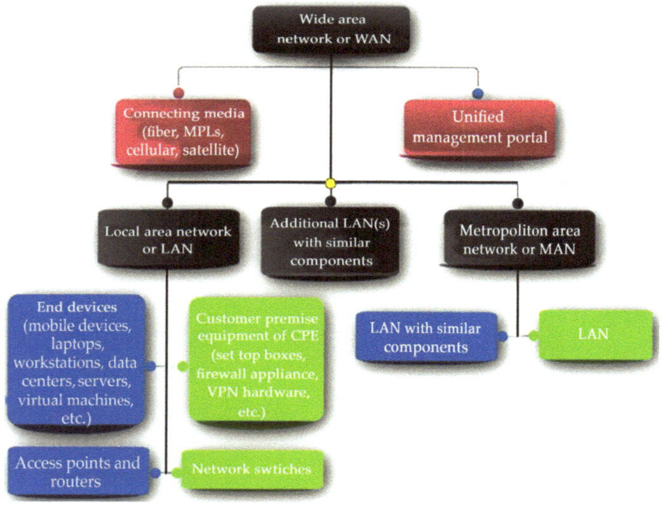

A: The exact design of your WAN architecture will vary based on your business requirements and the type(s) of WAN in use. However, seven architectural components are essential for WAN implementation:

1. **End devices**. End devices are computing systems that are being connected through wide area network technology.

2. **Customer premises equipment (CPE).** While most of the networking infrastructure used in WAN is owned by the carrier or service provider, CPE is owned by the enterprise and sits in your local environment.

3. **Access points and routers.** While access points and routers technically fall under CPE (as they are located within the LAN environment), they deserve special mention as indispensable architectural components of WAN. A router is your core LAN hub and manages data flow to and from your end devices.

4. **Network switches**. Network switches (also part of your CPE) sit between your access points and routers and the end devices to which they are connected.

5. **Local area network (LAN).** LAN is a key architectural component of a wide area network. All the components we discussed so far (end devices, CPE, access points, routers, and network switches) are part of your local area network environment.

6. **Connecting media**. The connecting media carries data packets in a WAN mesh architecture to and from different LAN components. There is a wide variety of media to choose from when setting up your WAN, including traditional MPLS lines, fiber optic cables, the cellular (3G, 4G, or 5G) spectrum, and satellite connectivity.

7. Metropolitan area network (MAN) – optional. A metropolitan area network or MAN is an optional component of WAN architecture. Instead of directly connecting two or more LAN environments, you can choose to connect LANs within a relatively small radius using a MAN.

8. Unified management portal – optional, but recommended. A unified WAN management portal is becoming increasingly commonplace in enterprise WAN implementations. This is because WAN can be difficult to orchestrate and manage, with each LAN hub responsible for network management for its own location.

3.2.4. WAN Management and Optimization

A wide area network (WAN) is a network that connects smaller campus and metropolitan networks spread across different locations into a single, distributed network by means of a variety of links, including private lines, virtual private networks (VPNs), wireless (cellular), MPLS, and the Internet. The locations they link may be a few miles apart or located halfway across the world. A wide area network (WAN) can be used in an organization to share corporate communications and resources by linking branch offices and even individual remote workers to the data center or headquarters.

The greater the distance between two devices, the longer it will take for data to travel between them because data transmission is still subject to the laws of physics. There is a direct correlation between distance and delay. Performance issues can also be brought on by network congestion and dropped packets. By improving the efficiency of data transmissions, WAN optimization can help with part of this. This is significant because wide area networks (WANs) can be costly. Consequently, technologies have emerged to minimize traffic over WAN links and guarantee efficient delivery of data. These optimization techniques include compression, caching (moving frequently used data closer to the end user), and de-duplication (short for reducing redundant data).

The ability to shape traffic allows for the prioritization of certain applications (like VoIP) over less urgent ones (like email), thereby enhancing WAN performance overall. This can be codified into quality of service settings that identify traffic classes based on the bandwidth allotted to each class, the kind of WAN connection each traffic type will use, and the priority each class receives in relation to the others.

3.2.4.1. WAN Optimization

Enterprise WAN performance problems are frequently caused by latency and bandwidth limitations. To combat them, WAN optimization appliances employ a number of strategies, such as traffic shaping, local caching, protocol optimization, deduplication, and compression. With the use of less expensive bandwidth connections, typically in the form of commercial internet services, along with traffic shaping and quality of service tools -- to increase reliability -- SD-WAN CPE or platforms offer an additional degree of application performance control.

3.2.4.2. WAN Security

Whenever end users will be using their devices, including those who work from home, the security of the WAN should be extended. Firewalls and antivirus programs should be used by end users who use WAN to guard against device compromises and illegal access. In addition to providing WAN connectivity, using a VPN has the added advantage of encrypting data. Network devices connected to a WAN from a remote location should also require users to establish a VPN connection. Furthermore, a key-exchange feature of SD-WAN is utilized for device authentication across various endpoints.

Keyword

Virtual private network (VPN) is a mechanism for creating a secure connection between a computing device and a computer network, or between two networks, using an insecure communication medium such as the public Internet.

It is not reasonable to expect a certain level of security from a WAN service provider, even though a WAN can be just as secure. A WAN system's complete security is not guaranteed, not even with a VPN in place. A hacker previously obtained access to Microsoft by breaking into a user's home device, which then followed the VPN back to Microsoft.

3.2.5. Types of WAN Connections and how WAN Connections Work

Wired and wireless technologies are both possible for WAN connections. T1s, carrier Ethernet, multiprotocol label switching, and commercial broadband internet links are examples of wired WAN services. Cellular data networks like 4G LTE as well as public WiFi and satellite networks are examples of wireless WAN technologies. Although most businesses still prefer wired network connections over WANs, wireless WAN technologies based on the 4G LTE standard are becoming more and more popular. WAN infrastructure can be either privately held or leased as a service from a third-party provider, like a cable company, internet service provider, telecommunications carrier, or private IP network operator. The service itself can run on a shared, public channel like the internet or a dedicated, private connection that is frequently supported by a service-level agreement. A mix of private and public network services is used by hybrid wide area networks. Software-defined WAN (SD-WAN) is designed to make hybrid WAN architectures easier for enterprises to deploy, operate, and manage. Using a combination of virtualization, application-level policies, and network overlays, on-site SD-WAN devices, software platforms, or customer premises equipment (CPE) perform two functions:

- They aggregate multiple public and private WAN links.
- They automatically select the most optimal path for traffic, based on real-time conditions.

The latter function has historically required network managers to manually reconfigure their networks anytime they wanted to shape the direction of traffic over multiple routes.

3.2.6. Wide Area Network (WAN)Standard

An extensive geographic network, such as the Internet, is referred to as a wide area network (WAN). Smaller local area networks (LANs) and metropolitan area networks (MANs) are contrasted with this. A MAN may cover a campus or provide services to city residents, as in the case of a citywide wireless or Wi-Fi network, whereas LANs are networks found in homes or offices. Although the Internet is a public wide area network (WAN), private or business models can be developed in a variety of ways. In essence, a private network consists of two or more LANs linked together.

In order to facilitate communication between LANs connected to a WAN, routers are used. Each data packet that travels over the WAN is read by the router, which is installed on the leased line. It then forwards the appropriate LAN to the appropriate packet's "envelopes," or headers. A device known as a switch forwards the data packet to the appropriate computer when it reaches the local area network (LAN). Therefore, for long-distance communication, the WAN functions as an interface between LANs. As there is no public traffic on a leased line, one that operates on it is considered private. Many businesses that need a WAN instead use an Internet Service Provider (ISP) to provide access because leased lines are costly. In this instance, a typical digital subscriber line (DSL) account is used for communication between each LAN in the WAN. An existing phone line is shared with the DSL Internet account and used for phone calls.

Public Internet lines are used by a DSL-based WAN. It is secured against intrusion by establishing a Virtual Private Network (VPN). When using a VPN, all communication over the Internet is encrypted while in transit and is only decrypted once it reaches its destination. Since the WAN is establishing a secure channel across a public area, this is known as "tunneling." Moreover, firewalls prevent hacker intrusion. This kind is probably the most widely used since it offers excellent advantages at a reasonable price. It has a high transfer rate and is an "always on" connection, so the WAN is always available. The most affordable kind of WAN connects to the Internet via a dial-up modem. Since DSL has dropped in price to the point where dial-up accounts can now compete, this is less common. A normal DSL connection can operate at up to 20 times the speed of a dial-up modem, which can only reach 56 kilobits per second (kbps). Additionally, dial-up connections are not able to share phone service. Lastly, a dial-up connection is not "always on." The effective reduction of uptime can occur when offices are located in different time zones. A wide area network (WAN) is a great tool for businesses to centralize productivity and access geographically dispersed resources. A rented space.

Did you know?

WANs are often built using leased lines. At each end of the leased line, a router connects the LAN on one side with a second router within the LAN on the other. Because leased lines can be very expensive, instead of using leased lines, WANs can also be built using less costly circuit switching or packet switching methods.

3.2.7. WAN Port

The local area network (LAN) and the wide area network (WAN) are the two main zones that make up most networks. A local area network, or LAN, can be found inside any type of building, be it a two-computer home or a high-rise office complex housing thousands of computers. The network outside of the local area network (LAN) includes the entire Internet as well as other internal networks. The gateway that allows data to move back and forth between a LAN and a WAN is called a WAN port.

On a network router, WAN ports are typically located for users. Four LAN ports and one WAN port are found on a typical home router. For the WAN port, they are referred to by some routers as an uplink, and for the LAN ports, as wired connections. This port splits data to multiple computers within the home network after receiving it from a high-speed Internet source, like a cable modem. Although four LAN ports are found on most home routers, there can be zero, an infinite number, or rarely more than eight. All five of these ports are visible as rectangular holes on the device's back. They are all made to be connected to a network cable. Though it otherwise has the same appearance as the LAN ports, the WAN port is typically positioned differently from the other ports to facilitate identification.

The router is where the two port types differ most significantly. Information from the Internet or an external network is received by the WAN port. The internal firewall and routing system of the router filter the data. After that, the data is transmitted to the appropriate LAN port or to a wireless source via a wireless connection. Routers have switching capabilities in addition to routing and firewalling capabilities. This enables communication between computers that are linked solely through LAN ports. The PCs are all connected to the same network because this switching feature gets around the router's built-in firewall. Users can expand the size of their network by using this feature to link multiple routers to one another.

Multiple internal networks that function independently of one another could be created if they connected several routers to one another via the WAN port. An example of this would be that three other routers are connected to a single router via its LAN ports, and it receives high-speed information from those routers at its WAN ports. With respect to one another, these internal networks would be completely separate entities with no more connection than if they were part of a network in an entirely different building.

3.2.8. Build a WAN

Creating a Wide Area Network, or WAN, entails setting up a link to your location through a third-party service provider. Various WAN technologies can be used based on your location and needs. For instance, much like a VPN, an MPLS network can be used to establish a single network from several physical locations. You need your own networking hardware, such as switches and routers, and a service provider contract in order to construct a wide area network (WAN).

1. To find out what kinds of WAN services are available, get in touch with a local service provider. Frame relay and T1 are common services. It's possible that business-class cable and DSL services are available in your area. The service provider establishes a demarcation point and installs their equipment at your location after you choose a desired service.
2. Get a router and attach the WAN connection to it. Even if the service provider installs a router as part of the wide area network (WAN), you will probably still require a separate router for local area network (LAN) access and control. It is your responsibility to use a router that can connect to the WAN circuit if the service provider does

not supply one. For instance, your router needs to have a T1 interface module if you bought a T1 connection.

3. Link your router to the network switch. All LAN connections are gathered by a network switch and connected to the router, which then routes the relevant traffic over the WAN connection. Using one or more Ethernet cables is the most typical method of connecting a switch to a router. Your router might have a built-in switch with enough ports to connect every device on it, depending on how your network is set up.

Did you get it?

1. What functions and features do WAN devices typically possess?
2. How are WAN ports configured and utilized in wide area network setups?

A CLOSER LOOK

Local Area Networks (LANs) and Wide Area Networks (WANs) are two fundamental types of computer networks, each serving distinct purposes and catering to different scales of connectivity. Despite their shared goal of facilitating communication and resource sharing, they exhibit several significant differences upon closer examination.

LANs are typically confined to a limited geographical area, such as a single building, office, or campus. They are characterized by high data transfer rates and low latency, making them ideal for facilitating fast communication and resource sharing among devices within their defined boundaries. LANs commonly utilize Ethernet or Wi-Fi technologies for connectivity, with devices interconnected through switches or wireless access points. Due to their localized nature, LANs are relatively easier to set up, manage, and maintain compared to WANs. They offer inherent security advantages as the network administrator has more control over access and monitoring within the confined environment.

In contrast, WANs span larger geographical areas, often connecting multiple LANs or individual devices across vast distances, such as between different cities, countries, or continents. WANs employ various technologies, including leased lines, satellite links, and fiber optics, to establish connections over long distances. The expansive reach of WANs introduces challenges such as higher latency and lower data transfer rates compared to LANs due to the increased distance and the involvement of multiple interconnected networks and devices. WANs are commonly used by organizations to facilitate communication between geographically dispersed branches, enable remote access for employees, and access centralized resources hosted in data centers.

One of the key differences between LANs and WANs lies in their ownership and management structures. LANs are typically owned, operated, and maintained by a single organization, such as a company, university, or government agency, allowing for centralized control and customization according to specific requirements. In contrast, WANs often involve collaboration between multiple entities, including Internet Service Providers (ISPs), telecommunications companies, and government agencies, making their management more complex and requiring adherence to standardized protocols and agreements for interconnection and data exchange.

Another critical aspect to consider is scalability. LANs are inherently scalable within their confined environment, allowing for the addition of devices and expansion of network capabilities as needed. However, scaling a LAN to cover larger geographical areas would require transitioning to WAN technologies and addressing the associated challenges of long-distance communication and connectivity. WANs, on the other hand, are designed to scale across vast distances, accommodating the growth and changing needs of organizations operating across multiple locations or serving diverse user bases.

CASE STUDY

CASE STUDY AND ANALYSIS OF WAN OPTIMIZATION PRE-REQUIREMENT

In today's world, the WAN network is congested with high traffic, which causes a lot of data loss and jitter. In order to provide a solution for this, a WAN Optimizer (e.g., Riverbed) was introduced over the WAN network to significantly improve network performance. However, there are many criteria that must be fulfilled to achieve a considerable amount of data transaction, including a decrease in the percentage of data loss over the network. These criteria will be analyzed during the discussion of the case study. Every organization has multiple applications running over the network, resulting in the available bandwidth being shared among them. If not balanced properly, this could lead to significant losses in business, data transactions, and application performance. Therefore, it is important to design this network in a way that ensures the organization's investment is satisfactory.

I. Criteria's involved in WAN Optimization

Whenever the concept of WAN is taken there are pre requisites that are taken into account like Network Infrastructure, Network Design (Head Office with other Branches), Cable used (Cat 5e, 6 within Organization, Fiber Optic Cable connecting branches, core switches), Model of Router, Model of Switches (Layer 2 or 3), Capacity of the organization, Application that will work on live environment which includes network security like ISA, Forefront, Business solution, etc., Servers, Data Base. How the calculations among them are carried out?

i) Network Bandwidth Consumed = TB – TC (1)

TB – Total Bandwidth provided by ISP

TC – Total bandwidth utilized by the organization during peak time and weekends/ non-working hours

ii) % of data loss = Data Loss / Total data transmitted *100 (2)

E.g. Data Loss = 5000Kbps Data Transmitted = 2500 Kbps

5000/2500 * 100 = 200% (Ratio becomes 2:1)

iii) Ratio between % of bandwidth consumed in internal network: % of bandwidth consumed over external network (This provides us the idea on how to manage the network performance during peak hours based upon which the prioritization should be done) (3)

iv) Network Performance

= Data transmission over Fiber optic + Data Transmission over Cat 6/5e Cables (4)

Data Transmission = Total data transmitted – Data loss (Calculate this for Fiber Optic and Cat 6/5e cables) (4(i))

% of network performance = Total Data transmission/ Total bandwidth provided * 100

v) % of service provided by ISP = (24*7 – Downtime) / (24*7) * 100 (5)

% of Service provided by ISP: % of overall Output (Expected along with fault tolerance)

vi) Total Consumption (%) = ABC*UBC*BW*DBC*UWBC (6)

ABC – Application Bandwidth Consumption UBCUser Bandwidth consumption BW- Bandwidth wastage DBC- Data Transaction Bandwidth Consumption UWBC – Unwanted Bandwidth Consumption.

vii) % of N/W used during peak hours : % of N/W usage in non-peak hours/ weekend

These are some of the criteria that will help the Infrastructure team design the network initially and put some of the operations of an application live to get an idea of the network consumption as a whole. Based on the overall performance, they can configure the WAN Optimizer, which will in turn accelerate the performance of the applications running live.

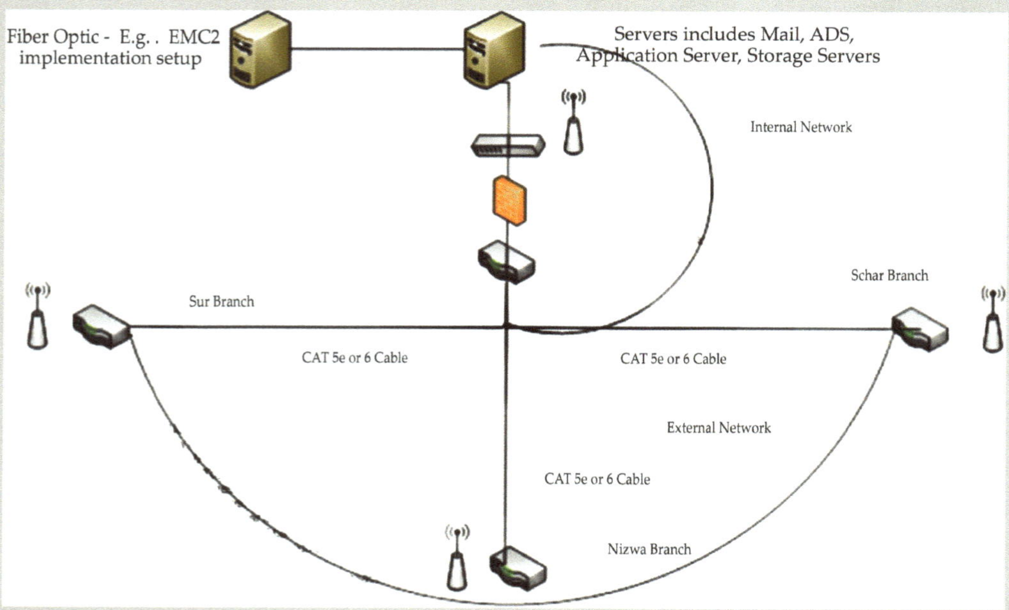

Figure 1. WAN optimization and performance (Source: Bhargav. Balakrishnan; Case study and analysis of WAN Optimization pre-requirements; https://arxiv.org/ftp/arxiv/papers/1109/1109.2285.pdf).

For example, Finacle is now widely used in the banking sector, where it will be integrated with Oracle Applications, Oracle Database, etc. Along with this, there are commonly used applications like Active Directory service, Exchange Servers, Anti-

Virus Servers, File Servers, SharePoint Servers, Web Servers, Blackberry Servers, etc. Therefore, the bandwidth consumed by these applications should be carefully studied by the network management, server management, and application management teams. Based on this, the router and WAN Optimizer should be configured to achieve the best overall output by minimizing data loss. Once data loss is reduced, transmission over the network becomes much faster, thereby reducing jitter and data loss to a greater extent. However, it is not possible to eliminate data loss and jitter completely, as there is always a certain amount of data loss and jitter, along with a reduction in network performance.

II. Case Study of Bank (Large Sectors)

Let us consider a Bank with 200 employees and three branches:

1. Head Office (Muscat) – 75
2. Sur Branch – 25
3. Sohar – 60
4. Nizwa – 40

So the above-mentioned applications in the topic criteria involved in WAN Optimization will be working along with certain other Backup Solution and Data Archiving, i.e., Veritas NetBackup and NetVault. Here, the Head Office will mostly have all the servers running the applications mentioned above. So, how is the network going to be maintained optimized, thereby providing the best results at the end of the financial year? The network diagram for this is shown below.

According to the network diagram above, the branches will depend on the services from the head office. Therefore, the prioritization of applications will come into play. In countries like Oman, the telephone exchange outside Muscat mostly provides a maximum bandwidth of 128Kbps leased line because the exchange can only support that amount of bandwidth. In this case, prioritization will have to be given to Finacle and Mail Servers as they are the main applications needed for processing data transmission with the clients, ensuring that reports can be generated without any issues by the end of the day. Internet access permissions can be granted for managerial level employees as they require certain other applications to communicate with the head office, such as Office Communicator and instant messenger. This way, application usage is balanced so that all data storages, transactions, and report updates are generated properly for the entire organization. This demonstrates how well the network is optimized by using a WAN Optimizer, which ultimately leads to organizational satisfaction with their investment, commonly referred to as return on investment.

To achieve this, the IT team should design the network in such a way that the above result is obtained constantly. The network design should incorporate redundancy, such as an MPLS connection that provides 24-hour support from the service provider, along with fault tolerance. In case one connection fails, the other connection will take over. However, the investment required is high for medium and small-level sectors.

This consideration is essential to ensure uninterrupted service in case of unplanned downtime by the ISP. The combination of the above information provides a solution on how to structure a network, prioritize, and implement the usage of WAN Optimizer. The entire IT team and managers should create a workflow chart on how to achieve the best throughput by optimizing the speed of applications. This falls under service transition, and any changes in applications, such as switching from Finacle to Fin Flex if it is lighter and more stable, should be considered based on the bank's requirements. After finalizing the report, the IT team should proceed with designing, testing (application in live environment), and execution.

A. Designing Phase & Test

During the design phase, the IT Team will have all the reports that were discussed. Initially, the team should start working on the core applications that will be widely used by the organization. Subsequently, all other common applications should be taken into account, and a statistical graph should be created to show the approximate bandwidth consumption by each application. An example of a statistical graph is shown below. In this graph, let's consider the consumption of Sharepoint portal and Finacle, which are used more frequently. Therefore, these applications should be prioritized based on their importance to the organization. These applications will be configured on WAN optimizer to ensure performance can be maintained. Backup should also be taken care of in WAN Optimization as it plays a role in storing and retrieving data. Therefore, these specific applications should be tested before being launched live. The calculations of the above formulas should be done in both test and live environments so that the IT team can have a clear understanding of the bandwidth consumption. These calculations can serve as a case study for future upgrades and references. Based on this, the IT Team will be able to determine how successfully they have implemented the infrastructure for the organization.

B. Live Environment

The organization should always conduct periodic tests on the performance of all applications over the network. Any identified flaws should be promptly analyzed and the information should be sent to the respective team. Based on this, the change advisory board should decide on an alternate solution, for example, if the bandwidth consumption is high during peak hours. The reasons for these issues should be discussed during meetings, such as: 1. Users downloading unwanted files from the internet 2. Certain applications utilizing excessive bandwidth, especially core applications 3. Data storage transmission between applications and the database 4. Anti-virus and firewall applications like ISA, Forefront Security, etc. These are common issues that need proper justification. To justify these issues, the team should prepare a case study on the application and conduct testing from all perspectives. For example, if it involves a database, consider how data is distributed over the network, such as network load balancing, to avoid performance issues. When structured in this manner, WAN Optimizer can enhance application performance. To achieve the best throughput with WAN Optimizer, certain prerequisites need to be met.

It is crucial to balance the performance of all applications over the network, especially for databases that primarily work on clustering.

The test results of all live servers should be presented to management every six months as a report to demonstrate how well the infrastructure is maintained within the organization.

C. Execution

This will be final phases after Live Testing of the critical applications. Here the reports of all the testing which were done in the live servers will be verified that the condition satisfies the usage of WAN optimizer and the respective applications for which this needs to be prioritized. How is the prioritization calculated?

1. Prioritization in % = Number of usage * Approx. time duration utilized /total no of employee * 100

   In approximate time duration time duration of peak hours with + or – extra hours.
2. Downtime in % = Total working hours(Application in WAN optimizer) / Total working hours *100 Downtime is unplanned downtime. Maintenance will be reduced in total working hours itself.
3. Percentage of transactions = Total of transaction done – Total no of lost transaction / Actual number of transaction * 100

So why above calculation are done for fixing a WAN Optimizer? What is need of these testing processes? Hardly the device is going to cost some 10 Lakhs Maximum with installation charges. The answer for this every inclusion of additional device needs a proper justification and at the time same the investment should have some output in the organizations overall result. These tests are conducted solely to ensure that the critical applications are brought under the umbrella of the WAN Optimizer, which will handle the performance of all applications configured under it. Subsequently, these tests should be conducted to verify if there are any changes in the processing speed of the desired applications. This will generate the final report for the management team, indicating that WAN optimization will enhance the performance of critical applications within the organization. Consequently, the organization can anticipate these results in the upcoming financial year.

When the Excel sheet containing the above graph is opened, there is a prioritization of core applications used in the banking sector. This scenario will be the same for other sectors as well. Therefore, when the WAN Optimizer is configured in this manner, the performance of the core applications will significantly improve, especially the daily backup of the entire banking process. It should be generated properly to avoid data loss in case of network performance interruptions, as the data transfer percentage depends on the type of cable used, particularly for backup purposes where fiber optic cables are utilized. In countries like India, the end-of-day (EOD) process can be cumbersome, making this optimization process quite relieving, as it reduces the need for constant monitoring.

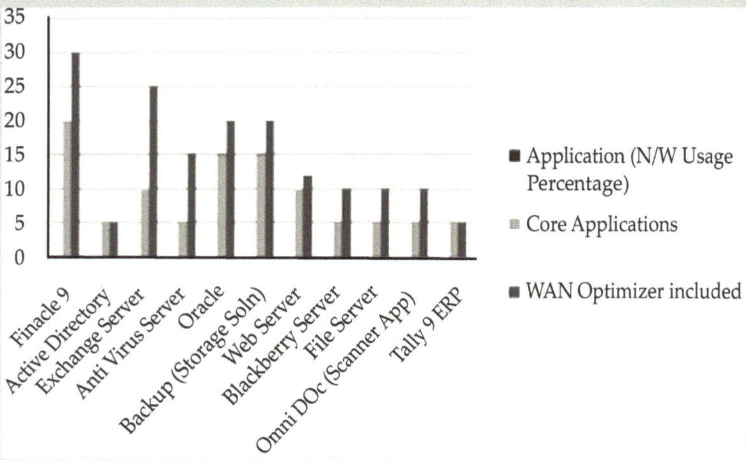

Figure 2. Live testing of WAN (Source: Bhargav. Balakrishnan; Case study and analysis of WAN Optimization pre-requirements; https://arxiv.org/ftp/arxiv/papers/1109/1109.2285.pdf).

III. Present Scenario

Many organizations have encountered WAN Optimization. However, to what extent have they been analyzed and utilized for organizational purposes? How satisfied are end users with the performance? Even though the network is optimized to enhance application performance, it depends on whether they use a wired or wireless network. This also significantly impacts application performance. Additionally, branch offices located in remote areas must also be taken into consideration. All these aspects need to be analyzed before conducting live testing. Once these network setups are confirmed, implementation becomes the next step. In the current scenario, how extensively are these reports prepared by the IT team to support the adoption of organizational policies? To what extent do organizations adhere to IT policies? Various policies such as group policies, internet restrictions, and USB restrictions need to be established to fully leverage WAN optimization benefits.

These policies need to be established, and comprehensive network testing must be conducted. Based on the results, a report should be generated. This report will then be reviewed by the change advisory board and approved, indicating that there are 99% fewer flaws and no fault tolerance in the current network infrastructure. Achieving this level of accuracy is crucial. However, many large organizations struggle to guarantee it. Achieving this is a complex task that requires time for testing to ensure that the network is optimized and that application performance is effectively shared across the network, reducing data loss and jitter compared to previous records without WAN optimization.

IV. Process Flow Diagram

The process flow of this implementation should be according to the above Step that, i.e., designing and test.

This workflow will give an idea of HOW ORGANIZED AN IMPLEMENTATION IS TAKEN. Since the implementation of WAN Optimization is interrelated with other networking devices, the notification should be generated as an email or SMS (SMS through Blackberry Enterprise Server). The clarification needs to be clearly documented for future reference if the organization is not benefiting in any way from the WAN Optimizer. This workflow involves proper approval at each stage by the IT Manager or CAB Member (Involves SLA Manager, Clients, Business Relationship Manager). So this kind of workflow will help in executing a task effectively and with proper authentication.

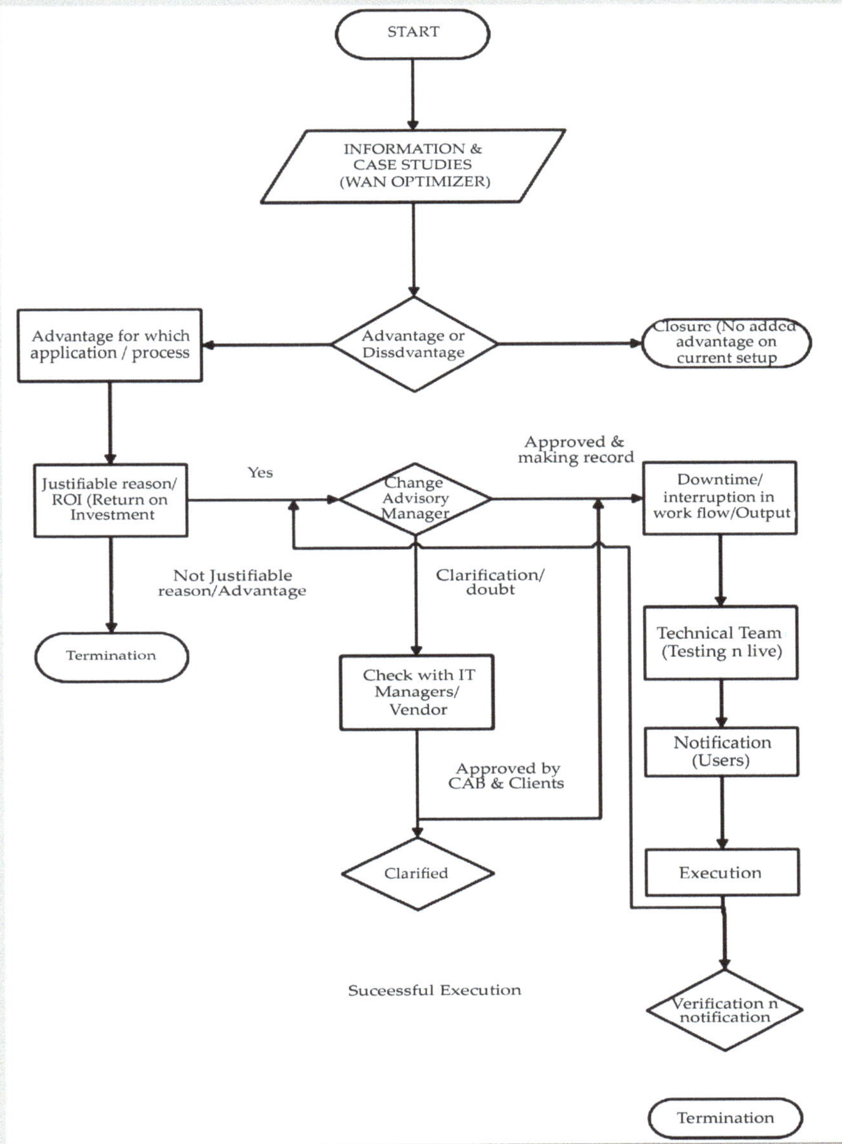

Figure 3. Process Flow Diagram of WAN (Source: Bhargav. Balakrishnan; Case study and analysis of WAN Optimization pre-requirements; https://arxiv.org/ftp/arxiv/papers/1109/1109.2285.pdf).

V. Key Advantage on Various WAN Optimizer In today's world there are various WAN optimizer and each of them have their own features let us some of them like Riverbed, Bluecoat, Juniper and Cisco.

A. Bluecoat

Works on the protocol CIFS (Common Internet File System) which can significantly reduce the number of round-trips required to satisfy a request, effectively minimizing delays associated with waiting for data retrieval while simultaneously reducing WAN usage. Another major advantage of CIFS protocol is CIFS Protocol Optimization is possible because ProxySG appliances have the ability to terminate user requests as if they were the server. They can then open a separate connection to the server that they can use to intelligently make requests on the client's behalf. The ProxySG appliance, acting as the client, is able to take advantage of the CIFS protocol in a way that the client cannot.

B. Riverbed

Riverbed's award-winning wide-area data services (WDS) solutions strategically enable IT to centralize and reduce operational overhead and expenses, while improving end-user satisfaction. Riverbed's products have been proven in some of the most demanding and complex networks in the world, with thousands of customers deploying Steelhead WDS solutions. Some key advantages of Riverbed Steelhead are speed, scalability, and accelerated key enterprise applications. Above all, there are some major advantages: IT infrastructure consolidation, serverless branch office, enhanced data protection, and enabling the mobile workforce. Key streaming processing data, application, transport, and management will improve the performance of key enterprise applications by 30%-40% compared to before. For example, if the current performance is 60%, it will be improved to 95% by using the Riverbed Steelhead.

C. Cisco

Cisco's WAAS has introduced the WAN Optimizer known as Wide Area Application Services. This offers significant advantages in terms of deployment and management compared to other WAN optimizers. The WAAS Central Manager is a web-based central management tool that simplifies configuration, provisioning, monitoring, fault management, logging, and reporting for up to 2,500 WAEs within a Cisco WAAS topology. Cisco's WAAS does not require any modifications to applications, clients, or servers to provide acceleration services.

Transparency: Transparency is crucial for many IT organizations when implementing a WAN optimization solution. It is essential that the network's functionality, such as security, QoS, or routing, remains intact. With WAAS not altering packet headers, it ensures a high level of transparency. This transparency impacts the Total Cost of Ownership (TCO) significantly.

Ease of Deployment and Management: Ease of Deployment and Management is another key benefit of Cisco's WAAS. By not modifying packet headers, WAAS minimizes the risk of disrupting IT operations, making it easier to deploy and manage compared to other solutions that may cause disruptions.

Moreover, WAAS supports auto-discovery, which checks for a peer acceleration appliance in the packet flow between the source and destination. This feature streamlines deployment by eliminating the need for IT organizations to set up an overlay network.

Integration: The point being that given Cisco's position in the enterprise networking marketplace, the chances are that the environment in which the WAN optimization solutions will be deployed will be a Cisco environment. Cisco is in the best position to ensure that its WAN optimization solution does not impact this environment.

Performance: Some of the comments that Miercom made about Cisco's WAAS include:

- Under favorable conditions (large WAN latency and highly compressible content) the WAAS V4.0 solution can provide impressive degrees of acceleration.
- The software demonstrated performance parity with these other products, and that in some key metrics provided superior compression, speed, and throughput.
- Unlike some of the other products in the market, Cisco's WAAS does not degrade.

So each WAN Optimizer manufacturing company tests their device on the aspect of fault tolerance, i.e., preventing any disturbance in the current infrastructure setup. In the same way, this case study needs to be carried out by the IT team in order to justify to management why they have selected this WAN optimizer and what the key advantage of that is.

SUMMARY

- A local area network (LAN) is a computer network in a limited physical area like a house, school, office building, or computer lab.
- A local area network, or LAN, is a type of network that can operate over a small physical area, like a few kilometers in size, which could be an office, factory, or collection of buildings.
- Local area networks (LANs) are widely used in the information age due to the advent of low-cost computers and the need for hardware resources and information sharing in office settings, leading to the development of affordable LANs.
- A server on a network provides services to workstations and clients. The main goal of a LAN server is data management. It ensures data is stored, secured, and retrieved.
- Servers are business-class PCs that offer collaboration tools, antivirus protection, messaging, and other services to the office.
- A local area network, or LAN, is a type of data communication network that links computers or terminals within a building or a constrained geographic area.
- Frame Relay is a WAN protocol that is only for internetworking Local Area Networks (LANs), or the transfer of data between LANs and WAN endpoints. It is based on packet switching technology.
- The connection between your router and the service provider must be made before you can use any type of WAN connection. The type of connection will determine how you proceed.
- A wide area network (WAN) is a network that connects smaller campus and metropolitan networks across different locations into a single, distributed network using various links such as private lines, virtual private networks (VPNs), wireless (cellular), MPLS, and the Internet.

MULTIPLE CHOICE QUESTIONS

1. Computer network that spans a limited physical area, usually ranging from a small office to a building is known as
   a. LAN
   b. WAN
   c. MAN
   d. PAN
2. Computer network which spans a large physical area, connecting several sites of an organization across cities, countries and continents is known as
   a. LAN
   b. MAN

   c. WAN
   d. PAN
3. Most common type of a computer network is
   a. PAN
   b. WAN
   c. LAN
   d. MAN
4. Modulator and demodulator as combine is known as –
   a. Modulus
   b. Modem
   c. Mod switch
   d. Mod access
5. Which of the following is an example of Personal Area Networking?
   a. Bluetooth
   b. WAN
   c. WLAN
   d. All of the above

REVIEW QUESTIONS

1. What are the characteristics of LAN technology?
2. What hardware devices are typically found on a LAN?
3. What are WAN devices and how do they differ from LAN devices?
4. How do you connect your Wide Area Network (WAN) devices?
5. How can WAN management and optimization be achieved?

Answer to Multiple Choice Questions

1. (a)   2. (c)   3. (c)   4. (b)   5. (a)

REFERENCES

1. Campbell, S., (2010). *A Wide Area Network (WAN) Tutorial [Technology Explained]*. [online] MakeUseOf. Available at: http://www.makeuseof.com/tag/technology-explained-wide-area-network-wan-tutorial/ (accessed on 05 April 2024).
2. Computerhope.com. (2016). *What is WAN (Wide Area Network)?* [online] Available at: http://www.computerhope.com/jargon/w/wan.htm (accessed on 05 April 2024).

3. Mitchell, B., (2015). *How 'Packet Switching' Works (Computer Networks).* [online] About.com Tech. Available at: http://compnetworking.about.com/od/networkprotocols/f/packet-switch.htm (accessed on 05 April 2024).
4. Mitchell, B., (2016). *What Is a Wide Area Network (WAN) and How Does it Work?* [online] About.com Tech. Available at: http://compnetworking.about.com/cs/lanvlanwan/g/bldef_wan.htm (accessed on 05 April 2024).
5. *Point to Point WAN: The Most Effective Way for Branch to Branch Transaction and Communication,* (2011). [Blog] Point to Point WAN. Available at: http://pointtopointwan.blogspot.com.au/ (accessed on 05 April 2024).
6. Symoens, J., (2000). *Preparing Exchange for High Availability-You Can Increase Uptime and Decrease Costs by Building a Redundant Groupware Configuration.* InfoWorld.
7. Winther, M., (2006). Avoiding the challenges of do-it-yourself broadband VPNs. *Business Communications Review.*

CHAPTER

4 Internetworks

LEARNING OBJECTIVES

After studying this chapter, you will be able to:

- Explain the principles of internetworking
- Define the internetwork architecture
- Discuss on IP addressing and architecture

INTRODUCTION

The original purpose of internetworking was to link different forms of computer networking technology. The term "computer network" refers to a group of two or more connected computers. Computer internetworking involves connecting two or more computer LANs, WANs, or network segments using routers and configuring them with logical addressing schemes and protocols like IP. The Internet Protocol is commonly used by interconnected computer networks, also known as Internetworking. There are two architectural models frequently used to explain the procedures and protocols in internetworking. Open Systems Interconnection is the industry standard reference model for internetworking (OSI).

Companies like Cisco, BBN, and other network product and service providers use the term "internetworking" to encompass all the concepts, technologies, and everyday items that allow people and their computers to communicate over different types of networks. For example, a user on a computer connected to a token ring local area network might want to communicate with a user on a computer connected to an Ethernet local area network in another country using a wide area network interconnection. Internetworking consists of standard internetwork protocols, relevant network devices, and routing tables necessary for this communication to take place.

Open Systems Interconnection (OSI) is the standard reference model for internetworking and can also be used as a model for intranetworking. Because all technologies can be related to the standard communication model, OSI makes it possible for any technology to be related to another technology. In order to make the problem of exchanging data across a network or a network of networks easier to understand and to make defining the boundaries between components easier, OSI offers a layering approach to the problem.

4.1. PRINCIPLES OF INTERNETWORKING

→Learning Objectives

- Understand the fundamental principles underlying internetworking
- Recognize the various challenges encountered in building and managing interconnected networks.
- Define internetwork addressing and its significance in facilitating communication between devices across interconnected networks.
- Explain the concept of a unit of internetworking and its role in establishing connections and data exchange between devices.

The term "internetworking" is a compound of the words "inter" and "networking," which denotes a connection between completely unrelated nodes or segments. The intermediary devices, which are similar to routers or gateways, establish this connection area unit. Catenet was the initial term for an internetwork. This connection frequently occurs within or between networks that are governmental, commercial, industrial, public, or private. As a result, an internetwork may consist of several small networks connected by intermediary networking devices that work together to form a single, large network. The term "internetworking" describes the services, goods, and methods that address the difficulty of creating and managing internetworks.

Every network node and phase is built with a similar protocol or communication logic, such as Internet Protocol (IP) or Transmission Control Protocol (TCP), to enable communication. Internetworking is the process of a network communicating with another network through continuous communication protocols. Internetworking was created to address the issue of sending an information packet over numerous links. There is a subtle distinction between Internetworking and network extension. A simple LAN extension is when two local area networks are connected via a switch or hub; connecting them via a router is an example of an Internetworking setup. The OSI-ISO model's Network Layer, or Layer Three, enforces internetworking. The Internet is the most prominent illustration of internetworking.

4.1.1. Principle

The process of connecting multiple networks via devices like routers and gateways is known as internetworking. These networks, owned by various organizations, use different technologies, ranging from small LANs to massive WANs. These networks can be public, private, government, commercial, or academic. The term "internetwork" or "internet" is commonly used to describe this network of networks. Networking is essential for computers of all sizes to communicate with each other, regardless of vendor, operating system, hardware platform, or geographic location. Internetworking involves tying together networks with different technologies using additional hardware and software. DARPA has funded research projects to develop standards for internetworking. Layering and other protocol suite concepts were first introduced to the networking community by the DARPA project ARPAnet, long before ISO took the lead in this area. DARPA persisted in investigating a suite of internetworking protocols. This can be observed in the early host-to-host protocol of the Network Control Program (NCP) to the TCP/IP protocol suite, which assumed its present form circa 1978. In 1975, the Defense Communications Agency (DCA) was given administrative responsibility for ARPAnet, which was declared an operational network. DARPA was widely recognized for having pioneered packet switching over radio networks and satellite channels. There was no TCP/IP developed yet.

Keyword

Network Control Program (NCP) was the name for the software on hosts which implemented the Network Control Protocol of the ARPANET.

The ARPAnet was essentially a leased-line network connected by Internet Message Processors (IMP), which are specialized switching nodes. By 1979, TCP/IP research had attracted a large number of researchers. This prompted DARPA to establish an unofficial committee to oversee and direct the development of the architecture and communication protocols.

The Internet Control and Configuration Board (ICCB) was the name of the committee. When DARPA began upgrading the machines in its research network ARPAnet to use the new TCP/IP protocols, it is possible to trace the earliest actual implementations of the Internet to that period. Following this shift, which took place between 1980 and 1983, DARPA mandated that TCP/IP be used by any computer that wished to connect to its ARPAnet. In 1983, the US military made TCP/IP the standard protocol and demanded that all networks connected to the ARPAnet follow the new guidelines.

The ARPAnet exceeded even its own founders' expectations in terms of success, and TCP/IP internetworking spread quickly. Consequently, new wide area networks (WAN) were established in the USA and linked via TCP/IP protocol to the ARPAnet. The set of interconnected networks was then expanded to include additional networks from around the globe, some of which were not even based on the TCP/IP protocols.

The world's largest network is currently made up of computing facilities connected to the Internet via separate sub-networks from regions such as Europe, Japan, and the United States of America. The Internet was established as the official global network in

1990, replacing ARPAnet. The development of a TCP/IP protocol implementation for Berkeley UNIX on the VAX, as well as the free distribution of the required code produced as a result of this project along with their UNIX operating system, was also funded by DARPA. In 1983, the TCP/IP protocol set was added to the Berkeley Software Distribution (BSD) for the first time (4.2BSD). TCP/IP quickly spread throughout academic institutions and research facilities as a result, and it is now the required communications subsystem for all UNIX connectivity. There are numerous BSD code updates available. These include 4.3BSD (1986), 4.4BSD (1993), 4.3BSD Tahoe (1988), and 4.3BSD Reno (1990).

4.1.2. Challenges in Internetworking

There is no guarantee that a useful internetwork will be implemented. Every area is crucial to building an affordable and efficient internetwork, and there are many demanding fields, especially in the areas of dependability, connectivity, network management, and adaptability. A select few are:

- The first difficulty arises when we attempt to link multiple systems to facilitate communication across various technologies. For instance, completely different websites may use entirely different media or run at varying speeds.
- In an internetwork, maintaining dependable service is another crucial consideration. Access to network resources needs to be consistent and dependable for both individual users and entire organizations.
- In an internetwork, network management should provide centralized support and advanced **troubleshooting** capabilities. The internetwork must have its configuration, security, performance, and other issues properly addressed for it to function properly.
- The most crucial aspect, flexibility, is crucial for a variety of reasons, including network expansion and the addition of new services and applications.

Keyword

Troubleshooting is a form of problem solving, often applied to repair failed products or processes on a machine or a system.

4.1.3. Internetwork Addressing

Devices can be established individually or as a group using internetwork addresses. Depending on the OSI layer and the protocol family, different addressing schemes apply. Media Access Control (MAC) addresses, network-layer addresses, and data-link layer addresses are the three types of internetwork addresses that are typically used.

4.1.3.1. Data Link Layer Addresses

Every physical network association of a network device is uniquely identified by its data-link layer address. Physical or hardware addresses are commonly used to refer to data-link addresses. Data-link addresses are associated with specific devices and are sometimes found within a flat address area. Their relationship is pre-established and typically fastened. End systems typically have a single data-link address because they have a single physical network association. Due to their multiple physical network connections, routers and other internet-connected devices typically have multiple data-link addresses.

Every physical network connection made by a network device is uniquely identified by its data-link layer address. Sometimes, physical or hardware addresses are used to refer to data-link addresses. A pre-established and usually fixed relationship between a data-link address and a particular device exists within a flat address space. End systems typically have one data-link address and one physical network connection. Since routers and other internet-connected devices frequently have several physical network connections, they also frequently have several data-link addresses. A data-link address serves as a unique identifier for each interface on a device, as shown in Figure 4.1.

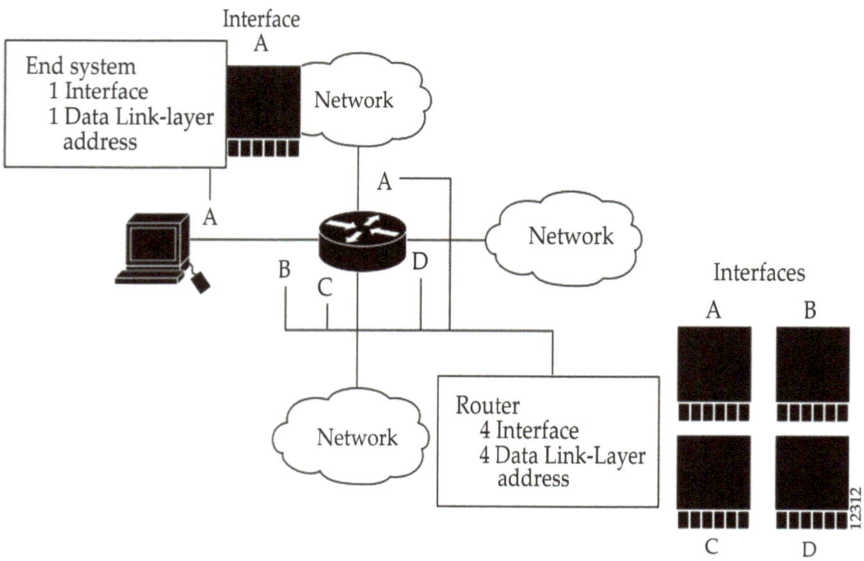

Figure 4.1. Each interface on a device is uniquely identified by a data-link address (Source: Scribd, https://image.slidesharecdn.com/internetworking-49-121020113333-phpapp02/75/internetworking49-15-2048.jpg?cb=1667679119).

4.1.3.2. MAC Addresses

A collection of data-link layer addresses is included in media access management (MAC) addresses. In LANs that use the IEEE MAC addresses of the data-link layer, MAC addresses define network entities. For each local area network interface, MAC addresses vary in specific ways. Twelve hexadecimal digits are used to express a MAC address, which has a length of 48 bits. The Organizational Unique Identifier is made up of the first six hexadecimal digits, which are typically used by the IEEE to identify the manufacturer or merchant (OUI). The final six positional notation digits represent either the interface serial variety or an additional price managed by the specific vendor. Because they are burned into read-only memory (ROM), MAC addresses are also known as burned-in addresses (BIAs). After the interface card initializes, MAC addresses are traced into random-access memory (RAM).

A subset of data-link layer addresses makes up media access control (MAC) addresses. In LANs that use the IEEE MAC addresses of the data-link layer, MAC addresses are used to identify network entities. Every LAN interface has a unique MAC address, just like the majority of data-link addresses. The relationship between data-link addresses, MAC addresses, and the IEEE sub-layers of the data-link layer is depicted in Figure 4.2.

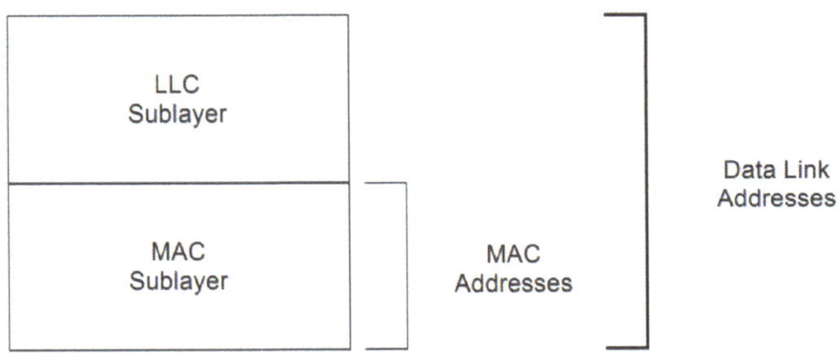

Figure 4.2. MAC addresses, data-link addresses, and the IEEE sub-layers of the data-link layer are all related (Source: Scribd, https://image.slidesharecdn.com/internetworking-49-121020113333-phpapp02/75/internetworking49-19-2048.jpg?cb=1667679119).

MAC addresses are expressed as 12 hexadecimal digits and have a length of 48 bits. The manufacturer or vendor is identified by the first six hexadecimal digits, which are managed by the IEEE, and together they make up the Organizational Unique Identifier (OUI). The interface serial number, or any other value managed by the particular vendor, is contained in the final six hexadecimal digits. Because MAC addresses are burned into read-only memory (ROM) and copied into random-access memory (RAM) upon interface card initialization, they are sometimes referred to as burned-in addresses (BIAs). The format of the MAC address is shown in Figure 4.3.

The techniques used by various protocol suites to ascertain a device's MAC address vary. MAC addresses are mapped to network addresses via Address Resolution Protocol (ARP), which is the most widely used of the three techniques. Network devices can discover the MAC addresses of other network devices thanks to the Hello protocol. MAC addresses can be produced by an algorithm or they can be included in the network-layer address.

Mapping network addresses to Media Access Control (MAC) addresses is known as address resolution. Several protocol suites implement the Address Resolution Protocol (ARP), which is used to carry out this process. The network device saves the data in the ARP cache after a network address and MAC address are successfully linked.

Because the destination's MAC address is already known, devices can send traffic there without generating ARP traffic thanks to the ARP cache.

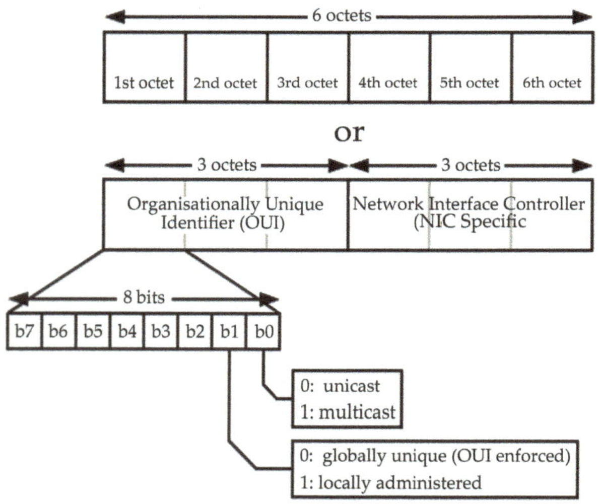

Figure 4.3. The MAC address contains a unique format of hexadecimal digits (Source: Wikipedia, https://upload.wikimedia.org/wikipedia/commons/thumb/9/94/MAC-48_Address.svg/800px-MAC-48_Address.svg.png).

Depending on the network environment, there are minor differences in the address resolution process. When End System A broadcasts an ARP request onto the LAN in an effort to find out the MAC address of End System B, address resolution on a single LAN starts. All of the LAN's devices receive and process the broadcast, but only End System B responds to the ARP request by giving End System A its MAC address in an ARP reply. After receiving the response, End System A stores End System B's MAC address in its ARP cache. Network addresses and MAC addresses are linked in the ARP cache. When End System A needs to communicate with End System B, it retrieves System B's MAC address from the ARP cache, sends the frame straight, and avoids using an ARP request in the process. However, when source and destination devices are connected to separate LANs that are connected by a router, address resolution functions differently. To find out End System Z's MAC address, End System Y sends out an ARP request across the LAN. Every device on the LAN receives and processes the broadcast, including Router X, which serves as a proxy for End System Z by determining that End System Z is situated on a separate LAN by consulting its routing table. After that, Router X responds to End System Y's ARP request by sending an ARP reply that appears to be from End System Z and includes its own MAC address. After receiving the ARP reply, End System Y stores Router X's MAC address in its ARP cache and adds it to the entry for End System Z. In order to send a frame directly to End System Z without utilizing ARP requests, End System Y first looks up Router X's MAC address in the ARP cache. Traffic from End System Y is received by Router X, which then forwards it to End System Z on the opposite LAN.

A network-layer protocol called Hello allows devices connected to a network to recognize one another and signal that they are still operational. For example, a new end system broadcasts Hello messages across the network upon powering up. Subsequently, devices connected to the network respond with "Hello," and to indicate that they are still operational, Hello messages are also sent at set intervals. Network devices can examine Hello-protocol packets to discover other devices' MAC addresses.

Three MAC addresses are known to function. Because the network layer either includes the MAC address in the network-layer address or determines the MAC address through an algorithm, MAC addresses in these protocol suites are predictable. Xerox Network Systems (XNS), Novell Internetwork Packet Exchange (IPX), and DECnet Phase IV are the three protocols.

4.1.3.3. Network-Layer Addresses

Network addresses, also known as virtual or logical addresses, can occasionally be found within a gradable address space. A network address and a device have a logical, non-fixed relationship that typically depends on either the physical properties of the network or on arbitrary groupings. For each network-layer protocol that end systems support, one network-layer address is required. For each supported network-layer protocol, routers and other internetworking devices require a single network-layer address for each physical network association.

An entity at the OSI layers' network layer is identified by its network-layer address. Network addresses, also known as virtual or logical addresses, are typically found in a hierarchical address space. A network address and a device have a logical, non-fixed relationship that is usually based on either physical network characteristics (e.g., the device is on a specific network segment) or groupings for which there is no physical basis (e.g., the device is a part of an AppleTalk zone). For each network-layer protocol that end systems support, one network-layer address is needed. This presupposes that there is just one physical network connection on the device. For each network-layer protocol supported by routers and other internetworking devices, one network-layer address is needed for each physical network connection. For instance, a router with three interfaces that are each running OSI, TCP/IP, and AppleTalk needs three network-layer addresses for every interface. Nine network-layer addresses are thus available to the router. The process of assigning a network address to each network interface for every supported protocol is shown in Figure 4.4.

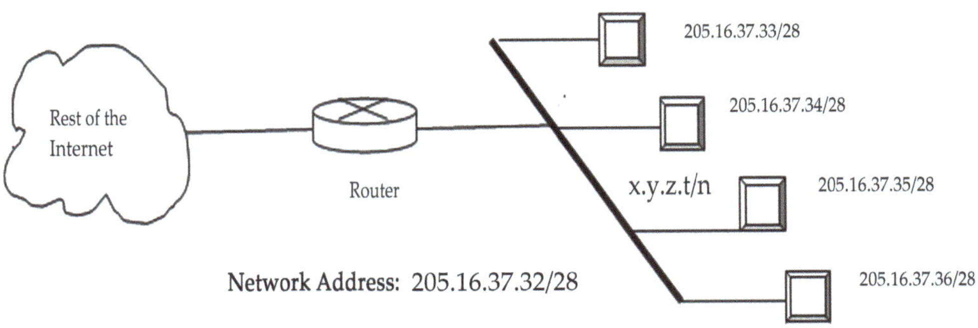

Figure 4.4. Each network interface must be assigned a network address for each protocol supported (Source: NotesforMsc, https://notesformsc.org/wp-content/uploads/2018/04/Network-Addresses.png).

4.1.4. Unit of Internetworking

The idea behind internetworking is to "build a large, global network by interconnecting different types of networks" so that any two hosts that are connected can exchange packets. A standardized protocol defining the format and handling of transmitted packets; components connecting the participating networks by routing packets to their destinations based on standardized addresses; and a standardized scheme to address packets to any host on any participating network are required to build an internetwork.

There are chiefly three units of Internetworking:

- Extranet;
- Intranet; and
- Internet.

The internet is not considered to be a part of the computer network or extranet, although it can serve as a portal for accessing parts of an extranet.

Remember

Intranets and extranets might or might not have connections to the net. If there is a connection to the net, the computer network or extranet area unit is usually shielded from being accessed from the net if it is not authorized.

- **Extranet**: An extranet is a network within a network that is limited to a single organization or entity, but it also has restricted connections to networks of one or more other organizations occasionally, but not always. It is the most basic form of internet work, typically confined to very private spaces. An extranet cannot consist of a single local area network (LAN), but it can be classified as a MAN, WAN, or other type of network. At least one reference to an external network should be included.
- **Intranet**: An intranet is a collection of interconnected computer networks managed by a single organization. They utilize IP-based tools, such as web browsers and file transfer programs, and leverage the Internet Protocol. This organization restricts access to the computer network to only authorized users and blocks access for everyone else. This network typically serves as an internal network for an organization or business. Large computer networks can typically support multiple internet servers to provide users with accessible data.
- **Internet**: A selective Internetworking that consists of a global network of public, academic, governmental, and private networks connected primarily by the Advanced Research Project Agency Network (ARPANET), created by the U.S. The World Wide Web (WWW), which is also housed by the Department of Defense and referred to as the "Internet" to distinguish it from other generic Internetworks, is another resource. Internet users and/or their service providers use IP addresses that are sourced from address registries that assign addresses.

Several major issues, including duplicate resource usage, unmanaged networks, and isolated local area networks, have led to the evolution of internetworking. Transmission issues between completely separate offices or departments were caused by isolated LANs. Due to resource duplication, each workplace or department required a dedicated support staff member in addition to constant hardware and code. Due to a lack of network management, there was no centralized approach to maintaining and debugging networks. Another way that networks are typically connected is through the Link Layer of the networking model, where businesses connect to one another. This layer is below the number of TCP/IP logical interfaces and is hardware-centric. Network switches and network bridges enable this kind of interconnection. Although this is sometimes mistakenly called "internetworking," the resulting system is really just a larger, single sub-network, and it doesn't require an internetworking protocol—similar to web protocol—to move between these devices.

Nevertheless, by segmenting the network into phases and using routers to logically split the segment traffic, one electronic network can also be reborn into an associate degree internetwork. The purpose of the Internet Protocol is to provide a somewhat erratic packet service throughout the network. The network's state is not maintained by intermediary network components, as per the design. Rather, this task is assigned to each communication session's endpoints. Applications should use an appropriate Transport Layer protocol, such as Transmission Control Protocol (TCP), which offers a dependable stream, to transfer data accurately. For tasks like video streaming or voice chat that require temporary service or don't require dependable information delivery, some applications use the simpler, connectionless User Datagram Protocol (UDP).

Did you get it?

1. **What are the various challenges encountered in building and managing interconnected networks?**
2. **Can you explain the concept of a unit of internetworking and its role in establishing connections and data exchange between devices?**

4.2. INTERNETWORK ARCHITECTURE

→Learning Objectives

- Demonstrate an understanding of how the Application Layer facilitates end-user applications' interaction
- Illustrate the transport Layer's role
- Explain the purpose and significance of the Internet Layer
- Explore various technologies and protocols operating at the Network Access Layer

An internetwork is a group of broadcast and packet-switching networks that work together as a single, sizable network thanks to the use of routers, switches, and bridges, which are intermediate networking devices. As a result, regardless of the network segment to which they are connected, all users and devices can communicate. An internetwork can be created by connecting various types of network technologies, as shown in Figure 4.5, through the use of routers and other networking devices.

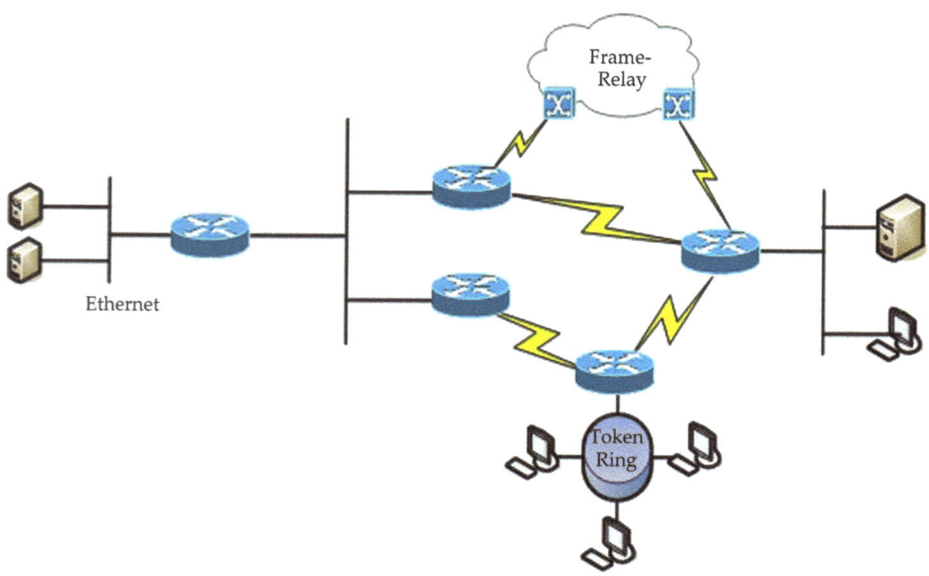

Figure 4.5. Internetworking flow meter (Source: CertificationKits, https://www.certificationkits.com/assets/images/stories/image16.jpg).

Local Area Networks (LANs) and Wide Area Networks (WANs) are two categories for the various network types that combine to form an Internetwork. A LAN is a network that is restricted to a small geographic area, like an office building or even a network of computers and devices in a home. There are numerous uses for a Local Area Network (LAN), including resource sharing, gaming, and teamwork. When a company owns a Local Area Network, everything from switches to cables is part of the network's infrastructure. Although a local area network can connect users at speeds of up to 10 Gbps, there is a distance restriction on the media.

Wide Area Networks (WAN) span large geographic areas, including entire countries, cities, and even continents. Multiple Local Area Networks that are spread out over several miles are connected by Wide Area Networks. An organization must purchase WAN service from a service provider or carrier due to the long distance connectivity. Wide Area Networks come in a variety of forms, including packet-switched, circuit-switched, and leased line networks. While Local Area Networks are owned by the organization itself and do not require any kind of connectivity service purchase, Wide Area Networks are contracted by businesses or organizations that need to connect multiple offices located across cities, countries, or even the entire world.

The TCP/IP Protocol Stack, also referred to as the Internet Protocol Suite, is a standard set of communication protocols that was created as a result of DARPA research and development for the ARPANET. This protocol suite was created in order to establish a common means of communication that would enable various network types with various computer systems to speak with one another. In order to facilitate computer communication over a network, the Internet Protocol Suite is a framework that specifies a set of general design guidelines and implementations of particular networking protocols. The Internet Protocol Suite architectural model, also known as the TCP/IP Model, is described in RFC 1122. A host must implement the layered set of protocols that make up the Internet protocol suite in order to communicate over the Internet.

The uppermost layer is called the Application Layer, and it describes the higher-level protocols, like File Transfer Protocol (FTP), Hyper Text Transfer Protocol (HTTP), and Simple Mail Transfer Protocol (SMTP), that are used by applications for network communication. Applications can communicate end-to-end through the transport layer.

There are two primary transport layer protocols:

- Transmission Control Protocol (TCP); and
- User Datagram Protocol (UDP).

TCP is a reliable connection-oriented transport protocol that provides flow control, re-sequencing, and end-to-end reliability. UDP is a connectionless ("datagram") transport protocol. To transmit datagrams (packets) from a host across network boundaries to the destination host identified by a network address (IP address) defined by the Internet Protocol (IP), a set of techniques, protocols, and specifications are detailed in the Internet Layer. Each computer on the Internet needs a unique IP address for identification, whether it is a host computer using services or a server providing services. The current version of the Internet Protocol used on the Internet is IP version 4 (IPv4). The 32-bit address specified by IPv4 allows for 4,294,967,296 unique addresses; however, due to the rapid growth of the Internet, this space is limited. The address space of IP version 6 (IPv6), intended to replace IPv4, is 128 bits, significantly larger than that of IPv4. The Network Access Layer, also known as the Link Layer or the Media Access Layer, defines protocols and specifications that the host must follow to communicate with its directly connected network.

Remember

All Internet transport protocols use the Internet Protocol (IP) to carry data from source host to destination host. IP is a connectionless or datagram internetwork service, providing no end-to-end delivery guarantees.

a. How the TCP/IP Protocols Handle Data Communications

A set of actions is started when a user issues a command that makes use of the TCP/IP application layer protocol. The local system's TCP/IP protocol stack processes the user's command or message. Subsequently, the command or message is transmitted through network media to the remote system's protocols. Each layer's protocols on the sending host supplement the original data with new information. Every layer of the sending host's protocols communicates with its peers on the receiving host. The TCP/IP protocol stack is used by two hosts to communicate, as seen in the figure below.

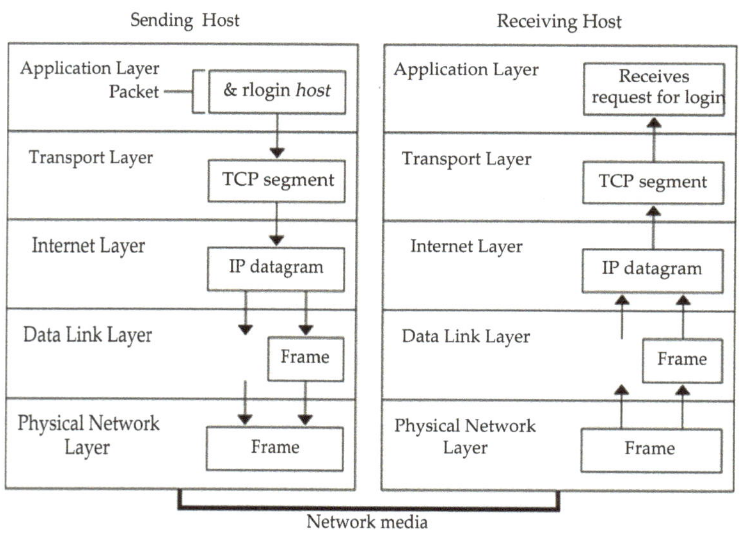

Figure 4.6. How information travels on internet? (Source: Medium.com, https://miro.medium.com/v2/resize:fit:720/format:webp/1*id6bv--a6s3oGk2uO0jnEg.jpeg).

The Internet, the most famous example of an Internetwork, is a global network that emerged from connecting various computer networks. It comprises both private and public networks of different sizes and types, serving diverse purposes and utilizing a wide array of technologies. The ARPANET, developed by the United States Defense Advanced Research Projects Agency (DARPA) in the 1960s, laid the groundwork for the Internet. In the 1980s, the government-sponsored military research project ARPANET became known to the public, leading to the rapid expansion and interconnection of various computer networks that eventually formed the Internet.

Did you know?

In 1977, ARPA demonstrated a three-way internetworking experiment, which linked a mobile vehicle in PRNET with nodes in the ARPANET, and via SATNET, to nodes at UCL. The X.25 protocol, on which public data networks were based in the 1970s and 1980s, was supplemented by the X.75 protocol which enabled internetworking.

b. Key Internet Services, and technologies and protocols that enable these services

The Internet of today is a widely dispersed global network that is accessible through multiple channels from any location. The Internet began as a defense research project and has since developed into a global network used for a variety of applications, including social networking, multimedia, and business/corporate communications. Using a variety of technologies and protocols, the Internet provides a wide range of services, some of which are covered below.

- *World Wide Web*: The Internet's World Wide Web (WWW) is a network of linked hypertext documents. A web browser allows users to view and use hyperlinks to navigate between web pages that may contain text, images, videos, and other types of multimedia. One of the main features that attracts people to the Internet is the vast number of websites, millions of them, offering various kinds of content. The Hyper Text Transfer Protocol (HTTP), an application layer protocol used by web browsers acting as HTTP clients to request information from web servers hosting websites, supports the entire World Wide Web. A website address is found using a Uniform Resource Locator (URL), and resources and information are requested from web servers via HTTP via URLs.
- *Email:* Email, also known as electronic mail, is a way to send and receive digital messages. One of the most widely used services provided by the Internet, next to the World Wide Web, is email. The email system, which enables message exchanges between Internet users, is based on a number of standards and protocols. Email transmission over Internet Protocol (IP) networks is facilitated by the Simple Mail Transfer Protocol (SMTP), an Internet standard. Email clients,

Keyword

Uniform Resource Locator, colloquially termed a web address, is a reference to a web resource that specifies its location on a computer network and a mechanism for retrieving it.

or end users, typically use Post Office Protocol (POP) or Internet Message Access Protocol (IMAP) to access their mailbox accounts on mail servers, while email servers use SMTP to send and receive mail messages.

- *Internet Infrastructure*: An Internet Service Provider (ISP) is a company that connects individual users or corporate private networks to the Internet. ISPs serve a large number of users through a variety of physical media, including DSL and wireless connections. These ISPs are referred to as local ISPs in an Internet infrastructure. While local ISPs can peer with one another, they typically peer with regional ISPs, which link several local ISPs together. Regional ISPs then peer with the larger provider known as the Network Service Provider (NSP). This may not, however, be taken to be the actual Internet infrastructure, as different peering, connections, and other complexities make it challenging to graph the entirety of the Internet.

4.2.1. Application Layer

In order to enable efficient communication between an application program and another application program on a network, the application layer offers services to the program. It is not appropriate to think of the application layer as an application in the sense that most people do. Rather, an application's application layer is a part that manages how the application communicates with other devices. The remainder of the application is hidden from the transmission process by this abstraction layer service. To finish its task, the application layer depends on every layer that comes before it. At this point, the application or data is displayed in a way that the user can comprehend visually.

Functions of the application layer:

- Ensures that the receiving device is identified, can be reached, and is ready to accept data.
- Enables, if appropriate, authentication to occur between devices for an extra layer of security.
- Makes sure necessary communication interfaces exist. For example, is there an Ethernet or Wi-Fi interface in the sender's computer?
- Ensures agreement at both ends about error recovery procedures, data integrity, and privacy.
- Determines protocol and data syntax rules at the application level.
- Presents the data on the receiving end to the user application.

Since the application layer in the OSI model is the one nearest to the end user, both the user and the application layer can communicate with the software program directly. Applications at the application layer are client-server based.

The application layer includes the following functions:

- **Identifying communication partners**: The application layer identifies the availability of communication partners for an application with data to transmit.
- **Determining resource availability**: The application layer determines whether sufficient network resources are available for the requested communication.
- **Synchronizing communication**: All

the communications occur between the applications require cooperation, which is managed by an application layer.

Services of Application Layers

- **Network Virtual terminal**: An application layer allows a user to log on to a remote host. To do so, the application creates a software emulation of a terminal at the remote host. The user's computer talks to the software terminal, which in turn, talks to the host. The remote host thinks that it is communicating with one of its own terminals, so it allows the user to log on.
- **File Transfer, Access, and Management (FTAM):** An application allows a user to access files in a remote computer, to retrieve files from a computer and to manage files in a remote computer. FTAM defines a hierarchical virtual file in terms of file structure, file attributes and the kind of operations performed on the files and their attributes.
- **Addressing:** To obtain communication between client and server, there is a need for addressing. When a client made a request to the server, the request contains the server address and its own address. The server response to the client request, the request contains the destination address, i.e., client address. To achieve this kind of addressing, DNS is used.
- **Mail Services**: An application layer provides Email forwarding and storage.
- **Directory Services:** An application contains a distributed database that provides access for global information about various objects and services.
- **Authentication:** It authenticates the sender or receiver's message or both.

A network diagram is usually used to guide the design of a computer network. This topology, which has seven layers of network functionality, is based on the Open Systems Interconnection model (OSI). Known as layer seven in OSI, the application layer is the highest level. The Hypertext Transfer Protocol (HTTP), email, and **File Transfer Protocol (FTP)** are among the communication protocols that are managed by the network layer. These applications allow email clients and web browsers to share files over a network.ile transfer protocol (FTP) are among the communication protocols that are managed by the network layer. These applications allow email clients and web browsers to share files over a network.

Keyword

File Transfer Protocol (FTP) is a standard network protocol used for the transfer of computer files between a client and server on a computer network.

A physical cable is the first step in a network, and a computer program is the last. In the course of a typical communication transfer, data is forced through multiple levels of transformations. To guarantee appropriate data quality and security regulations are followed, this procedure is required. Software protocols can now be more flexible thanks to the creation of the OSI model. There are seven layers in the OSI model. The transport, data link, network, session, presentation, and application layers are these. The layers communicate over a network by working in a hierarchical structure. Standard transmission control protocol (TCP/IP) is the Internet's primary communication language and is used by the majority of computer networks today. The OSI model serves as a guide for how network hardware and software should communicate in this network protocol. In the network topology, every layer in the model has a distinct role to play.

The hierarchical chaining of responsibility is the foundation of the OSI model. These guidelines compel every layer to transmit messages through the topology by adhering to predetermined handoff procedures. The presentation layer, the next tier down the hierarchy chain, has handoff rules that the application layer must abide by. The next level in the chain usually requires certain size requirements, format, and encryption before accepting a message. One common communication protocol on computers and mobile devices is instant messaging, or IM. Software that makes use of the application layer protocol is instant messaging (IM). Instant messaging software is made possible for businesses by the IM standard protocol. AOL Instant Messenger, Yahoo Mail, and MSN Messenger are a few of these products. At this layer, every program communicates over the network using the OSI standards.

One email program that makes use of the application layer is Microsoft Outlook. The task of converting software program messages into comprehensible computer messages falls under the purview of the lowest tier of the OSI model. The presentation layer, which manages the message's format and encryption, receives messages from the application layer.

4.2.2 Transport Layer

Data that must be transported beyond the confines of an address space must go through a transport layer. Unstructured byte sequences make up the data being transported from the perspective of the transport layer. A concrete transport mechanism is used to implement the transport layer. The transport layer's job is to provide a uniform interface to the presentation layer while abstracting from platform-specific transport mechanisms. Generally speaking, the transport layer is just an operating system's wrapper around network functions. Just like when the bank scenario is introduced, an analysis of requirements shows the features of the transport layer that serve as the foundation for a design:

1. The transport layer guarantees a reliable end-to-end connection between precisely two address spaces.
2. Data can be sent bi-directionally in the form of unstructured byte sequences of any length.
3. Different transport mechanisms should be supported.

4.2.2.1. Transport Layer Links Address Spaces

The details of the underlying transport mechanism are hidden above the transport layer, which ensures reliable end-to-end connections. Several transport protocols, such as TCP, currently offer reliable connections. It becomes more challenging to guarantee appropriate semantics above the transport layer when an unreliable transport mechanism is used at that layer. Requiring the transport layer to connect precisely two address spaces aims to simplify the middleware. Managing transport channels between different address spaces would be problematic without this restriction. Therefore, µORB only permits an application's objects to be split between exactly two address spaces.

The transport layer views data as unstructured, variable-length byte sequences exchanged between a client and a server. While the transport layer is not expected to continuously transmit media, multimedia applications require this capability. However, it is expected to support various transport mechanisms.

The following use case outlines the type of modeling needed at the class level:

1. The server establishes a communication end point and waits for a connection setup request.
2. The client creates a communication end point and connects it to the server.
3. The client sends data and waits for a response.
4. The server receives the data of the client and then sends a response.
5. After the client receives the response from the server, both close their communication end points

4.2.2.2. Applications Scenario of the Transport Layer

Keep in mind that the terms "client" and "server" do not refer to actual objects in this use case. Instead, they discuss the roles that are played in interactions with the transport layer, suggesting an uneven application of the transport layer. Based on the matching communication endpoints, clients and servers define a communications channel. An address designating the communication endpoints is a sign of the client and server's consent. Usually, a network address referring to the actual transport mechanism is included in a transport layer address. Address formats and details can vary amongst transport mechanisms. Thus, there isn't a format that is generally accepted.

4.2.2.3. Classes Buffer, Address, and Transport Model Transport Layer

To model the transport layer, three classes—Buffer, Address, and Transport—are introduced. The storage region connected to a specific memory chunk is represented by the class buffer. The unstructured byte sequences that are transferred between address spaces via a transport mechanism are contained in instances of this class. There are methods available for configuring and managing a memory chunk through the class Buffer's interface. A specific transport mechanism's address is represented by the class Address, and the transport mechanism itself is represented by the class Transport. This address serves as the transport mechanism's factory. Since they merely serve as the interface for the actual transport mechanism, the two classes are abstract in and of themselves. As a result, each transport mechanism requires the definition of two concrete classes: one for the address and another for the transport mechanism itself. The abstract base classes Address and Transport are the ancestors of these classes. A TCP-based transport mechanism in UML notation is displayed in Figure 4.7.

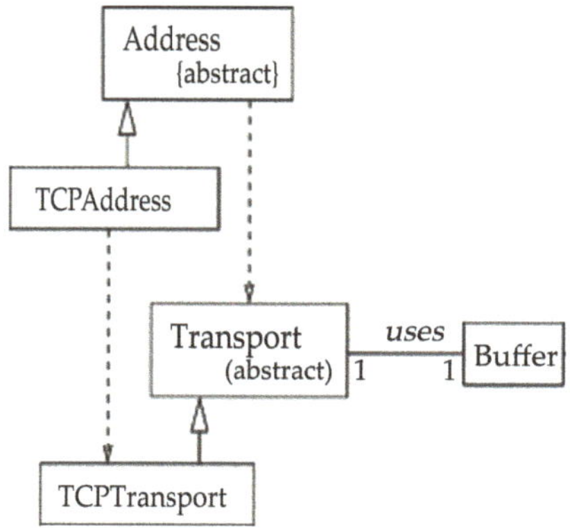

Figure 4.7. UML class diagram of transport layer (Source: ScienceDirect, https://ars.els-cdn.com/content/image/3-s2.0-B978155860648750005X-f04-02-9781558606487.gif).

4.2.2.4. Responsibilities of a Transport Layer

Keyword

User Datagram Protocol (UDP) is an alternative communications protocol to TCP used primarily for establishing low-latency and loss-tolerating connections between applications on the internet.

The second layer in the TCP/IP model is called the Transport Layer. In order to send messages to a host, it is an end-to-end layer. It is called an end-to-end layer because, in order to reliably deliver the services, it establishes a point-to-point connection between the source host and destination host as opposed to a hop-to-hop one. A segment is the data encapsulation unit used in the Transport Layer. TCP (Transmission Control Protocol), **UDP (User Datagram Protocol),** DCCP (Datagram Congestion Control Protocol), and other common protocols are utilized by the Transport Layer to improve its functionality.

Various responsibilities of a Transport Layer:

- **Process-to-process delivery***:* Just as the Data Link Layer needs the MAC address (a 48-bit address found inside each host machine's Network Interface Card) of the source and destination hosts in order to correctly deliver a frame, and the Network Layer needs the IP address in order to route packets appropriately, the Transport Layer also needs a port number in order to correctly deliver data segments to the appropriate process among the various processes that are running on a given host. Any client-server program can be uniquely identified by its port number, which is a 16-bit address.
- **End-to-end Connection between hosts**: TCP and UDP are primarily used by the transport layer to create this connection, which is also within its purview. TCP is a secure, connection-oriented protocol that builds a strong connection between two end hosts through a handshake protocol. TCP is used

in many different applications and guarantees dependable message delivery. On the other hand, UDP guarantees best-effort delivery and is a stateless, unstable protocol. It works well for applications like video conferences that need to send large amounts of data and don't care too much about flow or error control. Frequently, multicasting protocols make use of it.

- **Multiplexing and demultiplexing**: Multiplexing enables the use of several applications simultaneously over a network while a host is operating. This mechanism, provided by the transport layer, allows us to send packet streams from multiple applications over a network at the same time. After adding the appropriate headers, the transport layer transfers these packets—which are identified by their port numbers—from various processes to the network layer. Demultiplexing is also necessary at the receiving end in order to receive data originating from different processes. The appropriate process operating on the recipient's computer receives the data segments that transport receives from the network layer.
- **Controlling congestion**: Congestion occurs when there are too many sources attempting to send data over a network, causing the router buffers to overflow and packet loss. Consequently, the congestion is exacerbated by the sources' retransmission of packets. Congestion control is provided in this scenario by the Transport layer in various ways. It makes use of both closed-loop and open-loop congestion control to eliminate congestion in a network after it has already occurred. AIMD—additive increase multiplicative decrease—and the leaky bucket technique are two of TCP's congestion control mechanisms.
- **Data integrity and error correction**: The transport layer uses error detection codes, computes checksums, verifies that the received data is not corrupted, uses the ACK and NACK services to inform the sender whether the data has arrived, and verifies the integrity of the data. It also checks for errors in the messages that come from the application layer.
- **Flow control:** In the TCP/IP model, the transport layer acts as a conduit for data between the higher and lower layers. TCP also employs flow control techniques to prevent data loss from a fast sender and slow receiver. It utilizes the sliding window protocol, which is executed by the receiver informing the sender of the maximum amount of data it can receive by sending back a window.

4.2.3. Internet Layer

The Internet layer is in charge of organizing data that needs to be sent into IP datagrams, which are packetized data packets. These will have the data's source and destination addresses listed. The IP datagram routing is another function of this layer. Address Resolution Protocol (ARP), Reverse Address Resolution Protocol (RARP), Internet Group Management Protocol (IGMP), Internet Protocol (IP), and Internet Control Message Protocol (ICMP) are the primary protocols present at the Internet layer.

4.2.3.1. Static IP

An IP address that has been manually configured for a device is called a static IP (also called a fixed IP address; see view from 10:20 to 13:20). Because it remains constant without user intervention, the IP address is known as static. An IP address that matches the range selected for the task or provided by the IT department must be manually assigned when configuring a controller. It is necessary to manually assign a unique IP address to every device on the network. Static IP addresses have a significant drawback over dynamic ones: manually configuring the devices is required. This is usually done device-by-device.

4.2.3.2. DHCP

A client/server protocol called Dynamic Host Configuration Protocol gives an IP host its IP address and other relevant configuration data, such as the subnet mask and default gateway, automatically. With DHCP, IP addresses and other network configuration data can be distributed and updated automatically. When a client submits a request, a DHCP server usually replies with an address that is within the DHCP scope. If they are set up to do so, DHCP servers can offer more network-related information in addition to IP addresses. A valid range of IP addresses that can be leased or assigned to client computers on a specific subnet is known as a DHCP scope. A scope is set up in a DHCP server to ascertain the address pool of IPs that the server can offer to DHCP clients. The DHCP server can assign an address to a client, extend the lease term, recognize when the address is not in use, and reclaim it when an address has a dynamic lease.

A DHCP reservation, on the other hand, is a permanent IP address assignment. It is a particular IP address that is set aside for the exclusive use of a particular DHCP client within the scope of DHCP. In controls networks, lease reservations are preferred to dynamic leases. Sending and receiving data to other devices on the same network can depend on a controller's IP address. It will be simpler to configure and maintain the system if the IP address remains constant. In order to utilize lease reservations, you will require knowledge of the controller's MAC address. In order for the person in charge of the DHCP server to make sure every controller receives the IP address it is meant to have you will need to give them this.

4.2.4. Network Access Layer

The Data Link and Physical layers of the OSI reference model align with the Network Access layer of the TCP/IP model. It outlines the hardware and protocols needed to link a host to a real network and transfer data between them. In order to be delivered within the physical network, packets from the Internet layer are routed through the Network Access layer. The destination may be the network host itself, another host, or a router for additional forwarding. Therefore, the Network Access layer is restricted to the physical layer boundary, which is typically defined by a layer 3 device like a router, while the Internet layer has a view of the entire Internetwork.

There are numerous protocols that make up the Network Access layer. The most widely used protocols when the physical network is a local area network (LAN) are Ethernet and its numerous variants. Conversely, protocols like Frame Relay and Point-to-Point Protocol (PPP) are frequently used when the physical network is a Wide Area Network (WAN).

- The Network Access layer uses a physical address to identify hosts and to deliver data.
- The Network Access layer PDU is called a frame. It contains the IP packet as well as a protocol header and trailer from this layer.
- The Network Access layer header and trailer are only relevant in the physical network. When a router receives a frame, it strips off the header and trailer and adds a new header and trailer before sending it out to the next physical network towards the destination.

The TCP/IP protocol hierarchy starts at the Network Access layer. Because it is well hidden by the more well-known higher-level protocols like SMTP, HTTP, and FTP, as well as mid-level protocols like IP, TCP, and UDP, it is frequently disregarded by users. Encapsulating IP datagrams into network-transmitted frames and translating IP addresses into physical hardware addresses are among the tasks carried out at the network access layer. Software programs and drivers specific to particular hardware components handle a large portion of the work at the network access layer. Most of the time, configuration is as simple as choosing the right driver to load and TCP/IP as the protocol to use. Many computers have this driver software pre-installed and set up, or they have "plug-and-play" apps that allow them to configure themselves automatically.

Keyword

Network interface card (NIC) is a hardware component without which a computer cannot be connected over a network.

Configuring a Windows NT system to use a 3Com Etherlink III **network interface card (NIC)** with Ethernet is a good example of network access layer configuration. In a typical scenario, the operating system would identify the NIC during installation. If this doesn't happen, or if the card is added later, installing the card and picking the driver by selecting the card's manufacturer and model from a list of available drivers would be the main steps in the installation process. Certain cards may also need minimal hardware configuration, including deciding on an I/O port, setting the IRQ, and maybe utilizing the card's Twisted Pair or Coax connector. Upon selecting and configuring the appropriate driver for the card, the subsequent action involves choosing TCP/IP from a list of available protocols to be utilized on the interface. The network access layer configuration is finished after this. Numerous configuration programs proceed to configure DNS servers, IP addresses, netmasks, default gateways, and other parameters that are actually related to other layers and protocols automatically.

It's true that some network access layer protocols require a lot of configuration. Understanding the operation of the more common ones is beneficial. Network managers should know about serial point-to-point protocols like SLIP and PPP if they'll be handling remote access over serial communication lines, such as ISDN lines or POTS modems. Being aware of remote authentication protocols like TACACS and RADIUS is helpful if they'll be used on Network Access Server hardware, such as modem stacks or terminal servers.

Did you get it?

1. **What are the key Internet services, and what technologies and protocols enable these services?**
2. **Can you explain the classes Buffer, Address, and Transport model within the transport layer?**

FOCUS ON CAREERS

NETWORK ARCHITECT

A network architect is responsible for designing and building data communication networks. The networks they work on can range from smaller local area networks (LANs) to larger wide area networks (WANs), along with intranets. These professionals also manage the infrastructure of computer networks to ensure they operate effectively, including the installation of routers, cables, modems, and other necessary hardware and software. Network architects can find employment at organizations in numerous industries, including telecommunications, finance, insurance, and computer systems design services. This role is typically a senior IT position within an organization, often working alongside a team of IT specialists and communicating with management staff. These professionals use their understanding of the organization's business goals to develop network systems that meet them. If you are thinking about becoming a network architect, learning about the typical requirements for this career may help you assess whether this profession is a good fit for you:

Education and Training

To pursue a career as a network engineer, one typically needs to obtain at least a bachelor's degree in a relevant field. For instance, a degree in computer science, information systems, engineering, or mathematics may be considered. Coursework in computer-related fields provides individuals with hands-on experience, relevant skills, and knowledge necessary to carry out the typical job responsibilities of a network architect. Additionally, individuals learn about various technologies, software, and programs utilized in the industry. A bachelor's degree usually requires around four years to complete. Some employers or higher-level positions may mandate candidates with more advanced degrees, such as a master's or doctorate. One possibility is pursuing a Master of Business Administration degree in information systems. An MBA program encompasses both computer- and business-related coursework, including project management. An advanced degree could potentially facilitate career progression and showcase extensive expertise in the field. A master's program typically takes about two years to finish, while a doctorate may take four to six years.

Certifications

Network architects have several certifications they can obtain, often through specific software and product vendors. Many of these certifications have different levels that you can earn as you continue to advance your IT skills and knowledge. The certification you pursue may vary based on the types of systems or software used or required by your employer. You can research job openings in your field to understand the certifications sought by employers. Some examples of common certifications pursued by network architects include:

- Cisco Certified Network Professional (CCNP)
- Cisco Certified Architect (CCAr)
- CompTIA Network+
- ITIL Master
- Microsoft Technology Associate (MTA)
- Red Hat Certified Architect (RHCA)
- Salesforce Certified Technical Architect
- VMware Certified Professional (VCP)
- Zachman Certified – Enterprise Architect

Work Experience

When hiring for network architect roles, employers typically seek candidates with at least five years of professional experience working with IT systems. The amount of experience sought may vary by employer or role, with some requiring at least 10 years. You may gain relevant experience through internships as a student or entry-level jobs in the field. For example, individuals may work as network engineers, administrators, computer systems analysts, or database administrators. Demonstrating to potential employers that you have relevant work experience can prove that you have the skills and knowledge needed to perform the job effectively. When possible, you can also share any achievements from your prior roles to set yourself apart from other candidates.

Skills

Network architects need numerous technical skills to perform their job effectively, such as those related to computer operating systems, wireless systems, and security. They typically learn such skills and knowledge through their education, training programs, or on-the-job experience. Network architects also benefit from having several other skills, including:

- **Analytical thinking:** Network architects must examine networks to identify issues and develop potential solutions. They also use this skill to determine the appropriate hardware, software, and other equipment to utilize based on their organizations' resources and needs.
- **Attention to detail**: When designing complex data communication networks, network architects must consider numerous details. Having an attention to detail helps ensure they create comprehensive designs with accuracy and networks that function effectively.
- **Communication:** Network architects work with other IT professionals, and strong verbal and written communication and interpersonal skills can ensure

they convey information effectively and accurately. They may also use these skills to present plans and provide networking guidance to management staff.

- **Leadership:** Network architects may need to lead a team of IT specialists or computer engineers through the network implementation process or other necessary tasks. Leadership skills enable them to assign responsibilities and maintain the proper functioning of the network.
- **Organizational skills:** Depending on their job, network architects may need to manage numerous networks within an organization and keep these different systems organized to ensure they work well together. Organizational skills, such as time management and strategic planning, also help keep projects on schedule and budget.

4.3. IP ADDRESSING AND ARCHITECTURE

→Learning Objectives

- Define what an IP (Internet Protocol) address is and its significance in network communication.
- Describe the various types of IP addresses used in networking, such as unicast, multicast, and broadcast addresses.
- Explain the concept of website IP addresses and their role in hosting web content on the internet.
- Classify IP addresses based on their operational characteristics, such as static and dynamic IP addresses.
- Understand the basic functioning of IP addresses in routing data packets between devices on a network.
- Define static IP addresses and their role in network configuration, particularly in scenarios where consistent, unchanging addresses are necessary.
- Identify tools and techniques used to track and record IP addresses, such as network monitoring software and log files.
- Differentiate between public and private IP addresses in terms of their scope, accessibility, and usage.

An Internet Protocol address is represented by an IP address. A special address that serves as the device's network identification. It resembles a set of guidelines controlling the format of data transferred via a local network or the Internet. An IP address facilitates the Internet's ability to discern between various routers, PCs, and WebPages. It facilitates better visual communication between the source and the destination and acts as a unique machine identifier within a particular network.

IP address structure: IP addresses are displayed as a set of four digits- the default address may be 192.158.1.38. Each number on the set may range from 0 to 255. Therefore, the total IP address range ranges from 0.0.0.0 to 255.255.255.255.

IP address is basically divided into two parts: X1. X2. X3. X4

1. [X1. X2. X3] is the Network ID

2. [X4] is the Host ID

1. **Network ID**: This portion of the IP address on the left-hand side designates the particular network that the device is connected to. When a device is connected to a typical home network and its IP address is 192.168.1.32, it is called 192.168.1. The network ID will be one component of the address. Since it is usual to fill in the final digit that is not zero, we can state that the network ID of the device is 192.168.1.0.
2. **Hosting ID**: The portion of the IP address that the network ID did not take is the host ID. It identifies a particular device in that network (called the "host" in the TCP/IP world). Using the IP address 192.168.1.32 as an example again, the host ID will be 32, making it the only host ID on the 192.168.1.0 network.

4.3.1. Version of IP address

Currently there are 2 versions of IP addresses are in use i.e IPV4 and IPV6

1. **IPv4 (Internet Protocol Version 4):** It is the original Internet Protocol address version. IPv4 addresses have a 32-bit length. Regarding network security, Internet Protocol Security (IPSec) is optional in this case. Despite having 4,294,967,296 addresses, there is still a shortage of network addresses due to the rapidly growing number of network and virtual devices being used.
2. **IPv6 (Internet Protocol Version 6):** It is the most recent iteration of the IP address. IPv6 addresses have a bit count of 128. In terms of network security, Internet Protocol Security (IPSec) is required in this. It appears to be more than enough to support the trillions of internet-connected devices that are currently in use or will be in the future because it permits 3.4 x 10^38 unique IP addresses.

4.3.2. IP Address Types

IP addresses come in four varieties: public, private, fixed, and dynamic. These include their local network location, which should be used within the network, and their public IP address, which should be used online.

1. **Public IP address:** An IP address that is assigned by different servers and devices is known as a public IP address. When you connect these devices to your internet connection, this IP address is displayed on our homepage. The reason for this explanation is that not everyone is familiar with IP communication. Our objective is to simplify the process of obtaining necessary information for all individuals. Some even refer to this IP address as their external one. A public IP address that can be accessed over the Internet is unique and is assigned to a computer device, similar to a postal address used for mail delivery to your home. Servers that will use the public IP address include web servers, email servers, and any other server device with direct Internet access. The Internet Protocol address is unique to a single device and is globally unique.
2. **Private IP address**: The IP address of every device connected to your network over the Internet is unique. This includes not only PCs, iPhones, and iPads but also any Bluetooth-

capable devices like smart TVs, printers, and speakers. With the expansion of the Internet of Things, your home likely has more private IP addresses now. These devices need to be uniquely identified by your router, and most devices require some form of communication protocol. To differentiate each device within the network, your router assigns private IP addresses.

3. **Static IP Address:** An IP address that is static is not valid. In contrast, a dynamic IP address that is subject to change will be supplied by the Dynamic Host Configuration Protocol (DHCP) server. Although it can be modified as part of routine network administration, the static IP address is not dynamic. Once assigned, static IP addresses do not change over time and are therefore incompatible. Additionally, you can learn more about the device with the aid of this kind of IP.
4. **Dynamic IP Address:** It implies ongoing change. A dynamic IP address is one that is not constant and varies over time. You might have a dynamic IP address if you have active cable or DSL service. Because they are less expensive, Internet service providers give their clients dynamic IP addresses. Your IP address is pulled from the address pool and assigned to you, as opposed to being assigned a single permanent IP address. That number is returned to the pool and given a new number after a few days, weeks, or occasionally even months. If an ISP does offer a static IP address to a customer who resides there, it's usually at a higher cost. Though they can be inconvenient, dynamic IP addresses allow for easy and cost-free navigation with the correct software.

4.3.3. Types of Website IP address

Website IP addresses come in two types – Dedicated IP Address and Shared IP Address. Let's delve into both.

- **Dedicated IP address:** Each website is assigned a specific dedicated IP address that is unique to that domain. This means no other domain shares the same address. There are several benefits to having a dedicated IP address, such as increased speed and enhanced security, especially during high traffic periods. However, dedicated IPs are generally more costly compared to shared IPs.
- **Shared IP address:** A shared IP address is one that is not unique and is shared by multiple domains. For most users, a shared IP address suffices as common configurations do not require a dedicated IP address.

4.3.4. IP Address Classification Based on Operational Characteristics

Based on operational characteristics, IP addresses are classified as follows:

Broadcast addressing: Broadcasting involves sending audio or video data across a network. A broadcast packet is simultaneously sent to all users on a local network without the need to specify individual recipients. Users can choose to open, read, follow instructions, or delete these packets. This service is available in IPv4 and typically uses the IP address 255.255.255.255.

- **Unicast addressing**: This type of address identifies a specific node on the network. Unicast refers to the one-to-one transmission of data between network nodes, making it the most commonly used IP addressing type. Both data transmission and reception are possible with unicast addressing, available in both IPv4 and IPv6.
- **Multicast IP addresses:** These IP addresses mainly help to establish one-to-many communication. Multicast IP routing protocols are used to distribute data to multiple recipients. The class D addresses (224.0.0.0 to 239.255.255.255) define the multicast group.
- **Anycast addressing:** A packet is not sent to every network receiver when using anycast addressing for data. A data packet is sent to the nearest address when it is assigned to an anycast address.

4.3.5. IP Addresses Work

Computers can send and receive data over the internet with the help of an IP address. The majority of IP addresses are just numbers, but as more people use the internet, some addresses now include letters. IP addresses come in four varieties: static, dynamic, private, and public. Static and dynamic indicate permanence, while public and private indicate the network's location—private is used inside a network, whereas public is used outside of one.

A static IP address was generated by hand rather than assigned. Moreover, a dynamic IP address is one that is assigned by a (DHCP) server and is not fixed, unlike a static address. The most prevalent kind of internet protocol addresses is dynamic IP addresses. Only a limited period of time is allowed for dynamic IP addresses to be active before they expire. Either the computer will ask for a new lease on its own, or it might get a new IP address.

Remember

An IP address uniquely identifies a device on a network. You've seen these addresses before; they look something like 192.168.1.34.

An IP address is always a set of four numbers like that. Each number can range from 0 to 255. So, the full IP addressing range goes from 0.0.0.0 to 255.255.255.255.

Since an IP address is specific to the computer or user to whom it is assigned, it can be likened to a Social Security Number (SSN). Routers can determine where they are sending data over the internet by using these numbers. Additionally, they verify that the messages are reaching the appropriate devices. A router requires an IP address in order to deliver to the requested web address, much like the post office requires a mailing address to deliver a package.

4.3.5.1. The Subnet Mask

Thus, how does your device distinguish between the network ID and the host ID? They do this by using a second number that is always associated with an IP address. We refer to that figure as the subnet mask.

On most simple networks (like the ones in homes or small businesses), you'll see subnet masks like 255.255.255.0, where all four numbers are either 255 or 0. The position of the changes from 255 to 0 indicate the division between the network and host ID. The 255s "mask out" the network ID from the equation. IP addressing details are displayed together with a default gateway address in addition to the IP address itself and the corresponding subnet mask. This address may be known by a different name on the platform you are using. It may be referred to as the "gateway," "router address," "default route," or simply "router." These all refer to the same thing. When a device is supposed to send network data to a network other than the one it is currently connected to (one with a different network ID), it sends the data to the default IP address.

The simplest example of this is found in a typical home network

A router that is linked to the internet via a modem is probably present in a home network that has several devices connected to it. Your internet provider may provide a modem/router combo unit that includes the router, or it may be a stand-alone device. Passing (or routing) traffic back and forth between the computers and devices on your network and the more publicly facing devices on the internet is what the router does. Let's say you open your browser and go to www.howtogeek.com. Your computer contacts the IP address of our website with a request. Your PC sends traffic to your router, which acts as a gateway, and your router then forwards the request to our server because our servers are on the internet rather than your home network. You see our website load in your browser when the server sends the appropriate data back to your router, which subsequently routes it to the device that made the request.

Keyword

Router is a networking device that forwards data packets between computer networks.

Typically, routers are configured by default to have their private IP address (their address on the local network) as the first host ID. So, for example, on a home network that uses 192.168.1.0 for a network ID, the router is usually going to be 192.168.1.1. Of course, like most things, you can configure that to be something different if you want.

4.3.5.2. DNS Servers

There's one final piece of information you'll see assigned alongside a device's IP address, subnet mask, and default gateway address: the addresses of one or two default Domain Name System (DNS) servers. We humans work much better with names than numerical addresses. Typing www.howtogeek.com into your browser's address bar is much easier than remembering and typing our site's IP address.

DNS searches for human-readable information, such as website names, and converts them to IP addresses. It functions somewhat like a phone book. DNS accomplishes this by keeping track of everything on a network of connected DNS servers throughout the internet. For the purpose of sending their queries, your devices must be aware of the addresses of DNS servers.

The DNS server IP addresses are frequently the same as the default gateway address on a small or home network. When devices send DNS queries to your router, it routes them to the DNS servers that your router is set up to use. You can modify those to use different DNS servers if you'd like. By default, these are typically the DNS servers that your ISP offers.

4.3.6. Static IP Address

An Internet Protocol (IP) address is a unique numerical address that is assigned to computers when they connect to the Internet. Every computer on the Internet has a unique address, which allows computers to send and receive information in order to communicate with one another. All that a static IP address is is a "permanent" address that is linked to a single computer for a considerable amount of time. This is not the same as a dynamic IP address, which is given out randomly at the beginning of every session and typically varies from one to the next.

A person's Internet Service Provider (ISP) assigns their IP address. A sizable block of IP addresses that fall inside a particular range are assigned to each ISP. When clients log on to the Internet, the ISP server automatically assigns available IP addresses within that range to them. The dynamic IP address that was temporarily assigned returns to the pool for reassignment when an individual disables their Internet connection. Most people find that dynamically assigned IP addresses work well, but some people would rather have a static address. Having a static IP address has benefits in some circumstances. For instance, this kind of IP address is frequently preferred by those who play online games with distant players. The hosting server recognizes them when they join back into a game, restoring their score, position in the game, and other settings appropriately. A computer cookie that can be removed is less dependable than a static IP address. Every website has a static IP address, sometimes referred to as a Uniform Resource Locator or URL. A website wouldn't have a permanent address without a static address, which would force users to "follow it" around the Internet and make bookmarks meaningless. This brings up the most frequent reason for which someone chooses this kind of IP address: to host a website. One can create a website and serve as the server, hosting it on the Internet just like any other website, provided they have a static IP and 24/7 broadband access. The owner of a static IP can also host an email server and operate other services, such as forums or webcasts. Even though third parties offer all of these services, some people would rather take on the role of host. If the computer will be connecting to a Virtual Private Network (VPN) or enabling remote access through programs like Radmin™ or PCAnywhere™, then a static IP is also recommended. Provided that the remote computer in question has a static IP address, software that allows remote access only needs to be configured once. In the event that its address changes, the user will need to identify the remote IP address and update the software accordingly.

Unless a client specifically requests a static IP address, ISPs will automatically assign a dynamic IP address to them. Static IP addressing is typically more costly and perceived as less private by some. Since IP addresses are routinely logged by websites, an address that never changes gives data mining companies easy access to a fairly comprehensive profile of people's online browsing habits.

4.3.7. Track and Record IP Addresses

An IP address, also known as an Internet Protocol address, is a special number that is given to a computer when it connects to the Internet. Internet Service Provider (ISP) records can be used to trace an IP address back to a specific person. When users navigate the pages of nearly any website on the World Wide Web (Web), IP addresses are tracked and recorded. This is primarily due to two factors: site enhancement and security. Every website has a server to host it on. A request for a webpage at the specified location is sent by the user's browser to the server when they click to access a website. The webpage is sent back to the IP address that made the request by the server. After that, the visitor's computer screen loads the page.

The speed at which pages load for visitors may decrease if the server is overloaded with requests. When there are too many requests being made at once, the server will "crash" or go down, making the website momentarily unavailable. This might be classified as a Denial of Service (DoS) attack. An attack is known as a Distributed Denial of Service (DDoS) attack if it originates from a botnet, which is a collection of compromised computers. A malevolent cybercriminal may attempt to obtain data from password-protected databases containing credit card numbers and other customer information by breaking into a Web server. Those who are referred to as "script kiddies" may merely aim to damage a website by adding text or images.

Websites automatically track and log IP addresses, storing the numerical addresses in server logs, for all of the aforementioned reasons and more. Every request made by the IP address is noted and has a time stamp attached. Logs are regularly cleared of older data to make room for updated information. The duration that a website retains IP logs varies, is set by the site administrator, and depends on numerous variables. In order to determine which pages are the most popular, websites also monitor and log IP addresses. To boost website traffic, the website can expand on its most popular pages. Leaks in traffic can also be found by tracking IP addresses throughout the website.

IP addresses are typically referred to as "anonymous" data in website policies. Nonetheless, websites can still associate identities with IP addresses in a variety of ways—even if the address is dynamic and changes with every Web session—thanks to computer cookies. Additionally, a lot of websites have "Web bugs," which are a few pixels connected to an advertising company that can track and record IP addresses as they move from one website to another on the Internet, covertly assembling comprehensive surfing profiles of people over months or years. For a website to track and profile a visitor, registration is not required.

If cookies are enabled in the web browser, then every visit to a website is usually time-stamped and saved to a cookie. Every page and link that is viewed on the website is typically added to the cookie (along with the server logs). Cookies are often kept, but server logs are cleaned up. The duplicate cookie on the Web server remains after a user deletes a cookie from their computer. Even if the user is cautious to accept only temporary cookies or none at all, the server may be able to "identify" them when they return to the website later on thanks to a variety of system and software data that browsers frequently provide.

Because of these worries, a lot of astute internet users would rather browse in secret. Here, a proxy server is positioned in between the user's PC and the Internet. Every browser request is routed through the proxy and then sent to the Internet. Instead of logging the proxy's IP address, web servers return pages to it. After receiving the page, the proxy serves as a go-between by forwarding it to the surfer. Although the proxy server will track and record IP addresses, web servers do not have a record of the surfer's IP address. It's critical to ascertain whether a proxy service is actually anonymous before using it. Some proxy servers thwart the intent by sending the requester's IP address through their headers. It is only anonymous proxy servers that conceal this data. It is advised to personally verify through the proxy tools that are available because some proxies make false claims about being anonymous. Since the netizen's home country will not have jurisdiction over the proxy's logs, using international proxies can further enhance anonymity. Nevertheless, rather than shielding unlawful activity, proxy services are meant to support the preservation of freedom and privacy for legitimate activity.

To prevent records from accumulating on a single proxy server, users can maintain a list of proxies and quickly switch between them using the FoxyProxy add-on plug-in for the Firefox™ browser. Additionally, proxies can be linked by chaining two or three proxy servers together, but this slows down browsing. Moreover, requests are lost if a proxy server is unavailable. For proxy browsing, there are also various shareware applications available. Through an on-site interface, web-based anonymous services enable users to browse the internet. When using the website, a window displaying the requested pages opens. The website's IP address is the only one visible on the Internet. However, it is important to note that the website itself will log and monitor users' IP addresses.

4.3.8. Difference between Public and Private IP Addresses

All computers connected to a network, whether public (such as the World Wide Web) or private (such as those in a workplace), are uniquely identified by their Internet Protocol addresses, or IP addresses. Computers can locate and communicate with each other thanks to the IP addressing scheme. Each computer connecting to the Internet is assigned a public IP address, while computers within the same local area network (LAN) are recognized by their private addresses. This system operates similarly to how phone numbers work in an office environment. A company typically has a primary business number (the public IP address), and each employee may have a distinct extension that enables calls to be directed to the correct individual (the private IP address).

An IP address, a set of binary numbers, is used to identify a computer or other device on a network and provide information about it. In the more commonly used addressing scheme, IP Version 4 (IPv4), these numbers are typically expressed as four numbers separated by dots. A new addressing scheme, IPv6, was developed in the 1990s due to the limited and depleting number of addresses available in the IPv4 format. In this format, eight groups of four letters and numbers are used to represent IP addresses; groups with a zero value may be omitted. Groups are separated by colons. In IPv6, private addresses are known as "local-use."

- *Public Addresses:* The IP addresses that are public enable any two computers to recognize one another. A person's computer is typically assigned an address from a pool that has been reserved for her Internet Service Provider (ISP) to use for its clients when they connect to the Internet. The IP address of the server that hosts the website is generated when she types in a domain name, such as wisegeek.com. To determine where to send the requested site page, the server uses the computer's public IP address.

Keyword

Internet service provider (ISP) is an organization that provides services for accessing, using, or participating in the Internet.

- *Private Addresses*: A private network can be set up by connecting multiple computers or devices wirelessly or through cables. To enable file sharing and resource sharing across the network, each device is assigned a unique IP address. Different private networks may use the same addresses, as long as they are unique within their own network; this is because computers in different networks do not communicate directly with each other. Using private IP addresses as identifiers, a network router transfers data between the connected computers. A modem is usually used to link the private network or one of its computers to the Internet. **The Internet Service Provider (ISP)** assigns a public IP address to the router or firewall in the network; this single public IP address represents the entire network on the Internet. The router acts as a gatekeeper, directing requests from specific computer users to the Internet through a device called a Network Address Translator (NAT). The router decides how to send returned data to the public IP address.
- *Static and Dynamic:* A public IP address may be either dynamic or static. Websites and other online services are typically hosted on static IP addresses, which remain constant. Because they can facilitate communication, some Voice over IP (VOIP) users and gamers also favor static IPs. Every time a certain user connects to the Internet, a dynamic IP address is selected from a pool of available addresses. Since it's the default address type assigned to users of an ISP when they use its services, the majority of computers have dynamic public IP addresses.
- *Finding a Computer's IP Address*: Users can view the public IP address assigned to their computer or, occasionally, the IP addresses of other users, using a variety of online programs. Via the configuration dialogs on the network router, private IP addresses can also be seen. Before trying

to access or modify the data in a network router, inexperienced computer users might want to speak with a network administrator or another expert.

Did you know?

Classful network design served its purpose in the startup stage of the Internet, but it lacked scalability in the face of the rapid expansion of networking in the 1990s. The class system of the address space was replaced with Classless Inter-Domain Routing (CIDR) in 1993. CIDR is based on variable-length subnet masking (VLSM) to allow allocation and routing based on arbitrary-length prefixes.

4.3.8.1. Private Ranges

Within the range of publicly available IP addresses there are specific, excluded ranges withheld for private network use. In IPv4, the private IP ranges are as follows:

- 10.0.0.0 ... 10.255.255.255
- 172.16.0.0 ... 172.31.255.255
- 192.168.0.0 ... 192.168.255.255

In IPv6, site-local addresses—the equivalent of IPv4 private addresses—begin with FE followed by C, D, E, or F. Another type, called link-local, does not have a comparison in IPv4 and is only used for special purposes on physical networks. These also begin with FE, followed by 8, 9, A, or B.

4.3.8.2. Who Coordinates IP Addresses?

The global assignment of IP addresses and other associated protocols is governed by the Internet Assigned Numbers Authority (IANA). The Internet Corporation for Assigned Names and Numbers (ICANN) is currently in charge of IANA, which was previously an independent organization. The organization in charge of allocating and managing Internet domain names, such as those ending in .com and .org, is ICANN. The challenging task of connecting computers to each other so they can efficiently exchange information is facilitated by IP addresses, domain names, and other identifiers.

Did you get it?

1. Can you explain the concept of website IP addresses and their role in hosting web content on the internet?
2. What tools and techniques are used to track and record IP addresses, including network monitoring software and log files?

ROLE MODEL

Paul Baran: He was one of the two independent inventors of packet switching, which is today the dominant basis for data communications in computer networks worldwide, and went on to start several companies and develop other technologies that are an essential part of modern digital communication.

BIOGRAPHY

Paul Baran (born April 29, 1926, Grodno, Pol. [now Hrodna, Bela.]—died March 26, 2011, Palo Alto, Calif., U.S.) was an American electrical engineer and the inventor of the distributed network. He worked contemporaneously with British computer scientist Donald Davies on data packet switching across distributed networks. These inventions laid the foundation for the Internet.

In 1928, Baran's family moved to Philadelphia. He studied electrical engineering at Drexel University in Philadelphia (B.S., 1949) and at the University of California, Los Angeles (M.S., 1959). In 1959, he joined the RAND Corporation as a researcher, a think tank that provided analyses of various issues affecting public policy and national defense. At RAND, Baran focused on developing a method for U.S. authorities to communicate in case their centralized switching facilities were destroyed by a nuclear attack. Influenced by the principle that the human brain can recover lost functions by bypassing a dysfunctional area, Baran conceived a "distributed" network using digital technology. This network would have no centralized switches or dedicated transmission lines and would continue to operate even if several of its switching nodes were disabled.

For transporting messages across this system, Baran conceived of the idea of breaking large messages or units of computer data into "message blocks"—separate pieces of data that would be sent independently to the target destination, where they would be rejoined into the original message. By foregoing dedicated communication lines in favor of using any number of available circuits, Baran's system increased transmission capacity (bandwidth) and created a flexible, reliable, and robust communications network. Baran's work on message blocks appeared in a series of RAND studies published between 1960 and 1962. At about the same time, Davies in the United Kingdom invented a similar system employing what Davies called "packets," and packet switching, as this process came to be called, formed the basis for communication across modern networks. With digital computers as network nodes, Baran used a "rapid store and forward" design for packet switching, allowing for essentially real-time data transmission. In the 1970s, Baran became an informal consultant to ARPANET, a high-speed computer network created by the Defense Advanced Research Projects Agency (DARPA) to connect research institutes and laboratories supported by the Department of Defense across the United States. Baran's inventions provided the technical foundation for the eventual development at ARPANET of the Transmission Control Protocol/Internet Protocol (TCP/IP), a communications protocol that allowed a number of different networks designed by different vendors to form a "network of networks." ARPANET, based on Baran's packet switching, thus became the predecessor of the Internet.

Baran left RAND in 1968 and afterward was involved with developing discrete multitone technology (a crucial component of digital subscriber lines) and with contributing to developments in spread spectrum transmission (an essential component of wireless communication). Baran also founded Metricom, a wireless Internet service company, in 1986; Com21, a supplier of cable modem systems, in 1992; and GoBackTV, a company specializing in infrastructure equipment for television operators, in 2003.

SUMMARY

- The term "internetworking" is a compound of the words "inter" and "networking," which denotes a connection between completely unrelated nodes or segments. The intermediary devices, which are similar to routers or gateways, establish this connection.
- The process of connecting multiple networks via devices such as routers and gateways is known as internetworking. The various networks are owned by different organizations with vastly different network technologies.
- Each physical network connection of a network device is uniquely identified by its data-link layer address. Physical or hardware addresses are commonly used to refer to data-link addresses.
- Network addresses, also known as virtual or logical addresses, can sometimes be found within an address space that can be graded. A network address and a device have a logical, non-fixed relationship that typically depends on either the physical properties of the network or on arbitrary groupings.
- An internetwork is a group of broadcast and packet-switching networks that function as a single, large network thanks to the use of routers, switches, and bridges, which are intermediate networking devices.
- In order to enable efficient communication between an application program and another application program on a network, the application layer offers services to the program. It is not appropriate to think of the application layer as an application in the sense that most people do.
- A physical cable marks the beginning of a network, while a computer program wraps it up. During a regular data transfer process, information undergoes various transformations at different levels..
- The Internet layer organizes data into IP datagrams for transmission, containing source and destination addresses. It also handles routing of IP datagrams.

MULTIPLE CHOICE QUESTIONS

1. Network layer at source is responsible for creating a packet from data coming from another
   a. Station
   b. Link
   c. Node
   d. Protocol
2. Internet has chosen datagram approach to switching in the
   a. Data Link Layer
   b. Network Layer
   c. Physical Layer

d. Presentation Layer

3. In Internetwork, network layer is responsible for
   a. Host to User Link
   b. Host to Host Delivery
   c. User to Host IP
   d. Host to Server communication
4. Datagram network uses universal addresses defined in network layer to route packets from source to the
   a. Same source
   b. Layers
   c. Destination
   d. Application
5. Physical and data link layers of a network operate
   a. Locally
   b. Seperately
   c. Unjointly
   d. Independently

REVIEW QUESTIONS

1. Identify the challenges to internetworking.
2. Give an overview on internetwork addressing.
3. What are the importance of application layer and transport layer in internetworking?
4. How to IP addresses work?
5. Define the TCP/IP network architecture.

Answer to Multiple Choice Questions

1. (d) 2. (b) 3. (b) 4. (c) 5. (b)

REFERENCES

1. Advances in Internetworking, Data & Web Technologies, (2017). *The 5th International Conference on Emerging Internetworking, Data & Web Technologies, EIDWT-2017*. Wuhan, China.
2. Comer, D., (2013). *Internetworking with TCP/IP* (Vol. 1, 6th edn.). Saddle River, NJ: Pearson.
3. Coulouris, G., Dollimore, J., Kindberg, T., & Blair, G., (2012). *Distributed Systems: Concepts and Design*. Addison-Wesley.

4. Kozierok, C., (2005). *The TCP IP Guide: A Comprehensive, Illustrated Internet Protocols Reference*. San Francisco: No Starch Press.

5. Medhi, D., (2007). *Network Routing: Algorithms, Protocols, and Architectures*. San Francisco: Morgan Kaufmann Publishers.

6. Osterlow, H., (2012). *IP Routing Primer Plus*. Indianapolis: Sams Publishing.

7. Peterson, L. L., & Davie, B. S., (2012). *Computer Networks: A Systems Approach.* Elsevier, Inc.

CHAPTER

5

Networking for Clusters

LEARNING OBJECTIVES

After studying this chapter, you will be able to:

- Explain the principles of internetworking
- Define the internetwork architecture
- Discuss on IP addressing and architecture

INTRODUCTORY EXAMPLE

CLUSTER NETWORKS WITH INSTANCE POOLS

Cluster networks with instance pools are a modern approach to efficiently managing resources in cloud computing environments. This paradigm combines the concepts of cluster networking and instance pooling to enhance scalability, reliability, and cost-effectiveness. In this configuration, a cluster network refers to a group of interconnected servers or virtual machines (instances) that collaborate to perform various tasks or services. These instances are organized into pools, which are sets of identical or similar instances configured to handle specific workloads or applications.

One key aspect of cluster networks with instance pools is their dynamic nature. Instances within a pool can be added or removed based on demand, allowing the system to automatically scale resources up or down in response to changing requirements. This elasticity ensures optimal resource utilization and performance efficiency, as resources are provisioned and de-provisioned as needed. Additionally, instance pools can improve fault tolerance and reliability by distributing workloads across multiple instances. If one instance fails or becomes unavailable, the workload can be seamlessly transferred to another instance within the pool, minimizing downtime and service interruptions.

Furthermore, cluster networks with instance pools offer cost benefits by optimizing resource usage. Instead of provisioning separate instances for each workload, organizations can leverage shared pools of instances, reducing the total number of resources required. This consolidation leads to lower infrastructure costs and better overall resource utilization. Additionally, cloud providers often offer pricing models based on resource usage, allowing organizations to pay only for the resources they consume.

INTRODUCTION

A cluster network is an ultra-low latency, high-bandwidth network that connects a pool of GPU-optimized instances or high-performance computing (HPC) instances. Every node in the cluster is a simple machine made of metal that is situated near other nodes. Similar to on-premises HPC clusters, a remote direct memory access (RDMA) network between nodes offers latency as low as single-digit microseconds.

Cluster networks are designed for highly demanding parallel computing workloads. For example:

- Computational fluid dynamics simulations for automotive or aerospace modeling
- Financial modeling and risk analysis
- Biomedical simulations
- Trajectory analysis and design for space exploration
- Artificial intelligence and big data workloads

The instance pools feature serves as the foundation for cluster networks. Although you can monitor, add tags, and resize the underlying instance pool, the cluster network manages the majority of instance pool operations.

5.1. CLUSTER-BASED NETWORKS

→Learning Objectives

- Identify the components and characteristics of cluster-based network architectures
- Implement and configure routing protocols to facilitate efficient data transmission and communication within cluster-based networks

Large dynamic networks can be controlled more effectively by using resources thanks to cluster-based network control structures. They make excellent candidates for ad hoc networks as a result. Cluster-based architectures come in various varieties. In particular, the link-cluster architecture is made for managing transmission in ad hoc networks. The clustering techniques used for backbone formation are virtual subnet architecture and Near-Term Digital Radio Network (NTDR) architecture. The preferred method for increasing routing efficiency in cluster-based networks is hierarchical routing, whether it is strict or quasi-hierarchical.

An entity with dynamically changing states in an unpredictable way is a communication network. A network must be able to modify its behavior to account for variations in its inherent characteristics, such as connectivity, capacity, and offered load, in order to achieve performance targets set for user traffic. The following goals are in competition with each other for control functions that govern the network's performance:

- Quick and accurate response when adapting the network's behavior to the current network state.
- Minimal use of network resources during and after the adaptation process.

Self-organizing controlled structures work better for networks with fluctuating connectivity (e.g., mobile networks) or those that are large with numerous configuration parameters. Nodes construct and maintain these structures, leading to increased network availability, faster response to state changes, and reduced risk of configuration errors. Depending on the control functions to be carried out, the size of the network, and the anticipated frequency and magnitude of changes in network state, the proper network control structure and algorithms for using this type of structure are selected.

Applicability of these structures and algorithms to ad hoc networks is also investigated, particularly on routing functions. A cluster-based control network improves efficiency of resource use by creating contexts for:

- Managing wireless transmission among multiple nodes to reduce channel contention.
- Forming routing backbones to reduce network diameter.
- Abstracting network state information to reduce its quantity and variability.

5.1.1. Cluster Based Network Architectures

The cluster based control structures used in ad hoc networks to achieve specific purposes are described below.

5.1.1.1. Link-Cluster Architecture

Broadcast environments with multiple access use this kind of architecture. Different node clusters are arranged so that transmissions are controlled without contention, which lowers interference. All network nodes in this architecture autonomously group together into interconnected clusters. As seen in Figure 5.1, each cluster consists of a cluster head, one or more gateways, and zero or more regular nodes. The cluster head distributes resources among the clusters and plans transmissions. Adjacent clusters are linked by gateways. A gateway can form an indirect connection between two clusters by joining one and creating a link to a member of the other, or it can form a direct connection between two clusters as members of both. As a result, the architecture may have clusters that overlap or are disjoint.

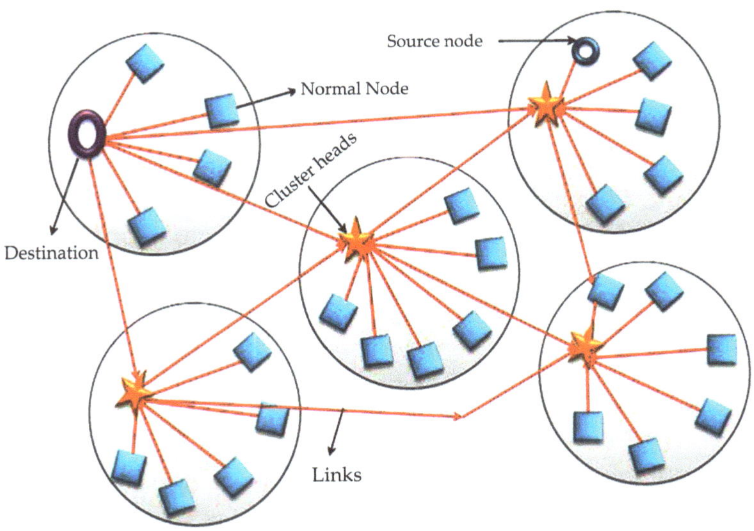

Figure 5.1. The Link-Clustered Architecture (Source: Springer, https://media.springernature.com/m685/springer-static/image/art%3A10.1007%2Fs12083-021-01175-6/MediaObjects/12083_2021_1175_Fig1_HTML.png).

Nodes establish a link-clustered architecture over a physical network by the following:

1. Discovering neighbors with bi-directional connectivity by broadcasting a list of those neighbors that they can hear and by receiving broadcasts from neighbors.

2. Electing cluster heads and forming clusters.
3. Agreeing on gateways between clusters.

5.1.1.2. Cluster Heads

For the purpose of electing cluster heads, at least two algorithms—identifier-based clustering and connectivity-based clustering—have been proposed. Both algorithms can be implemented centrally or distributedly. In the centralized version, the cluster head for the cluster that consists of that node and its one-hop neighbors is determined by looking at the node with the greatest number of neighbors (connectivity-based) or the lowest number of neighbors (identifier-based). A node that has the lowest or highest numbered identifier in its neighborhood elects itself when using the distributed version of identifier-based clustering. If a node is the most highly connected among all of its neighbors who are not chosen to be cluster heads, it becomes a cluster head in the distributed version of connectivity-based clustering. The literature also describes variants of clustering algorithms that, for the two methods mentioned above, always form disjoint clusters. In those situations, cluster heads serve as coordinators of intra-cluster transmission only, not as facilitators of cluster formation.

5.1.1.3. Node Mobility

To ensure accurate transmission scheduling, cluster membership must be updated in line with node movements within the network. Whenever a node joins or leaves a cluster, the clustering algorithms as described by Baker, Ephremidis, Wieselthier, Gerla, and Tsai recalculate the cluster membership, cluster head, and gateway status. In the cluster recompilation approach, identifier-based clustering proves to be more stable than connectivity-based clustering. This is attributed to the potential for more frequent changes in a node's cluster head status when utilizing connectivity-based clustering. The algorithm that minimizes cluster changes reduces the number of cluster head status alterations caused by node movements. Changes in cluster head status only occur when two cluster heads come within range of each other, leading one of them to relinquish their cluster head status, or when a regular node moves out of range of any other node and assumes the role of cluster head for its own cluster. Lin and Gerla also propose cluster maintenance strategies to minimize the impact of node movements on the existing cluster set.

Keyword

Connectivity-based clustering is based on the core idea of objects being more related to nearby objects than to objects farther away.

5.1.1.4. Routing

A naturally occurring routing backbone made up of cluster heads, gateways, and the links connecting them is provided by the link-clustered architecture. Nevertheless, cluster heads could become clogged as hubs for traffic, and each one could end up being a communication breakdown point for the cluster as a whole. For this reason, routing algorithms do not use link-clustered architecture as their routing control architecture. Rather, every node creates and chooses routes, distributes and gathers routing data. In a link-clustered architecture, clusters serve as a routing backbone and are primarily used to define regions for transmission management.

5.1.1.5. Near-Term Digital Radio (NTDR)

Large tactical networks are where Network Near-Term Digital Radio (NTDR) networking is meant to be applied and deployed.. This is one of the backbone formation clustering techniques. As seen in Figure 5.2, NTDR generates a collection of clusters, each with a cluster head, which are connected to form a routing backbone. It is similar to link-clustered architecture in that it consists of a single level of clusters with nodes within one hop of a cluster head. NTDR architecture is not the same as link-clustered architecture in the following ways, though. Cluster heads serve as intermediaries for direct communication between clusters. All communication within the cluster must pass through the cluster head, with the exception of nodes that are adjacent to each other and only require a single hop.

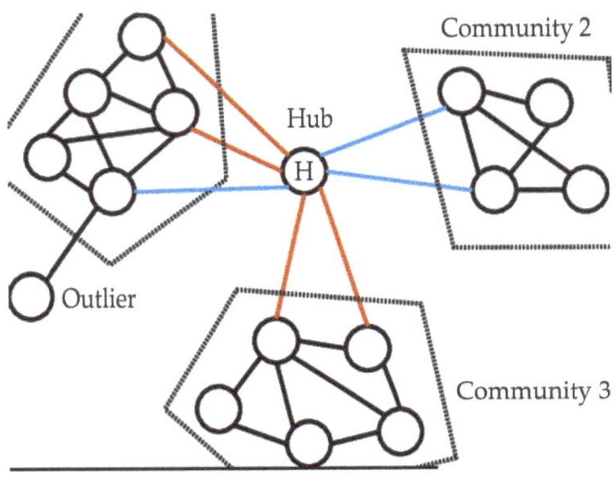

Figure 5.2. The NTDR Network Architecture (Source: Researchgate, https://www.researchgate.net/profile/Symeon-Papadopoulos/publication/284104416/figure/fig4/AS:667840692617225@1536237037913/Hub-specificity-calculation-Blue-lines-indicate-visual-edges-with-weight-exceeding-th-d.png).

Any node has the ability to take over as cluster head quickly in the event that frequent node movements or cluster head outages necessitate changes in node interconnectivity. By periodically broadcasting and receiving beacons, each node maintains bi-directional connectivity with its neighbors.

5.1.1.6. Cluster Heads

If an NTDR node receives beacons advertising two different partition identifiers or does not receive any beacons from any cluster heads, it elects itself as a cluster head. The NTDR algorithm uses the following mechanisms to limit the number of nodes simultaneously attempting to become cluster heads:

- Each node that detects one of the conditions for becoming a cluster head waits a short random time interval and tests the conditions again. If the condition persists following the waiting period, the node assumes the role of a cluster head.
- Each new cluster head immediately issues beacons in quick succession proclaiming its status.

5.1.1.7. Cluster Affiliation

A node seeking cluster affiliation prefers clusters in which

- The node and the cluster head belong to the same organization.
- The signal from the cluster head is transmitted at low power but received at high strength.
- The resulting cluster size is relatively small.
- A cluster member remains affiliated with its chosen cluster head until one of the following occurs:
- The cluster head relinquishes its role.
- The cluster head's beacons no longer list the member.
- The received signal strength from the cluster head is unacceptably low.

5.1.1.8. Routing

The cluster heads in the NTDR network are in charge of keeping the backbone stable, so they keep an eye on it and share information about any changes with one another. To communicate with other cluster heads, each cluster head generates link state information about its links and membership information about its cluster. It floods the backbone with data and uses that data to compute routes to other network nodes. A "resistance" metric, which quantifies the likelihood of interference that upcoming transmissions over the links may experience, is included in the link state. Cluster heads use Dijkstra's shortest path-first (SPF) algorithm to calculate least resistance routes to destinations.

5.1.1.9. Virtual Subnet Architecture

In a multihop mobile wireless network, the virtual subnet architecture uses a number of disjoint routing backbones to provide fault-tolerant connectivity and load balancing. The network is first split into a number of physical subnets of disjoint clusters based on the node locality. Virtual subnets, which span all physical subnets, are created by grouping together members of various physical subnets.

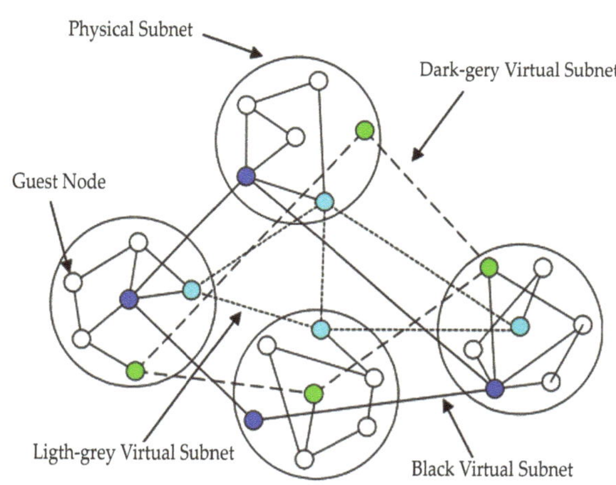

Figure 5.3. The virtual Subnet Architecture (Source: Semanticscholar, https://d3i71xaburhd42.cloudfront.net/df535cc40f672e2f9003a73de4ac8facb58f9e5a/3-Figure3-1.png).

To minimize interference, distinct frequencies are assigned for communication between adjacent physical subnets and all virtual subnets. In the network, the maximum number of virtual subnets, Q, and the maximum number of physical subnets, P, are predefined. As illustrated in Figure 5.3, every node belongs to exactly one physical subnet and zero or more virtual subnets. If a node communicates regularly with the members of multiple virtual subnets, it may be considered a member of those subnets.

The prefix of a node's address, which represents the physical subnet, and the suffix of its address, which represents the virtual subnet, allow it to be uniquely identified as a node within this cluster-based control structure. A node will have multiple addresses and address suffixes if it is a member of multiple virtual subnets. An ad hoc network can be organized and used with multiple overlaid routing backbones using the virtual subnet architecture. Therefore, before it could be realized as an actual ad hoc network, a full set of networking algorithms compatible with this architecture, such as subnet clustering, frequency assignment, distribution of address and routing information, computing of routes, and packet forwarding, would need to be specified.

5.1.1.10. Node Mobility

A node might have to join a new virtual subnet and another physical subnet when it moves to remain connected to the network. If all nearby physical subnets have reached their virtual subnet limits, the node can connect as a "guest" to one of them. If there's space available, the node can then become a member. It will then inform all members of its new physical and virtual subnets about its new address. The source node uses a unique identifier to distribute an address query within its physical subnet before trying to communicate with the destination node. If the destination is associated with a virtual subnet represented by a member of the source's physical subnet, the destination's address will be sent back to the source. Otherwise, the source will distribute the address query within its virtual subnet. If the destination is currently linked to a physical subnet indicated by some, the destination's address will be returned.

5.1.1.11. Routing

When there are multiple routes available within a virtual subnet architecture, a source can more quickly and effectively find a different route to their destination and, as a result, maintain their current session even when nodes move and the network's connectivity changes. Two approaches are recommended for multiple forwarding. First, there is direct routing, where packets are forwarded to the destination based only on source and destination addresses from the source. Packets are forwarded through a node if it is discovered in a manner that allows it to be a part of both the destination's virtual subnet and the source's physical subnet, as indicated in Figure 5.4(a). As seen in Figure 5.4(b), packets are routed via a node that is a member of both the destination's physical subnet and the source's virtual subnet if the destination node is a guest of a physical subnet.

However, in the presence of highly mobile nodes, this straightforward routing might not be feasible. The second technique is long-path routing, which helps the network support divided subnets and distribute traffic load evenly among nodes by randomly distributing the routes chosen over the space of feasible routes. One of the virtual subnets contained in its physical subnet is randomly selected by the source. Packets will be routed to a node that is a member of both the selected virtual subnet and the physical subnet of the source if it is not a member of that virtual subnet. As seen in Figure 5.5(a), routing is then carried out to a member node of the destination's physical subnet as well as the virtual subnet of choice. As demonstrated in Figure 5.5(b), if the source is a part of the selected virtual subnet, it will arbitrarily choose a different physical subnet from its own that is represented within the virtual subnet and route packets through it to the destination.

Remember

If every subnet is connected, long-path routing generates at most Q+P-1 distinct routes from a source to a destination. The number of possible routes increases when there are partitioned subnets because each intermediate node along the route might have to choose at random the next hop subnet to route around such partitions.

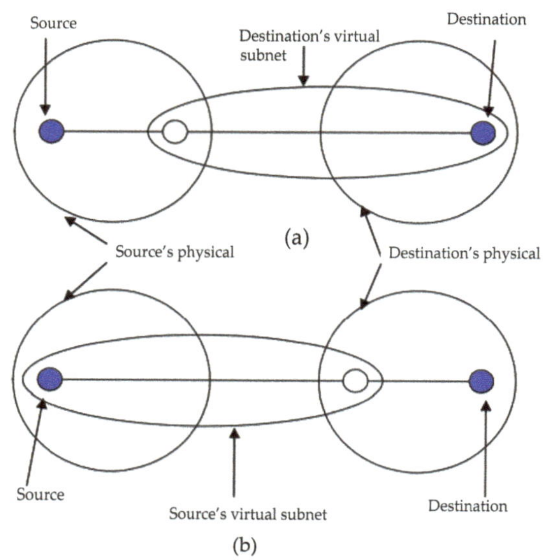

Figure 5.4. Direct Routing (Source: Semanticscholar, https://d3i71xaburhd42.cloudfront.net/df535cc40f672e2f9003a73de4ac8facb58f9e5a/4-Figure4-1.png).

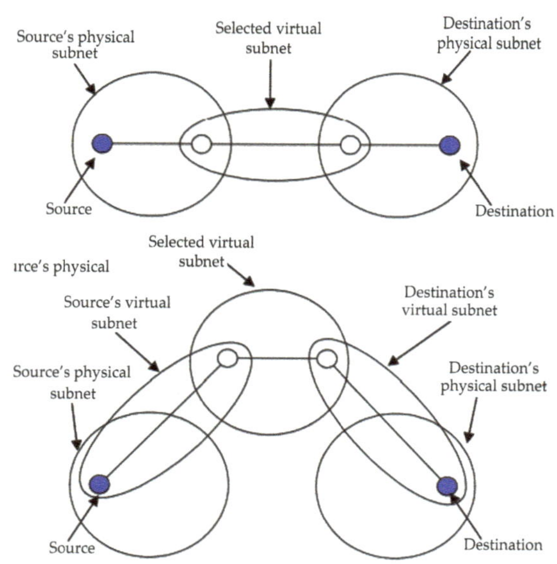

Figure 5.5. Long-Path Routing (Source: Semanticscholar, https://d3i71xaburhd42.cloudfront.net/df535cc40f672e2f9003a73de4ac8facb58f9e5a/5-Figure5-1.png).

Consequently, a route's length may grow significantly. Nonetheless, nodes can shorten routes by providing additional details about their interconnectivity and utilizing those details to choose a shorter path. As a result, nodes may choose a routing strategy that combines the first two mentioned above.

5.1.2. Routing in Cluster-Based Networks

The inherently dynamic nature of ad hoc networks poses challenges in the design of effective yet efficient routing functions. Routing functions are the focus of this section.

5.1.2.1. Hierarchical Routing

A hierarchical cluster-based control structure is a network consisting of N nodes organized into an m-level hierarchy of nested clusters of nodes, as shown in Figure 5.6, such that all level-i clusters are disjoint for 0≤i<m.

Every node is a cluster at level 0. They are organized into level-1 clusters, which are then organized into level-2 clusters, and so on, until all level-(m-1) clusters are finally organized into a single level-m cluster that is made up of every node. This kind of nested cluster structure uses a hierarchical addressing scheme. The concatenation of the labels of the level-(m-1) through level-0 clusters that contain the node is how the address is expressed. For instance, the address of node z in the clustering hierarchy shown in Figure 5.6 is x.y.z, with u acting as the implicit prefix. The disjointness criterion is not a prerequisite for routing schemes to function properly in the presence of non-ancestral clusters.

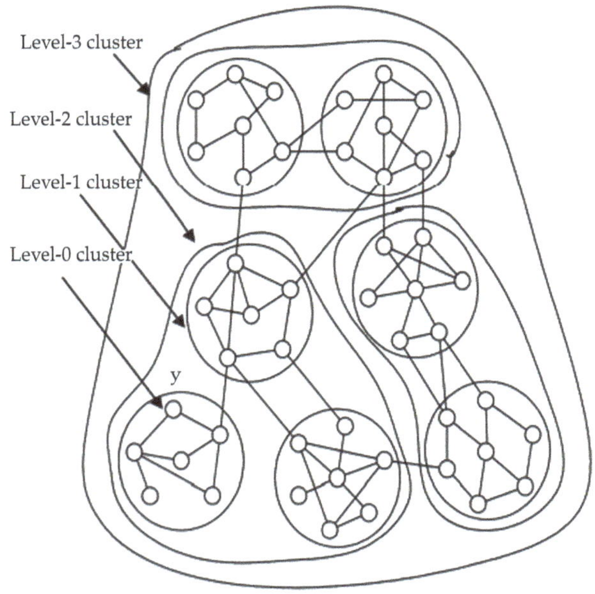

Figure 5.6. The Nested Cluster Architecture (Source: Semanticscholar, https://d3i71xaburhd42.cloudfront.net/df535cc40f672e2f9003a73de4ac8facb58f9e5a/5-Figure6-1.png).

One can categorize the hierarchical routing scheme as strictly hierarchical or quasi-hierarchical. The following example clarifies how they differ from one another. Assume for the moment that the lowest-level cluster, ck, contains a session's source and destination. A packet is routed directly from the source, s0, to the boundary of dk-1, the level-(k-1) cluster of the destination, d0, when using quasi-hierarchical routing. After that, the packet is routed straight to the dk-2 boundary, the level-(k-2) cluster of d0, and so on, until it is ultimately routed straight from the d1 boundary to d0. A packet is routed indirectly from s0 to the edge of sk-1, s0's level-(k-1) cluster, using strict-hierarchical routing. Initially, the packet is sent straight from s0 to s1's edge. It is then routed via s2's level-1 clusters until it reaches the s2 boundary, and so on, until it reaches the sk-1 boundary. The packet is routed through level-(k-1) clusters in ck to reach the boundary of dk-1 after it reaches the boundary of sk-1. The packet is then routed through dk-1's level-(k-2) clusters to get to dk-2's border, and so on, until it is ultimately routed to di.

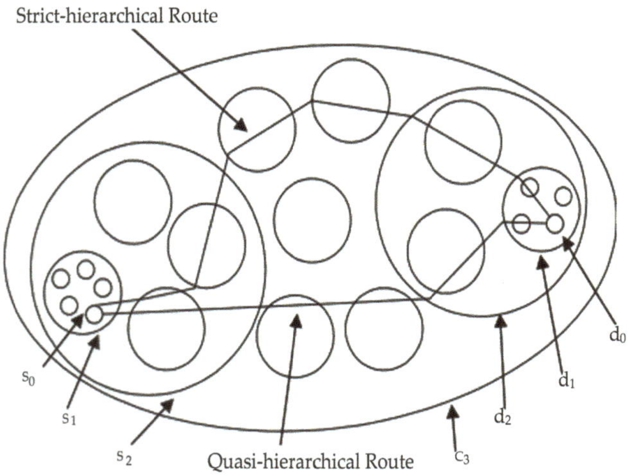

Figure 5.7. Quasi-hierarchical Routing versus Stricthierarchical Routing (Source: Semanticscholar, https://d3i71xaburhd42.cloudfront.net/df535cc40f672e2f9003a73de4ac8facb58f9e5a/6-Figure7-1.png).

5.1.2.2. Quasi-Hierarchical Routing

The quasi-hierarchical category includes the majority of hierarchical cluster-based routing systems. Moreover, the distance vector routing technique is the basis for nearly all quasi-hierarchical routing schemes. In this case, the objective is to determine the next hop on the minimum-cost route from a node to each level-i cluster within the node's level-(i+1) cluster, for $0 \leq i < m$. The information about routing inside the cluster is not distributed outside the cluster.

Link-state routing can also serve as the foundation for quasi-hierarchical routing. Nodes create, share, and utilize hierarchical routing information in the following ways when using this scheme. Every node in a level-1 cluster floods its link-state information, which is expressed as the link cost to its neighboring nodes, to other nodes in the cluster. Next, using Dijkstra's SPF algorithm, each node creates a minimum-cost route to every other node in the cluster. Every gate node on a cluster boundary computes every other gate for the cluster using intra-cluster link-state information. Next, a gate builds link-state information in the form of costs over virtual links to "neighboring" gates, both in the gate's immediate vicinity and in neighboring clusters that are directly connected to it. This link-state data is flooded by the gate to every other gate in every level-1 cluster. Next, every gate within the network creates the least expensive paths to every other gate, and consequently, to every other cluster within the network. Additionally, every gate floods all other clusters with its minimum costs through its intra-cluster nodes. A node can ascertain the n by fusing this intra-cluster link-state information with the inter-cluster cost information.

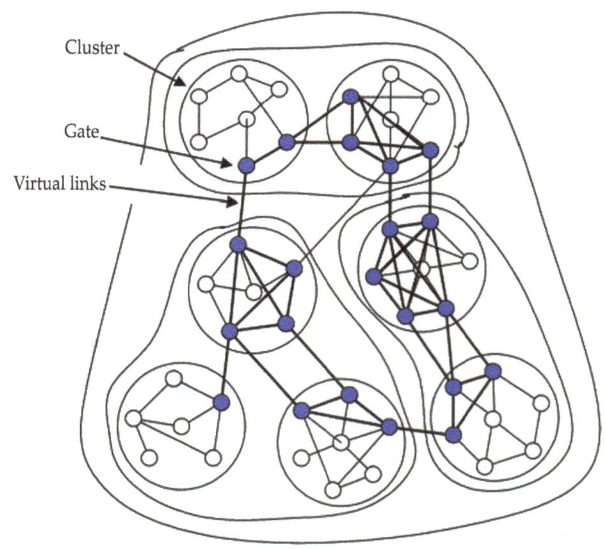

Figure 5.8. The Link-State Routing Architecture with Gates (Source: Citeseerx, https://d3i71xaburhd42.cloudfront.net/df535cc40f672e2f9003a73de4ac8facb58f9e5a/6-Figure8-1.png).

Large tactical packet radio networks can use hybrid routing schemes, such as distance-vector and link-state quasi-hierarchical routing schemes. This hybrid plan was proposed for the **SURAN (Survivable Adaptive Networks)** initiative. The next hop on the least-cost route to each destination is ultimately determined by each node using distance-vector routing in this scheme; however, for destinations outside of its cluster, the distance-vector routing information is partially derived from link-state data between clusters and superclusters. Certain nodes are used as routing focal points in quasi-hierarchical routing schemes like landmark routing and regional node routing. When a packet is being forwarded from source to destination, the focal nodes assist other nodes in making decisions about it. Every level-k cluster, also known as a "k-region," has one or more k-regional nodes, with the exception of the top-level m-region, when using regional node routing. Figure 5.9 below shows the addressing scheme and node affiliations to regions.

Keyword

Survivable Adaptive Networks (SURAN) refer to networks designed to withstand and adapt to various types of disruptions or attacks, ensuring continuity of critical communication and services.

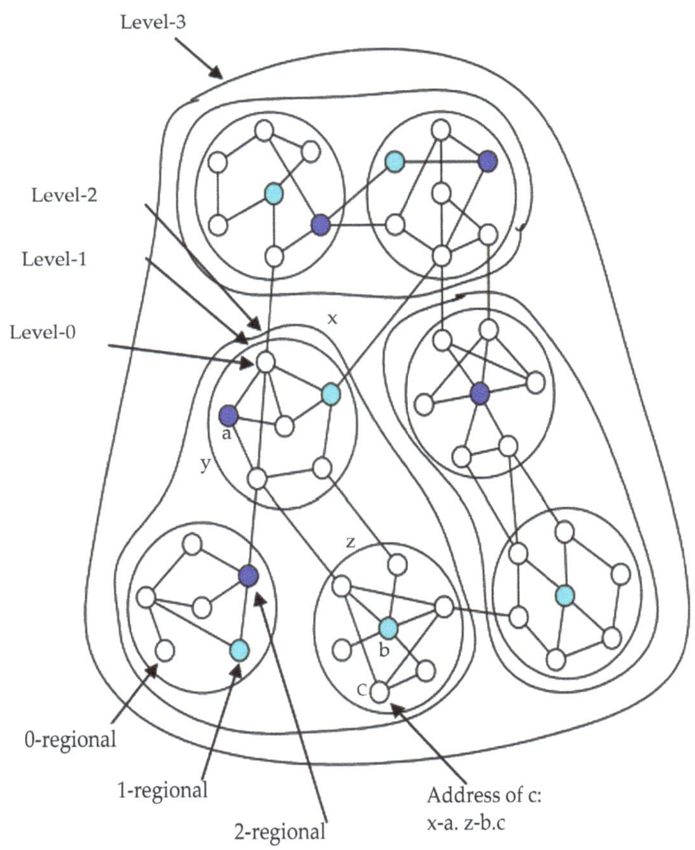

Figure 5.9. The Regional Node Routing Architecture (Source: Citeseerx, https://citeseerx.ist.psu.edu/document?repid=rep1&type=pdf&doi=df535cc40f672e2f9003a73de4ac8facb58f9e5a).

With landmark routing, each level-i landmark, x, defines a level-i cluster consisting of all nodes that are within the radius of ri(x) node hops from x, where 0 < ri(x) ≤ ri and ri is the maximum radius permitted for the level-i cluster. Each level-m landmark has a radius that is at least as large as the diameter of the network, and each node is a level-0 landmark. For $0 < i \leq m$, more than one level-i landmark is also a level-(i+1) landmark, and for each such landmark, y, ri+1(y) > ri(y).

5.1.2.3. Strict-Hierarchical Routing

Because it is resilient to changes in the network state, strict-hierarchical routing is a preferred method in mobile wireless networks. Comparing the robustness to quasi-statistical routing, higher route costs and packet forwarding overhead result from the robustness. Using either the distance-vector or the link-state approach, a representative of a level-i cluster, c, gathers its routing data and distributes it to representatives of other level-i clusters within its level-(i+1) cluster. Within its level-(i+1) cluster, c's representative calculates the next-hop clusters and minimum-cost routes from c to any other level-i clusters using routing information similarly obtained from other clusters. The representative of c then sends the cluster boundary information, route cost, and next-hop cluster information to every node inside c.

There are two key differences between strict-hierarchical routing and quasi-hierarchical routing with respect to forwarding information. The first difference concerns the number of forwarding table entries a node must consult to determine the next-hop node to a destination. With quasi-hierarchical routing, the next hop to level-i cluster c' stored in the forwarding table is always a node which is a neighbor of node x. With strict-hierarchical routing, the next hop to c' stored in the forwarding table is always a cluster at level $j \leq i$, as explained below. For an entry for c' to appear in x's forwarding table, c' and x's level-i cluster, c, must be siblings within x's level-(i+1) cluster. If c' and c are non-neighboring siblings, the next hop to c' is a level-i cluster that is a neighbor of c. If c' and c are neighboring siblings, the next hop to c' is a level-j cluster, where $0 \leq j < 1$, that lies on the boundary of c and contains at least one node, y, with a direct link to c'. With quasi-hierarchical routing, a node can determine the next hop to any destination using a single forwarding table entry, whereas with strict-hierarchical routing, a node may have to consult up to 2m-1 forwarding table entries to determine the next-hop node to a destination. In practice, m remains small.

The expenses of the routes that the forwarding entries are derived from are the subject of the second distinction. Since the cost to reach the level-i cluster, c', from x is calculated as the sum of the individual link costs, it is always the true minimum cost when using quasi-hierarchical routing. The total of each cluster cost for each level-i in the route from c to c' is the cost to reach c' from x when using strict-hierarchical routing. As a result, the latter routing is probably going to produce more expensive routes than the former one. For the SURAN packet radio network, the strict-hierarchical routing scheme below was selected due to its ability to maintain routes in the face of dynamically changing nodes and links. To find the lowest cost routes and next-hop nodes to every node in its cluster and to every neighboring cluster within its supercluster, each node employs distance vector routing. The cluster head, also known as the super-cluster head, is a node within each cluster or supercluster, as depicted in Figure 5.10. This node is in charge of creating and disseminating routing information about the cluster to all other clusters or superclusters within the same supercluster (or network).

Did you know?

A 2003 measurement study of Internet routes found that, between pairs of neighboring ISPs, more than 30% of paths have inflated latency due to hot-potato routing, with 5% of paths being delayed by at least 12 ms. Inflation due to AS-level path selection, while substantial, was attributed primarily to BGP's lack of a mechanism to directly optimize for latency, rather than to selfish routing policies.

The connectivity and cost to each neighboring clusterhead (or super-clusterhead) are determined by each clusterhead (or super-clusterhead). It then inundates all clusterheads (or super-clusterheads) within its supercluster (or network) with this link-state data. The number of node hops to the neighboring clusterhead (or superclusterhead), the number of cluster hops to the neighboring superclusterhead, and the value 1 to indicate inter(super)cluster connectivity only are among the suggested costs from one clusterhead (or super-clusterhead).

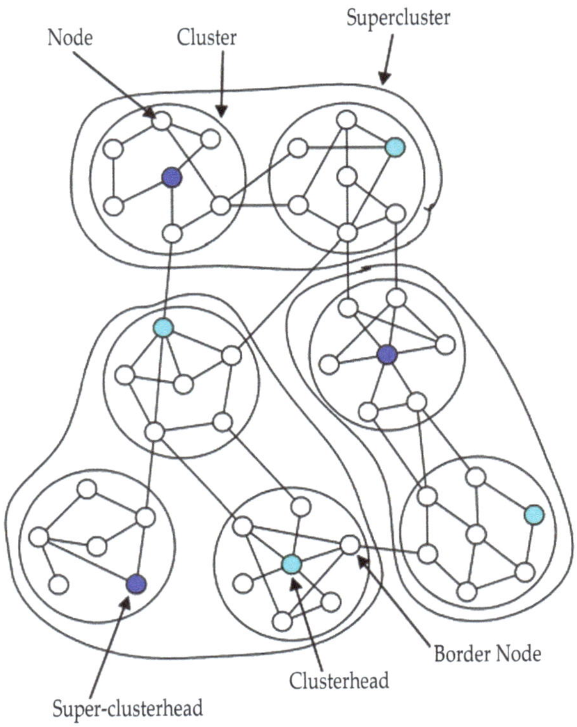

Figure 5.10. The SURAN Routing Architecture (Source: Citeseerx, https://citeseerx.ist.psu.edu/document?repid=rep1&type=pdf&doi=df535cc40f672e2f9003a73de4ac8facb58f9e5a).

In tactical packet radio networks, a hybrid strict-hierarchical routing scheme is employed in large networks. Regarding forwarding table entries, this routing scheme is strict-hierarchical; however, with regard to the granularity and dissemination of routing information, it is quasi-hierarchical. In order to find the least expensive route and the next hop that corresponds to each node in its level-1 cluster, each node engages in distance-vector routing. It also adds the discovery of the level-1 cluster's boundary nodes and their connectivity to neighboring clusters. The next hop is a neighboring node, and route cost within a level-1 cluster is expressed in terms of the number of node hops. Global routing nodes supply the data needed for routing outside of a node's level-1 cluster. A global routing node serves as a cluster representative in each level-1 cluster. The quasi-hierarchical routing process is carried out by global routing nodes.

The link-based strict-hierarchical routing schemes described below were designed to provide quality of service routing in large dynamic networks. Both schemes have the following features:

- Nodes represent and distribute routing information according to the link-state approach, at all levels of the clustering hierarchy.
- Nodes select routes with the objective of satisfying individual users' service requests given the constraints imposed by the current state of the network, and they forward packets as directed by the sources.

Keyword

Virtual gateway allows resources that are outside of your mesh to communicate to resources that are inside of your mesh.

In the context of providing quality of service, the destination-based packet forwarding used by hierarchical routing schemes up to this point is insufficient. Source-directed forwarding increases the likelihood of successful packet delivery by guaranteeing that various nodes make forwarding decisions consistent with the route chosen by the source, in addition to providing quality of service. Furthermore, smaller forwarding tables are typically the outcome of source-directed forwarding. A node does not need to keep up a forwarding table when using explicit-route forwarding. A node's forwarding table size in virtual-circuit forwarding is directly correlated with the number of virtual circuits it participates in. The number of destinations for which a node has received routing information directly relates to the size of the node's forwarding table when using destination-based forwarding.

A strict hierarchical routing scheme, or MMWN, is created for large mobile wireless networks that support multimedia. The MMWN nested-cluster architecture is shown in Figure 5.11. Every node in this architecture is a level-0 cluster, but the number of ancestral clusters varies between two different nodes. As a result, a cluster may be connected to more than one level in the clustering hierarchy, and the maximum level connected to the single cluster that contains every other cluster is how the height of the hierarchy is expressed. As long as two clusters share the same parent cluster, they are regarded as siblings even if they appear at different levels of the clustering hierarchy. If at least one pair of border nodes, one in each cluster, have a direct link, then sibling clusters may form a connecting virtual gateway. The border nodes in each of the two clusters along with their connecting links make up a *virtual gateway*. The endpoints of a virtual link that spans a cluster are two virtual gateways that are connected to the cluster. At least one QoS manager is present in every cluster, producing abstracted link-state data such as connectivity to the cluster, services (e.g., disperses the data to other clusters, and transfers the data (delay, throughput, loss rate) throughout the cluster and to nearby clusters. A cluster's QoS manager broadcasts link-state updates to every node in the parent cluster.

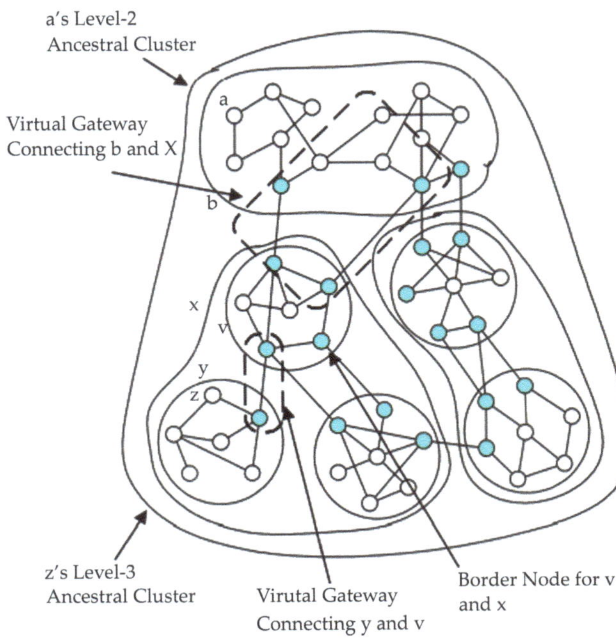

Figure 5.11. The MMWN Routing Architecture (Source: Citeseerx, https://citeseerx.ist.psu.edu/document?repid=rep1&type=pdf&doi=df535cc40f672e2f9003a73de4ac8facb58f9e5a).

A node makes an effort to create routes that are compatible with the users' service requests and the network's existing capabilities using this link-state information. There exists an opportunity to greatly minimize the amount of network state data that needs to be dispersed, processed, and stored across a network by utilizing hierarchical cluster-based control structures. It is accomplished by abstracting away the specifics of a cluster's connectivity and services, and expressing the cluster's state in this way. However, balancing the abstraction's fidelity and size is necessary to build a workable abstraction for a cluster whose features vary widely or often. All abstraction techniques, however, have in common that a cluster's connectivity and services are expressed in terms of the cluster's neighboring clusters, which serve as the cluster's entry and exit points.

Did you get it?

1. **How does NTDR differ from traditional analog radio technologies, and what are its key advantages?**
2. **How can quasi-hierarchical routing be implemented and optimized to improve network performance and scalability?**

5.2. CLUSTERING PROTOCOLS

→Learning Objectives

- Define clustering protocols in the context of network communication
- Explain the LEACH (Low Energy Adaptive Clustering Hierarchy) clustering protocol and its significance in wireless sensor networks.
- Explore the concept of clustering and routing protocols tailored for wireless sensor networks (WSNs).
- Identify the essential components and resources required to establish a cluster networking environment.

As the object is being tracked, the clustering protocol simplifies the transfer of information between cluster heads regarding the object's current state and the uncertainty of its target position. The topology of the hierarchical, non-overlapping sensor node clusters is specified by clustering protocols. A robust clustering method is essential for sensor networks to self-organize. An effective clustering protocol ensures clusters with nearly equal radii and optimally positioned cluster heads. Route discovery among cluster heads is sufficient to establish a workable route in a clustered network since each node is connected to a cluster head. Clustering can reduce the number of transmissions and facilitate multihop route discovery for large sensor networks compared to a flat, non-clustered network.

5.2.1. Classification of Clustering Protocols

Techniques for clustering can be decentralized or centralized. Each sensor node must transmit its unique data, including its location and energy level, to the central base station in order to use centralized clustering algorithms. A base station determines the number of clusters, their sizes, and the positions of the cluster heads using a predetermined algorithm. It then assigns a new duty to each node. Assuming that sensor networks could have thousands of nodes, it is not feasible, if not impossible, for a base station to gather data about each node in the network before setting up a route. For big sensor networks, centralized clustering is therefore not an option. A clustering algorithm should be able to form clusters without the assistance of the base station and knowledge of node positioning, since a sensor node starts a clustering process without any knowledge about its location relative to the corresponding base station. While location-finder devices can also be used for this purpose, they are frequently too expensive or add excessive network overhead.

Clusters are formed using decentralized clustering techniques independently of centralized base stations. Each sensor node has a probability of p to become a cluster head, and it can be achieved by an energy-efficient hierarchical clustering algorithm that broadcasts its candidacy to nodes that are within k hops of the cluster head. There are limits to a hierarchical structure with an arbitrary number of levels because wireless sensor nodes have a limited transmission range. Upper-level cluster heads may become so separated from one another as the number of hierarchical levels rises that they are unable to communicate. Two examples of decentralized clustering protocols are the Decentralized Energy Efficient Cluster Propagation (DEEP) protocol and the Low-Energy Adaptive Clustering Hierarchy (LEACH) algorithm.

5.2.2. LEACH Clustering Protocol

The Low-Energy Adaptive Clustering Hierarchy (LEACH) protocol is a decentralized clustering algorithm that lacks a strategy for defining the positioning and distribution of cluster heads, making it an incomplete energy-optimization solution. By periodically re-clustering and altering the network topology, LEACH is an application-specific protocol architecture that seeks to extend network lifetime. LEACH is divided into rounds consisting of a clustering phase and a steady-state phase for data collection. At the start of each round, a sensor node randomly chooses a number between 0 and 1 and then compares this number to a calculated threshold called T(n). If T(n) is larger than the chosen number, the node becomes a cluster head for the current round. The value T(n) is calculated using the following formula:

$$T(n) = \begin{cases} \frac{p}{1 - p(r mod(1/p))} \text{for } n \in G, \\ 0 \end{cases} otherwise$$

where p is the ratio of the total number of cluster heads to the total number of nodes, r is the number of rounds, and G is a set of nodes that have not been chosen as cluster heads for the last 1/p rounds. For the first round (r=0), T(n) is equal to p, and nodes have an equal chance to become cluster head. As r gets closer to 1/p, T(n) increases, and nodes that have not been selected as cluster head in the last 1/p rounds have more chance to become

Remember

The LEACH algorithm is distributed because it can be carried out locally at each node through computation and communication, as opposed to transmitting the location and energy level of every node to a single point. Nevertheless, there is no energy consumption optimization, and cluster heads are selected at random.

cluster head. After 1/p – 1 rounds, T(n) is equal to 1, meaning that all the remaining nodes have been selected as cluster head. Thus, after 1/p rounds, all the nodes have had a chance to become a cluster head once. Since being the cluster head puts a substantial burden on the sensor nodes, this ensures that the network has no overloaded node that runs out of energy sooner than the others.

Following their self-selection, cluster heads begin to promote themselves to other sensor nodes. A sensor node begins to determine which cluster head it corresponds with when it receives advertisements from multiple cluster-head candidates. Every node pays attention to the signals from the advertisements and selects the candidate whose signal is received with the highest power. By doing this, every sensor node is guaranteed to select the nearest candidate to lead the cluster.

5.2.3. Clustering and Routing Protocol for Wireless Sensor Networks

WSNs are used in a wide range of industries, including manufacturing automation, industry, data collection during wartime, and agricultural environment monitoring, primarily for the perception and transmission of environmental data. A WSN is always made up of one or more sink nodes (SNs), which are responsible for uploading and collecting data, and hundreds of ordinary nodes (ODs). The primary responsibility of the OD is to perceive environmental data, which it then transmits to the SN via a predetermined method to complete the communication. The OD is inexpensive, but its processing power is constrained. ODs are typically distributed randomly throughout the detection space. In certain instances, the installation of some or all nodes at the specified location will be done by hand. For instance, in the context of gathering data during a war, optical distribution (OD) is typically achieved through aircraft sprinkling, whereas in the context of gathering data on underwater detection, nodes are typically placed artificially in their surroundings. Since OD runs solely on batteries, its energy supply is finite and cannot be increased. The two nodes were chosen based on the similarities and differences between their initial energies.

Routing protocols refer to the means of data collection and transmission in a network. Numerous researchers have put forth different WSN routing protocols in recent years. These routing protocols can be separated into single-hop and multi-hop categories based on the data transfer between OD and SN. Whereas in the single-hop routing protocol, OD only communicates with SN via single-hop, in the multi-hop routing protocol, OD and SN can communicate via single-hop or multi-hop. The hierarchical routing protocols originated when the Low-Energy Adaptive Cluster Hierarchical (LEACH) [1] protocol suggested the clustering technique for sensor network development. WSNs divide the OD distributed into two categories: member nodes (MN) and CH. The primary duty of MN is to gather data and forward it via a single hop to the relevant CH. The CH compiles data and sends the message in a single or multiple hop fashion to the SN.

As WSNs develop, certain issues are discovered. To begin with, one of the main issues limiting the network's lifespan is the imbalance in network load. Within the WSNs, nodes with the same starting energy are dispersed, and during each data collection round, the energy consumption of each node varies. High energy consumption nodes die more quickly, reducing network coverage or causing SN to become an island, which ultimately results in the failure of WSNs. Second, the issue of "hot point," which arises from the phenomenon of network load imbalance, is the situation in which certain nodes in the network experience significantly higher network loads than other nodes because of issues with routing protocols or node distribution. These two issues cannot be avoided by any protocol in WSNs where nodes are assigned at random. The only way to lessen it is to try balancing the network load as much as possible using different techniques.

When it comes to WSN research, the majority of researchers presume that the application environment is two-dimensional. Most WSNs are still used in 3D application scenarios in real life, despite the fact that there is one application scenario that can be thought of as a 2D environment with minimal fluctuation. It is possible to use the 2D routing protocol in a 3D environment. Under the same circumstances, the LEACH protocol's performance in 2D and 3D space is simulated. It is discovered that the lifetime of the LEACH protocol in 3D space is decreased by roughly 21% when compared to the LEACH protocol in 2D space. It is established that the traditional protocol's 2D approximation of the environment is illogical. Nodes in a 3D environment typically use more energy than those in a 2D environment because of issues with the 3D environment's structure. It is easy to demonstrate that SN is at the center of the network if there are an equal number of nodes uniformly distributed in the sphere with radius R and in the circular plane area. In both environments, it is not difficult to find through the formula of the circular area S=2πr2 and the formula of sphere volume V=4/3πr3. The proportion of the number of nodes with a distance less than r to the total number of nodes is reduced from (r/R)2 in 2D space to (r/R)3 in 3D space, that is to say, in 3D space nodes with a distance less than R have only r/R in 2D space. The number of nodes in the area closer to SN decreases more obviously. When the network coverage is broad, the total number of nodes close to the SN in 2D WSNs will be several times that in 3D WSNs.

The average distance between a node and the sink increases when the percentage of nodes that are close to the sink decreases. The LEACH protocol shows a positive correlation between node energy consumption and inter-node distance. The average distance will eventually rise, which will result in higher energy usage and a shorter lifespan for the LEACH protocol. Not only that, but when the multi-hop routing protocol was used, the number of nodes near the convergence node decreased, which also decreased the network's load balance. It is inevitable to designate the nodes within one hop of the SN as the relay nodes in the majority of multi-hop routing protocols. The network load imbalance gets worse when the number of relay nodes decreases because the load on the remaining relay nodes increases. It is critical to develop an energy optimization protocol for load balancing in order to address the issues of energy consumption and load imbalance in 3DWSNs.

The time for each node to broadcast CH claim information is computed based on its residual energy and the average distance between it and surrounding nodes. It is preferred for nodes to be CH if they have a small average distance from the surrounding nodes and a relatively high residual energy. Between CH and MN, two additional identity nodes are added in an effort to balance the network's load and lower energy consumption. The secondary SCH serves as the standby CH, and the other is the load transfer node (LTN), which distributes the communication load among

CH nodes. The CH and SCH nodes are generated in the order specified during the initial clustering process. The SCH nodes immediately take on the role of the new CH during the ensuing clustering process, and only new SCH nodes are created. This protocol generates routing tables by using SN, which has powerful computing power, in place of OD. Through directed flooding, the CH node notifies SN of its location and remaining energy during the network's initial clustering. Each CH's routing table is created by the SN. In accordance with the routing table, the CH node adds data information to the SN node. Consequently, when clustering for the first time in the route construction method, CH nodes only need to let SN nodes know where they are. This greatly lowers the energy consumption during the route construction process because the newly generated CH in the subsequent process only needs to wait for the routing table created by SN nodes. SN uses the fragile collection ant colony algorithm to create the routing table that corresponds to each CH. We propose a load balancing routing algorithm for WSNs called the fragile collection ant colony algorithm. We include the fragile coefficient of every edge, based on the ant colony routing algorithm, so that the ant takes into account the energy of each node along the path in addition to the path's overall length. We compare various routing protocols under the network energy consumption model and the 3D sphere wireless sensor model. The protocol performs better than other protocols in terms of load balancing and network lifetime, according to the results.

5.2.3.1. Work Process

The LEACH protocol is unavoidable when it comes to WSNs. The clustering mechanism is proposed by the LEACH protocol. The CH selection process in the LEACH protocol is comparatively straightforward because it was the first to apply clustering to a WSN. Even so, the introduction of the clustering concept significantly lowers the single-hop distance between any two nodes in the entire network. By creating a random number and establishing the cluster probability, the LEACH protocol chooses CH. To prevent a node from acting as the CH continuously, the nodes that have served as CHs are unable to run for the CH positions in the following round. The CHs are distributed randomly by the LEACH protocol, and it is not possible to influence or direct this process. Only fuzzy control, which modifies the clustering probability, can limit the total number of CHs. This can easily result in a situation where the MN of a particular CH is excessively high, disrupting the network's load balance.

Since LEACH cannot reasonably choose CHs at random, a new clustering algorithm is developed after LEACH. The hybrid energy-efficient distributed (HEED) [4] protocol represents the clustering technique used to calculate CHs. The HEED protocol takes into account the impact of both the nodes' residual energy and the WSN's overall network energy. The selection of CH nodes goes from completely equal probability to unequal probability random, as the nodes with larger residual energy have a higher probability of becoming CH. The remaining energy of nodes influences the choice of CHs to some degree. However, when calculating the clustering probability, the average energy of all the nodes in the network is taken into account. All other nodes must provide energy information to nodes. Consequently, nodes' energy consumption rises. Energy consumption is higher in large-scale networks or networks with a high node density. Nonetheless, it makes sense to calculate the likelihood of nodes turning into CHs using their residual energy.

There are additional clustering techniques. For instance, the dynamic hierarchical clustering in 3D WSNs (3DHCP) energy-optimization clustering routing protocol uses the clustering technique of first determining the ideal number of clusters in the network. The network is divided into the ideal number of clusters, and then appropriate nodes are identified in each region to become CHs. In this way, the network's overall energy consumption is decreased, and its load balance is improved. However, the time required for this clustering method is lengthy, and the size of each cluster cannot be guaranteed. Clusters in the network with a wide size gap are simple to form.

There are two types of routing protocols: single-hop and multi-hop. The aforementioned LEACH, HEED, and 3DHCP protocols are examples of single-hop routing protocols, and situations where there are few nodes and limited network coverage are typical application scenarios for them. The single-hop routing protocol will use a lot more energy if the network coverage is widespread. Using a multi-hop routing protocol makes more sense when there is extensive network coverage. Through the energy-efficient uneven clustering (EEUC) protocol, the nodes have multi-hop communication with the SN. Data is directly transferred to the SN by CHs with communication capabilities after the clustering phase. Other CHs utilize a greedy algorithm to determine their next-hop by calculating the distance from other nodes, on the assumption that data forwarding to the SN completes the communication. In order to balance the network's load and lower energy consumption, the EEUC protocol uses multi-hop and non-uniform clustering.

However, it employs the "use and throws" clustering technique. Following clustering, the CH gathers and transmits node data to the SN; if the cluster fails right away, the network will initiate a fresh round of CH selection. Frequent replacement of the CH prevents the "hot point" issue that arises when a node serves as CH for an extended period of time; however, excessive clustering also increases total energy consumption and shortens network life. Next, we conduct experiments to ascertain this protocol's ideal clustering period.

In actuality, building multi-hop routing for some of the existing multi-hop WSN protocols is not too difficult. For instance, in order to guarantee data transmission in the SN direction, the sending CH chooses the relay node when the EEUC protocol builds the routing path by measuring the distance between the candidate CH and itself. Through flooding, the Advanced Zonal Stable Election Protocol (AZ-SEP) protocol connects CHs located far from the SN to the SN. However, in recent years, researchers have discovered that the network's load balance and energy consumption will be impacted by the routing system's construction. As a result, numerous novel approaches to route building are put forth. For instance, the Unequal Clustering Routing Protocol (UCNPD) takes into account energy balancing based on network partition and distance and expands nodes' sensing range while increasing the routing path's consideration factors when establishing communication between clusters. In the building inter-cluster routing stage, UCNPD adopts a reasonable approach to increase the sensing range of nodes and uses the nodes' remaining energy as the deciding factor for next-hop selection. Nonetheless, the growth of.

Additionally, the route construction process gradually applies the sophisticated *path planning algorithm.* Using an enhanced ant colony algorithm (PEG-ant) protocol,

PEGASIS in WSN creates a routing chain connecting every node by applying the ant colony algorithm. The PEGASIS protocol in the 3D application environment is enhanced by the PEG-GA (PEGASIS in 3DWSN) protocol, which links nodes into the chain using a genetic algorithm rather than a greedy one to produce the node chain with the shortest length.

The ant colony algorithm is used in the adaptive periodic threshold-sensitive energy-efficient sensor network (APTEEN) protocol to create multi-hop routing. The network's performance has somewhat improved as a result of these protocols. However, in order to use the routing algorithm to build routing, the OD must have a large amount of computing and storage capacity. Additionally, building inter-cluster routing will require more energy to run. Since the node is widely dispersed throughout the network, an increase in OD costs will result in a significant rise in the network's overall cost. As a result, we suggest a way to create routing paths using SN without raising the price of common nodes.

Keyword

Path planning algorithms are used in various fields such as robotics, computer graphics, video games, and navigation systems to find an optimal path from a starting point to a goal while avoiding obstacles or considering constraints.

The ant colony algorithm, a well-developed path search algorithm, can be used to create routing paths since it is frequently used to resolve point-to-point path planning and the traveling salesman problem (TSP). To better adapt to the environment of WSNs, there are a few differences between the application conditions of the ant colony algorithm and WSNs that need to be addressed.

Nodes in a cluster determine how long it will take to send cluster head claim information by calculating their distance and relative energy from other nodes in the cluster. To balance the network load and lower the energy consumption of the network routing path construction process, we have introduced two new roles, SCH and LTN, to the cluster. Regarding the creation of routing paths, we suggest a novel approach that shifts the responsibility for path construction from OD to SN. According to simulation results, the suggested cluster routing protocol improves network load balance and efficiently lowers network energy consumption.

This makes the following main contributions.

- The reasons for the performance degradation of the two-dimensional wireless sensor network routing protocol in three-dimensional wireless sensor networks are analyzed.
- A new model for measuring the fitness value of the cluster head is proposed. Considering the relative distance between the nodes and the surrounding nodes, the nodes with a smaller average distance from the surrounding nodes have a higher probability to become cluster heads.

- The SN replaces the OD and cooperates with the cluster head update mechanism to generate a routing table corresponding to each cluster head.
- A new path-finding algorithm based on the ant colony algorithm is proposed, which is more suitable for wireless sensor network routing construction. The algorithm not only considers the total length of the generated path but also the energy of the nodes that the path passes through.

5.2.4. Prepare Cluster Networking Infrastructure

This part describes the cluster network preparation required for the installation of an Exasol cluster.

5.2.4.1. Setup a Basic Network

A public network (CSCN) and a cluster-internal network (CICN) are the minimum components of the basic network configuration. Every node also features an interface for out-of-band management, or lights out management.

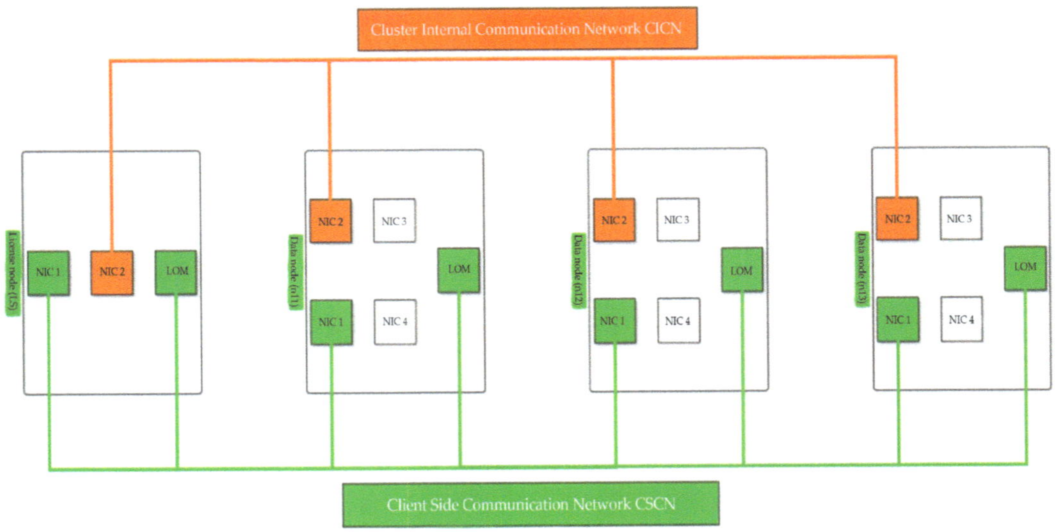

Figure 5.12. Basic network setup (Source: Exasol, https://docs.exasol.com/db/7.1/resource/images/administration/on%20premise/installation/network_simple_1_844x410.png).

5.2.4.2. Private Network (CICN – Cluster Internal Communication Network)

Create a dedicated and isolated VLAN (for example, called "VLAN CICN") and connect a NIC of each cluster member to it (license node and all data nodes). For the CICN, configure the following:

- Disable STP (Spanning Tree Protocol)
- Disable EEE (Energy Efficient Ethernet)
- (Optional) Disable Flow-Control to optimize performance for less network latency.

The CICN VLAN must not be routed.

- CICN IP Address Numbering: The CICN is an IPv4 Class A network by default. Using cluster-internal DHCP, IP addresses are assigned. The Number setting in EXA operation configuration refers to the final octet of the node's IP address. For instance, the node's private IP address is 27.1 if its internal number is 15. 0:15. The Node ID and Internal ID are other names for this number.

5.2.4.3. Public Network (CSCN – Client Side Communication Network)

You can set up a public network in two ways:

- Create a dedicated VLAN (for example, called "VLAN CSCN") and connect an NIC of each cluster member to it (license node and all data nodes).
- Use an existing VLAN and connect an NIC of each cluster member to it (license node and all data nodes).

5.2.4.4. CSCN IP Address Numbering

The CSCN may be a class C private network or an IPv4 class A network. 10.50 is the IP address range by default. 0 points out of 24. The External Number setting is used to find the last octet of the node's IP address when configuring nodes in EXA operation. The last octet of the public network IP address is modified to include the External Number that was assigned to the node.

Keyword

Cluster internal communication network refers to the infrastructure that enables communication among the nodes within a cluster computing environment. In a cluster, multiple interconnected computers (nodes) work together to perform a task or execute a computation.

Example. Client-Side Network Address + External Number = Client-Side Node IP Address

If you plan to use EXA2EXA for data transfer, the public IP addresses of the nodes must be a continuous, consecutive address block.

Public Network Access	Network Mask	External Number	Node IP Address
10.70.0.50	255.255.255.0 (24)	34	10.70.0.84
10.70.0.70	255.255.255.0 (24)	1	10.70.0.71

Source: Exasol

5.2.4.5. Setup Additional Networks (Optional)

Depending on the need for link bonding or network fail-safety, there are two approaches to implement more network interfaces.

Communication between clients and cluster members can be facilitated by implementing either of these two approaches. For the cluster internal communication network (CICN), both approaches are shown in the example that follows. Access to every CICN network is required for the license node. If the license node has fewer physical network interfaces than the data nodes, add VLAN tagging (802.1q) to the CICN interface of the license server.

5.2.4.6. Private Failover Interface (For Network Fail Safety)

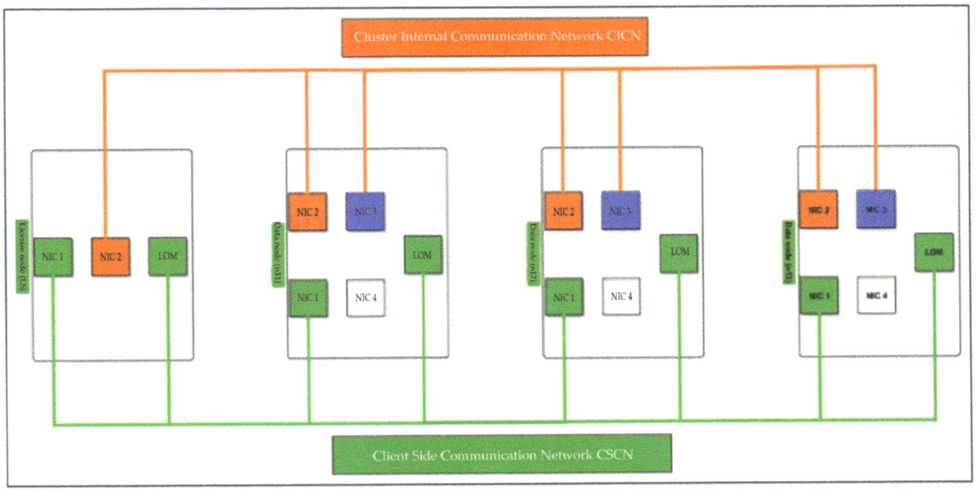

Figure 5.13. Add 3rd NIC of each cluster member to existing VLAN 'CICN' (Source: Exasol, https://docs.exasol.com/db/7.1/resource/images/administration/on%20premise/installation/network_failover_1_799x392.png).

5.2.4.7. Private Bonding Interface (for link bonding)

Create a new dedicated and isolated VLAN 'CICN_2':

- Add 3rd NIC of each cluster member to it
- Disable Flow-Control
- Disable STP (Spanning Tree Protocol)
- Disable EEE (Energy Efficient Ethernet)

For multiple internal networks, each needs to have different IP address numbering. For example:

- Private1 27.1.0.0/16
- Private2 27.65.0.0/16
- Private3 27.66.0.0/16

Internal traffic must not be rooted.

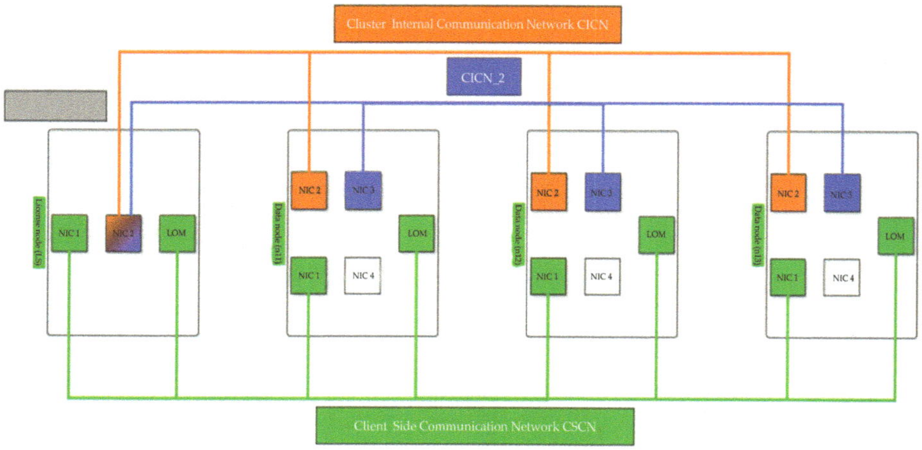

Figure 5.14. Create a new dedicated and isolated VLAN (Source: Exasol, https://docs.exasol.com/db/7.1/resource/images/administration/on%20premise/installation/network_bonding_1_810x378.png).

5.2.4.8. Network Switch Configuration

The following features must be disabled on the switch ports connected to the cluster to maximize network performance:

- IEE802.3az: Energy-Efficient Ethernet (EEE) ("no interface A1-A24 energy-efficient-ethernet")
- IEEE 802.3x: Flow-Control ("no interface A1-A24 flow-control").

5.2.4.9. Configure VPN Tunnel for Exasol Support

If you opt for Exasol to provide support via VPN, you will need to configure a site-to-site VPN tunnel. The proposed setup is an IPSec tunnel with the following phases:

- Phase 1: AES 256 / SHA1 / DH-Group 5: MODP 1536; Lifetime: 7800 seconds
- Phase 2: AES 256 / SHA1 / PFS-Group 5: MODP 1536; Lifetime: 3600 seconds

For maintenance tasks, the following service/ports need to be accessible, at least on the cluster's public and LOM IP addresses:

- TCP/20 (SSH)
- TCP/22 (Cluster-SSH)
- TCP/443 (HTTPS access to EXAoperation and the LOM web interface)
- ICMP ECHO REQUEST/REPLY (ping)
- UDP/123 (NTP)

If you mandate Exasol to monitor clusters or to perform incident management, additional ports will be required.

Did you get it?

1. Design network solutions by selecting appropriate clustering protocols based on specific requirements and constraints.
2. Examine the functionalities and objectives of clustering and routing protocols in WSNs.

5.3. NETWORKS AND INTER-CONNECTION/ SWITCHING DEVICES

→Learning Objectives

- Define the role and function of a Network Interface Card (NIC) in computer networking
- Define the purpose and functionality of a repeater in networking
- Explain the role of a hub in network connectivity and data distribution
- Analyze the role of bridges in improving network performance, reducing collisions, and enhancing security
- Describe how switches operate at the data link layer to forward data packets based on MAC addresses
- Design and implement router configurations to optimize network routing, security, and performance

A modern network needs a lot of interconnection devices, ranging from the interface that connects a single computer to other computers through a phone line or LAN cable to the big, intricate switching devices that link two or more complete networks. The following is a list of the primary types of interconnection devices used in computer networks.

5.3.1. Network Interface Card (NIC)

A network interface card (NIC) must be installed on any device connected to a network that needs to send and receive data. They are often installed into one of the expansion slots on the computer in the same manner as a sound or graphics card, and are also referred to as network adapters. A transceiver—a transmitter and receiver combined—is part of the NIC. A network device can send and receive data over the transmission medium with the help of a transceiver. Every NIC is manufactured with a distinct 48-bit Media Access Control (MAC) address burned into its ROM. An Organizationally Unique Identifier

(OUI), a block code that uniquely identifies the manufacturer of NICs, is made up of the first 24 bits. The Institute of Electrical and Electronics Engineers (IEEE) oversees the issuance of OUIs to organizations. The manufacturer's sequential number is comprised of the final 24 bits. The MAC address, which uniquely identifies the network adapter, is also referred to as a hardware address or physical address.

It is used by many data link layer communications protocols, including Ethernet, the 802.11 wireless protocol, and Bluetooth. The use of a 48-bit address allows for 248 (281,474,976,710,656) unique addresses. A MAC address is usually shown in hexadecimal format, with each octet separated by a dash or colon, for example: 00-90-47-03-B6-C4.

Did you know?

The NIC is both a physical layer and data link layer device, as it provides physical access to a networking medium and, for IEEE 802 and similar networks, provides a low-level addressing system through the use of MAC addresses that are uniquely assigned to network interfaces.

5.3.2. Repeater

Signal strength will decrease (attenuation) as it passes through a transmission medium. A repeater is a type of network device that lacks intelligence. It receives a signal on one port, regenerates it, and then retransmits it on all of its remaining ports. Repeaters can join two network segments together to increase a network's length (but not its capacity). Repeaters are not useful for connecting network segments that use distinct network access methods or for expanding a network beyond the bounds of its underlying architecture. However, they may be able to link segments of bridges with varying data rates and various media types. Operationally, a repeater is at the physical layer. Its task is to prolong the time that a signal can be transmitted over the same network by regenerating the signal over it before it gets too weak or distorted. It is imperative to acknowledge that repeaters do not enhance the signal strength. They replicate the signal bit by bit and regenerate it at the original strength when it starts to fade. This gadget has two ports.

5.3.3. Hub

An Ethernet network uses hubs. Every port on the hub retransmits a signal that is received at any other port. Hub-using network segments are frequently referred to as having a star topology, where the hub serves as the star's wiring center.

Because each network device has a separate connection to the hub, using a hub offers a certain level of fault tolerance as only one device is impacted by a failed connection. Additionally, it is simpler to expand the network because a single hub—which is frequently linked to a network backbone—can add a large number of new devices. Hubs may be passive or active. An active hub regenerates incoming frames prior to retransmitting them and has its own power supply. Each output port can link a channel up to 100 meters (the maximum permitted length for twisted pair cables) because signals are regenerated. Passive hubs don't generate the signal; they just relay it.

5.3.4. Bridge

Bridges are useful for connecting multiple LAN segments of the same kind (e.g., Token-Ring to Token-Ring or Ethernet to Ethernet). Similar to repeaters, bridges can increase a network's length, but because each port on a bridge has a unique MAC address, they can also increase a network's capacity. In an Ethernet network, bridges that are powered on begin by analyzing the source addresses of incoming frames from all connected network segments in order to determine the topology of the network. They accumulate a routing table over time. The bridge does not need to move an incoming frame to another network segment unless the source and the destination are on separate network segments. The bridge must be able to identify which segment the destination device is on if the source and destination are on separate segments.

The bridge monitors all traffic on the segments it connects, cross-referencing each frame's source and destination addresses against its routing table. The routing table is empty when the bridge first starts up, but as data is sent back and forth, the bridge adds each incoming frame's source MAC address to the table and links it to the port on which the frame arrives. The bridge quickly builds a comprehensive image of the network topology in this way. An incoming frame will be forwarded to all attached segments if the bridge is unsure of its destination segment, with the exception of the segment from which it originated. By segregating intra-segment traffic and acting as a filter, bridges reduce the volume of traffic on individual segments. This can significantly improve reaction times.

Remember

Managed hubs give administrators the ability to remotely enable or disable specific ports, and intelligent hubs have the ability to automatically close ports if a predetermined threshold of packet errors is exceeded.

Ethernet bridges are considered to operate at the data link layer of the OSI Reference Model because they decide whether or not to forward frames based on the destination MAC address. Although they effectively isolate intrasegment traffic, lowering overall network traffic and speeding up network response times, Ethernet bridges are sometimes referred to as transparent due to the transparency of both their existence and operation to network users.

5.3.4.1. Bridging Loops

When more bridges are added to the network to offer a degree of redundancy and fault tolerance by providing alternate paths through the network, a potential issue could occur. Loops may arise if there are multiple paths connecting any two segments at the same time. Bridges can be easily confused in the very basic example shown in the diagram below. For instance, these bridges would continuously forward a broadcast message from A, consuming valuable network bandwidth and preventing the transmission of other frames on both segments.

By putting redundant links into standby mode, which can be activated in the case of a primary link failure and offer a new path through the network, a Spanning Tree Algorithm (STA) can remove loops. The algorithm needs to be dynamic in order for the bridges to be able to recognize changes in topology and generate a new spanning tree accordingly. When the bridges are initially powered on and whenever a change in the network topology is noticed, the spanning-tree calculation takes place. Configuration messages are used to facilitate communication between the bridges and are sent back and forth at regular intervals (usually every few seconds). The other bridges will rerun the algorithm if a bridge fails because they will notice that its configuration messages are missing.

5.3.4.2. The Spanning Tree Algorithm (Ethernet)

The spanning tree technique disables loops in a network by putting bridge ports into a standby (blocking) state that, in an active state, would result in loops. In the event that a link fails to offer an alternative path across the network, a standby port can be reactivated. The spanning tree algorithm builds a loop-free topology using graph theory as a foundation. According to graph theory, a spanning tree of edges keeps a connected graph connected but free of loops, given any connected graph made up of nodes and edges joining pairs of nodes.

Every bridge represents an edge, and every LAN segment represents a node. This makes it possible for the network's bridges to generate a spanning tree using a straightforward algorithm. Bridges can register a change in network topology and obtain a new spanning tree by rerunning the STA, demonstrating the dynamic nature of the algorithm. According to the algorithm, every bridge must have a unique identity, as does every port on every bridge. Each port is typically identified by its MAC address, and the algorithm uses one of the bridge ports—prefixed by a two-byte priority—to identify the bridge itself. Network administrators have the ability to assign an arbitrary cost to each bridge port on the network. The algorithm can then use this cost to decide which ports are put into standby mode and which are left open, based on which ports have the lowest cost. A default value is applied if no cost value is specified. The network with five segments that redundant bridges have caused loops within is depicted in the diagram below.

The root bridge is chosen initially in a spanning-tree computation; this is typically the bridge with the lowest identifier. For the purpose of clarity, the simplified bridge identifiers (B1-B5) are used in the diagrams on this page, and B1 will be the root bridge. Next, one needs to identify a root port (R) on every other bridge. This is the port that has the lowest root path cost to reach the root bridge (the cost of each bridge port that must be crossed on a specific root path will determine this). Lastly, for every LAN segment, designated bridges and their designated ports are identified. The bridge on the segment that offers the root path at the lowest cost is designated. The port that links a segment to its designated bridge is known as the designated port. The bridge with the lowest bridge identifier number is used when two or more bridges have the same root path cost. All but one of the bridges attached to each LAN segment are removed using the STA, eliminating loops while maintaining connectivity. The outcome of applying the STA to the network that was previously depicted is displayed in the following updated diagram. The ports company is in the STA's list.

When a change in the network topology is detected or the bridge is powered on, the spanning-tree calculation takes place. Bridges must communicate with one another in order for this to occur, and *bridge protocol data units (BPDUs)* are used to send configuration messages. The bridge and port identifiers of the sending bridge are contained in a configuration message, which also identifies the bridge that the sender believes to be the root bridge.

It also includes the age of the data in the configuration message and the root path cost from the sending bridge to the root bridge. Every few seconds, on average, bridges exchange configuration messages. In the event of a bridge failure, which results in a topology change, neighboring bridges will detect this and send topology change messages to start a spanning-tree recalculation.

Keyword

Bridge Protocol Data Units (BPDUs) are frames that contain information about the spanning tree protocol (STP).

5.3.4.3. Frame Format

The format of the IEEE 802.1d configuration message is illustrated in Figure 5.15. The fields of the bridge configuration message are described below.

- Protocol identifier – contains the value zero.
- Version – contains the value zero.
- Message type – contains the value zero
- Flags – only the first two bits are used. The topology-change bit , if set, signals a topology change, and the topology-change acknowledgment bit , if set, acknowledges receipt of a configuration message with the topology-change bit set.
- Root ID – identifies the root bridge using its 2-byte priority followed by its 6-byte ID.
- Root path cost – the root path cost from the bridge sending the configuration message to the root bridge.
- Bridge ID – identifies the bridge sending the message using its 2-byte priority followed by its 6-byte ID.
- Port ID – identifies the port from which the configuration message was sent.
- Message age – indicates when the configuration message should be deleted.
- Maximum age – contains the value zero.
- Hello time – indicates the time period between root bridge configuration messages.
- Forward delay – the time bridges should wait before transitioning to a new state after a topology change.

Topology-change messages are only 4 bytes long and consist of the protocol identifier field , the version field , and the message type field which contains the value 128.

8	5	8	32	32	32	32	32	11 Bit
Type	Flags	Hop count	RREq ID	Destination address	Destination Seq Nbr	Source address	Source Seq Nbr	Destination region

Figure 5.15. Bridge configuration message format (Source: Research gate, https://www.researchgate.net/profile/Soufiene-Djahel-2/publication/280317385/figure/fig3/AS:287057567076355@1445451265758/Format-of-the-new-RREQ-packet.png).

5.3.4.4. Route Bridging (Token Ring)

The source-route bridging (SRB) algorithm, which IBM created for Token Ring networks, gets its name from the fact that the sending device inserts routing information into each and every inter-segment frame. forwards frames by using the routing data contained in the frame as a guide. Below is an example of a basic source-route bridging network.

Let us assume that computer A wishes to transmit a frame to computer B. Initially, A does not know if B is located on the same ring or a separate one. Therefore, A sends a test frame. If B does not acknowledge the test frame, A assumes that B is on a different segment. Subsequently, A sends out an explorer frame. The explorer frame is forwarded to any additional segments connected to each bridge that receives it (in this case, B1 and B4). As the explorer frame traverses the network, each bridge appends route information to it. Upon reaching B, each explorer frame receives a unique reply that is routed based on the accumulated route information. After receiving the replies, A must choose one of the listed routes for future transmissions to B, following predefined criteria.

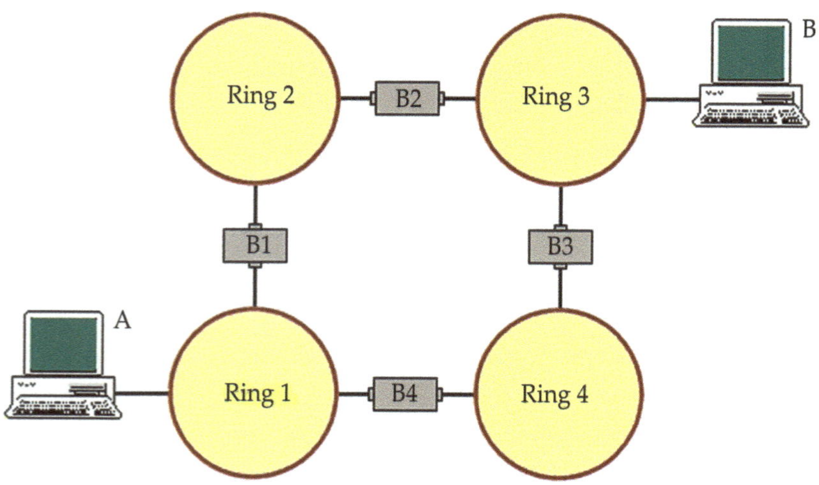

Figure 5.16. A simple source-route bridging network (Source: https://www.vikramuniv.ac.in/files/academic/e-Resources2020-21/engg2020-21/BE_8_SEM_EL_CN-DLL_SWITCHING-AMIT_THAKUR.pdf).

Typically, the route provided in the first reply is selected, although other factors such as the maximum frame size allowed and the number of hops on a specific route may also influence the decision. Once a route is chosen, it is inserted into the routing information field (RIF) of frames destined for B. Only frames addressed to devices on different segments contain a routing information field. Indicating the presence of routing information in the frame is done by setting the most significant (leftmost) bit in the Source Address field. This bit is referred to as the routing information indicator (RII) bit.

5.3.4.5. Frame Format

The location of the routing information field within a Token Ring data/command frame is shown below, together with its detailed structure.

The routing information field consists of a single routing control field and a number of routing descriptor fields. These fields and their subfields are described below.

- Routing control field – contains the following subfields:
  - Routing type (3 bits) – indicates one of three possible types of routing control:
  - Specifically routed – used when the source node supplies the route in the RIF's header.
  - All paths explorer – used to find a remote node. Route information is collected as the frame traverses the network.
  - Spanning-tree explorer – used to find a remote node. Only bridges in the spanning tree forward the frame, reducing the number of frames used for route discovery.
- Length (5 bits) – specifies the total length of the routing information field in bytes.
- Direction bit – indicates the direction in which the route is being traversed, and determines whether bridges read the ring and bridge number combinations in the route designators from right to left (forward) or left to right (reverse).
- Largest frame (6 bits) – indicates the largest frame size that can be handled by the specified route.
- Reserved bit – not used
- Routing descriptor fields – contains the following subfields:
  - Ring number (12 bits) – identifies a ring segment (must be unique within the network)
  - Bridge number (4 bits) – identifies a bridge (only has to be unique if the bridge it identifies is parallel with another bridge connecting two rings).

A maximum of 14 routing descriptor fields may be present in the routing information field. Every route consists of a series of bridge and ring numbers that alternate and begin and end with a ring number. For every explorer frame that a bridge receives, it adds its bridge number and the number of the ring that the frame is forwarded onto (the first bridge additionally adds the ring number of the ring that it receives the frame from, and the last bridge number always equals zero).

5.3.5. Switch

Hubs and bridges in Local Area Networks have been superseded by the relatively new network device known as switches. An internal address table is used by a switch to route incoming data frames to the port that corresponds to their final MAC address. Switches are useful for interconnecting different network segments or several end-user devices, like workstations. A workgroup switch is a term frequently used to describe a switch that links end-user devices. Each connected device is essentially given its own network segment by the dedicated full-duplex links that switches provide. This greatly lowers the amount of intra- and inter-segment collisions.

A floor switch is a higher-level switch that connects several network segments that are on the same floor of a building (or on the same campus) and each has its own workgroup switch. Floor switches, workgroup switches, routers, and other high-level network devices are frequently connected by far more powerful switches. These devices, which go by the name "core switches" frequently, ought to be able to handle the amount of traffic that moves through the network.

5.3.6. Router

A sophisticated device is required to manage the flow of traffic between multiple interconnected networks with different network protocols and architectures in a network environment. This type of device, commonly referred to as a router but also known as an intermediate system at times, must be capable of determining the optimal route to forward incoming packets, or datagrams, to the destination network. Routers gather information about the networks they are linked to and can share this information with other routers on the same network. The accumulated data, which includes the routing information itself and the current status of various network links, is stored in the router's internal routing table. Through specialized routing protocols, routers exchange this routing data.

In many cases, hosts or end-systems refer to computers and other end-user devices connected to networks that form an internetwork. A network host will direct a datagram to its local router (also known as the default gateway) if it cannot route the datagram to a host on another network. As a datagram travels from an end-system on the source network to an end-system on the destination network, it may traverse multiple networks and, consequently, multiple routers. Each intermediate router makes a determination regarding the best next hop. Routers serve as the central element of packet-switching networks. The process by which the router forwards the incoming datagram to one of its output ports in this manner is referred to as switching. Routers utilize the IP address contained in a datagram to ascertain the destination network address, unlike bridges and switches, which focus on MAC addresses.

Did you get it?

1. Explain the role of a hub in network connectivity and data distribution
2. Design and implement router configurations to optimize network routing, security, and performance

A CLOSER LOOK

Cluster networks are groups of high-performance computing (HPC), GPU, or optimized instances that are connected with a high-bandwidth, ultra-low-latency network. Each node in the cluster is a bare metal machine located in close physical proximity to the other nodes. A remote direct memory access (RDMA) network between nodes provides latency as low as single-digit microseconds, comparable to on-premises HPC clusters.

Cluster networks are designed for highly demanding parallel computing workloads. For example:

- Computational fluid dynamics simulations for automotive or aerospace modeling
- Financial modeling and risk analysis
- Biomedical simulations
- Trajectory analysis and design for space exploration
- Artificial intelligence and big data workloads

Oracle Cloud Infrastructure offers two types of cluster networks. In both cases, the networks are groups of bare metal instances that are connected with an ultra-low latency network.

- Compute clusters allow you to manage instances in the cluster individually. When you create a compute cluster, you create an empty RDMA network group. After the group is created, you can add instances to the group or delete instances from the group. If you want to manage instances in the RDMA network independently of each other or use different types of instances in the network group, use compute clusters.
- Cluster networks with instance pools enable you to use instance pools to manage groups of identical instances in the RDMA network group. If you want predictable capacity for a specific number of identical instances that are managed as a group, use cluster networks with instance pools.

SUMMARY

- A cluster network is an ultra-low latency, high-bandwidth network that connects a pool of GPU-optimized instances or high-performance computing (HPC) instances.
- The networks whose connectivity fluctuates frequently (e.g., mobile networks) or are large with many configuration parameters work better with self-organizing controlled structures. Because nodes construct and maintain them, they offer greater network availability, a quicker reaction to state changes, and a lower chance of configuration errors.
- Broadcast environments with multiple access utilize this architecture. Node clusters are organized to control transmissions without contention, reducing interference..
- Large tactical networks are the intended application and deployment context for Network Near-Term Digital Radio (NTDR) networking. This is one of the backbone formation clustering techniques.
- The cluster heads in the NTDR network are responsible for keeping the backbone stable, so they monitor it and share information about any changes with one another.
- The quasi-hierarchical category includes the majority of hierarchical cluster-based routing systems. Moreover, the distance vector routing technique forms the basis for nearly all quasi-hierarchical routing schemes.
- A node strives to create routes that align with the users' service requests and the network's existing capabilities using this link-state information.
- Techniques for clustering can be decentralized or centralized. Each sensor node must transmit its unique data, including its location and energy level, to the central base station to utilize centralized clustering algorithms.

MULTIPLE CHOICE QUESTIONS

1. What is a primary benefit of cluster networking?
   a. Reduced hardware costs
   b. Increased latency
   c. Limited scalability
   d. Single point of failure
2. Which of the following accurately describes a cluster network?
   a. A network where all devices communicate through a central server
   b. A network where multiple interconnected servers work together to provide services
   c. A network topology with a linear connection between devices
   d. A network consisting of isolated, non-communicating segments

3. In cluster networking, what is the purpose of load balancing?
    a. To increase latency
    b. To overload certain servers for better performance
    c. To evenly distribute workloads across multiple servers
    d. To reduce the number of servers in the cluster
4. Which of the following is a characteristic of high availability in cluster networking? Single point of failure
    a. Redundancy and failover mechanisms
    b. Limited scalability
    c. Increased latency
    d. Single point of failure
5. What role does fault tolerance play in cluster networking?
    a. It increases the chances of system failures
    b. It ensures that the network operates at maximum capacity
    c. It allows the network to continue operating even if some components fail
    d. It reduces the need for load balancing

REVIEW QUESTIONS

1. What is the role of routing in cluster-based networks?
2. How can clustering protocols be classified?
3. What are the considerations in clustering and routing protocol design for wireless sensor networks?
4. What functions does a Network Interface Card (NIC) serve?
5. How does the Spanning Tree Algorithm apply to Ethernet networks?

Answer to Multiple Choice Questions

1. (a) 2. (b) 3. (c) 4. (b) 5. (c)

REFERENCES

1. Charles, E., (2001). Perkins: Chapter 4. *Ad Hoc Networking*. Addison Wesley. ISBN 0-201-30976-9.
2. Kalashnikov, D. V., & Mehrotra, S., (2004). *Learning Importance of Relationships for Reference Disambiguation*. RESCUE.
3. McDonald, D. W., (2003). Recommending collaboration with social networks: A comparative evaluation. In: *Proceedings of the SIGCHI Conference on Human Factors in Computing Systems* (pp. 593–600). ACM Press, Ft. Lauderdale, Florida, USA.

4. Tho, Q. T., Hui, S. C., & Fong, A. C. M., (2003). A web mining approach for finding expertise in research areas. In: *Cyberworlds, 2003; Proceedings. 2003 International Conference* (pp.310–317). Oxford University Press.
5. Bathelt, H., & Glückler, J. (2011). The Relational Economy: Geographies of Knowing and Learning. Oxford University Press.
6. Ketels, C. (2013). Cluster Reinvention and Regional Economic Development. In M. Porter, C. Ketels, & M. Delgado (Eds.), Competitiveness in the Global Economy: A Multi-Disciplinary Perspective (pp. 235-258). Harvard Business School Publishing.
7. Martin, R., & Sunley, P. (2003). Deconstructing clusters: Chaotic concept or policy panacea? Journal of Economic Geography, 3(1), 5-35.

CHAPTER

6

Distributed Network Systems

LEARNING OBJECTIVES

After studying this chapter, you will be able to:

- Elaborate the client-server model in a distributed computing system
- Examine the extensions to the client-server model
- Discuss on service discovery
- Explain the characteristics of a distributed system

INTRODUCTORY EXAMPLE

ISTRIBUTED NETWORK IN MODERN COMPUTING

Distributed network systems are a fundamental architectural approach in modern computing that distribute tasks or resources among multiple nodes, enabling scalability, fault tolerance, and efficient resource utilization. These systems are characterized by decentralization, where no single node or entity controls the entire network, and nodes communicate and collaborate autonomously to achieve common goals. One prominent example of a distributed network system is blockchain technology, which underpins cryptocurrencies like Bitcoin and Ethereum. In a blockchain network, transactions are recorded and validated by a decentralized network of nodes, each maintaining a copy of the ledger. Through cryptographic techniques and consensus algorithms such as Proof of Work (PoW) or Proof of Stake (PoS), blockchain networks ensure the integrity and immutability of data without the need for a central authority. This decentralization enhances security and eliminates single points of failure, making it resilient to attacks and censorship.

Another example of distributed network systems is content delivery networks (CDNs), which optimize the delivery of web content to users by strategically distributing it across a network of servers located in various geographic regions. CDNs cache static content such as images, videos, and scripts on edge servers closer to end-users, reducing latency and improving load times. By distributing content across multiple nodes, CDNs can handle high traffic volumes efficiently, ensuring a smooth and responsive user experience even during peak demand periods. Companies like Akamai, Cloudflare, and Amazon CloudFront provide CDN services, leveraging distributed architectures to enhance the performance, reliability, and security of websites and web applications.

Peer-to-peer (P2P) networks are another type of distributed network systems where nodes in the network act as both clients and servers, sharing resources or tasks directly with each other without the need for central coordination. P2P networks are commonly used for file sharing, with protocols like BitTorrent allowing users to distribute and download files across a decentralized network of peers. Each peer contributes bandwidth and storage capacity, enabling efficient distribution of large files while reducing the load on individual servers. Similarly, communication applications like Skype use P2P architectures to facilitate direct communication between users, leveraging the collective resources of network participants to establish connections and transmit data without relying on centralized servers. Distributed file systems also demonstrate distributed network systems, providing storage resources across multiple nodes in a network, typically for enterprise or cloud computing environments. Examples include Google File System (GFS), Apache Hadoop Distributed File System (HDFS), and Amazon Simple Storage Service (S3). These distributed file systems partition and replicate data across multiple nodes, ensuring high availability, durability, and scalability. By distributing data storage and processing tasks across a network of nodes, distributed file systems can handle large volumes of data and support parallel processing, enabling efficient data analysis, backup, and retrieval operations.

INTRODUCTION

A computer network that is dispersed over several networks is known as a distributed network. This provides a single data communication network that each network can manage independently or in concert. In addition to facilitating shared communication among nodes in the network, a distributed network frequently shares processing.

Distributed computing architecture, which divides enterprise IT infrastructure resources across multiple networks, processors, and intermediary devices, includes distributed networks. Network management software powers distributed networks by combining and allocating network bandwidth, controlling access, managing and tracking data routing, and performing other essential networking tasks.

Different remote users can receive specialized applications from distributed networks and processing. This implies that numerous people may access an application that is hosted and run on a single machine. An example of a distributed network is a client/server computing architecture, in which numerous connected remote users access the application from various networks, while the server provides the resource.

6.1. THE CLIENT-SERVER MODEL IN A DISTRIBUTED COMPUTING SYSTEM

→Learning Objectives

- Understand features and issues of client-server model in distributed computing.
- Explore cooperation mechanisms between clients and servers in client-server architecture.
- Differentiate types of cooperation in client-server interactions and analyze chained servers concept.
- Investigate advantages and challenges of deploying and managing multiple servers in client-server environment.

A distributed computing system is a collection of data and application programs spread over separate personal computers linked by a communication network. Users access services by running necessary programs on multiple computers with data stored in various locations.

Challenges in distributed computing include formalizing progress and managing processes that may work together or against each other. The client-server model is suitable for distributed computing, handling distribution issues, explaining computation processes, and enabling software development. In this model, the client requests a service, the server provides it, and responds after completing the task.

Printing, email, file services, authentication, naming, database services, and computing services are among the services that a distributed computing system can offer from the user's perspective. Appropriate servers offer these services. Clients compete for these servers because there are only a limited number of servers (implied by a limited number of resources on which these servers were implemented).

Figure 6.1 illustrates the relationship between this conceptual framework and its concrete application. The client and server, as well as the request and response, are the main components of the model that are displayed. Two separate computers are used in this instance to run the client and server processes. By exchanging requests and answers, they engage in virtual (logical) communication. These two processes send physical messages to each other in order to accomplish this virtual communication. This suggests active participation in the service delivery on the part of computer operating systems and distributed computing systems' communication networks.

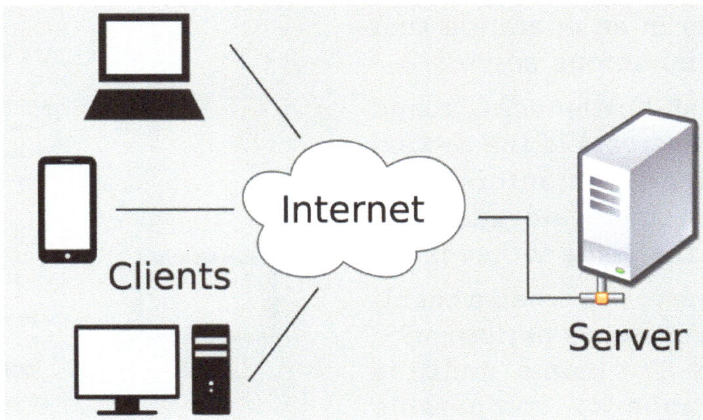

Figure 6.1. The basic client-server model (Source: Wikipedia, https://upload.wikimedia.org/wikipedia/commons/thumb/c/c9/Client-server-model.svg/1024px-Client-server-model.svg.png).

A more detailed client-server model has three components:

- *Service:* A service is a software entity that runs on one or more machines. It provides an abstraction of a set of well-defined operations in response to applications' requests.
- *Server*: A server is an instance of a particular service running on a single machine.
- *Client*: A client is a software entity that exploits services provided by servers. A client can but does not have to interface directly with a human user.

6.1.1. Features and Problems of the Client-Server Model

The client-server model's simplicity, modularity, extensibility, and flexibility are its key components. A sign of simplicity is when the data flow and the control flow closely align. A collection of computer operations can be arranged and integrated into a distinct service to achieve modularity. Additionally, any collection of data that has operations on it can be arranged into a distinct service. By introducing new services in the form of additional servers, the client-server model-based distributed computing system can be readily expanded. It is simple to change or even remove servers that do not meet user requirements. All that needs to be maintained are the client-server interfaces.

There are three major problems of the client-server model:

- One server has centralized control over all resources, which is the cause of the first. This implies that the failure of the computer supporting a server results in the failure of that control element. Such a solution is unacceptable if a server's control function is essential to the system's functionality (e.g., as an authentication server, a file server, or a name server). As a result, the dependability of all computers and devices as well as communication lines determines the availability and reliability of an operation that depends on numerous servers.

- The potential bottleneck caused by individual servers is the second issue. As more computers with potential customers are added to the system, the issue worsens.
- The third issue arises when a client-server based system's performance is improved by using multiple implementations of comparable functions to maintain consistency. Additionally, this increases the overall costs of a distributed computing system.

6.1.2. Cooperation between Clients and Servers

It is highly likely that you are familiar with the terms "client" and "server" if you have worked in the tech industry for any amount of time. Understanding the relationship between the two is essential for comprehending many aspects of common applications or webpages. The field of computer science is built on this model. We will now review the model, examine its significance, as well as its benefits and drawbacks.

- **The Client:** The client is the other half of this partnership. Additionally, the client is a computer unto itself. When this computer retrieves data from the server, it does so as a client. When you use your laptop to check your emails, for example, your laptop becomes the client and retrieves the data from the mail server. Every kind of computer goes through this procedure again when requesting information from servers. As such, your phone, laptop, and even smartwatch can serve as clients.

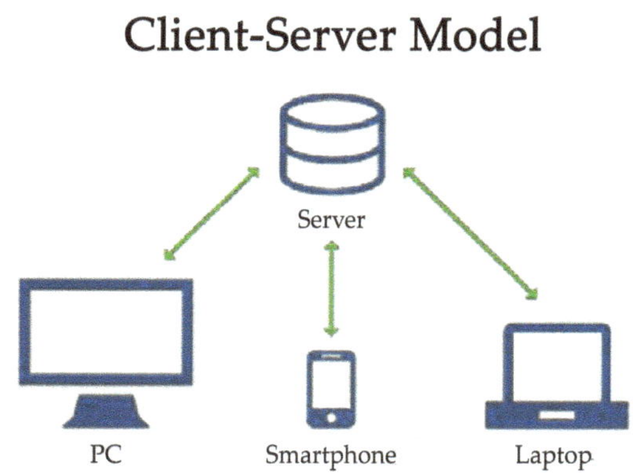

Figure 6.2. Cooperation functionality between client and server (Source: TechTerms, https://medium.com/@joshjnunez09/the-client-server-relationship-9ac90fadb3d2).

- **The Relationship:** We can delve further into the relationship's process now that you have a clearer grasp of each component. Like in a lot of other relationships, every component has a distinct function. For example, one or more clients can receive a function or service from the server. These customers are the ones who are requesting this service. Only when both roles are performing their duties is this relationship feasible. A request-response messaging pattern is the exchange of messages between the two parties. The server is required to respond to requests sent by the client. There are several benefits to this kind of relationship. One benefit is that all the necessary data can be stored on the server in one location. This makes granting authorization and protecting your data much simpler. To make matters worse, efficient access to the data is possible even when the server is not physically close to the client. Lastly, because the client-server model is independent of all other models, upgrading the modes is simple. One of the model's few drawbacks is that if a client sends in an excessive number of requests, the server may quickly become overloaded.

6.1.3. Cooperation Type and Chained Server

Users wouldn't expect top-notch, cost-effective, and reliable services from a system with just one server and one client. To handle multiple clients simultaneously, a single server is necessary. The most basic form of cooperation between clients and servers is sharing, which reduces system costs and enhances the efficient use of resources. A printing service exemplifies a service that depends on this collaboration. In Figure 6.3, a printer server is depicted serving n clients connected via a local area network. There are two main ways clients and servers can collaborate in a distributed computing system. In the first scenario, a client requests a temporary service. The second involves a customer scheduling multiple calls to be directed to a specific serving procedure. This implies that long-term connections between the client and server are essential.

Keyword

Authorization is the function of specifying access rights/privileges to resources, which is related to general information security and computer security, and to access control in particular.

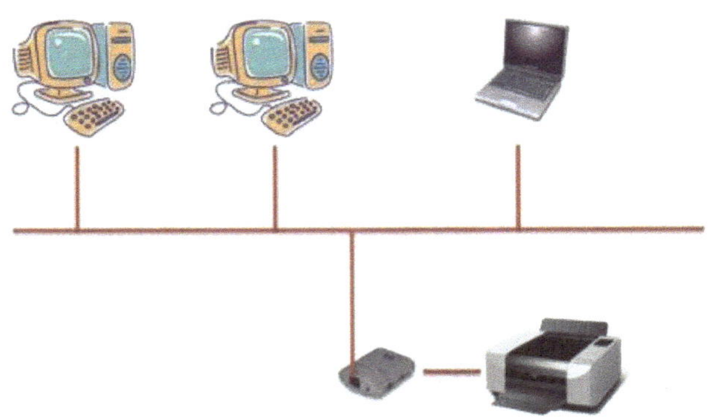

Figure 6.3. Printing service (a service example) (Source: What-is-my-computer.com, https://www.what-is-my-computer.com/images/what-is-a-print-server.jpg).

6.1.4. Multiple Servers

A distributed computing system has the following functions:

- Improve performance through parallel execution of programs on a cluster (sometimes called a network) of workstations,

- Decrease response time of databases through data replication,
- Support synchronous distant meetings,
- Support cooperative workgroups,
- Increase reliability by service multiplication, etc.

Numerous servers must contribute to the overall application in order for it to carry out these tasks. This suggests that using several services is necessary. Moreover, it would necessitate sending multiple simultaneous requests to different servers in certain situations. As the following paragraphs demonstrate, different applications will call for different semantics in order for clients and servers to cooperate.

6.1.4.1. Cooperation in the Systems Supporting Parallel Execution

Certain program components may run as separate processes on different computers in a distributed computing system that supports parallel execution. In order to accomplish this, a process (parent) that orchestrates the parallel processing of distinct processes (children) sets them to run on particular idle computers while it awaits the computation of results. In this instance, there is a one-to-many communication pattern where the parent process serves as a client and the child processes serve as servers. However, until all children return their responses, the parent process comes to an end. This example demonstrates that in order to enhance the collaboration between clients and servers, two questions need to be addressed: first, who is in charge of identifying idle computers that can host servers, and second, who is in charge of installing those servers on distant computers and organizing responses.

6.1.4.2. Cooperation in the Systems Supporting a Distributed Database

Supporting a distributed database has similarities to the semantics of collaboration between a client and several servers in a distributed computing system. Every operation carried out on a group of databases has to be finished successfully in order to commit the transaction. In order to complete a transaction, a client process sends operation requests to the appropriate databases (servers) and then waits for the operations' outcomes. Although the client process is capable of performing other tasks, the transaction cannot be committed until all database servers have responded. In this instance, setting up servers on unused computers is not necessary because servers that are currently operating on dedicated computers already exist. The question of who has access to these database servers, the client process, or another organization acting on the client's behalf, remains, though.

6.1.4.3. Cooperation in the Systems Supporting a User Application

In a distributed computing system that supports a user application, cooperation between a client and several servers can take on distinct meanings. Finding a database server that houses pertinent data, gaining access to it, processing it, and printing it are all necessary for this. Three servers—a database server, a printer server, and a service discovery server—must be active in order to support the application. The application software-running client process calls each server in turn, one after the other, and then waits for a response before moving on to the next server. Again, there's no need to install servers on unused PCs in this scenario. But the same problem still exists, i.e., who is capable of handling these database servers, the client procedure, or another organization acting on the client's behalf.

6.1.4.4. Cooperation in the Systems Supporting Mission Critical Applications

Reliability in distributed computing systems requires a different kind of cooperation between a client and multiple servers, especially when supporting mission-critical applications. In this scenario, a request made to a collection of servers ought to result in the same replies from each of them. A fault-tolerant transaction-oriented database or a redundant computational server on a spacecraft are two examples of such a system. In any event, the client will only accept identical operation results. These illustrations demonstrate how, in an effort to increase efficiency and dependability, distributed computing systems have shifted from the traditional one-to-one client-server model to the one-to-many and chain models. Additionally, the problems found when debating the client-server model's one-to-many communication pattern show that certain active entities that are client-server model extensions can have a significant impact on and support client and server cooperation. These topics are covered in the sections that follow.

Remember

Distributed computing refers to a system where processing and data storage is distributed across multiple devices or systems, rather than being handled by a single central device. In a distributed system, each device or system has its own processing capabilities and may also store and manage its own data.

Did you get it?

1. **What are the mechanisms of cooperation employed in systems supporting parallel execution?**
2. **How does cooperation manifest in systems designed to support mission-critical applications?**

6.2. EXTENSIONS TO THE CLIENT-SERVER MODEL

→Learning Objectives

- Explore the concept of agents and their role in facilitating indirect client-server cooperation within distributed systems.
- Understand the principles and components of the three-tier client-server architecture in distributed computing environments.

The client-server model is a foundational architectural design used in computer networking that facilitates the communication and exchange of data between multiple devices over a network. In this model, the interaction between computers is structured into two distinct roles: the client and the server.

At its core, the client-server model operates on a principle of division of labor, where specific tasks are assigned to each participant. The client, typically a software application or device, initiates requests for services or resources from another program or computer known as the server. The server, on the other hand, is a specialized system designed to provide the requested services or resources to the client.

The interaction between clients and servers follows a request-response pattern. When a client requires a service or resource, it sends a request to the server. This request contains information about the desired service or resource, such as the type of operation to be performed and any necessary parameters. Upon receiving the request, the server processes it, executes the requested operation, and formulates a response. This response contains the requested data or confirmation of the completed operation, which is then sent back to the client.

One of the key advantages of the client-server model is its scalability and flexibility. By distributing tasks between clients and servers, the model allows for efficient resource allocation and utilization. Servers can be dedicated to specific functions or services, such as file storage, database management, or web hosting, while clients can access these resources as needed without having to manage the underlying infrastructure themselves. This separation of concerns simplifies system administration and maintenance, as changes or updates can be made to individual components without affecting the entire network.

Additionally, the client-server model promotes a centralized approach to data management and security. Servers act as central repositories for data and resources, which can be accessed and managed through controlled channels. This centralized control enables administrators to enforce access restrictions, implement security protocols, and monitor network activity more effectively, reducing the risk of unauthorized access or data breaches.

However, the client-server model is not without its limitations. One potential drawback is the reliance on a single point of failure—the server. If the server experiences downtime or becomes overwhelmed with requests, it can disrupt service for all connected clients. To mitigate this risk, redundant servers and load balancing techniques can be implemented to distribute workload and ensure high availability.

A study into the involvement of other entities in the provision of services, an interface between a client and server, and the behavior of a client after sending a request to a server can specify the need for expanding the client-server model.

6.2.1. Agents and Indirect Client-Server Cooperation

Direct or indirect cooperation is possible between a client and server. In the first scenario, a client and a server exchange requests and responses without the involvement of a third party. In the client-server model, indirect cooperation necessitates the request and provision of a service by two extra entities, referred to as agents. A similar extension is seen in Figure 6.4.

These agents' functions can range from a basic communication module that conceals communication network details to an entity that handles resource management and cooperative servers, mediates disputes between clients and servers, and resolves heterogeneity problems. A client can send direct requests to multiple servers in order to explicitly invoke desired servers. In this scenario, the user application programmer needs to focus on managing server cooperation and communication in addition to the application itself. Writing communication and resource management software is costly, time-consuming, and prone to mistakes. The user interface is not transparent to the client process, and the interface between the server and the client varies depending on the application.

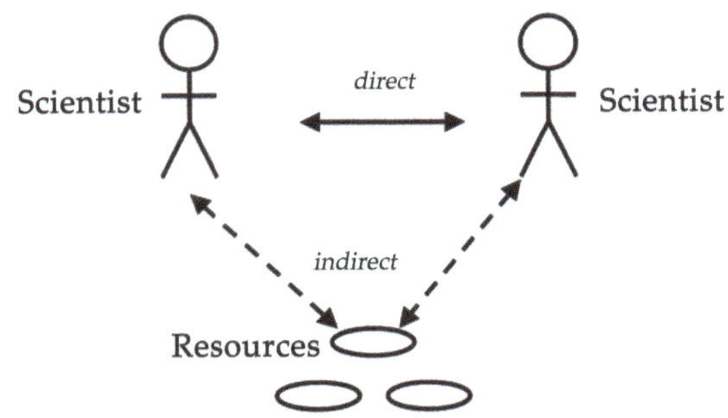

Figure 6.4. Indirect client-server cooperation (Source: Researchgate, https://www.researchgate.net/profile/Tran-Vu-Pham-2/publication/260388648/figure/fig1/AS:669403502878734@1536609640717/Direct-and-indirect-support-for-collaborations.ppm).

Additionally, clients may implicitly request more than one service. As a result, the client needs to contact a general server with just one request. Based on the data included in the request, this invoked server will work with other servers to create the requested service. The invoked server replies to the client after the involved servers have finished any necessary processing. An agent with the right design can carry out this coordination function. The cooperation between the client and the server is predicated on a single, clearly defined interface, despite the complexity of such an agent. Additionally, the client receives transparency, which lessens the application's complexity.

A straightforward communication system that uses a direct, one-to-one message protocol can facilitate cooperation between a client and several servers. Despite being straightforward, this communication model performs poorly because it requires sending separate messages to each of the servers involved. When a one-to-many communication pattern is employed, the overall performance of a communication system supporting message delivery in a client-server based distributed computing system can be significantly increased. In this instance, the client process sends a single request—specified by a single group name—to each server. Although it's not necessary, multicasting at the physical/data link layer does make this system better.

Q: How the browser interacts with the servers in while using client-server model?

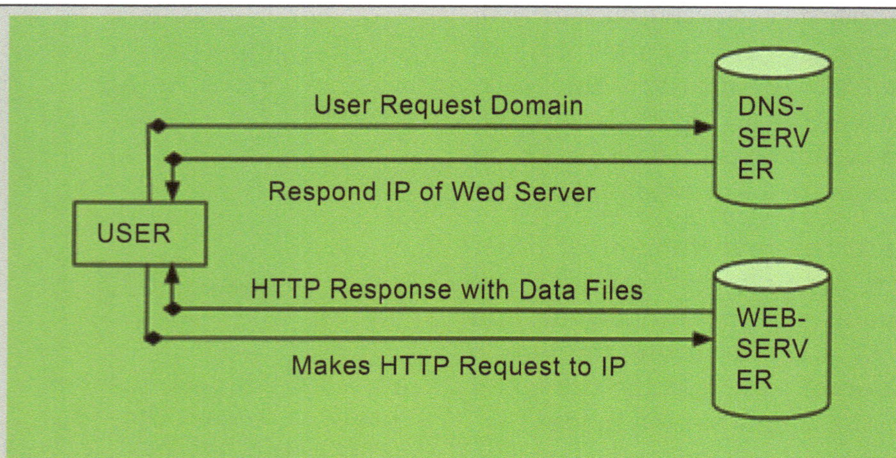

A: The Client-server model is a distributed application structure that partitions task or workload between the providers of a resource or service, called servers, and service requesters called clients. In the client-server architecture, when the client computer sends a request for data to the server through the internet, the server accepts the requested process and deliver the data packets requested back to the client. Clients do not share any of their resources.

There are few steps to follow to interact with the servers a client.

- User enters the URL(Uniform Resource Locator) of the website or file. The Browser then requests the DNS(DOMAIN NAME SYSTEM) Server.
- DNS Server lookup for the address of the WEB Server.
- DNS Server responds with the IP address of the WEB Server.
- Browser sends over an HTTP/HTTPS request to WEB Server's IP (provided by DNS server).
- Server sends over the necessary files of the website.

- Browser then renders the files and the website is displayed. This rendering is done with the help of DOM (Document Object Model) interpreter, CSS interpreter and JS Engine collectively known as the JIT or (Just in Time) Compilers.

6.2.2. The Three-Tier Client-Server Architecture

The user interface (presentation), functional process logic (business rules), computer data storage, and data access are all developed and maintained as separate modules, usually on different platforms, in a three-tier architecture, a client-server software architecture pattern. The creator of it is John J. Donovan in Open Environment Corporation (OEC), a Cambridge, Massachusetts-based tools company he founded. The three-tier architecture is meant to enable any of the three tiers to be upgraded or replaced independently in response to changes in requirements or technology, in addition to the standard benefits of modular software with well-defined interfaces. For instance, only the user interface code would be impacted by an operating system change in the presentation tier. The functional process logic, which can be comprised of one or more independent modules operating on a workstation or application server, and the RDBMS, which is a database server or mainframe that houses the computer data storage logic, are typically used by the user interface, which runs on a desktop PC or workstation and uses a standard graphical user interface. If there are multiple tiers within the middle tier, the overall architecture is referred to as an n-tier architecture.

Keyword

Resource management software describes the digital tools used to allocate, assign, and track employees, finances, and equipment across projects.

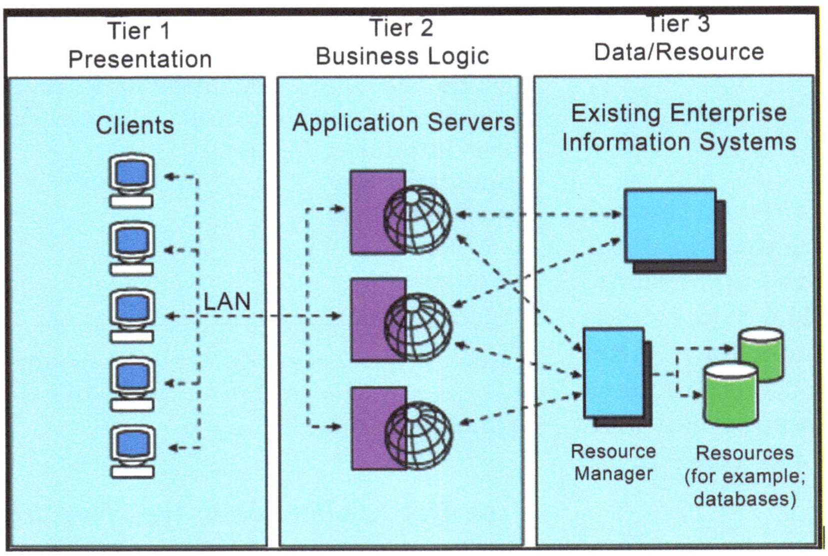

Figure 6.5. Examples of three-tier configurations.

Source: https://www.setgetweb.com/p/WAS8/images/thtrcs.gif

A well-known software application architecture known as "three-tier architecture" divides programs into three logical and physical computing tiers: the application tier, which processes data, the data tier, which stores and manages application data, and the presentation tier, which is the user interface. The main advantage of a three-tier architecture is that separate development teams can work on each tier concurrently since each tier is supported by its own infrastructure. and can be modified or expanded as necessary without affecting the tiers below it. An established software application design pattern called "three-tier architecture" divides an application into the following three logical and physical computing tiers:

Presentation Tier

It is the highest tier of the architecture and the user interface. Its function is to receive client requests and provide information to them. It uses a web browser to communicate with other tiers and displays output on the browser. When it comes to Web-based tiers, languages like HTML, CSS, and JavaScript are used in their development.

Application Tier

As the information/request obtained through the presentation tier is processed in detail here, it is the middle tier of the architecture referred to as the logic tier. The data storage server is also a point of contact for it. After handling and formatting the client's request, it returns it to them. Languages like PHP, Java, Python, and others are used in its development.

Data Tier

It is also referred to as the Database Tier and is the final tier of the architecture. It serves as a repository for the information that has been processed and can be retrieved as needed in the future. Database servers such as Oracle, MySQL, DB2, and so forth are included in it. Middle-tier I facilitates the exchange of information between the Presentation Tier and Data-Tier. E. Application Level.

Table 6.1. The basics diffraction between Tiers vs. layer

Tier	Layer
Tier refer to the physical operation of components.	Layer refers to the logical separation of an application.
Tiers are physical separated and running on the different machines are servers.	Layers are logically separated but running on the same servers or the machines.
Scalability of an application is very high.	Scalability of an application is medium.
Common tiers in a multi-tier architecture include the presentation tier (user interface), application tier (business logic), and data tier (database).	Each layer focuses on specific responsibilities, such as presentation, business logic, and data access, within a single tier.

Source: https://www.geeksforgeeks.org/three-tier-client-server-architecture-in-distributed-system/

Three-Tier Application In Web Development

The three architectures and web applications will have the same tiers; the only distinction is in their names.

1. **Web Server:** A web server is a type of presentation tier in a three-tier architecture, also known as a UI (User Interface) tier. Depending on the needs of the user—for example, an e-commerce site where users can add items to their shopping cart, enter payment information, or create an account—this content can be static or dynamic.
2. **Application Server:** The application tier is a middle tier that houses all of the logic needed by the company to process user inputs and other data. It will carry out logical operations such as updating a customer's profile with new information or querying the inventory database to retrieve product availability.
3. **Database server:** The back-end tier of a web application houses all of the data, so databases like MySQL, Oracle, DB2, or PostgreSQL are typically found here.

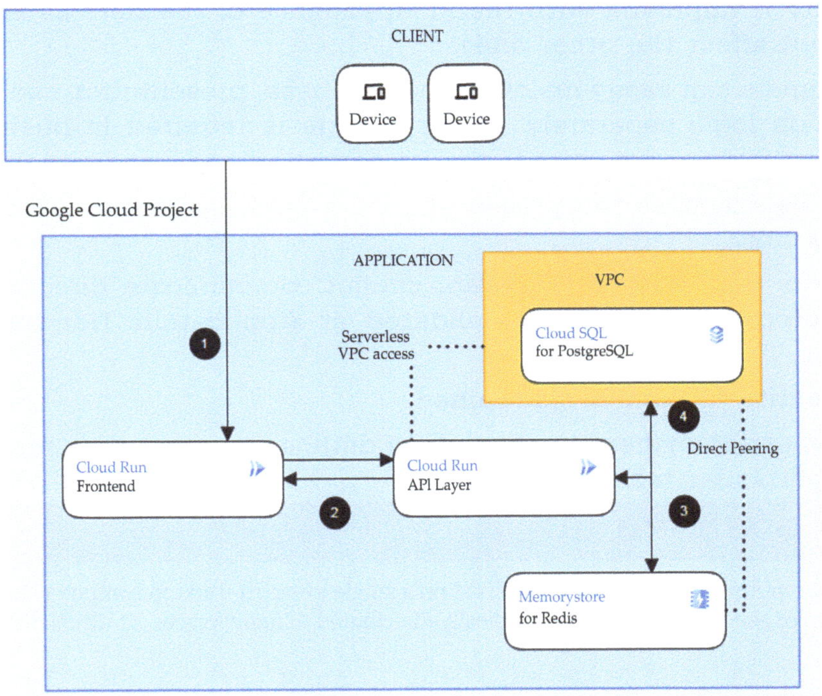

Figure 6.6. An example implementation for creating a three-tier web application.

Source: https://www.gstatic.com/pantheon/images/solutions/three_tier_web_app_v6.svg

Benefits of a tree-tier app architecture

A three-tier architecture offers enhanced availability, performance, and horizontal scalability. Three tiers allow for the simultaneous development of each component by distinct programming teams using different languages from those of the other tier developers. An enterprise or software packager can more easily evolve an application as new needs and opportunities arise thanks to the 3-tier model, which allows tier programming to be changed or relocated without affecting other tiers. Critical components or applications that are already in place can be contained within the new tier they are a part of, either permanently or temporarily. N-tier programs are another name for 3-tier application programs. The letter n represents several tiers in this context.

- Logical separation is maintained between Presentation Tier, Application Tier, and Database Tier.
- Enhancement of Performance as the task is divided on multiple machines in distributed machines and moreover, each tier is independent of other tiers.
- Increasing demand for adding more servers can also be handled in the architecture as tiers can be scaled independently.
- Developers are independent to update the technology of one tier as it would not impact the other tiers.
- Reliability is improved with the independence of the tiers as issues of one tier would not affect the other ones.
- Programmers can easily maintain the database, presentation code, and business/ application logic separately. If any change is required in business/application logic then it does not impact the presentation code and codebase.
- Load is balanced as the presentation tier task is separated from the server of the data tier.
- Security is improved as the client cannot communicate directly with Database Tier. Moreover, the data is validated at Application Tier before passing to Database Tier.
- The integrity of data is maintained.
- Provision of deployment to a variety of databases rather than restraining yourself to one particular technology.

Did you know?

Prior to the 1980s, computing was typically centralized on a single low-cost desktop computer. But today, computing resources (computers or servers) are typically physically distributed in many places, at which distributed networking excels.

Did you get it?

1. **What role does the client typically play in the client-server model when it comes to user interface and presentation processing?**
2. **How does the server contribute to data access processing within the client-server model?**

6.3. SERVICE DISCOVERY

→Learning Objectives

- Understand the concept of hardwiring computer addresses and its significance in networking.
- Explain the broadcast approach in networking and its use for communication between devices.
- Describe the name server approach and its role in resolving domain names to IP addresses.
- Analyze the broker-based location lookup method and its application in distributed systems.
- Explore the concept of client-server interoperability and its importance in heterogeneous network environments.
- Define client/server computing and identify its key components and characteristics.

To request a desired service, a client needs to know if there is a server that can provide it, what those characteristics are, where it is located, and its name. This is the service discovery problem. It is not necessary to determine whether a desired server exists in a simple distributed computing system with a small number of servers. All of the servers that are available are known in advance. This suggests that the scope of service discovery is limited to identifying the server that offers the required service. However, in a sizable distributed computing system that is a federation of several dispersed computing systems, with numerous service providers that dynamically offer and withdraw these services, it is necessary to ascertain whether a suitable service (e.g., a high-quality, extremely quick color printer) is available at a specific time, along with its name and location.

One of the most crucial aspects of a distributed computing system is transparency. It is important to note that in a distributed computing system managed by a distributed operating system, a client should only be aware of the name of a server or an agent acting on the server's behalf. In contrast, a client in a distributed computing system that is controlled by a collection of centralized operating systems and their extensions needs to be aware of its name and location in order to access remote resources and services. The absence of transparency is the cause.

Service discovery is achieved through the following modes:

- Server computer address is hardwired into client code;
- Broadcast is used to locate servers;
- Name server is used to locate services; and
- Brokers are used to locate servers.

6.3.1. Hardwiring Computer Address

All that is needed for this method is the server's location, which takes the form of its computer address. It is only useful in extremely small, straightforward systems, though, where the destination computer is only hosting one server process. An operating system can therefore deliver an incoming request to the right place.

A more sophisticated naming scheme forms the basis of an alternative variation of this methodology, in which requests are routed through processes as opposed to computers. Each process in this instance is identified by a pair <computer_address, process_name>. In addition to the server's name, a client receives the server computer's address. Since the user is aware of the server's location, this solution is not location transparent. When a server needs to be moved to a different computer and a pair of computers, the lack of transparency can cause issues. <computer_address, process_name> is ingrained in the client code.

6.3.2. Broadcast Approach

This method assigns a unique name to each process (e.g., for this purpose, an extremely lengthy identifier can be employed). To send a request, a client needs to know the name of the destination, specifically the server. This is insufficient, though, since the server's computer's operating system needs to be aware of its address. To achieve this, every computer connected to a network will receive a unique locate request from the client's operating system that includes the server's name. When an operating system discovers the name of the server in the list of processes it is running, indicating that the server is running on its machine, it responds with a "here I am" message that includes the address (location). After receiving the response, the operating system of the client can cache—or save—the server's computer address for use in subsequent communications. Although all computers on a network are involved in processing the locate request, this method is transparent but has a high broadcast overhead.

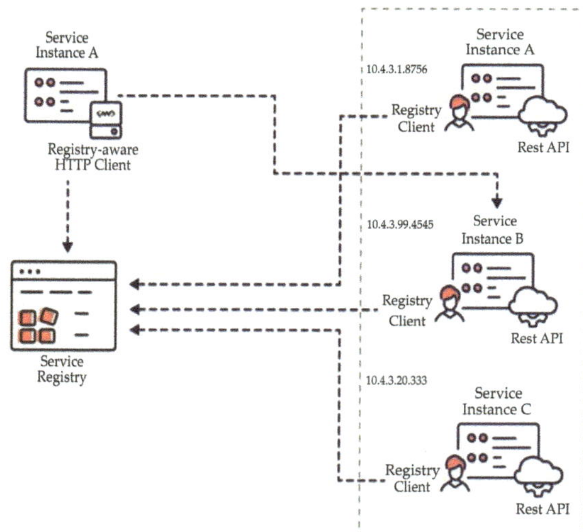

Figure 6.7. Service discovery -- broadcast approach (Source: Middleware.io, https://middleware.io/wp-content/uploads/2021/09/Client-Side-Service-Discovery-768x713.jpg).

The cooperation between clients, servers, and operating systems supporting them in a distributed computing system using the broadcast approach to locate servers is illustrated in Figure 6.7.

6.3.3. Name Server Approach

This method reduces the broadcast overhead but is quite similar to the broadcast-based method. The client's operating system sends a "where is" request to a name server—a specialized system server—asking for the address of the machine running the desired server to locate the desired server. All operating systems are aware of the name server's location (computer address) and name. The name server returns the requested server's address in a response. Upon receiving the response, the client's operating system can store the server's computer address for future communications.

When comparing this approach to the broadcast-based method, it is transparent and much more effective. However, due to the centralized nature of the name server, it may become a bottleneck and impact the overall performance of a distributed computing system. Additionally, this method lacks reliability; if a name server computer crashes, a distributed computing system cannot operate. Collaboration among clients, servers, and the supporting operating systems is essential in a distributed computing system utilizing the server.

6.3.4. Broker-Based Location Lookup

To access a desired service in a distributed computing system that uses any of the aforementioned server location approaches, a client needs to be aware of all the servers that are present in the system, their names, and, in the case of non-transparent systems, the locations of the servers (addresses). There may be a lot of servers in a large distributed computing system. In addition, distinct attributes pertaining to the services that they offer can distinguish servers of the same kind (e.g., a black and white printer and a color printer are two types of laser printers). Servers can also be dynamically revoked and offered by certain users. The identities, characteristics, and constantly fluctuating availability of each of these servers are not visible to the user. A server must exist that could assist users in resolving these issues. A broker is the term for this server. Therefore, a broker is a server that:

> **Keyword**
>
> **Service Management** focuses on providing value to the customer and also on the customer relationship.

- allows a client to identify available servers which can be characterized by a set of attributes that describe the properties of a desired service;
- mediates cooperation between clients and servers;

- allows service providers to register the services they support by providing their names, locations, and features in the form of attributes;
- advertises registered services and makes them available to clients; and
- withdraws services dynamically.

A name server approach's server location lookup is extremely similar to that of a broker-based approach. A broker and a name server, on the other hand, differ conceptually in important ways. A broker relieves clients of the burden of memorizing the path names or ASCII names of every server (and eventually their locations), while also enabling clients to identify server attributes and availability. As a result, a broker is a server that combines naming and *service management* functions. There exist two fundamental categories of brokers, representing distinct modes of collaboration between clients and servers:

6.3.4.1. Forwarding Broker

Cooperation between a client and a server mediated by this broker is as follows:

- Step 1: The broker receives from a client a service inquiry in the form of a set of attributes that characterize a desired service, and a server operation request;
- Step 2: If a matching server is available, the broker sends the server operation request to that found server; otherwise, it sends a failure response to the client;
- Step 3: the server sends back a response to the broker;
- Step 4: the broker passes the response to the client.

The forwarding broker possesses advantages and disadvantages of a system with a centralized server. This means that all requests to servers and their responses are going through this broker.

Direct Broker

Cooperation between a client and a server mediated by this broker is as follows:

- Step 1: The broker receives from a client a service inquiry in the form of a set of attributes that characterize a desired service;
- Step 2: If a matching server is available, the broker sends back a name and a server computer address to the client; otherwise, it sends a failure response;
- Step 3: The client sends the server operation request to the server;
- Step 4: The server sends back a response to the client.

Despite the fact that the direct broker also possesses advantages and disadvantages of a system with a centralized server, its performance is better than that of the forwarding broker because only service inquiry messages are sent to this broker.

6.3.5. Client-Server Interoperability

Because software writing is expensive, server reusability is a crucial concern for both users and software manufacturers. In a homogeneous environment, this problem might be easily fixed because software interfaces can be used to make client access mechanisms compatible, with static compatibility determined by types and dynamic compatibility by protocols. Because they are not entirely compatible, cooperation between heterogeneous clients and servers is far more challenging. Making them interoperable is therefore the problem. The capacity of two or more software components to work together despite variations in language, interface, and execution platform is known as interoperability.

Client-server interoperability has two components: interoperation mechanisms and an interoperation unit. A procedure is the fundamental building block of cooperation. However, software components might need higher-granularity units of interaction. Additionally, it might be necessary to preserve the functional and temporal properties.

There are two major mechanisms for interoperation:

- *Interface Standardization:* The objective of this mechanism is to map client and server interfaces to a common representation. The advantages of this mechanism are: (i) it separates communication models of clients from those of servers, and (ii) it provides scalability, since it only requires m + n mappings, where m and n are the number of clients and servers, respectively. The disadvantage of this mechanism is that it is closed.
- *Interface Bridging:* The objective of this mechanism is to provide a two-way mapping between a client and a server. The advantages of this mechanism are: (i) openness, and (ii) flexibility — it can be tailored to the requirements of a given client and server pair. However, this mechanism does not scale as well as the interface standardization mechanism, as it requires m * n mappings.

6.3.6. Client/Server Computing

The idea of dividing up related processing across multiple resources has gained popularity as networks of computing resources have become more commonplace. Many techniques have developed over time to make this distribution easier. Client/server computing is one of the most widely used distributed models. The modular programming model is expanded upon by the client/server model. A program's design can be divided into discrete modules that can be independently programmed and tested through the use of modular programming. A main module and one or more auxiliary modules make up a modular program. Clients and servers make up a client/server model, just like in a modular programming model. Typically, a computer network connects the various computers that the clients and servers use to operate. The called component is the server, and the calling component is the client.

Through the network, a client application communicates with a server to ask it to do a particular task. Input-output devices, local disks, and other peripherals are managed by the client. Requests from clients that are sent over the network are received by the server program. After receiving those requests, servers take certain actions. Only the results are sent back to the client after the majority of the data has been processed on the server. As a result, there is less network traffic between the client computer and the server. Network performance is further enhanced. In addition to managing information distribution, the server optimizes resource usage.

Whether a client communicates with the server directly or whether an intermediary process is introduced between the client and the server is a crucial design consideration for large client/server systems. Web applications typically use N-tier architecture to forward requests to additional enterprise services. Small environments are where the two-tier architecture is most commonly utilized because it is simpler to implement. Three-tier architecture is more scalable than two-tier architecture, though.

An intermediary process links the clients and servers in the three-tier architecture. For improved speed and scalability, the middleman can gather frequently used server data. A client PC, an application server, and a database server are typically the three main parts of a database-based 3-tier client/server architecture. The middle tier server that manages the business application is called the application server. The middle tier server retrieves the data from the database server and forwards it to the client. Creating a three-tier client/server application requires middleware. An *Application Program Interface (API)* is provided by database-oriented middleware to access a database. The popular Java Database Connectivity (JDBC) classes can be used to help an applet or servlet access multiple databases without taking into account the database's internal features.

Keyword

Application programming interface (API) is a way for two or more computer programs or components to communicate with each other. It is a type of software interface, offering a service to other pieces of software.

The issue of authentication must also be addressed by servers for security reasons. Sensitive information kept on a server by an unauthorized client could be accessed in a networked environment. Cryptographic techniques like public key encryption and special authentication servers are used to provide client authentication. Replicating vital servers can occasionally be done to attain fault tolerance and high availability. Clients can still access the other replicas hosted on separate servers in the event that one fails.

It is simpler to change or replace any tier in a three-tier architecture without impacting the other tiers. Improved load balancing is achieved by separating the functionality of the database and application. Furthermore, without negatively affecting the clients, the server tiers can implement the required security policies.

The "proxy server model," a three-tier client/server architecture (Figure 6.7), is frequently used to enhance Internet retrieval performance. In order to allow requests to run concurrently, the intermediary process known as the proxy server divides up client requests among multiple servers. A client establishes a connection with the proxy server and requests a service, like a web page hosted on a web server. The request is evaluated by the proxy server according to its filtering policy. It might, for instance, filter traffic based on a protocol or IP address. The proxy presents the resource by connecting to the relevant server and requesting the necessary service for the client if the filter authenticates the request.

Sometimes a proxy server will fulfill the request without getting in touch with the designated web server. This is made possible by storing frequently visited pages in the proxy's cache. The proxy can serve frequently accessed files back to a requesting browser without having to visit the external site each time by maintaining local copies of those files; this significantly enhances the end user's experience with performance. A "proxy-cache server" is the term used to describe a proxy server that has the capacity to cache data. A stand-in is occasionally.

Did you get it?

1. **How does the broker-based location lookup method function, and what are its applications in distributed systems?**
2. **What is the definition of client/server computing, and what are the key components and characteristics associated with this model?**

6.4. CHARACTERISTICS OF A DISTRIBUTED SYSTEM

→Learning Objectives

- Understand the concept of fault tolerance and its importance in ensuring system reliability and resilience.
- Explain scalability in the context of computing systems and its implications for accommodating growing workloads or user demands.
- Define predictable performance and discuss strategies for achieving consistent and reliable system response times.
- Explore the concept of openness in software and systems, including the benefits of interoperability and accessibility.
- Analyze security considerations in computing environments, including threats, vulnerabilities, and strategies for safeguarding data and resources.
- Discuss transparency in system design and operation, including mechanisms for providing visibility and insight into system behaviors and processes.

Distributed systems are characterized by several key features that distinguish them from centralized or standalone systems. These characteristics define the architecture, behavior, and capabilities of distributed systems, enabling them to achieve scalability, fault tolerance, and efficient resource utilization. One fundamental characteristic of distributed systems is decentralization, where multiple autonomous nodes collaborate to perform tasks or provide services without relying on a central coordinator. This decentralization fosters resilience and flexibility, as nodes can operate independently and adapt to changes in the network topology or workload distribution without affecting the system's overall functionality.

Another important characteristic of distributed systems is concurrency, which refers to the ability to perform multiple tasks or processes concurrently across different nodes in the network. Concurrency enables distributed systems to handle multiple requests simultaneously, improving throughput and responsiveness. However, managing concurrency requires mechanisms for synchronization and coordination to ensure consistency and integrity of shared resources or data accessed by multiple concurrent processes.

Scalability is a critical characteristic of distributed systems, allowing them to accommodate growing workloads or user demands by adding more nodes to the network. Scalability can be achieved through horizontal scaling, where additional nodes are added to distribute the workload, or vertical scaling, where existing nodes are upgraded to handle increased capacity. Distributed systems must be designed to scale efficiently, ensuring that adding or removing nodes does not introduce bottlenecks or degrade performance.

Fault tolerance is another key characteristic of distributed systems, enabling them to continue operating even in the presence of node failures, network partitions, or other types of faults. Distributed systems achieve fault tolerance through redundancy, replication, and distributed consensus mechanisms that enable nodes to detect and recover from failures autonomously. By replicating data or services across multiple nodes and implementing fault detection and recovery mechanisms, distributed systems can maintain availability and reliability in the face of failures.

Heterogeneity is a characteristic commonly found in distributed systems, where nodes may vary in terms of hardware, operating systems, programming languages, or communication protocols. Heterogeneity introduces challenges related to interoperability, data consistency, and resource management, requiring distributed systems to support diverse environments and integrate seamlessly with different technologies.

Finally, distributed systems exhibit transparency, which refers to the extent to which the distribution of resources and processes is hidden from users and applications. Transparency encompasses aspects such as location transparency, where the physical location of resources is abstracted from users, and access transparency, where users can access distributed resources as if they were centralized. Achieving transparency simplifies the development and deployment of distributed applications, enabling users to interact with distributed systems seamlessly without needing to be aware of the underlying complexities of the network architecture.

A distributed system must possess the following characteristics to deliver utmost performance for the users:

6.4.1. Fault-Tolerant

Distributed systems are composed of numerous hardware and software components, all of which will eventually fail. These types of component failures can result in service disruptions. Therefore, systems should be able to recover from component failures without errors. Fault tolerance is designed to prevent system failures even in the presence of faults to ensure continuous service. If a system can hide errors, it is considered fault tolerant. The objective of any fault-tolerant system is to enhance its dependability and availability. The system's ability to operate until a certain point is known as its reliability. Dependable systems prevent data loss even in the event of component failures. The time a system is available for use is referred to as its availability. Redundancy is typically employed to achieve fault tolerance, involving components that are not essential for the system's basic operation. There are three types of redundancy: time, software, and hardware. Hardware redundancy is achieved by adding extra hardware components to take over the functions of failed components.

6.4.2. Scalable

When a distributed system is scaled to a larger size, some parts of the system still function as intended. Three factors determine a system's scale: the quantity of users and other entities it contains, the separation between its farthest nodes, and the number of organizations that have administrative control over certain areas of the system. The three dimensions of scale have a variety of effects on distributed systems. A few of the components that are impacted are naming, authorization, communication, remote resource utilization, authentication to confirm an individual's identity, and user observation mechanisms. To control scale, three strategies are used: caching, replication, and distribution.

Resources are replicated multiple times during replication. Its application to file services, naming, and authentication lightens the burden on individual servers and raises the overall availability and dependability of the services. The locations of the replicas and the methods used to maintain consistency between them are the two key aspects of replication. The reason for replicating a resource determines where replicas should be placed in a distributed system. A service's replicas are dispersed throughout the system if it is being replicated in order to minimize network latency when the service is accessed. Replicas may be positioned close to one another if most users are local and if the service is being replicated to increase availability or distribute the load across several servers. Any modifications made to the object should be apparent to all users of the system. As an illustration, the system updates any replica it finds, and that replica then distributes the updates to the others as they become available. Timestamps, or the date and time the update was generated, are used to distinguish between copies of an inconsistent update if they are received by various replicas in different orders.

A distributed service's data can be expanded across multiple servers through distribution, another method for controlling scale in distributed systems. By spreading the data among several servers, the size of the database that each server needs to maintain is decreased, which cuts down on the amount of time required for database searches. Additionally, distribution divides the load among the servers, limiting the amount of requests that each can handle. The load on servers can be efficiently managed if requests are routed to servers according to their power. Assigning data to servers near their most frequently used location can help minimize network traffic. If cached copies are accessible from lower-level servers in a tree-structured system, the higher levels can be skipped.

Another crucial method for creating scalable systems is caching. The strain on servers and the network is reduced by caching. Accessing data that has been cached is quicker than making a new request. Replication and caching differ in that the latter is a temporary storage of data. When consistency cannot be ensured, consistency is preserved by nullifying cached data rather than propagating updates on it. As the client typically handles caching, there are fewer repeated requests made to the network services. On the servers running those services, caching may also take place. It is quicker to read a file from the file server's memory cached copy than from the client's local disk.

6.4.3. Predictable Performance

A range of performance indicators, including system utilization, network capacity, throughput (the speed at which data is sent or received over a network), response time (the amount of time that passes between the end of a request or inquiry on a computer system and the start of a response), etc., are used in order to evaluate the performance. The capacity to deliver desired responsiveness on time is known as predictable performance.

6.4.4. Openness

The quality that guarantees a subsystem is always available for communication with other systems is called "openness." Software systems known as web services are made to facilitate networked, interoperable machine-to-machine communication. These protocols enable scalability and extension of distributed systems. A scalable, open system is preferable to one that is totally closed and independent. The openness of a distributed system is achieved without relying on the heterogeneity of the underlying environment, including hardware and software platforms. As a result, each service in the system is equally available to all clients, whether they are local or remote. New service implementation, installation, and debugging shouldn't be too difficult in a system with an openness characteristic.

Remember

A distributed networking system is composed of processes, threads, agents, and distributed objects. Merely distributed physical components are not enough to suffice as a distributed network; typically distributed networking uses concurrent program execution.

6.4.5. Security

By enforcing the appropriate security measures, distributed systems should enable communication between users, programs, and resources on various computers. The primary goals of the security features are to ensure availability, integrity, and confidentiality. Privacy, or confidentiality, is the defense against revelation to unauthorized parties. Confidentiality violations can range from upsetting to disastrous. Integrity shields against corruption and modification. Availability maintains the resource's usability. The integrity of databases and other resources is frequently compromised by hacking incidents. The term "denial of service" refers to an attack that targets availability. Nonrepudiation and access control are two more crucial security issues. Ensuring that users can only access resources and services to which they are legally entitled is made easier by maintaining access control. Additionally, it makes sure that users don't lose access to resources that they have a right to. Protection against denial by one of the parties to a communication is offered by nonrepudiation. The security measures implemented ought to ensure that various system users are utilizing resources in an appropriate manner.

6.4.6. Transparency

Rather than being seen as a group of collaborating parts, distributed systems should be viewed as a whole by users and application developers. The locations of computer systems that are involved in concurrent operations, data replication, failures, system recovery, and resource discovery from multiple sites. are concealed from users. Transparency allows the system to appear and function like a typical centralized system, concealing from its users the fact that it is distributed. In a distributed system, the transparency can be used in various ways (Figure 6.8).

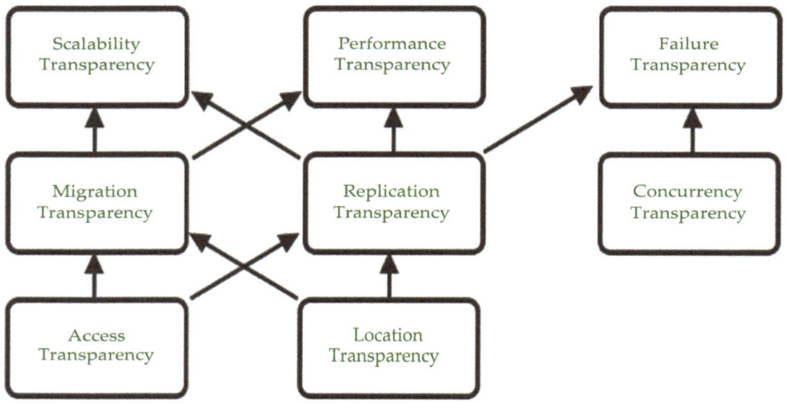

Figure 6.8. Transparency in Distributed Systems (Source: Geeksforgeeks, https://media.geeksforgeeks.org/wp-content/uploads/20220527122938/Dimensionsoftransparency.jpg).

- Access transparency facilitates the users of a distributed system to access local and remote resources using identical operations (e.g., navigation on the web).
- Location transparency describes names used to identify network resources (e.g., IP address) independently of both the user's location and the resource location. In other words, location transparency enables a user to access resources from anywhere on the network without knowing where the resource is located. A file could be on the user's own PC or thousands of miles away on other servers.
- Concurrency transparency enables several processes to operate concurrently using shared information objects without interference between them (e.g., Automatic Teller Machine network). The users will not notice the existence of other users in the system, even if they access the same resources.
- Replication transparency enables the system to make additional copies of files and other resources for the purpose of performance and/or reliability, without the users noticing. If a resource is replicated among several locations, it should appear to the user as a single resource (e.g., Mirroring – Mirror sites are usually used to offer multiple sources of the same information as a way of providing reliable access to large downloads).
- Failure transparency enables applications to complete their tasks despite failures occurring in certain components of the system. For example, if a server fails, but users are automatically redirected to another server and the user never notices the failure, the system is said to exhibit high failure transparency. Failure transparency is one of the most challenging types of transparency to achieve since it is difficult to determine whether a server has actually failed or is simply responding very slowly. Moreover, achieving full failure transparency in a distributed system is generally unfeasible due to the unreliability of networks.
- Migration transparency allows resources to move from one location to another

without changing their names (e.g., Web Pages). Users should not be aware of whether a resource or computing entity can move to a different physical or logical location.

- Performance transparency ensures that load variation does not result in performance degradation. This can be achieved through automatic reconfiguration in response to changes in the load (e.g., load distribution).
- Scalability transparency enables the system to remain efficient even with a significant increase in the number of users and connected resources (e.g., World-Wide-Web, distributed database).

Did you get it?

1. **What does scalability mean in the context of computing systems, and how does it impact the ability to handle increasing workloads or user demands?**
2. **How can you analyze security considerations in computing environments, including identifying potential threats and vulnerabilities, and implementing strategies to protect data and resources?**

FOCUS ON CAREERS

WIRELESS NETWORK ENGINEER

A Wireless Network Engineer job description includes installing, configuring, and maintaining wireless network equipment, network management, and security, including 802.11 b/g/n/ac standards and industry best practices for implementing high-density WIFI solutions. Moreover, to put it concisely, a Wireless Network Engineer needs to assess, plan, and develop several operational capabilities for wireless telecommunications. As more companies continue to embrace Wireless LAN, the demand for wireless network engineers has grown manifold in the recent past. The proliferation of mobile applications, which require testing in a wireless environment, is also one of the other reasons why enterprises need their services more. Research indicates that 60% of enterprise-level managers report utilizing freelancers in their workforce. But with the emergence of Software Defined WAN (SD-WAN) DevOps, the advent of 5G, and virtualization, it is necessary for Wireless Network Engineers to be open to reskill themselves, as it could likely bring about changes that might change the way they operate. It is, however, averred by experts that despite all the changes that may take place in the networking landscape, the demand for Wireless Network Engineers will continue to rise.

Wireless Network Engineer Job Description

To become a freelance Wireless Network Engineer, aspirants need to be well-versed in wireless equipment, wireless LAN (WLAN) standards, design, and protocols. Wireless Network Engineer job descriptions will require excellent analytical and problem-solving skills. They should also have good communication skills as they would need to work alongside vendors, network technicians, and customers.

Wireless Network Engineers need to be available round-the-clock to support mission-critical applications. They should have strong customer service skills.

The responsibilities and duties of a Wireless Network Engineer include the following:

- Devise, plan, deploy, and improve wireless networks from the beginning to implementation by collaborating with vendors, managers, and network engineers.
- Understand client requirements to be able to cater to their appropriate needs.
- Manage firewalls, such as Palo Alto, Juniper, or Cisco ASA.
- Handhold other in-house engineers to train them on wireless technologies, besides guiding other non-technical people.
- Use tools to evaluate to test and tweak wireless products, such as routers, switches, hubs, bridges, virtual private networks (VPNs), and network amplifiers, among others.
- Design and validate the performance, quality, and reliability of the RF link.

- Design and implement WLANs and other wireless networks.
- Write manuals and document current network procedures.
- Have extensive knowledge of routing protocols (OSPF, EIGRP, and BGP).Make use of enterprise monitoring tools (SolarWinds and Splunk).
- Optimize network performance by supervising performance, addressing network problems and breakdowns, and partnering with network engineers to optimize the network.
- Develop and implement policies and classify and oversee access to protect network systems.
- Ensure that all equipment, including servers and other network products, is well-connected.
- Devise and support radio frequencies (RF) link performance, reliability, and quality.
- Enable data and system protection by developing and maintaining mechanisms for backing up and retrieval.
- Collaborate with different teams to ensure the optimized performance of VoIP and other wireless telecommunication devices.
- Work with the security team to evaluate threats, troubleshoot issues, and comply with appropriate security configuration standards of their organizations.
- Design and deploy changes to the configurations of clients as per the applicable change management process.
- Proactively handle all network security solutions.
- Utilize testing and diagnostic tools to assess and modify equipment.

Wireless Network Engineers Job Prospects

As more companies continue to embrace Wireless LAN, the demand for wireless network engineers has recently grown. The proliferation of mobile applications, which require testing, is also one of the reasons why enterprises need their services more.

With the emergence of Software Defined Networking (SDN), DevOps, 5G, and virtualization, it is necessary for an engineer to be open to reskilling themselves, as it could likely bring about changes that will alter the way networks operate.

It is, however, asserted by experts that despite all the changes that may take place in the networking landscape, the demand for Wireless Network Engineers will continue to grow.

Wireless Network Engineer Training & Educational Qualifications

Most employers would look for Wireless Network Engineers who have undergone wireless network engineer training to earn a bachelor's degree or an equivalent in mathematics, engineering, or computer science. They should have a certification in Cisco Certified

Network Professional (CCNP) Wireless or Certified Wireless Network Professional (CWNP) or Aruba Certified Mobility Associate (ACMA).

Since it is a skill set that requires experience, a minimum experience of five years in WAN/LAN engineering is mandatory for an aspirant.

Through wireless network engineer training, they should become adept with wireless technologies, such as Wi-Fi, WiMax, and WAP. Wireless Network Engineer Training should have a thorough knowledge of 802.11n and 802.11a. They should be able to understand scripting languages, such as Bash, Perl, or Python.

Engineers should have extensive knowledge of both wired and wireless networking.

Wireless Network Engineer Salary

According to Indeed, the average earnings of a Wireless Network Engineer (CCNP certified) range in a senior position from about $87,772 per year to $106,566 per year in the United States. While their average annual earnings are $83,998 per year, freelancers earn $24.57 per hour, says Payscale. There are numerous additional factors that make up the salary of a Wireless Network Engineer.

SUMMARY

- A group of linked computers is referred to as a computer network. Nodes designate computers connected to a network. Computers can be linked wirelessly using radio waves or through cabling, typically an Ethernet cable..
- Wide Area Networks (WANs) link computers and local networks to larger networks across larger geographical regions, such as continents.
- An assembly of computing hardware, including computer systems, connected via communication channels to enable resource sharing and communication among users, forms a computer network.
- The fundamental idea behind OSI is that communication between two endpoints in a network can be separated into seven different groups, or layers, of related functions. Every user or program that communicates uses a device capable of providing those seven levels of functionality.
- Routing protocols are designed for internet routers to use.
- In a ring topology, each device has a unique connection to the two devices on its sides..
- Every device in a star topology has a dedicated point-to-point link that connects it to the hub, or central controller.
- Hostname is a special device name that is assigned to each device in the network. In the Administrator Mode command prompt, type "hostname" and hit "Enter" to see your machine's hostname.

MULTIPLE CHOICE QUESTIONS

1. In distributed system each processor has its own
   a. local memory
   b. clock
   c. both local memory and clock
   d. none of the mentioned
2. If one site fails in distributed system
   a. the remaining sites can continue operating
   b. all the sites will stop working
   c. directly connected sites will stop working
   d. none of the mentioned
3. A dynamic connection that grows into dynamic networks of networks, is called
   a. Cyber cycle
   b. Internet of things
   c. Cyber-physical system
   d. Multithreading

4. Parallel computing is also known as
   a. Parallel computation
   b. Parallel processing
   c. Parallel distribution
   d. Parallel development
5. Connections that grows exponentially into a new dynamic network of networks, is known as
   a. Dynamic
   b. Static
   c. Transparent
   d. Opaque

REVIEW QUESTIONS

1. Define the client-server model in a distributed computing system.
2. Explain the cooperation between clients and servers.
3. What are the extensions to the client-server model?
4. Discuss the three-tier client-server architecture.
5. What is broadcast approach?

Answers of Multiple Choice Questions

1. (c) 2. (a) 3. (b) 4. (b) 5. (a)

REFERENCES

1. Robert, R., Chris, A., & Jay, L., (2003). A solver for the network testbed mapping problem. *ACM SIGCOMM Computer Communications Review, 32*(2), 65–81.
2. Jonathon, D., Robert, R., John, B., & Jay, L., (2006). *Automatic IP Address Assignment on Network Topologies.* Technical Report FTN-2006-02.
3. David, S. A., Leigh, S., Mike, H., Tim, S., & Jay, L., (2006). Automatic online validation of network configuration in the Emulab network testbed. *Third IEEE International Conference on Autonomic Computing (ICAC 2006).*
4. Ang, B. S., Chiou, D., Rosenband, D. L., Ehrlich, M., Rudolph, L., & Arvind, (1998). StarT-voyager: A flexible platform for exploring scalable SMP issues. In: *Proceedings of SC98: High Performance Networking and Computing*. Orlando, Florida.
5. Arpaci-Dusseau, C., (1998). *Implicit Coscheduling: Coordinated Scheduling with Implicit Information in Distributed Systems*. PhD thesis, University of California at Berkeley.

6. Adem, E. G., David, B., Emin, G. S., & Robbert, V. R., (2015). *Configuring Distributed Computations Using Response Surfaces*. Middleware, Vancouver, Canada.
7. Alysson, N. B., Eduardo, A., Miguel, C., & Joni, S. F., (2008). DepSpace: A Byzantine Fault-Tolerant Coordination Service. *Proceedings of the 3rd ACM SIGOPS/EuroSys European Systems Conference – EuroSys'08.*
8. Jonathon, D., Robert, R., Junxing, Z., Daniel, G., Sneha, K., & Jay, L., (2006). Flexlab: A realistic, controlled, and friendly environment for evaluating networked systems. *Fifth Workshop on Hot Topics in Networks (HotNets-V).*
9. Shashi, G., Rob, R., & Jay, L., (2005). Integrated network experimentation using simulation and emulation. *First International Conference on Testbeds and Research Infrastructures for the Development of Networks and Communities (Tridentcom 2005).*
10. Shashikiran, B. G., (2005). *Issues in Integrated Network Experimentation Using Simulation and Emulation*. Thesis, University of Utah.
11. David, J., Tim, S., Russ, F., Daniel, M. F., Leigh, S., Robert, R., & Jay, L., (2006). *Mobile Emulab: A Robotic Wireless and Sensor Network Testbed*. IEEE INFOCOM 2006.
12. Arora, N. S., Blumofe, R. D., & Plaxton, C. G., (1998). Thread scheduling for multiprogrammed multiprocessors. In: *Proceedings of the 10th Symposium on Parallel Algorithms and Architectures* (pp. 119–129). Puerto Vallarta, Mexico.
13. Jonathon, D., Robert, R., John, B., & Jay, L., (2005). *Optimizing IP Address Assignment on Network Topologies*. Technical Report FTN-2005-04, University of Utah.
14. Bruno, V., Nuno, N., Henrique, M., & Paulo, V., (2010). Randomized consensus in wireless environments: A case where more is better. *Third International Conference on Dependability*. Venice, Italy.
15. Nitin, G., Alan, J. D., & Johannes, E. G., (2008). SEMMO: A scalable engine for massively multiplayer online games. *Talk. International Conference on Management of Data.* Vancouver, Canada.
16. Vincent, G., Ymir, V., Ken, B., Anne-Marie, K., & Robbert, V. R., (2007). *Sliver, a Fast Distributed Slicing Algorithm.* Technical Report.
17. David, J., Daniel, G., & Jay, L., (2008). Towards a high quality path-oriented network measurement and storage system. *Proc. of the Ninth Passive and Active Measurement Conference (PAM 2008).*
18. Michael, P. K., Priya, N., Kevin, A., & Jay, L., (2006). Towards finger pointing in the Emulab dynamic distributed system. *Third USENIX Workshop on Real, Large Distributed Systems (WORLDS 2006).*
19. David, J., Tim, S., Russ, F., Dan, F., Rob, R., & Jay, L., (2005). *TrueMobile: A Mobile Robotic Wireless and Sensor Network Testbed.* Technical Report FTN-2005-02, University of Utah.

CHAPTER

7

Wireless Network Security

LEARNING OBJECTIVES

After studying this chapter, you will be able to:

- Define the synopsis of wireless technology
- Examine the development of wireless LANS
- Learn about the wireless personal area networks

INTRODUCTORY EXAMPLE

WIRELESS NETWORK SECURITY IN AN ORGANIZATION

Wireless network security in an organization is a critical aspect of ensuring the confidentiality, integrity, and availability of sensitive information and resources. It encompasses various measures, protocols, and best practices designed to protect the organization's wireless infrastructure from unauthorized access, data breaches, and cyber threats.

To begin with, implementing robust authentication and encryption mechanisms is essential. Strong authentication protocols like WPA2-Enterprise or WPA3, coupled with complex pre-shared keys (PSKs) for smaller deployments, help verify the identity of users and devices before granting access to the network. Encryption protocols such as AES (Advanced Encryption Standard) ensure that data transmitted over the wireless network remains secure and cannot be intercepted or tampered with by unauthorized parties.

Furthermore, controlling access to the wireless network is vital for minimizing security risks. This can be achieved through techniques such as MAC address filtering, where only devices with pre-approved MAC addresses are allowed to connect, and disabling SSID broadcasting to make the network less visible to potential attackers. Segmenting the wireless network into separate virtual LANs (VLANs) based on user roles or departments adds an extra layer of security by restricting the lateral movement of threats within the network.

Regular monitoring and intrusion detection play a crucial role in identifying and mitigating security threats in real-time. Intrusion detection systems (IDS) or intrusion prevention systems (IPS) can analyze network traffic patterns and detect suspicious activities or unauthorized access attempts. Additionally, deploying wireless intrusion detection/prevention systems (WIDS/WIPS) helps monitor the airwaves for rogue access points, unauthorized clients, or other malicious activities that could compromise network security.

Employee awareness and training are also essential components of a comprehensive wireless network security strategy. Educating users about the risks of connecting to unsecured wireless networks, the importance of using strong passwords, and the dangers of phishing attacks can significantly reduce the likelihood of security incidents resulting from human error or negligence.

Finally, regular security audits, vulnerability assessments, and penetration testing should be conducted to identify weaknesses in the wireless network infrastructure and address them promptly. Updating firmware, patches, and security configurations for wireless devices and access points is crucial for staying ahead of emerging threats and vulnerabilities.

INTRODUCTION

A few advantages that wireless communications provide to users and organizations are enhanced productivity, reduced installation costs, and portability and flexibility. With a wide range of applications and needs in mind, wireless technologies offer a diverse range of capabilities. The threats to wireless network security are categorized into nine groups in this chapter: malicious hackers, industrial espionage, malicious code, threats to personal privacy, employee sabotage, fraud and theft by authorized or unauthorized users of the system, loss of physical and infrastructure support, and errors and omissions. Potential risks to wireless networks are all represented by the aforementioned. But the immediate threats to wireless communications are industrial and foreign espionage, fraud and theft, hostile hackers, and malicious code. Given how portable wireless devices are, theft is more likely to happen. Fraud and theft can be committed by both authorized and unauthorized users of the system, though the former are more likely to do so. It is simpler for users to communicate when they are aware of the resources and security vulnerabilities in the system.

7.1. SYNOPSIS OF WIRELESS TECHNOLOGY

→Learning Objectives

- Understand the fundamentals of wireless communication technologies
- Recognize various types of wireless devices such as smartphones, tablets, laptops, and IoT devices
- Understand the risks associated with unsecured wireless networks and unauthorized access
- Explore the latest trends and advancements in wireless communication technologies.
- Gain an understanding of FIPS and its significance in information security standards

In the simplest terms, wireless technologies allow for the communication of one or more devices without the need for network or peripheral cabling or physical connections. Whereas wired technologies use cables, wireless technologies use radio frequency transmissions to transfer data. Wireless technologies cover a broad spectrum, from sophisticated systems like wireless local area networks (WLAN) and cell phones to basic gadgets like wireless microphones, headphones, and other non-processing, non-storing devices. They also include wireless hi-fi stereo headsets, some cordless computer keyboards and mice, and remote controls that use infrared (IR) technology. All of these devices require a direct line of sight to break the connection.

7.1.1. Wireless Networks

A wireless network is one that is set up so that computers and other network devices can communicate with one another using radio signal frequency. It is also known as a WLAN or WiFi network at times. These days, this network is becoming more and more popular because it requires no cabling and is simple to set up. Without the use of cables, computers can be connected to any location in your house.

Here's a brief explanation of how it operates: Suppose you have a wireless router installed and two PCs, each with a wireless adapter. The binary data will be converted to radio frequency and sent via wireless router when the computer sends out the data. After that, the signal will be decoded back to binary data by the receiving computer. Using a wireless network, you can access the internet via either a DSL modem or a broadband cable. If you've heard of a wireless hotspot, it's a place where you and other people can connect to a wireless network using wireless devices.

The two main components are wireless router or access point and wireless clients. Simply purchase a wireless router and connect it to your cable or DSL modem if you haven't already set up a wired network. After that, you create a basic wireless network by installing wireless cards into each computer and configuring wireless clients.

7.1.1.1. Wireless LANs

A wireless local area network, also known as a wireless LAN, is made up of two or more computers connected to the same radio frequency. This is in contrast to a wired LAN, where every computer on the network is physically connected to the server's network switch or hub via an Ethernet cable. Every network starts with a primary computer, also called a server, and a number of connected devices, also referred to as clients. Two Ethernet network interface cards (NICs) and network-supporting software are usually installed on the server. Since Windows 98 Special Edition (SE), Microsoft Windows operating systems have included built-in networking capabilities; however, third-party networking software is also accessible. A desktop computer could be the server and a laptop the client in a basic home wireless LAN. Assume for the moment that the desktop computer is connected to a high-speed digital subscriber line (DSL) for Internet access. The desktop computer must be physically linked to a wireless DSL modem in order to share the Internet connection via a wireless local area network (WLAN). A network switch or router may also be integrated into the wireless DSL modem. These two devices maintain data flow to the appropriate network machine. Should they not be integrated into the modem, they will need to be bought independently.

> **Keyword**
>
> **Multiple-Input Multiple-Output (MIMO)** is a wireless technology that uses multiple transmitters and receivers to transfer more data at the same time.

Physical Ethernet cables are used to connect the desktop server to the DSL modem, switch, and router. But the clients don't need any cabling. Instead, a wireless NIC needs to be installed on every computer. This could be an internal wireless NIC, a USB device, or a PCMCIA NIC. A tiny antenna is a feature of many wireless NICs, but not all of them. Radio waves can be used by machines to send and receive data once the wireless LAN has been configured on the server and client. Because the client can stay mobile anywhere within the network's broadcasting range, a wireless LAN is incredibly convenient. With a laptop, one can work from any room in the house—mostly even the backyard—and still share the server's network connection.

Mobile employees have instant access to the office via a wireless LAN. Additionally, it saves money by eliminating the need to run Ethernet cables throughout an entire building, enabling simple desktop connectivity between clients. One of the key benefits of a wireless local area network (LAN) is its ease of installation, as there are no wires needed to reach the clients. In addition to being less expensive, wireless LANs offer greater flexibility than wired LANs. A wired network has fewer security measures to prevent intrusion, and wireless LANs can be slower and less dependable when interference is present. These are the two main drawbacks of wireless LANs. On the other hand, as technology advances, dependency rates also do. Certain wireless local area networks (LANs) can rival wired networks. Wireless technology standards are denoted by letter designations. 54 megabits per second are possiblwith the wireless "g" standard (mbps). The most recent iterations of *multiple input multiple output (MIMO)* technology enable rates to approach 100 mbps.

7.1.1.2. Ad Hoc Networks

Wireless networks have been classified into two categories since their inception: ad hoc networks and infrastructure networks, which include some LANs. The Latin term "ad hoc" means "for this purpose." Ad hoc networks, then, are networks that are designed specifically for that purpose. They are frequently made quickly and for a single, fleeting purpose. These networks typically consist of a collection of workstations or other wireless devices that exchange data directly with one another. Consider these ties as impromptu networks that are open to anyone in a particular location.

An ad hoc network is one in which no access points allow participants to exchange data. Infrastructure networks route data via a central information hub, which may be a computer's hardware or software. For instance, office networks typically use a server that business workstations connect to in order to obtain their information. On the other hand, ad hoc networks bypass a central information hub.

These networks are usually created between participants and are closed networks, meaning they do not connect to the Internet. However, if one of the participants is connected to a public or private network, other network members may share this connection. This will make it possible for additional users on the impromptu ad hoc network to establish an Internet connection. Due to their ability to enable wireless gaming between players, ad hoc networks are frequently found on portable gaming systems such as the Nintendo DS and Sony PSP. Customers can access new game demos through the store's own ad hoc network by creating networks within certain retail establishments. Peer-to-peer networking for the wireless era is what an ad hoc network is. Network environments for early Windows computers were created using peer-to-peer or workgroup style networks. In a smaller office setting, this allowed the early computers to connect to each other and share information without the need for domains and the associated extra overhead and management.

7.1.2. Wireless Devices

Any type of communication equipment that can transmit data to another device without the need for a physical wire is referred to as a wireless device. Wireless headphones with a receiver connect to a transmitter that is connected to the sound source, such as a television, using either radio frequency (RF) or infrared technology. Generally speaking, though, a wireless device is a networking device that can transmit data to other wireless network equipment even when it is not physically connected.

There are many different kinds of wireless technologies in today's world, where people value having constant access to the Internet and to one another. Local area networks (LANs) are broadcast by wireless routers with integrated modems, hubs, and switches in homes and offices, enabling nearby computers to connect. A LAN typically spans 300 feet (91.44 m) or more, though the actual broadcasting distance varies greatly depending on numerous factors. A printer, other office supplies, or a fast Internet connection are just a few examples of the network resources that any computer on the network can share. A wireless network card or adapter needs to be installed on a computer in order for it to connect to a wireless LAN (WLAN). A network card is an internal wireless device designed to operate using the same protocol or language as wireless routers. Nevertheless, in the interim, compatibility problems arise as these protocols sporadically develop into new standards. In cases where an internal wireless device is unable to support the protocol used by the router, an external wireless adapter can be inserted into an external port. Although ExpressCard® formats are also available for wireless network adapters, laptop users have an additional option in addition to the more popular USB dongle.

Perhaps a Personal Area Network (PAN) contains another kind of wireless device. A Personal Area Network (PAN) is established through the use of Bluetooth® technology, which allows connections between personal digital devices over extremely short distances—a few feet, on average—though the standard is 30 feet (9.14 m). Networks of the Bluetooth® variety are incredibly versatile and practical. It saves the trouble of setting up shared resources over a LAN by allowing print jobs to be sent from a laptop to a nearby printer. Moreover, it is employed to link Apple products, PDAs, and cell phones with Bluetooth® capability to one another as well as to other Bluetooth®-enabled devices like computers, headsets, and standalone speakers. A Bluetooth® network can operate "within" a LAN without interfering since it operates on a different frequency spectrum than LANs.

7.1.1.3. Personal Digital Assistants

A portable electronic gadget used for communication and personal organization is called a personal digital assistant (PDA). PDAs typically have memory cards for removable storage, touch screens that allow for finger or stylus input, organizational software like an address book and calendar, and ways to connect to a personal computer via a cable or a wireless protocol like Bluetooth®. The majority allow you to add apps, like games or business software.

PDAs come in a wide variety, occupying a space between laptop computers and cell phones in terms of both functionality and size. Typically, they are compact enough to fit easily in a pocket or belt loop. A smartphone is a PDA that has cell phone functionality; these are by far the most common kind of PDAs available.

One of the key benefits of PDAs is their capacity to replace numerous heavy paper organizational tools with one handy device. A software suite used for personal organization is referred to as a "personal information manager" (PIM). While some PIMs run on PCs or other platforms, this suite is typically included with a personal digital assistant. A calendar, address book, notepad, calculator, to-do list, and other small apps resembling those in a paper-based personal organizer are commonly included in this software. Software for spreadsheets and word processing may also be included in more advanced bundles. Earlier on in the history of the device class, PDAs themselves were also referred to as "Personal Information Managers.""

Remember

Restrict access by MAC address. Many will tell you that MAC address restriction doesn't provide real protection but, like hiding your wireless network's SSID, restricting the MAC addresses allowed to connect to the network helps ensure you are not one of the "low hanging fruits" that people prefer to attack.

A number of operating systems (OS), called mobile operating systems, have been created specifically for PDAs. Many mobile operating systems are based on familiar computer operating systems — such as Microsoft Windows®, Mac OS®, or Linux® — that have been heavily modified to run using a mobile device's limited hardware and interface elements. Others are built from scratch with the electronic device in mind. While the PC market has historically been dominated by Windows®, no single OS holds a clear majority in the mobile market. When personal digital assistants rose to popularity in the late 1990s and early 2000s, many popular devices by Handspring™ and Palm®, Inc. ran Palm OS®, which featured a simple interface and primitive handwriting recognition software called Graffiti™. With the introduction of the Palm Pre™, the operating system was succeeded by Palm webOS™. Microsoft's mobile OS is called Windows Mobile®; Apple's is called iPhone® OS. Symbian™ OS and the Google-initiated Android™ are other mobile operating systems.

A minor backlash emerged in popular culture as a result of the personal digital assistant's quick ascent to fame and early connotations as a status symbol for the business class. The cheeky Hipster PDA was designed by self-help author Merlin Mann. It is a set of index cards with a ballpoint pen and binder clips holding them together. A user base has emerged to support the "device" as a result of the concept becoming popular with some people.

7.1.1.4. Smart Phones

In addition to the basic function of placing calls, smartphones offer additional features. A smartphone is typically thought of as a mobile phone rather than a landline, even though the term can be appropriately used to refer to any kind of phone. As mobile devices have advanced in sophistication over time, the idea of the "smartphone" has grown. In 1992, IBM created the first mobile phone that could be categorized as a smartphone. Renamed Simon, the gadget debuted at COMDEX that year and went on sale to the general public the following year. The functionality included several useful features previously exclusive to desktop and laptop computers. Simon added an email feature, a basic notepad, a calculator, and fax and email capabilities. Not too long after, the user could also play a few games on the device and view the current times in major cities across the globe with the help of a handy world clock. There were several kinds of cutting-edge mobile phone devices available on the market for the balance of the 1990s. On many smartphones, touch screens started to take the place of keypads. New model releases brought with them increasingly complex email and gaming features. The quality of the speakerphone feature on many smartphone models started to compete with that of handset speakerphones. A feature-rich communication tool, the smartphone serves many purposes today. New developments in smartphone technology include the addition of Internet access. Nowadays, people can browse the web just as easily as they would on a desktop or laptop. The clarity and integrity of the phone's basic audio signal have been improved by numerous smartphone manufacturers concurrently. This makes it possible to use the smartphone to make a basic phone call and still expect clear, sharp sound quality, even with all the extra features added.

7.1.3. Wireless Security Threats and Risk Mitigation

Security risks are generally divided into nine categories by An Introduction to Computer Security, which range from mistakes and omissions to threats to individual privacy. These all stand for possible dangers to wireless networks. But the more pressing issues with wireless communications are theft of devices, denial of service attacks, hostile hackers, malicious code, theft of service, and foreign and industrial espionage. Because wireless devices are so portable, theft is more likely to happen. The system's users, both authorized and unauthorized, have the potential to commit fraud and theft, but authorized users are more likely to do so. Users find it easier to commit fraud and theft because they may be aware of the resources available to them and the security holes in the system. Hackers who enter a system without authorization with malicious intent, also known as crackers, typically do so for personal gain or malicious intent. Typically, malicious hackers are people who are not affiliated with any agency or organization, though they can also be users there. Through wireless device eavesdropping, these hackers may be able to access the wireless network access point.

If successful, attacks stemming from these threats jeopardize an agency's systems and, more crucially, its data. The main goals of all government security practices and policies are to ensure availability, confidentiality, integrity, and authenticity. Information must be shielded from unauthorized, unexpected, or inadvertent alteration, according to NIST Special Publication (SP) 800-26, Security Self-Assessment Guide for Information Technology Systems. The following are among the requirements for security:

- *Authenticity:* A third party must be able to verify that the content of a message has not been changed in transit.
- *Nonrepudiation:* The origin or the receipt of a specific message must be verifiable by a third party.
- *Accountability:* The actions of an entity must be traceable uniquely to that entity.

Network availability is "the property of being accessible and usable upon demand by an authorized entity."

The information technology resource (system or data) must be available on a timely basis to meet mission requirements or to avoid substantial losses. Availability also includes ensuring that resources are used only for intended purposes.

The risks associated with operating a wireless network are the same as those associated with operating a wired network (or any network, for that matter) plus the additional risks brought about by flaws in wireless protocols. Agencies must implement security procedures and policies that help reduce these risks to a manageable level in order to mitigate them. For example, before implementing wireless networks, they must conduct security assessments to identify the specific risks and weaknesses that these networks will bring into their environments. They should take into account current security policies, known threats and vulnerabilities, laws and regulations, safety, dependability, system performance, the life-cycle costs of security measures, and technological requirements when conducting the assessment. Following the completion of the risk assessment, the agency can start organizing and putting into practice the safeguards it will use to protect its systems and reduce security risks to a manageable level. Because malicious threats and computer technologies are always evolving, the agency should regularly review the policies and procedures it has put in place. (For further in-depth details regarding risk mitigation and.)

- All the vulnerabilities that exist in a conventional wired network apply to wireless technologies.
- Malicious entities may gain unauthorized access to an agency's computer or voice (IP telephony) network through wireless connections, potentially bypassing any firewall protections.
- Sensitive information that is not encrypted (or that is encrypted with poor cryptographic techniques) and that is transmitted between two wireless devices may be intercepted and disclosed.
- Denial of service (DoS) attacks may be directed at wireless connections or devices.
- Malicious entities may steal the identity of legitimate users and masquerade as them on internal or external corporate networks.
- Sensitive data may be corrupted during improper synchronization.
- Malicious entities may be able to violate the privacy of legitimate users and be able to track their physical movements.
- Malicious entities may deploy unauthorized equipment (e.g., client devices and access points) to surreptitiously gain access to sensitive information.
- Handheld devices are easily stolen and can reveal sensitive information.
- Data may be extracted without detection from improperly configured devices.
- Viruses or other malicious code may corrupt data on a wireless device and be subsequently introduced to a wired network connection.
- Malicious entities may, through wireless connections, connect to other agencies for the purposes of launching attacks and concealing their activity.
- Interlopers, from inside or out,

may be able to gain connectivity to network management controls and thereby disable or disrupt operations.

Malicious entities may use a third-party, untrusted wireless network services to gain access to an agency's network resources.

Internal attacks may be possible via ad hoc transmissions.

Agency representatives must be aware of liability concerns for the loss of confidential data or for any attacks coming from a compromised network, just like with wired networks.

7.1.4. Emerging Wireless Technologies

Today, with the global mobile traffic expected to increase nearly 11 times between 2013 and 2018, there is a strong need for more efficient use of bandwidth and faster mobile speeds. The market is being dominated by smart devices with high processing power and network connectivity; there are currently 7 billion wireless devices in use. With the advent of the *Internet of Things (IoT),* where smart sensing and machine-to-machine communication are expected to skyrocket in the next ten years (with applications to smart environments, smart health, etc.), this number is expected to rise by an order of magnitude. ( ). All of this indicates that there are fundamentally new problems that need to be solved using knowledge from information theory, computer science, mathematics, and economics.

Keyword

Internet of Things (IoT) is a name for the aggregate collection of network-enabled devices, excluding traditional computers like laptops and servers.

A new wireless standard called "5G" will be developed over the next five years with the goal of increasing system capacity by orders of magnitude in order to address these issues. Current technologies will not be sufficient to enable this, and fundamentally new ideas must be developed to deal with the anticipated proliferation of IoT devices. In this workshop, basic new concepts in wireless networks and their mathematical applications will be examined. While there are numerous conferences and workshops focused on wireless systems and implementations, none that we are aware of will bring together traditionally unrelated fields like computer science, applied mathematics, information theory, and wireless networks. Researchers working on a number of fundamental topics that could have a significant influence on wireless networks in the future will be brought together for this workshop. Information theoretic and entropy inequalities, coding theory, probabilistic analysis—which includes the analysis of (randomized) algorithms—convex optimization, stochastic geometry, random matrices, and other mathematical tools will all be used.

7.1.5. Federal Information Processing Standards

FIPS 140-2 defines a framework and methodology for NIST's current and future cryptographic standards. The standard provides users with the following:

- A specification of security features that are required at each of four security levels
- Flexibility in choosing security requirements
- A guide to ensuring that the cryptographic modules incorporate necessary security features
- The assurance that the modules are compliant with cryptography-based standards.

According to the Secretary of Commerce, FIPS 140-2 is now required and enforceable for U.S. government organizations. When a federal agency concludes that cryptography is required to protect sensitive data, the standard is particularly applicable. The standard is applied in the design and implementation of cryptographic modules that are operated, or have been operated, by federal departments and agencies. FIPS 140-2 is relevant whether the module is used as a standalone device or integrated into a product or application. Both Bluetooth and 802.11 security as it exists now do not adhere to the FIPS 140-2 standard.

Cryptography is used by federal agencies, businesses, and the general public to secure communications and data used in electronic commerce, critical infrastructures, and other application areas. These systems and products use cryptographic modules to offer cryptographic functions like identification, authentication, confidentiality, integrity, and nonrepudiation. For security assurance, the cryptographic module must be adequately tested and validated against accepted standards. The public and federal agencies alike gain from the use of products that have been verified and tested. Insufficient testing can lead to insecure products due to flaws like shoddy design, subpar algorithms, or improper cryptographic module implementation.

The Cryptographic Module Validation Program (CMVP), developed by NIST in 1995, verifies cryptographic modules in accordance with FIPS 140-2, Security Requirements for Cryptographic Modules, and other standards based on FIPS cryptography. NIST and the Canadian government's Communications Security Establishment (CSE) collaborated to create the CMVP. The federal agencies of both nations accept products that have been verified to comply with FIPS 140-2 for the protection of sensitive data. Cryptography module vendors test their products in independent, approved testing facilities. As the program's validation authorities, NIST's Computer Security Division and CSE work together to verify the test findings. FIPS 140-2 compliance testing is currently carried out by six laboratories that have been accredited by the National Voluntary Laboratory Accreditation Program (NVLAP).

Did you get it?

1. **Explain the importance of device compatibility and interoperability in wireless networks.**
2. **Discuss the implications of adopting emerging wireless technologies on network performance, security, and scalability.**

7.2. DEVELOPMENT OF WIRELESS LANS

→Learning Objectives

- Explore the role of WLAN in providing flexible and mobile connectivity within organizations.
- Discuss the scalability and flexibility offered by WLAN for accommodating changing business needs.
- Learn about the security mechanisms and protocols available for securing 802.11 Wireless LANs.
- Identify the security requirements and compliance standards applicable to WLAN deployments.
- Explore the latest advancements in WLAN security standards and technologies.

A wireless LAN, or wireless local area network, consists of two or more computers linked through the same radio frequency. In contrast, a wired LAN requires physical connections via Ethernet cables to a server's network switch or hub. Each network begins with a main computer, known as a server, and multiple connected devices, called clients. Two Ethernet network interface cards (NICs) and network-supporting software are usually installed on the server. Since Windows 98 Special Edition (SE), Microsoft Windows operating systems have included built-in networking capabilities; however, third-party networking software is also accessible. A desktop computer could be the server and a laptop the client in a basic home wireless LAN.

Imagine if the desktop computer is hooked up to a high-speed DSL for Internet access. To spread the Internet connection through a wireless LAN, the desktop computer needs to be physically connected to a wireless DSL modem. The wireless DSL modem might have a network switch or router built in to keep the data flowing to the right network device. If these aren't part of the modem, you'll have to get them separately. Physical Ethernet cables connect the desktop server to the DSL modem, switch, and router. Clients require wireless NICs like internal, USB, or PCMCIA. Many wireless NICs have a small antenna.

With a laptop, one can work from any room in the house—mostly even the backyard—and still share the server's network connection. Mobile staff members can instantly connect to the office via a wireless LAN. Additionally, it provides simple, easy desktop connectivity between clients without incurring the high cost of running Ethernet cable throughout a building. One of the primary benefits of a wireless LAN is its ease of installation, as there are no wires leading to the clients. In addition to being less costly than wired LANs, wireless LANs offer greater flexibility. Wireless local area networks (LANs) have two drawbacks: they can be slower and less dependable than wired networks when interference is present, and they require additional steps to secure against intrusion. However, as technology advances, dependency rates also tend to improve. Certain wireless LAN configurations are competitive with wired networks.

Remember

Radio waves can be used by the machines to send and receive data once the wireless LAN has been configured on the server and client. Because the client can stay mobile anywhere within the network's broadcasting range, a wireless LAN is incredibly convenient.

Wireless technology standards use letter designations. The "g" standard allows speeds of up to 54 mbps. Recent MIMO technology versions can achieve rates close to 100 mbps. This corresponds to the speed of a typical hard-wired network and DSL connection. The slower technologies of the earlier wireless LAN standards "a" and "b".

7.2.1. Purpose of Wireless LAN

The Federal Communications Commission (FCC) initially opened up the RF spectrum to industry in the mid-1980s, which is when WLAN technology and the WLAN sector began. Growth was comparatively slow in the 1980s and early 1990s. But WLAN technology is growing at a very rapid rate right now. The more bandwidth made available by the IEEE 802.11 standard is the main driver of this expansion. Table 7.1 gives an overview of some of the most important features of WLAN and 802.11 technology.

Table 7.1. Key Characteristics of 802.11 Wireless LANs

Characteristic	Description
Physical Layer	Direct Sequence Spread Spectrum (DSSS), Frequency Hopping Spread Spectrum (FHSS), Orthogonal Frequency Division Multiplexing (OFDM), infrared (IR).
Frequency Band	2.4 GHz (ISM band) and 5 GHz.
Data Rates	1 Mbps, 2 Mbps, 5.5. Mbps (11b), 11 Mbps (11b), 54 Mbps (11a)
Data and Network Security	RC4-based stream encryption algorithm for confidentiality, authentication, and integrity. Limited key management. (AES is being considered for 802.11i.)
Operating Range	Up to 150 feet indoors and 1500 feet outdoors.9
Positive Aspects	Ethernet speeds without wires; many different products from many different companies. Wireless client cards and access point costs are decreasing.
Negative Aspects	Poor security in native mode; throughput decrease with distance and load.

7.2.1.1. Frequency and Data Rates

In order to provide wireless networking technology similar to the long-established wired Ethernet, IEEE developed the 802.11 standards. The 802.11 WLAN family's most extensively used standard is IEEE 802.11a. It uses OFDM technology and operates in the licensed 5 GHz band. The widely used 802.11b standard uses direct sequence spread-spectrum technology to function in the unlicensed 2.4. GHz–2.5. GHz Industrial, Scientific, and Medical (ISM) frequency band. Since the ISM band is accessible everywhere, it has grown in popularity for wireless communications. Up to 11 Mbits per second of transmission are possible with the 802.11b WLAN technology. This makes it marginally faster than regular Ethernet and much faster than the original IEEE 802.11 standard, which transmits data at up to 2 Mbps.

7.2.1.2. 802.11 Architecture

The Basic Service Set (BSS) and the Extended Service Set (ESS) are the two types of services that are defined by the IEEE 802.11 standard. The fundamental component of a wireless LAN is the BSS. A BSS is made up of mobile or fixed wireless stations, as well as maybe a central base station (e.g., an AP). A station can communicate with other BSS members when it is a part of the BSS.

A BSS without an AP is an isolated network that is unable to communicate with other BSSs. We refer to these BSSs as Independent BSSs (IBSS). IBSSs typically consist of a limited number of stations that are set up for a particular function and for a brief amount of time (e.g., establishing a transient network to facilitate a solitary conference room meeting). Another name for IBSSs is ad hoc networks. The usage of an AP sets infrastructure BSSs apart from ad hoc networks. In an infrastructure BSS, all communications—including those between mobile nodes within the same service set—take place over APs. The coverage distance from the AP defines the boundaries of an infrastructure BSS. A single AP's coverage area is referred to as a cell. The AP needs to be able to reach every mobile station.

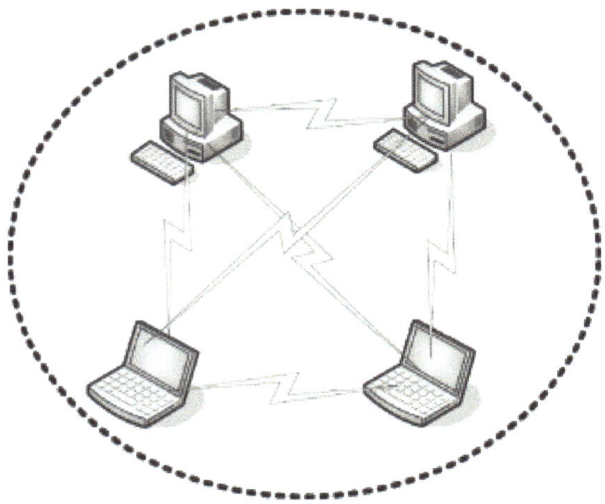

Figure 7.1. Independent and Infrastructure Basic Service Sets (Source: ScienceDirect, https://ars.els-cdn.com/content/image/3-s2.0-B9781856177474000056-gr3.jpg).

802.11 enables the creation of wireless networks with arbitrarily large coverage by connecting BSSs to an ESS. BSSs are connected via a backbone network to form an ESS. An ESS's Service Set Identifier (SSID), which acts as a network name for its users, is assigned to each AP in the system. The way APs in an ESS function allows the outside world to communicate with a station using its MAC address without having to worry about where it is in the ESS. Three BSSs that correspond to three APs are shown in Figure 7.2. Between BSS 2 and BSS 3, as well as between BSS 1 and BSS 2, there is an equal amount of overlap. In order to ensure that stations can move seamlessly from one BSS to another, this overlap is required. In the figure, frames are delivered to a station by the router using its MAC address as the destination; only the associated AP can deliver the frame to that station.

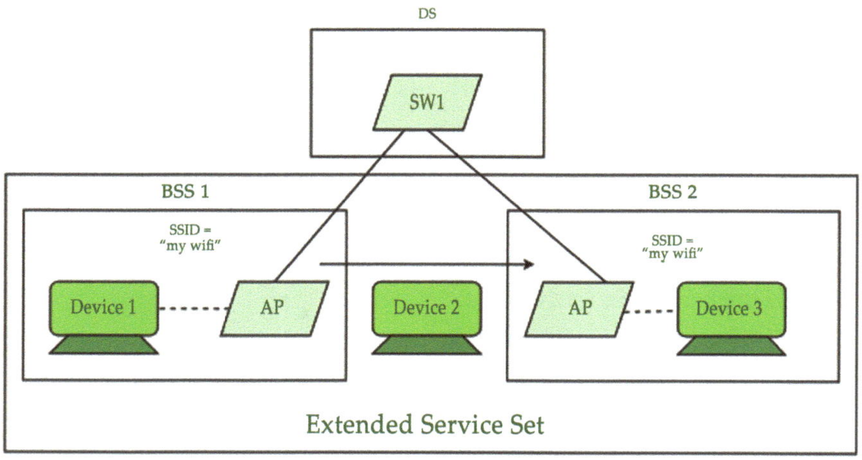

Figure 7.2. Extended service set (Source: Geeksforgeeks, https://media.geeksforgeeks.org/wp-content/uploads/20201105165935/fffd1.png).

Typically, the main driver behind the deployment of an 802.11 network is mobility support. At the link layer, IEEE 802.11 permits mobility between BSSs. It is ignorant of all activity occurring above the link layer, though. Stations will search for and try to associate with an AP with the strongest signal and the least amount of network traffic when they move between BSSs. In this manner, a mobile station can move between APs in the network without experiencing a loss of connectivity. This phenomenon is commonly known as roaming.

7.2.1.3. Wireless LAN Components

A wireless station and an access point are the two pieces of hardware that make up a WLAN. A laptop or notebook PC with a wireless network interface card (NIC) is commonly referred to as a station, or client. Additionally, a desktop computer or a portable electronic device (e.g., PDA, or specialized gadget like a barcode scanner) or hardware found in a kiosk on a production line or other place that is open to the public. With the exception of using wireless NICs to connect to network access points, wireless laptops and notebooks, also known as "wireless enabled," are identical to laptops and notebooks. Usually, the wireless NIC is installed in the client.

A USB port or a PCMCIA slot is a type of connector used for memory cards in computers. In order to connect to the WLAN, the NICs use radio signals. Usually made up of a radio, a wired network interface (like 802.3), and bridging software, the access point (AP) serves as a bridge between wireless and wired networks. The AP aggregates several wireless stations onto the wired network, acting as a base station for the wireless network.

7.2.1.4. Range

The sharing of data between wireless devices or computers is known as long-range wireless. Wireless technology, commonly referred to as WiFi, enables users to connect from up to 40 miles away (about 64.37 km) and transmits data at high speeds. Computer data is transformed into radio waves and sent through the air in wireless technology. These waves are detected by a wireless router, which converts them back into data. The technology behind this process is comparable to that of walkie-talkies, cell phones, and other two-way communication devices. Long-range wireless has a high speed that allows for the transfer of more data in less time. Even though wireless technology is quick, there are situations when even faster performance is required. Typically, power amplifiers or specialized antennas can increase the connection speed and range.

However, adding boosters can have a drawback in that they not only increase speed but also increase the connection's susceptibility to threats and other technical issues. The obstruction of line of sight (LOS) by long-range wireless is a minor additional concern. This means that users in cities have to take into account obstacles like radio stations, buildings, and microwave signals, while residents in more rural areas are more likely to be concerned about trees and signal loss from being too far outside of the connection range. Millions of people use wireless technology worldwide. Wireless technology is used by companies and educational institutions for coverage establishment, remote support, and research completion. Long-range wireless is used in homes for local WiFi networks, remote access, and hard-to-reach rural locations. There are public WiFi hotspots where people can use a wireless transmitter to connect to the Internet when they're not at home or at work. One needs the required hardware in order to use a wireless connection to access the Internet. Almost all laptops manufactured after the year 2000 have a wireless transmitter installed. Users typically have the option of buying a wireless adapter for desktop and laptop computers that might not be wirelessly compatible. Wireless adapters are made to fit into PC card slots and Universal Serial Bus (USB) ports.

7.2.2. Benefits

WLANs offer four primary benefits:

- User Mobility: Users can access files, network resources, and the Internet without having to physically connect to the network with wires. Users can be mobile yet retain high-speed, real-time access to the enterprise LAN.
- Rapid Installation: The time required for installation is reduced because network connections can be made without moving or adding wires, or pulling them through walls or ceilings, or making modifications to the infrastructure cable plant. For example, WLANs are often cited as making LAN installations possible in buildings that are subject to historic preservation rules.
- Flexibility: Enterprises can also enjoy the flexibility of installing and taking down WLANs in locations as necessary. Users can quickly install a small WLAN for temporary needs such as a conference, trade show, or standards meeting.
- Scalability: WLAN network topologies can easily be configured to meet specific application and installation needs and to scale

from small peer-to-peer networks to very large enterprise networks that enable roaming over a broad area.

The WLAN market has been growing steadily over the past few years, and WLANs are still becoming more and more popular, thanks to these core advantages. WLANs are starting to show promise as a substitute for conventional wired solutions. To carry out their regular business operations, hospitals, colleges, airports, hotels, and retail stores, for instance, already use wireless technologies.

7.2.3. Security of 802.11 Wireless LANs

It is very difficult to control which computers or devices are receiving the wireless network signal because of the RF signal nature of the network. In order to prevent eavesdropping and other network threats, software link-level protection—which employs cryptography—is therefore necessary for wireless. Exclusively WEP is available for wireless network security in the original 802.11 standard.

7.2.3.1. Access Control List

In a wireless network, the most basic security feature is the access control list. This mechanism provides protection mostly by filtering out unknown users and necessitates loading the MAC addresses of authorized clients into the access point. The Access Point will only accept communication from those MAC addresses that have registered; any communication from unregistered MAC addresses will be rejected.

This mechanism does not protect the confidentiality or integrity of wireless network traffic, nor does it offer any other protection other than access control to the network behind the access point, as its name suggests. As a result, any wireless network that is only secured by this method is extremely weak and susceptible to network attacks. Furthermore, it turns out that it is relatively simple to temporarily change the MAC address on almost any wireless network interface (at least in Windows and UNIX/Linux OS), rendering this security mechanism useless as an access control measure. MAC spoofing is the process of altering the MAC address to pretend to be another person or device. To perform MAC spoofing in UNIX/Linux OS, we simply need to run one command.

```
ifconfig eth0 hw ether 00:01:02:03:04:05
```

Where:

eth0 is the network interface we want to modify.

00:01:02:03:04:05 is the MAC address we want to specify with numbers in hex number format.

In Windows environment, we need the help of tools designed specially for this intention. There are at least two tools available for MAC spoofing:

a. SMAC3, from KLC Consulting, and
b. MAC Makeup4 (freeware), from H&C Works

Both feature an intuitive graphical user interface, work with Windows XP and 2000, don't require drivers to be installed, and work almost with any network interface card—including wireless ones. Anyone can obtain a list of registered MAC addresses on their own with the use of wireless analyzer utilities, which enables anyone to use this information to gain access to an unprotected wireless network. With the ability to passively monitor or sniff wireless network traffic, wireless analyzers are incredibly potent tools for learning vital details about wireless networks.

Did you know?

Norman Abramson, a professor at the University of Hawaii, developed the world's first wireless computer communication network, ALOHAnet. The system became operational in 1971 and included seven computers deployed over four islands to communicate with the central computer on the Oahu island without using phone lines.

7.2.3.2. WEP (Wired Equivalent Privacy)

At first, the 802.11 standard only defined WEP (Wired Equivalent Privacy) as a link-level security option. Its primary goal was to safeguard the integrity and confidentiality of wireless network traffic. WEP gets its name from the fact that it was intended to offer similar secrecy to a conventional wired network. To achieve the required level of security, data is encrypted using WEP. To encrypt data packets, WEP employs the RC4 stream cipher with a 64- or 128-bit key. WEP can also be used as an access control mechanism because, once enabled, it only allows communication between the Access Point and nodes that have a shared secret key, rejecting all other nodes.

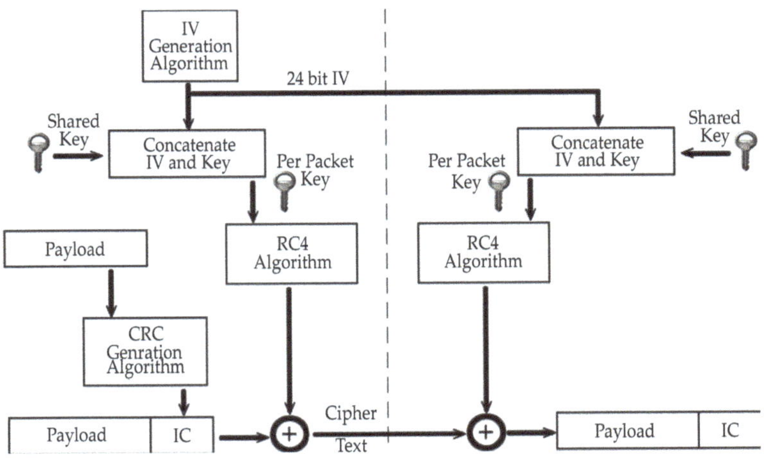

Figure 7.3. WEP Encryption/Decryption Process. (Black) Common steps, (Red) Encryption Process, (Blue) Decryption Process (Source: Researchgate, https://www.researchgate.net/profile/Abdel-Karim-Al-Tamimi/publication/303417816/figure/fig9/AS:627929046335490@1526721359103/WEP-encryption-and-decryption-processes.png).

Every wireless client on a WEP-protected network needs to have the same secret key as the access point in order to function. This secret key may take the form of a passphrase or a string of characters produced by a wireless configuration software. The most crucial requirement for every member of the wireless network is that they all have the same WEP secret key. Although WEP uses a 64- or 128-bit key to encrypt data, the actual effective key is smaller because a portion of the WEP key is transmitted in clear text along with the data packet. This is especially true when using cards from multiple manufacturers. The shared secret key (the static portion of the key) and the dynamic Initialization Vector (IV) value are concatenated to form the WEP key, which is the key used to encrypt the data packet. In order to give the WEP key liveness, the transmitter wireless network interface selects the Initialization Vector (IV), a dynamic 24-bit value that offers more than 16 million possible keys at random. WEP keys must be live since every message needs to be encrypted using a unique key. The duration of the mutual.

A data packet that reaches the link level in a wireless network protected by WEP is encrypted before being sent over the air. The wireless network interface first selects an IV value at random and concatenates it with the shared secret key to create the WEP Key (IV + secret key). This is how data packet encryption is carried out. The selection criteria for the wireless network interface are not specified in the 802.11 standard. As a result, the manufacturer determines how the wireless network interface determines the IV value. When the WEP Key is prepared, the RC4 stream cipher uses it to generate a pseudo-random string that matches the length of the data packet. When the wireless network interface performs a logical XOR operation between the data packet and the pseudo-random string, encryption occurs. The link-level headers, IV value, and encrypted data packet are combined and sent to the recipient to complete the WEP-protected data packet. The procedures for encrypting messages and decrypting a data packet protected by WEP are the same. The recipient reads the IV value before repeating the encryption process when decrypting a WEP-protected data packet. The data is decrypted by executing a second logical XOR operation between the encrypted data packet and the pseudo-random string, canceling the effect of the first logical XOR operation. This is possible because a specific WEP key (the same IV and shared secret key) will always produce the same pseudo-random string, making it possible to regenerate the same pseudo-random string.

When the WEP was designed, it was thought to be sufficiently secure. However, later research revealed an inherent weakness in the WEP mechanism. Since then, a number of tools have been created to successfully crack the WEP shared secret key, making it unsecure.

7.2.3.3. WEP Key Recovery

A serious cryptographic flaw in the WEP protocol makes it possible for an attacker to obtain the shared secret key. This flaw involves taking advantage of the fact that a specific IV value generates weak WEP keys. The first bytes of the pseudo-random string may have some correlation with the WEP key when encryption is performed with a weak WEP key. There is a 5-6 percent certainty probability that each weak key will leak one byte of the shared secret key. The attacker needs to collect a significant number of raw WEP-protected data packets (roughly 5 million to 10 million packets) in order to increase the likelihood that the shared secret key will be successfully cracked because the certainty level is low. This flaw was revealed in the paper "Weaknesses in the Key Scheduling Algorithm in RC4" by Fluhrer, Mantin, and Shamir.

A number of WEP cracking tools have already been available for some time. Wepcrack and Airsnort8 are a couple of the first tools that take advantage of the FMS vulnerability. Other tools, such as brute-force attacks and optimizations for requiring fewer weak WEP-protected data packets, have more capabilities. Among the tools are

Dwepcrack, Aircrack, and Airjack. Although most of these tools are designed to operate on UNIX/Linux, some have already been adapted for Windows OS. By passively capturing a significant amount of wireless network traffic, attackers can potentially obtain the shared secret key by utilizing any of these WEP cracking tools. The wireless network is completely vulnerable as soon as the attacker manages to get their hands on the shared secret key.

7.2.3.4. IV Collision

An additional method of getting into a wireless network without the shared secret key is to passively capture a lot of data packets, but this time the attacker is searching for IV collisions. When two or more data packets are encrypted using the same IV value—and thus, the same WEP key—this is known as an IV collision. An attacker can remove encryption by performing a logical XOR with the two encrypted data packets when an IV collision is detected. The XOR of the two data packets is the outcome. If the attacker has sufficient time and employs analytical and statistical techniques, they may be able to retrieve the contents of the two packets. When more packets encrypted with the exact same WEP key are intercepted and used for the recovery, the effort and time needed to recover the contents of the data packets decrease. It should be noted that recovering a pseudo-random string for a specific WEP key is simple if this attack is successful. After that, an attacker could store all of the pseudo-random strings in a record and use them for network access, packet forging, and decryption.

Aware of the WEP key vulnerability, some manufacturers of wireless interface cards provide updates for their cards that prevent the use of weak IVs for encryption, thereby addressing the weak key vulnerability. Reducing the number of WEP keys by avoiding some IVs exacerbates the IV collision weakness.

7.2.3.5. Dynamic WEP

An attacker must intercept a significant number of data packets in order to decipher the shared secret key before they can gain physical access to a WEP-protected network. It will be much more difficult to crack the secret key if the wireless network is able to alter the shared secret key each time before the attacker receives enough data packets. Therefore, regularly changing the shared secret key is a way to stop a potential secret key recovery without aggravating any other vulnerability. Because the current WEP mechanism lacks an automatic key rotation system that could support this solution, using it could be very problematic.

To accomplish this, automatic key delivery and recurring rekeying can be facilitated by utilizing the 802.1x protocol. For user authentication and authorization, the 802.1x protocol is responsible. When a user is approved and authenticated, the authentication server generates the WEP key..

7.2.3.6. WPA (Wi-Fi Protected Access)

The Wi-Fi Alliance has released WPA as a solution while a final security protocol is being standardized. The next 802.11 wireless network security protocol standard, 802.11i, is the foundation of this security protocol. The three primary parts of WPA are TKIP, 802.1x, and MIC. Every element was created and put into place with a specific 802.11 vulnerability in mind.

Significant security enhancements were put into place, like the 802.1x protocol for network access control and the key hierarchy that essentially neutralizes and safeguards the WPA main key from attacks. By using key hierarchy, WPA avoids using the main key for encryption directly. Rather, the main key (Pairwise Master Key) is used to generate other temporal keys, like session keys and group keys, and then the session key is used recursively to generate the encryption key for each packet. In order to prevent replay attacks, the IV is also extended from 24 to 48 bits in length and given a new function as a sequence counter. Using a specially created cryptographically protected hashing function rather than the CRC32 linear function improves packet integrity protection.

7.2.3.7. TKIP (Temporal Key Integrity Protocol)

This protocol fixes the majority of critical vulnerabilities and is a direct replacement for WEP. Maintaining compatibility with current 802.11 hardware allowed for software upgrades, which was part of its intended purpose. The fact that each packet is generated by a per-packet key mixing function rather than by concatenating the IV and the shared secret key is one of the most significant improvements over WEP.

Since the majority of cryptographic features are hard-coded into the hardware of the wireless network interface, software upgrades are not possible. Owing to these constraints, the WPA protocol makes use of certain hardcoded functions from the WEP protocol in order to maintain performance and compatibility. Certain functions, such as the output function of the RC4 stream cipher, are hardcoded into the wireless network interface and cannot be altered. TKIP reuses the RC4 stream cipher to circumvent this issue, but it modifies how the shared secret key is used. The shared secret key is only used as a seed for creating additional keys; it is not used to access the cipher directly. This strategy reduces the likelihood that any attack will reveal the shared secret key. The session key is the first key to be generated. The per-packet key is generated using this key as a seed.

7.2.3.8. Security Features of 802.11 Wireless LANs per the Standard

The three basic security services defined by IEEE for the WLAN environment are as follows:

- Authentication: A primary goal of WEP was to provide a security service to verify the identity of communicating client stations. This provides access control to the network by denying access to client stations that cannot authenticate properly. This service addresses the question, "Are only authorized persons allowed to gain access to my network?"
- Confidentiality: Confidentiality, or privacy, was a second goal of WEP. It was developed to provide "privacy achieved by a wired network." The intent was to prevent information compromise from casual eavesdropping (passive attack). This service, in general, addresses the question, "Are only authorized persons allowed to view my data?"
- Integrity: Another goal of WEP was a security service developed to ensure that messages are not modified in transit between the wireless clients and the access point in an active attack. This service addresses the question, "Is the data coming into or exiting the network trustworthy—has it been tampered with?"

It is important to note that the standard did not address other security services such as audit, authorization, and nonrepudiation. The security services offered by 802.11 are described in greater detail below.

7.2.3.9. Authentication

Open-system authentication and shared-key authentication are the two ways that wireless users trying to connect to a wired network can be "validated" according to the IEEE 802.11 standard. *Cryptography* underpins one method of authentication (shared-key authentication), but not the other.

Keyword

Cryptography is the process of hiding or coding information so that only the person a message was intended for can read it.

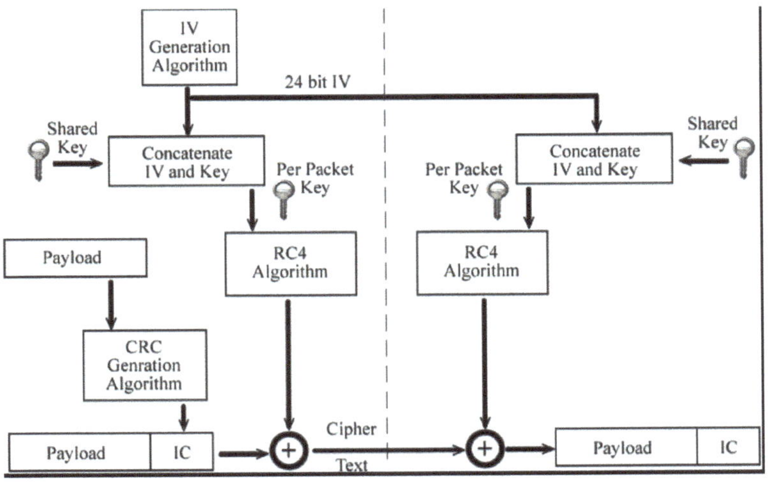

Figure 7.4. Taxonomy of 802.11 Authentication Techniques (Source: Researchgate, https://www.researchgate.net/profile/Karen-Scarfone/publication/238668444/figure/fig7/AS:484492956704776@1492523530652/1-Taxonomy-for-Pre-RSN-and-RSN-Security.png).

Since the access point accepts the mobile station without confirming the station's identity, the open-system authentication technique is not really authentication. Furthermore to be mentioned is the fact that the authentication process is one-way, validating only the mobile station. The mobile station needs to have faith that the AP it is speaking to is legitimate. Figure 7.4 shows a taxonomy of the methods for 802.11.

A client using Open System authentication is considered authenticated if it merely provides its MAC address in response to an access point's two-message exchange. The client simply replies with the appropriate fields in the message exchange; they are not actually validated during the exchange. It is evident that open-system authentication is highly vulnerable and essentially invites unwanted access in the absence of cryptographic validation. According to the 802.11 specification, only open-system authentication is necessary.

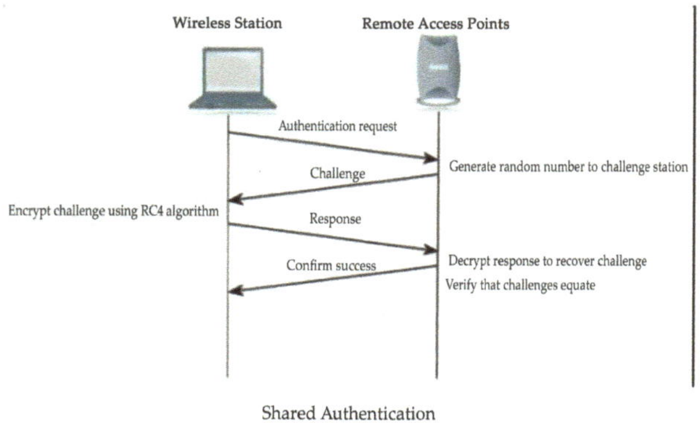

Figure 7.5. Shared-key Authentication Message Flow (Source: Medium.com, https://miro.medium.com/v2/resize:fit:640/format:webp/1*olfHTS-hoqEtiSDIXxxipA.png).

One cryptographic method of authentication is shared key authentication. It is a straightforward "challenge-response" system that asks clients if they are aware of a shared secret. In this scheme, which is conceptually shown in Figure 7.5, the wireless client receives a random challenge generated by the access point. The challenge, also known as a "nonce" in security jargon, is encrypted by the client using a shared cryptographic key with the AP, and the client then sends the result back to the AP. The client computes a result, which the AP decrypts. Access is granted only if the decrypted value matches the transmitted random challenge. The RC4 stream cipher, created by MIT's Ron Rivest, is the algorithm used for both the cryptographic computation and the creation of the 128-bit challenge text. It should be mentioned that the just-described authentication method lacks mutual authentication and is a simple cryptographic technique. In other words, there is no guarantee that a client is interacting with a genuine AP and wireless network since the client does not authenticate the AP. Not to mention, straightforward unilateral challenge-response schemes have been around for a while.

7.2.3.10. Privacy

The 802.11 standard uses cryptographic methods for the wireless interface to support privacy (confidentiality). The RC4 symmetrickey stream cipher algorithm is also used by the WEP cryptographic technique for confidentiality in order to produce a pseudo-random data sequence. To the data to be transmitted, this "key stream" is simply added modulo 2 (exclusive-OR-ed). Data can be shielded from disclosure during transmission over a wireless link by using the WEP technique. To secure traffic such as Transmission Control Protocol/Internet Protocol (TCP/IP), Internet Packet Exchange (IPX), and Hyper Text Transfer Protocol (HTTP), WEP is applied to all data above the 802.11 WLAN layers.

According to the 802.11 standard, WEP can only support shared keys with a cryptographic key size of 40 bits. Numerous vendors do, however, provide nonstandard WEP extensions that support key lengths ranging from 40 to 104 bits. A keysize of 128 bits is supported by at least one vendor. For example, a 128-bit RC4 key can be created from a 104-bit WEP key with a 24-bit Initialization Vector (IV). Generally speaking, a cryptographic technique's security is increased when the key size is increased, barring any other circumstances. Long keys may not, however, always be able to boost security due to poor implementations or designs. Studies have indicated that when considering robust designs and implementations, brute-force cryptanalysis (code breaking) is rendered impossible for key sizes larger than 80 bits. The keyspace of over 1026 possible keys for 80-bit keys is larger than what is currently possible to compute. The majority of WLAN deployments in use today rely on 40-bit keys. Furthermore, regardless of keysize, recent attacks have demonstrated that the WEP approach for privacy is regrettably susceptible to some attacks.

7.2.3.11. Integrity

A method for guaranteeing data integrity for messages sent between wireless clients and access points is also described in the IEEE 802.11 specification. The purpose of this security service was to reject any messages that had been altered by a hostile party "in the middle." This method employs a basic encrypted Cyclic Redundancy Check (CRC) methodology. A CRC-32, or frame check sequence, is calculated on each payload before transmission, as shown in the above diagram. The cipher-text message is then obtained by encrypting the integrity-sealed packet using the RC4 key stream. Decryption and CRC recalculation are done on the receiving end after the message has been received. The CRC calculated with the original message and the one computed at the receiving end are compared. The packet would be rejected if the CRCs do not equal, indicating that the message was "received in error," which would be an indication of an integrity violation caused by an active message spoofer. Unfortunately, regardless of key size, the 802.11 integrity is susceptible to some attacks, just like the privacy service. In conclusion, the basic weakness in the WEP integrity scheme lies in the fact that the straightforward CRC is not a "cryptographically secure" mechanism.

Remember

IEEE 802.11 is used in most home and office networks to allow laptops, printers, smartphones, and other devices to communicate with each other and access the Internet without connecting wires.

Unfortunately, key management—the life cycle handling of cryptographic keys and related materials—is not covered by the IEEE 802.11 specification. Thus, those using WLANs are responsible for creating, distributing, storing, loading, escrowing, archiving, auditing, and destroying the content. The 802.11 network's users are primarily responsible for managing their keys, which is arguably the most important component of any cryptography system. Consequently, the WLAN environment may be exposed to numerous vulnerabilities.

Weak keys (all zeros, all ones, based on easily guessed passwords, or other similar trivial patterns) and non-unique, factory-default, and never-changing WEP keys are some examples of these vulnerabilities. WEP-secured WLANs also do not scale well since key management was not addressed in the original 802.11 specification, leaving the key distribution unresolved. In a large WLAN environment, the task is daunting if an enterprise realizes it needs to frequently change keys and make them random. As an illustration, a sizable campus might have up to 15,000 APs. It is a significant task to generate, distribute, load, and manage keys in an environment this size.

7.2.3.12. Problems with the IEEE 802.11 Standard Security

The 802.11 WLAN standard's standardized security has this vulnerability. WLANs based on 802.11 employ the WEP protocol, as previously mentioned. In response, WEP protects traffic using the RC4 cryptographic algorithm and a variable-length key. Once more, 40-bit WEP cryptographic keys are supported by the 802.11 standard. However, some suppliers have used 128-bit or even 104-bit keys in their products. The real key used in the RC4 algorithm is 152 bits for the 128-bit WEP key after the 24-bit IV is added. Noteworthy is the fact that some vendors generate keys based on a user's keystrokes; when done correctly, with appropriate random processes, this can yield a strong WEP key. As a result, the effective key size is usually smaller than with other vendors who base WEP keys on user-selected passwords. Security flaws that allow malevolent users to breach WLAN security have been found by multiple teams of computer security experts. These comprise statistical analysis-based passive attacks to decrypt traffic, active attacks to introduce new traffic from unapproved mobile stations (i.e., based on plain text that is known), ongoing attempts to decrypt traffic (i.e., dictionary-building attacks), and deceiving the access point attacks. Once sufficient traffic on a busy network has been analyzed, the dictionary-building attack can be launched.

Security problems with WEP include the following:

A well-known security flaw in wireless networks is the use of static WEP keys, which allows multiple users to potentially share the same key for extended periods of time. The WEP protocol's absence of any important management clauses is partially to blame for this. The key could be compromised along with all the other computers that share it if a laptop or other computer were lost or stolen. Furthermore, if every station uses the same key, an eavesdropper may have quick access to a lot of traffic for analytic attacks like the ones shown in numbers 2 and 3 below.

The IV in WEP is a 24-bit field that is transmitted in a message's clear text section. When used for cryptography, this 24-bit string—which is used to start the key stream produced by the RC4 algorithm—is a comparatively small field. When an IV is reused, it generates identical key streams that protect data, and in a busy network, its short length ensures that these streams will repeat after a short while. Furthermore, the 802.11 standard is silent on the setting or modification of IVs, so different wireless NICs from the same vendor might produce identical IV sequences or some might even employ a fixed IV. Because of this, hackers are able to capture network activity, identify the key stream, and utilize it to crack the ciphertext.

The RC4 encryption key contains the IV. Due to a flaw in the RC4 key schedule and the fact that an eavesdropper is aware of the first 24 bits of each packet key, a successful analytic attack can recover the key after only a small amount of traffic has been intercepted and examined. The attack script and open source code for this attack are accessible to the general public. Cryptographic integrity is not protected by WEP. To verify packet integrity and acknowledge packets with the correct checksum, the 802.11 MAC protocol employs a noncryptographic Cyclic Redundancy Check (CRC).

It is risky and frequently results in vulnerabilities when noncryptographic checksums and stream ciphers are combined, as is the case with WEP. By methodically altering the packet, CRC sending it to the AP, and noting whether the packet is acknowledged, the attacker can currently decrypt any packet. Because of the potential for interactions with other protocol levels that could reveal cipher details, it is now deemed dangerous to design encryption protocols without cryptographic integrity protection. These attacks are frequently subtle.

Keep in mind that just one of the four issues mentioned above is dependent on a cryptographic algorithmic flaw. Therefore, using a more powerful stream cipher would not solve these issues. For instance, the third issue on the above list results from an implementation flaw in the RC4 stream cipher that is made public by a badly thought out protocol. Table 7.2 provides a summary of some of the issues with WEP and 802.11 WLAN security.

Table 7.2. Key Problems with Existing 802.11 Wireless LAN Security

Security Issue or Vulnerability	**Remarks**
1. Security features in vendor products are frequently not enabled.	Security features, albeit poor in some cases, are not enabled when shipped, and users do not enable when installed. Bad security is generally better than no security.
2. IVs are short (or static).	24- bit IVs cause the generated key stream to repeat. Repetition allows easy decryption of data for a moderately sophisticated adversary.
3. Cryptographic keys are short.	40- bit keys are inadequate for any system. It is generally accepted that key sizes should be greater than 80 bits in length. The longer the key, the less likely a comprise is possible from a brute-force attack.
4. Cryptographic keys are shared.	Keys that are shared can compromise a system. As the number of people sharing the key grows, the security risks also grow. A fundamental tenant of cryptography is that the security of a system is largely dependent on the secrecy of the keys.
5. Cryptographic keys cannot be updated automatically and frequently.	Cryptographic keys should be changed often to prevent brute-force attacks.
6. RC4 has a weak key schedule and is inappropriately used in WEP.	The combination of revealing 24 key bits in the IV and a weakness in the initial few bytes of the RC4 key stream leads to an efficient attack that recovers the key. Most other applications of RC4 do not expose the weaknesses of RC4 because they do not reveal key bits and do not restart the key schedule for every packet. This attack is available to moderately sophisticated adversaries.

7. Packet integrity is poor.	CRC32 and other linear block codes are inadequate for providing cryptographic integrity. Message modification is possible. Linear codes are inadequate for the protection against advertent attacks on data integrity. Cryptographic protection is required to prevent deliberate attacks. Use of noncryptographic protocols often facilitates attacks against the cryptography.
8. No user authentication occurs.	Only the device is authenticated. A device that is stolen can access the network.
9. Authentication is not enabled; only simple SSID identification occurs.	Identity-based systems are highly vulnerable particularly in a wireless system because signals can be more easily intercepted.
10. Device authentication is simple shared-key challenge-response.	One-way challenge-response authentication is subject to "man-inthe-middle" attacks. Mutual authentication is required to provide verification that users and the network are legitimate.
11.The client does not authenticate the AP.	The client needs to authenticate the AP to ensure that it is legitimate and prevent the introduction of rogue APs.

7.2.4. Security Requirements and Threats

The WiFi, or 802.11 WLAN, market is growing and has a lot of momentum right now. It appears that many organizations will implement 802.11 WLAN technology in the upcoming years.

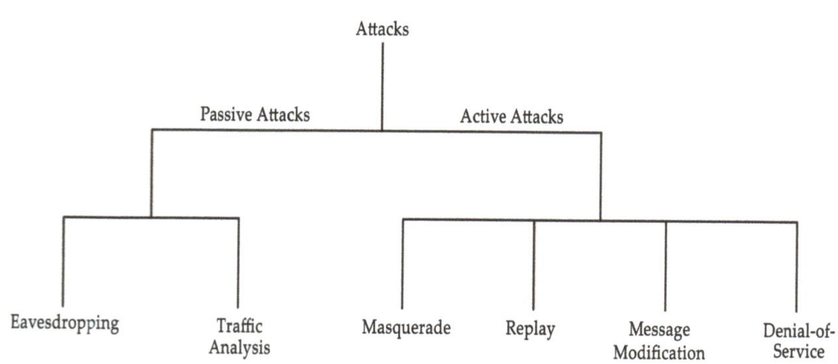

Figure 7.6. Taxonomy of Security Attacks (Source: Researchgate, https://www.researchgate.net/profile/Shaurya-Gupta-10/publication/342685632/figure/fig2/AS:945114490875906@1602344262858/Taxonomy-of-Security-Attacks.png).

Numerous establishments—such as shops, medical facilities, airports, and commercial businesses—aspire to profit from "going wireless." Nevertheless, despite enormous success and growth, not everything about 802.11 WLANs has been favorable. Numerous papers and reports detailing attacks on 802.11 wireless networks that put organizations at risk for security have been published. To assist users and organizations in understanding some of the attacks against WLANs, Figure 7.6 offers a general taxonomy of security attacks.

Network security attacks are typically divided into passive and active attacks. These two broad classes are then subdivided into other types of attacks. All are defined below.

- *Passive Attack:* An attack in which an unauthorized party gains access to an asset and does not modify its content (i.e., eavesdropping). Passive attacks can be either eavesdropping or traffic analysis (sometimes called traffic flow analysis). These two passive attacks are described below.
- *Eavesdropping:* The attacker monitors transmissions for message content. An example of this attack is a person listening into the transmissions on a LAN between two workstations or tuning into transmissions between a wireless handset and a base station.
- *Traffic analysis:* The attacker, in a more subtle way, gains intelligence by monitoring the transmissions for patterns of communication. A considerable amount of information is contained in the flow of messages between communicating parties.
- *Active Attack:* An attack whereby an unauthorized party makes modifications to a message, data stream, or file. It is possible to detect this type of attack but it may not be preventable. Active attacks may take the form of one of four types (or a combination thereof): masquerading, replay, message modification, and denial-of-service (DoS). These attacks are defined below.
- Masquerading: The attacker impersonates an authorized user and thereby gains certain unauthorized privileges.
- Replay: The attacker monitors transmissions (passive attack) and retransmits messages as the legitimate user.
- Message modification: The attacker alters a legitimate message by deleting, adding to, changing, or reordering it.
- Denial-of-service: The attacker prevents or prohibits the normal use or management of communications facilities.

Keyword

Denial-of-service (DoS) attack is a malicious attempt to overwhelm an online service and render it unusable.

The risks associated with 802.11 are the result of one or more of these attacks. The consequences of these attacks include, but are not limited to, loss of proprietary information, legal and recovery costs, tarnished image, and loss of network service.

7.2.4.1. Loss of Confidentiality

The quality of confidentiality is the ability to prevent information from being accessed or revealed to unauthorized individuals, organizations, or processes. For most companies, this is typically a fundamental security requirement. Confidentiality in a wireless network poses a more complex security challenge due to the broadcast and radio nature of wireless technology. Adversaries can access network resources without the need to physically connect a network cable. Additionally, the distance over which transmissions occur may be uncontrollable. Consequently, traditional physical security measures become less effective.

Passively eavesdropping on native 802.11 wireless communications can pose a significant risk to a company. An adversary could potentially intercept and collect sensitive data, including configuration details, network IDs, passwords, and proprietary information. This risk arises from the possibility of an "insider" threat or the potential for 802.11 signals to extend beyond the building. With the extended range of 802.11 broadcasts, adversaries might be able to intercept transmissions from nearby roads or parking lots. Exploiting this vulnerability is relatively straightforward using a wireless network analyzer tool, or sniffer, for two main reasons: (1) WLAN technology's confidentiality features are often left disabled, and (2) numerous security vulnerabilities exist in 802.11 technology.

These days, wireless packet analyzers are easily accessible on the Internet thanks to programs like WEPcrack and AirSnort. One of the earliest programs designed to automate network analysis was AirSnort. Regretfully, it is also frequently employed to breach wireless networks. Vulnerabilities in the key-scheduling algorithm included in the original WEP standard and used for RC4 implementation can be exploited by AirSnort. All that AirSnort needs to do this is a computer with a wireless network card and the Linux operating system. Once at least 100 MB of network packets have been sniffed, the software computes the encryption keys while passively monitoring the WLAN data transmissions. This much data can be collected in as little as three or four hours on a highly saturated network; in several days if traffic volume is low. For instance, after about 10 hours, a busy data access point transmitting 3,000 bytes at 11 Mbps will run out of 24-bit IV space. Data integrity and confidentiality could be readily jeopardized if an attacker manages to recover two cipher texts that were created using the same key stream after ten hours. Once the packets on the network have been broadcast, monitoring poses an additional risk to confidentiality breaches caused by simple eavesdropping. An adversary can observe traffic when an access point is linked to a hub rather than a switch by using a laptop in promiscuous mode. All network traffic is typically broadcast by hubs to all devices that are connected, making the traffic open to unauthorized monitoring. Conversely, switches have the ability to be set up so that specific connected devices are not allowed to intercept broadcast traffic from other designated devices. Data meant for both wired and wireless clients could be intercepted by a wireless device monitoring broadcast traffic, for instance, if a wireless access point were linked to an Ethernet hub. As a result, organizations connecting to wireless access points ought to think about utilizing switches rather than hubs.

WLANs also run the risk of losing their confidentiality after an ongoing attack. As user names and passwords are sent over a wireless connection, sniffing software—as previously mentioned—can obtain them, along with any other data that is traversing the network. An adversary might be able to use a false identity to access a wired network from an access point (AP). Once "on the network," the hacker can use tools that are readily available to the public or that they have purchased to scan the network. The malicious eavesdropper then gains access to network resources and private company data by using the user name, password, and IP address information.

Finally, there's a security risk from rogue APs. A rogue AP could be physically and covertly inserted into a closet, under a conference room table, or into any other hidden space inside a building by a malicious or careless user. Unauthorized users might then be able to access the network through the rogue AP. The rogue AP can successfully persuade wireless clients of its legitimacy and force them to send traffic through it as long as it is situated close to the WLAN users and is configured to look alike to them.

The wireless communication between wireless clients and an authorized AP can be intercepted by a rogue AP. To intercept the client traffic, it merely needs to be configured with a stronger signal than the current AP. APs that are set up to permit access without authorization can also be used by a malevolent user to access the wireless network. It's also crucial to remember that malevolent users don't always deploy rogue access points. Rogue APs are frequently set up by users who wish to utilize wireless technology without the IT department's consent. Furthermore, because rogue APs a.

Remember

Monitor your network for intruders. You should always make sure you have an eye on what's going on, that you are tracking attack trends. The more you know about what malicious security crackers are trying to do to your network, the better the job of defending against them you can do.

7.2.4.2. Loss of Integrity

Issues with data integrity that arise in wired networks also occur in wireless networks. Integrity can be challenging to achieve because wireless and wired communications are commonly used by organizations without sufficient cryptographic protection of data. For instance, a hacker can jeopardize data integrity by altering or removing information from an email from a wireless system account.

This could be harmful to a company if crucial emails are shared widely among the recipients. The lack of strong message integrity in the 802.11 standard's current security features makes other active attacks that jeopardize system integrity possible. A linear CRC is all that the WEP-based integrity mechanism is. When cryptographic checking techniques like message authentication codes and hashes are not used, message modification attacks are possible.

7.2.4.3. Loss of Network Availability

A denial of service (DoS) attack, like jamming, is involved in a denial of network availability. When a malevolent user intentionally emits a signal from a wireless device to overpower authorized wireless signals, this is known as jamming. Emissions from microwave ovens and cordless phones can also unintentionally cause jamming. Communication breaks down as a result of jamming because reputable wireless signals are unable to interact with the network. Another source of a DoS is non-malicious users. For example, a user may download large files and inadvertently monopolize a wireless signal, thereby preventing other users from accessing the network. Agency security policies should therefore restrict the kinds and volumes of data that users can download via wireless networks.

Other Security Risks

More users are looking for ways to connect remotely to the networks within their own organizations as a result of the widespread use of wireless devices. The use of untrusted, third-party networks is one such technique. For instance, wireless networks are frequently available in conference centers, enabling attendees to connect to the Internet and then their own companies. Airports, hotels, and even some coffee shops are starting to provide their patrons with 802.11-based publicly accessible wireless networks. For an extra layer of security, these networks even offer VPN capabilities.

These untrusted public networks present three main risks: 1) they are open to the public and can therefore be accessed by anyone, including malevolent users; 2) they act as a bridge to the user's own network, making it possible for anyone on the public network to attack or gain access to the bridged network; and 3) they use high-gain antennas to enhance reception and expand coverage area, making it easier for malevolent users to intercept user signals. Unless their organizations take action to safeguard both their users and themselves, users may introduce vulnerabilities into company networks and systems by connecting to them via an untrusted network. Usually, users must gain access to resources that are classified as either public or private by their organizations. Transport Layer Security (TLS), the Internet Engineering Task Force-standardized version of Secure Sockets Layer (SSL), is one application layer security protocol that agencies might want to think about utilizing to protect their public resources. In the majority of agencies, though, this is not required because the information is already available to the public. Agencies should think about securing their connections to private resources by utilizing a VPN solution, as this will help stop eavesdropping and unauthorized access.

Finally, social engineering and dumpster diving are issues as well, just like with any network. When preparing to implement a wireless network, an organization should take network security into account from every angle.

7.2.5. Emerging Security Standards and Technologies

Standards organizations have reacted to the uproar over vulnerabilities in 802.11 WLANs, much like the security industry. The IEEE and the Internet Engineering Task Force (IETF) are both active. Three distinct projects are being worked on by the IEEE to enhance WLAN security. In the first, as a long-term security solution, the IEEE 802.11 Task Group i (TGi) has suggested substantial changes to the current IEEE 802.11 standard. On the basis of the recently published Advanced Encryption Standard (AES), the TGi is defining new ciphers. Although it will require new hardware and protocol modifications, the AES-based solution will offer a very reliable solution in the future. TGi's current design requirements include the ability to detect replay attacks and prevent forgeries, two of the most common issues with WEP.

The TGi's temporary fix for WEP's issues, WiFi Protected Access (WPA), is the second effort to enhance WLAN security. To solve the issues without needing to modify hardware, the team is developing the Temporal Key Integrity Protocol (TKIP), which will only require firmware and software driver changes. The third initiative from IEEE is the June 2001 approval of IEEE 802.1X-2001, a new standard that provides a generic framework for port-based network access control and key distribution. IEEE 802.1X defines the encapsulation of EAP (defined in RFC 2284) over IEEE 802 media, allowing mutual authentication between an AP and a station. The IEEE 802.11i draft standard specifies extra capabilities needed for the safe implementation of IEEE 802.1X on 802.11 networks because IEEE 802.1X was designed primarily for use with IEEE 802 LANs and not for use with WLANS. Using an EAP method that supports mutual authentication, key management, and dictionary attack resistance are a few of these requirements. Furthermore, 802.11i specifies a "four way" key management handshake that is used to confirm that the station has been authenticated to both the AP and, if one is present, a back-end authentication server. This handshake is also used with the TKIP and AES ciphers. Therefore, it is crucial that IEEE 802.1X implementations on 802.11 implement both the fundamental IEEE 802.1X standard and the IEEE 802.11i enhancements in order to provide sufficient security.

Did you know?

IEEE 802.11i enhances IEEE 802.11-1999 by providing a Robust Security Network (RSN) with two new protocols: the four-way handshake and the group key handshake. These utilize the authentication services and port access control described in IEEE 802.1X to establish and change the appropriate cryptographic keys.

IEEE 802.1X can be used with a backend authentication server or fully implemented on the AP (by supporting one or more EAP methods within the AP). Diameter, Kerberos, RADIUS, and other authentication protocols are supported by the IEEE 802.1X standard. RADIUS provides authentication, authorization, and accounting for Network Access Server (NAS) devices, such as dial-up, xDSL, and 802.11; it is detailed in RFC 28652869 and RFC 3162. The 802.1X standard can be implemented using various EAP types, such as EAP-TLS (defined in RFC 2716, supporting fast reconnect, mutual authentication, and key management via certificate authentication) for Ethernet LANs and EAP-MD5 (defined in RFC 2284, supporting only one-way authentication without key exchange). The IETF is currently working on a new generation of EAP techniques that will address problems with wireless authentication and key management. Additional security features like identity protection, secure ciphersuite negotiation, cryptographic protection of the EAP conversation, tunneling of other EAP methods, etc., are supported by these methods. The reader is encouraged to visit the IEEE 802.11 standards website for the most recent updates on each specification's status.

Did you get it?

1. **What are the cost savings and operational efficiencies associated with WLAN deployments?**
2. **What emerging encryption protocols, authentication methods, and intrusion detection/prevention systems are available for WLANs?**

7.3. WIRELESS PERSONAL AREA NETWORKS

→Learning Objectives

- Gain an understanding of the fundamentals of Bluetooth technology
- Define the useful benefits of WPAN
- Explore strategies and best practices for securing Bluetooth devices and mitigating potential security threats

Ad hoc networks are a relatively new wireless communication paradigm in which access points and base stations are not part of a fixed infrastructure. Ad hoc networks rely on a system of mobile routers connected by wireless links that allow devices to communicate with one another, allowing devices to maintain random network configurations created "on the fly." In an ad hoc network, devices manage and exchange resources in addition to controlling the network configuration. Ad hoc networks and peer-to-peer (P2P) networks are comparable in that they both rely on decentralized networking, where data is kept locally at the end user's location as opposed to in a centralized database. Ad hoc networks, on the other hand, are different from P2P networks in that the former rely on the device hardware to request and share information, while the latter rely on a routing mechanism to direct information queries. Ad hoc networks enable devices to connect to wireless personal area networks (PANs) and use wireless applications, like file sharing and address book synchronization. These networks can be expanded to include network and Internet access by combining them with other technologies. When connected to a Bluetooth network with another device that is capable of 802.11, Bluetooth devices—which normally do not have access to network resources—can establish a connection within the corporate network and access the Internet.

7.3.1. Bluetooth Technology

Nowadays, Bluetooth technology serves as the foundation for most ad hoc networks. An open standard for short-range digital radio is called Bluetooth. It is marketed as a low-profile, low-cost, low-power technology that offers an ad hoc means of establishing small wireless networks. Bluetooth is regarded as a wireless PAN technology that provides dependable and quick voice and data transmission. Untethered Bluetooth devices function as a bridge to current networks and do away with the need for cables. Bluetooth can be used to connect almost any device to any other device. An example is the connection between a PDA and a mobile phone. The goal of Bluetooth is to connect disparate devices (PDAs, cell phones, printers, faxes, etc.) together wirelessly in a small environment such as an office or home. According to the leading proponents of the technology, Bluetooth is a standard that will ultimately—

- Eliminate wires and cables between both stationary and mobile devices
- Facilitate both data and voice communications
- Offer the possibility of ad hoc networks and deliver synchronicity between personal devices.

With some variations, Bluetooth is intended to function in the unlicensed ISM (industrial, scientific, and medical applications) band, which is accessible in the majority of the world. Table 7.3 provides a summary of Bluetooth's features. While Bluetooth-enabled devices can find each other automatically, users must take action to connect with other devices and create networks. Like any other ad hoc network, Bluetooth networks are created in an arbitrary and transient manner. The master-slave relationship that is maintained between the network devices is one of the characteristics that sets Bluetooth networks apart. A "piconet" is a master-slave network that consists of up to eight Bluetooth devices. In a piconet, up to seven slave devices are directly connected to the network that has one device designated as the master. The network is configured and controlled by the master device, which also establishes the network's hopping scheme. Within a Bluetooth piconet, devices use the same frequency hopping pattern and share the same channel. A slave in one network can function as the master for another, even though only one device can serve as the master for each network.

Table 7.3. Key Characteristics of Bluetooth Technology

Characteristic	Description
Physical Layer	Frequency Hopping Spread Spectrum (FHSS).
Frequency Band	2.4 – 2.4835 GHz (ISM band).
Hop Frequency	1 ,600 hops/sec.
Data Rate	1 Mbps (raw). Higher bit rates are anticipated.
Data and Network Security	Three modes of security (none, link-level, and service level), two levels of device trust, and three levels of service security. Stream encryption for confidentiality, challenge-response for authentication. PIN-derived keys and limited management.
Operating Range	About 10 meters (30 feet); can be extended to 100 meters.
Throughput	Up to approximately 720 kbps.
Positive Aspects	No wires and cables for many interfaces. Ability to penetrate walls and other obstacles. Costs are decreasing with a $5 cost projected. Low power and minimal hardware.
Negative Aspects	Possibility for interference with other ISM band technologies. Relatively low data rates. Signals leak outside desired boundaries.

The dynamic network topologies of Bluetooth networks are managed by mobile routers. Additionally, the routers manage the data transfer between devices that can maintain a direct link. These networks need to be dynamically reconfigured to accommodate the devices' erratic movements. Through the use of routing protocols, Bluetooth is able to create and sustain these dynamic networks.

Similar to WLAN devices and other IEEE 802.11 compliant devices, Bluetooth transceivers operate in the 2.4. GHz ISM band. Frequency hopping (FH) spread spectrum system is used by Bluetooth transceivers, which use *Gaussian Frequency Shift Keying (GFSK)* modulation. The system hops 1,600 times per second across 79 frequencies in a quasi-random manner. A Bluetooth network can have a maximum theoretical bandwidth of 1 Mbps. The networks' inability to handle such data rates, however, is actually due to communication overhead. It is anticipated that Bluetooth 2.0 will offer up to 2 Mbps of maximum bandwidth.

Bluetooth networks are capable of supporting one channel that transfers both synchronous speech and asynchronous data simultaneously, or they can support one channel that transfers asynchronous data and up to three simultaneous synchronous speech channels. Circuit-switching and packet-switching technologies are combined in Bluetooth. The benefit of Bluetooth packet switching is that it enables devices to route multiple information packets via a single data path. The fact that this approach doesn't use up all the resources on a data path makes it simpler for distant devices to keep data flowing through a scatter-net.

Keyword

Gaussian Frequency Shift Keying or GFSK is an extension of the FSK modulation scheme where the frequency of the modulated signal will not instantaneously change at the beginning of each symbol period of the binary data.

7.3.1.1. Brief History

Ericsson Mobile Communication was the original architect of Bluetooth, which bears the name of the Danish king Harald Bluetooth from the tenth century. The Bluetooth SIG was established in 1998 by IBM, Intel, Nokia, and Toshiba and is responsible for overseeing the specification. Initially, the SIG was established as a way to track advancements in radio technology and the establishment of an open, worldwide standard. The Bluetooth SIG is made up of more than 2,000 organizations today, including prominent figures from the computer and telecommunications sectors who are spearheading the advancement and marketing of Bluetooth technology. When Bluetooth was first developed, its main purpose was to replace cables in wireless communication systems. To improve wireless connectivity, SIG members intend to create a wide variety of consumer electronics with Bluetooth capabilities. Cell phones, PDAs, laptop computers, modems, cordless phones, pagers, PC cards, fax machines, and printers are just a few of the many gadgets that are expected. The IEEE 802.15 Personal Area Network (PAN) Working Group, which was established in the beginning of 1999, has now standardized Bluetooth. There are many links to other websites on the Bluetooth SIG website.

7.3.1.2. Frequency and Data Rates

Bluetooth was intended to function in the unlicensed 2.4 GHz–2.4835 GHz ISM frequency band, just like the 802.11 WLAN standard. In order to mitigate interference caused by the many other technologies that use this frequency range, Bluetooth employs a frequency-hopping spread-spectrum (FHSS) technology. By shifting frequency roughly 1,600 times per second, the FHSS scheme makes use of 79 distinct radio channels. The process is repeated continuously, using one channel for 625 microseconds, then hopping in a pseudo-random order to another channel for another 625 microsecond transmission. As previously mentioned, because the ISM band is free of license and accessible everywhere, it has gained popularity for wireless communications.

Bluetooth technology can transmit data at up to 1 Mbps in the ISM band, with a throughput of about 720 kbps. The data rates are still three to eight times faster than the average speed of parallel and serial ports, respectively, even though they are lower than those of 802.11 wireless LANs. For many of the applications that Bluetooth was designed for, this rate is fast enough. Furthermore, even faster data rates are expected to become available in the future.

7.3.1.3. Bluetooth Architecture and Components

A slave radio can communicate with a master radio via Bluetooth. Bluetooth radios are symmetric, meaning that one device can function both as a slave and a master. A fixed 48-bit unique device address (BD_ADDR) is assigned to each radio. Piconets are ad hoc networks made up of two or more radio devices. A piconet's units are all connected via the same channel. A master device and one or more slaves are present in every piconet. A piconet can contain up to seven active slaves at once. As a result, a 3-bit active device address uniquely identifies each active device in a piconet. It is possible for inactive slaves in disconnected modes to stay inside the piconet.

The only person who can start a Bluetooth communication link is a master. Nevertheless, the slave may ask for a master/slave switch to take control of the connection once it has been established. It is forbidden for slaves to speak with one another directly. All communication takes place between the master and the slave. Additionally, slaves in a piconet need to align their internal clocks and frequency hops with the master's. A distinct frequency hopping sequence is used by each piconet. Time Division Multiplexing was used by radio devices (TDM). In a piconet, the slaves may transmit on odd-numbered slots, while the master device transmits on even-numbered slots. A scatternet is made up of several piconets with overlapping coverage areas. While slaves may participate in multiple piconets on a time-division multiplex basis, each piconet may have a single master. A device can function as a slave in multiple piconets or as a master in one and a slave in another.

7.3.1.4. Range

Three distinct classes of power management are offered by Bluetooth. The highest power devices, known as Class 1, have an operating range of up to 100 meters (m) and run at 100 milliwatts (mW). The lowest power Class 3 devices operate at 1 mW and have an operating range of 1/10 meter to 10 meters. Class 2 devices operate at 2.5 mW and have an operating range of up to 10 meters. Table 7.4 provides an overview of these three operating power levels.

Table 7.4. Device Classes of Power Management

Type	Power	Power Level	Operating Range
Class 1 Devices	High	100 mW (20 dBm)	Up to 100 meters (300 feet)
Class 2 Devices	Medium	2.5 mW (4 dBm)	Up to 10 meters (30 feet)
Class 3 Devices	Low	1 mW (0 dBm)	0.1–10 meters (less than 30 feet)

In Figure 7.7, the three Bluetooth ranges are shown. The shortest range, as demonstrated, might be useful for tasks like changing out cables (e.g., mouse or keyboard), syncing files, or exchanging business cards. Like with the data rates, it is expected that even longer ranges will be attained in the future. The high-powered range can travel up to 100 m, or roughly 300 feet.

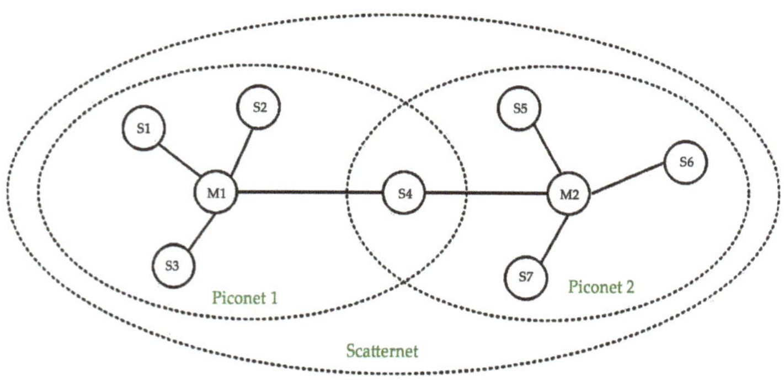

Figure 7.7. Bluetooth Operating Range (Source: Geeksforgeeks, https://media.geeksforgeeks.org/wp-content/uploads/20190322083717/bluetootharchitecture.jpg).

7.3.2. Benefits

Users can benefit from Bluetooth in five main ways. Bluetooth is becoming increasingly appealing due to its ad hoc untethered communication method, which can lead to lower costs and more efficiency. Both home users and business users in large organizations find the efficiencies and cost savings appealing.

Benefits of Bluetooth include—

- **Cable replacement**: For a range of interconnections, Bluetooth technology takes the place of cables. These consist of those of auxiliary equipment (i.e., USB at 12 Mbps (USB 1.1) up to 480 Mbps (USB 2.0); printers and modems, typically at 4 Mbps; wireless headsets and microphones that interface with PCs or mobile phones; mouse and keyboard computer connections.

- **Ease of file sharing**: File sharing between Bluetooth-enabled devices is made possible via Bluetooth. For instance, laptops that are Bluetooth compatible during a meeting allow participants to share files. Another example is the use of a mobile phone with Bluetooth compatibility as a wireless modem for laptops. The laptop communicates with the mobile phone through Bluetooth, and the phone connects to a network. This allows the laptop to have full networking functionality without requiring an electrical interface to connect to the mobile device.
- **Wireless synchronization**: Automatic wireless synchronization with other Bluetooth-capable devices is made possible by Bluetooth. For instance, PDAs, laptops, mobile phones, and other devices can synchronize the private data found in address books and date books.
- **Automated wireless applications**: Automatic wireless application functions are supported by Bluetooth. In contrast to local synchronization, automatic wireless applications communicate with the LAN and Internet. A person working offline on emails, for instance, might be traveling or otherwise not within their usual service area. After returning to a service location, the person will email the files that are queued in the laptop's inbox (i.e., upon landing), would turn on a cell phone or any other gadget that could establish a network connection. After the person logs on, the laptop would then automatically start a network join by using the phone as a modem and send the emails.
- **Internet connectivity**: Many different kinds of devices and apps support Bluetooth. Mobile phones, PDAs, laptops, desktop computers, and fixed telephones are a few of these gadgets. When these technologies and devices work together to leverage each other's capabilities, internet connectivity is made possible. For instance, a laptop can ask a smartphone to establish a dial-up connection via Bluetooth, and the laptop can use that connection to access the Internet.

Office equipment is anticipated to include Bluetooth built-in (e.g., laptops, printers, fax machines, and PCs), communication appliances (e.g., pagers, headsets, cell phones, and handsets), as well as household appliances (e.g., microwave ovens, DVD players, cameras, and refrigerators). In addition, Bluetooth finds use in smart homes, banking, electronic payment systems, vending machines, wireless conference rooms and offices, in-car communications, and parking.

Did you know?

The development of the "short-link" radio technology, later named Bluetooth, was initiated in 1989 by Nils Rydbeck, CTO at Ericsson Mobile in Lund, Sweden. The purpose was to develop wireless headsets, according to two inventions by Johan Ullman, SE 8902098-6, issued 1989-06-12 and SE 9202239, issued 1992-07-24.

7.3.3. Security Requirements and Threats

Bluetooth provides a number of advantages and benefits. Before implementing the technology, organizations must, however, not only address the security risks associated with Bluetooth but also assess the vulnerabilities of the devices they allow to connect to Bluetooth networks. Organizations must specifically focus on security issues related to network availability, data integrity, and confidentiality. Additionally, Bluetooth devices are more susceptible to unintentional security breaches as they are typically managed by users who may have lower security awareness compared to administrators.

7.3.3.1. Confidentiality Loss

For a comprehensive overview of security attacks, refer to Figure 7.7 in the 802.11 wireless section. This will help in understanding some of the attacks that target Bluetooth. Compromised Bluetooth devices pose the primary threat to confidentiality. When a component of a Bluetooth piconet is compromised (e.g., in the possession of an unauthorized individual), sensitive data may be accessed by the malicious party. Moreover, the compromised device may retain information or network privileges that could jeopardize the broader network. In such cases, the compromised device may request data as part of a deliberate network attack in addition to receiving regular traffic. The fact that Bluetooth networks require device authentication rather than user authentication for resource access is a distinguishing feature of this compromise. Once authenticated, the device does not need further authentication and gains immediate access to resources. The security of Bluetooth devices is inherently compromised. Wireless microphones, for instance, can be used as bugging tools by malevolent users. While successful attacks on PCs using Back Orifice and Netbus have been reported, such attacks have not been documented because Bluetooth is not yet widely used commercially. A malevolent user may be able to access other Bluetooth devices and networks with little to no security if they have a program like Back Orifice installed on a device connected to the Bluetooth network. It is possible to use these same programs against Bluetooth networks and devices. Because the system authenticates the devices rather than the users, Bluetooth devices are even more vulnerable. This means that a compromised device has the ability to access the network and compromise the network itself as well as the devices connected to it..

Bluetooth networks are vulnerable to unauthorized remote users. Users at a distance are not always bound by the same security regulations as those in person. Whether they are traveling or at home, they routinely use insecure links. They send user IDs and passwords during the connection process, which a malevolent user can intercept with a network sniffer. A malicious user does not need to be physically close to the user in order to intercept traffic because there is no secure perimeter as is usually present in an office setting. All of the devices in that Bluetooth network are open to attacks as soon as the device or link is compromised. For instance, a malicious user can request and receive sensitive data from a compromised device, and they can monitor data traffic via a compromised link. A compromised device may also be used to access the network if the malicious user manages to learn the password and user IDs for the targeted network. In this case, it takes several security lapses before a malevolent user is able to access the network. Mitigating the risk of such an attack would involve implementing additional security layers on top of Bluetooth and Bluetooth secure links. An additional risk to Bluetooth devices that use unit keys—generally the more basic "dumb" devices—comes from the man-in-the-middle attack. The security encryption key that a network device (Device A) uses to monitor traffic between itself and another network device (Device B) is obtained by the man-in-the-middle (Device C) in this attack. Device A only needs to share its unit key—a static key that is specific to each device—separately with Devices C and B in order for the attack to succeed. There may be no connection at all between Devices A and B and Devices A and C, and there may even be a difference in the degree of secrecy. But once Device C is aware of the unit key, it can determine the encryption key and surreptitiously monitor communication between Devices A and B by using a fictitious device address. There is no expensive or specialized equipment needed for the man-in-the-middle attack. The attack can be carried out by a skilled malevolent user who has access to the unit key and can impersonate a Bluetooth address to generate the encryption key. Such attacks rely on prior knowledge about the Bluetooth devices that are being targeted. However, this does not always mean that malicious users cannot use rand.

The attack is depicted in Figure 7.8. Device A, a reliable PDA, exchanges confidential data with Device B, a reliable laptop. Device A connects to Device C, an untrusted PDA, during the connection with Device B in order to exchange personal contacts from A's PDA address book. Using Device A's unit key and a fictitious address, Device C can monitor traffic between Devices A and B after connecting to Device A. This makes Device C the man-in-the-middle. It's possible that the owner(s) of Device A or Device B won't ever be aware that their data is being monitored, which poses the greatest risk.

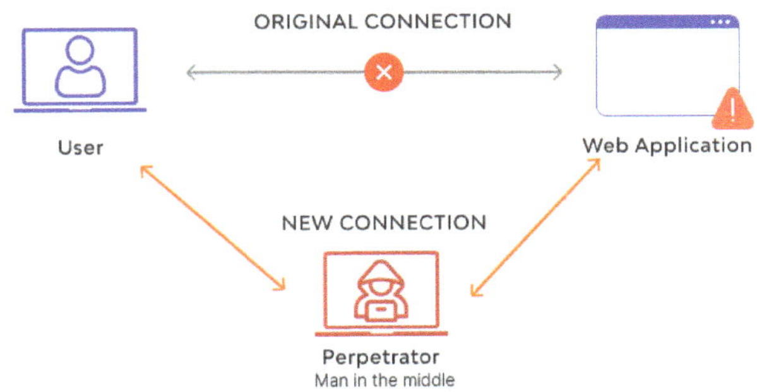

Figure 7.8. Man-in-the-Middle Attack Scenarios (Source: Wallarm, https://uploads-ssl.webflow.com/5ff66329429d880392f6cba2/605cab5ff8f386ea033ae16c_Man-in-the-Middle)%20Attack.jpg).

Network administrators cannot see Bluetooth devices, and there is currently no software available to monitor these intrusions. In an ad hoc network, it doesn't really matter if users from various organizations enforce different security policies. Every device connected to the ad hoc network is vulnerable to each other's security flaws. Since network administrators are unlikely to be in charge of Bluetooth devices, users should be mindful of the security risks when using them in settings where sensitive data is processed. While agencies should take privacy concerns into account when implementing Bluetooth technologies, privacy violations are not a direct threat to security. Every Bluetooth gadget has a distinct address (BD_ADDR), which is utilized to record every device's involvement in the network. In order to guarantee device authentication (i.e., because the address that is logged belongs to the device and not to the user, an individual can refuse to participate in the network since we lack evidence of who was using the device. But it also enables organizations to keep an eye on and record what.

7.3.3.2. Loss of Integrity

When users' or organizations' data is tainted, there are violations of integrity. The immediate result is a compromised network, much like in the case of a confidentiality or disclosure threat. Beyond this, though, are threats to network integrity that include information being added, altered, or deleted and then transmitted through the network without the user's or network administrator's knowledge. Data on user devices and files on the network are both susceptible to corruption. For instance, a malevolent user may use a PDA or other untrusted device to access the address book of a different PDA or laptop. But unlike a disclosure threat, where information would only be monitored, the malicious user changes the contact details without the owner's knowledge or even erases them entirely. Such attacks may cause the agency (or user) to lose faith in its data and system if they go unnoticed. It is recommended that users confirm that their Bluetooth product prohibits automatic data synchronization in order to stop any information from being changed without the user's consent.

7.3.3.3. Loss of Availability

Network availability and "usability upon demand" for authorized users and devices are lost as a result of DoS and DDoS attacks. DoS attacks prevent authorized users from accessing network applications and system resources. Aside from the standard DoS attacks (e.g., Signal jamming attacks (such as flooding techniques) can also target Bluetooth devices, LANs, and Internet services. Bluetooth devices are susceptible to interference because they share bandwidth with cordless phones, microwave ovens, and other wireless networks. Malicious users have the ability to obstruct the information flow (i.e., employing devices that broadcast in the 2 GHz ISM band to skew the network's information and interfere with the routing protocol. Ad hoc network devices are not able to negotiate the dynamic topologies of the network when the routing protocol is disrupted. Jamming may occur more frequently for remote users than for on-site users. The same interference that users face in the office must also be dealt with by remote users. Additionally, because the remote environment is uncontrolled, it is more probable that distant devices will be near other devices (e.g., other ISM band and Bluetooth devices) that are purposefully or.

An attack due to battery exhaustion is another risk connected to ad hoc devices. This attack uses a device's battery to try and disable it. The device receives frequent requests from a malevolent user requesting either the creation of a network or data transfers (presuming the user is a member of the network topology). This kind of attack doesn't jeopardize network security, but in the end, it keeps the user from accessing the network since it breaks the device.

Did you get it?

1. What are the architecture and components of Bluetooth technology?
2. What are the implications of a loss of confidentiality in communications?

ROLE MODEL

Norman Manuel Abramson: An American engineer and computer scientist, most known for developing the ALOHA net system for wireless computer communication.

BIOGRAPHY

Norman Abramson, the leader of a group of scientists and engineers who pioneered the development of wireless computer networks, passed away on December 1 at his residence in San Francisco. He was 88.

The cause of his passing was skin cancer that had spread to his lungs, as reported by his son, Mark.

Professor Abramson's project at the University of Hawaii was initially intended to transmit data to schools on the distant Hawaiian islands through a radio channel. However, the solution he and his team developed in the late 1960s and early 1970s would prove to be widely applicable; some of their technology is still utilized in today's smartphones, satellites, and home WiFi networks.

The technology they invented enabled numerous digital devices to exchange data over a shared radio channel. It was a straightforward approach that did not necessitate intricate scheduling of when each data packet would be transmitted. If a data packet was not received, it was simply retransmitted. This method deviated from telecommunications practices at the time, but it was effective.

"It was an incredibly bold idea, truly innovative engineering," remarked Vinton Cerf, a computer scientist at Google and the co-author, alongside Robert Kahn, of the technical standards for connecting computer networks on the internet.

The wireless network in Hawaii, which commenced operations in 1971, was named ALOHA net, incorporating the Hawaiian greeting or farewell. It served as a smaller, wireless counterpart to the more renowned ARPA net, the precursor to the internet, which enabled university researchers to communicate over a network and send messages via landlines. The ARPA net was overseen by the Pentagon's Advanced Research Projects Agency, which also supported the ALOHA net.

"The early wireless work in Hawaii is vastly underappreciated," said Marc Weber, an internet historian at the Computer History Museum in Mountain View, Calif. "Every modern form of wireless data networking, from WiFi to your cellphone, goes back to the ALOHA net."

Professor Abramson has been called the father of wireless networking. But it was a shared paternity. The project included graduate students and several faculty members, notably Frank Kuo, a former Bell Labs scientist who came to the University of Hawaii in 1966, the same year Professor Abramson arrived.

His deepest expertise was in communication theory, the subject of his Ph.D. thesis at Stanford University. The fundamental design ideas behind ALOHA net were his. In a 2018 oral history interview for the Computer History Museum, Professor Kuo recalled, "Norm was the theory and I was the implementer, and so we worked together pretty well."

ALOHAnet owed a lot to surfing. Professor Abramson was presenting a paper at an academic conference in Tokyo in the days when flights from San Francisco to Tokyo had to stop midway in Honolulu. Professor Abramson, who was raised in Boston, had not been to Hawaii before and decided to spend a few days there on the way home.

He rented a surfboard. "I got on, I learned how to surf, and I said, Boy, I could stand some of this," he recalled in 2013 in an oral history interview with the Computer History Museum.

Within a year, after the University of Hawaii offered him a tenured professorship, he and his family moved to Hawaii. "My father was really wrapped up in his work, but he surfed nearly every day," Mark Abramson said.

That the ALOHAnet technology became so widely used was partly because Professor Abramson and his team had shared it freely and welcomed other scientists to Hawaii.

"We had done no patenting, and ALOHA was published in scientific papers," putting their work in the public domain, Professor Abramson said in the oral history, adding: "And that was fine with me. I was too busy surfing to worry about that sort of thing."

Norman Manuel Abramson was born in Boston on April 1, 1932, to Edward and Esther Abramson. His father was a commercial photographer, his mother a homemaker. Norman and his sister, Harriet, grew up in the Dorchester neighborhood, home to mostly Jewish immigrants, like his parents, at the time. His father was from Lithuania, his mother from Ukraine.

Norman was educated in Boston's public schools, at the elite Boston Latin School and the English High School, where he excelled in math and science. He went on to Harvard University, where he took a course taught by Howard Aiken, a mathematician and early pioneer in computing. It was a computer course long before the discipline of computer science existed, and he enjoyed his first taste of programming.

Professor Abramson majored in physics at Harvard, then earned a master's degree in physics from the University of California, Los Angeles, and his doctorate in electrical engineering from Stanford, in 1958. He briefly worked in industry and had postdoctoral teaching stints before he went to Hawaii. He retired from the University of Hawaii in 1994.

In addition to his son, Mark, he is survived by his wife, Joan Abramson; his sister, Harriet Schannon; and three grandchildren. His daughter, Carin Wethington, died in 2014.

Some of the data-networking techniques developed by Professor Abramson and his Hawaii team proved valuable not only in wireless communications but also in wired networks. One heir to his work was Robert Metcalfe, who in 1973 was a young computer scientist working at Xerox PARC, a Silicon Valley research laboratory that had become a fount of personal computer innovations.

Mr. Metcalfe was working on how to enable personal computers to share data over wired office networks. He had read a 1970 paper, written by Professor Abramson, describing ALOHAnet's method for transmitting and resending data over a network.

"Norm kindly invited me to spend a month with him at the University of Hawaii to study ALOHAnet," Mr. Metcalfe recalled in an email.

Mr. Metcalfe and his colleagues at Xerox PARC adopted and tweaked the ALOHAnet technology in creating Ethernet office networking. Later, Mr. Metcalfe founded an Ethernet company, 3Com, which thrived as the personal computer industry grew.

"Norm, thank you," Mr. Metcalfe concluded in his email. "Aloha!""

SUMMARY

- A wireless network is one that allows computers and other devices to communicate using radio signal frequency. It's also referred to as a WLAN or WiFi network sometimes.
- A wireless LAN, or wireless local area network, consists of two or more computers linked to the same radio frequency. In contrast, a wired LAN requires each computer to be physically connected to the server's network switch or hub via an Ethernet cable.
- Physical Ethernet cables are used to connect the desktop server to the DSL modem, switch, and router. But the clients don't need any cabling.
- Since their beginning, wireless networks have been categorized into ad hoc networks and infrastructure networks, which encompass LANs. The term "ad hoc" in Latin means "for this purpose." Ad hoc networks are designed for specific purposes, often created quickly and for a temporary use.
- A minor backlash appeared in popular culture due to the rapid rise to fame of the personal digital assistant and its early associations as a status symbol for the business class.
- A wireless local area network, or WLAN, consists of two or more computers connected to the same radio frequency. In contrast, a wired LAN has computers physically connected to the server's network switch or hub via Ethernet cables.
- A WLAN comprises a wireless station and an access point. A laptop or notebook PC with a wireless network interface card (NIC) is commonly known as a station or client.

MULTIPLE CHOICE QUESTIONS

1. Which of the following is a fundamental security protocol used to secure wireless networks?
   a. WEP
   b. WPA2
   c. WEP2
   d. WPA
2. What does WEP stand for in the context of wireless network security?
   a. Wired Equivalent Privacy
   b. Wireless Encryption Protocol
   c. Wi-Fi Encryption Protection
   d. Wireless Enhanced Privacy
3. Which of the following authentication methods is considered the most secure for wireless networks?
   a. WPA-PSK

   b. WEP
   c. WPA2-Enterprise
   d. MAC Filtering

4. What does SSID stand for in the context of wireless networks?
   a. Secure Server Identifier
   b. Service Set Identifier
   c. Secure Signal Detection
   d. System Security Identifier

5. Which of the following is a common method used to prevent unauthorized access to a wireless network?
   a. Enabling WPS (Wi-Fi Protected Setup)
   b. Broadcasting SSID
   c. Disabling encryption
   d. MAC address filtering

REVIEW QUESTIONS

1. What are Ad Hoc Networks?
2. How are Personal Digital Assistants (PDAs) relevant in wireless networking?
3. What are some examples of Emerging Wireless Technologies?
4. What components constitute Wireless LANs?
5. How is the security of 802.11 Wireless LANs ensured?

Answer to Multiple Choice Questions

1. (b) 2. (a) 3. (c) 4. (b) 5. (d)

REFERENCES

1. Andy, D., (2002). *Emerging Technology: Wireless LAN Standards.* NetworkMagazine.com. http://networkmagazine.com/article/NMG20020206S0006 (accessed on 05 April 2024).
2. Bajwa, M. I., (2004) *Wireless Network Security*. Directed Study Project, Strayer University, Herndon.
3. Vacca, J. R. (2013). Computer and Information Security Handbook (2nd ed.). Morgan Kaufmann.
4. Rappaport, T. S. (2002). Wireless Communications: Principles and Practice (2nd ed.). Prentice Hall.
5. Stallings, W. (2017). Wireless Communications & Networks (2nd ed.). Pearson.

6. Russell, D. L., Ganguly, A., & Liscano, R. (2016). Wireless Security: Models, Threats, and Solutions. CRC Press.
7. Pirzada, A. A., & McDonald, C. (2007). Network Security: A Beginner's Guide (2nd ed.). McGraw-Hill.

Index

FSC
www.fsc.org
MIX
Papier | Fördert
gute Waldnutzung
FSC® C083411

Kolibri 360 GmbH
Ferdinand-Jühlke-Straße 7
99095 Erfurt, Deutschland
produktsicherheit@kolibri360.de